# Hard Times

# HARD TIMES

*The Adult Musical
in 1970s New York City*

Elizabeth L. Wollman

OXFORD
UNIVERSITY PRESS

# OXFORD
UNIVERSITY PRESS

Oxford University Press is a department of the
University of Oxford. It furthers the University's objective
of excellence in research, scholarship, and education
by publishing worldwide.

Oxford   New York
Auckland   Cape Town   Dar es Salaam   Hong Kong   Karachi
Kuala Lumpur   Madrid   Melbourne   Mexico City   Nairobi
New Delhi   Shanghai   Taipei   Toronto

With offices in
Argentina   Austria   Brazil   Chile   Czech Republic   France   Greece
Guatemala   Hungary   Italy   Japan   Poland   Portugal   Singapore
South Korea   Switzerland   Thailand   Turkey   Ukraine   Vietnam

Oxford is a registered trademark of Oxford University Press
in the UK and certain other countries.

Published in the United States of America by
Oxford University Press
198 Madison Avenue, New York, NY 10016

© Oxford University Press 2013

Library of Congress Cataloging-in-Publication Data
Wollman, Elizabeth L., 1969–
Hard times : the adult musical in 1970s New York City
/Elizabeth L. Wollman.
p.  cm.
Includes bibliographical references and index.
ISBN 978-0-19-974748-1 (hardback)
1. Musicals—New York (State)—New York—20th century—History and criticism.
2. Theater—New York (State)—New York—History—20th century.   I. Title.
ML1711.8.N3W62   2012
792.609747'109047—dc23
2012002815

9 8 7 6 5 4 3 2 1

Printed in the United States of America
on acid-free paper

For Mom, Dad, and Philip

# CONTENTS

# ACKNOWLEDGMENTS

This book was a hoot to research and write, and I am grateful to the many people, organizations, and institutions that made the experience so rewarding. My thanks, first and foremost, to Byron Werner, whom I have never met face to face but who felt compelled, many years ago, to mail me a recording of *Let My People Come* after our mutual friend, Jim Cowdery, mentioned to him that I was researching rock musicals for a previous project. I am not sure how Byron made the leap from "rock musicals" to "The Cunnilingus Champion of Company C," but I am eternally grateful that he did. I thank him for the cassette, and Jim for getting it to me.

Jonathan Ward, who coined the term *adult musicals*, JD Doyle, who hosts the radio program *Queer Music Heritage*, and the dearly departed playwright and activist Doric Wilson were all wonderful about sharing information, giving advice, and helping me connect with informants in the early stages of research. Elizabeth Mariko Murray at the Museum of Sex, Ann Butler at the Fales Collection at the Bobst Library, New York University, K. Kevyne Baar at the Tamiment Archives at the Bobst Library, Jennifer Steward at the Broadway League, and Karen Nickeson, Annemarie van Roessel, and Jeremy Megraw at the New York Public Library at Lincoln Center were all enormously helpful; my thanks to these individuals and the organizations they represent. Ron Mandelbaum at Photofest and Tom Lisanti at the New York Public Library were both very patient with me as I chose (and then decided against, and then chose new) images to use in this book. Gail Merrifield Papp granted me permission to cite from her late husband's correspondence with Myrna Lamb; Edward G. Carmines granted me access to his late brother's script for *The Faggot*. My thanks also to Jeff Haller, Eric Richardson, and Jeremy Aufderheide for sharing with me materials from their private collections.

My informants deserve extra-special mention here because their words shaped this book. My heartfelt thanks to Adrienne Barbeau, Joanne Baron, Susan Hulsman Bingham, Jacqui Ceballos, Ze'eva Cohen, Tobie Columbus, Gretchen Cryer, Peter Del Valle, Boni Enten, Ed Gaynes, Lee Goldsmith, Lawrence Hurwit, Bruce Kimmel, Alan Kootsher, Larry Kornfeld, Myrna Lamb, Mario Manzini, David Newburge, Robert Patrick, Peachena, Barry Pearl, Harvey Perr, Fred Silver, Bill Solly, Steve Sterner, and Earl Wilson Jr. for their patience, candor, and willingness to share their memories and opinions as well as programs, old photos, news clippings, scores, scripts, and recordings.

I work with colleagues who are kind, respectful, helpful, and lots of fun to blow off steam with. My thanks to past and present members of Baruch College's Department of Fine and Performing Arts, and especially to current chair Anne Swartz, former chair Terry Berkowitz, and office manager Skip Dietrich. Daniel Borenstein and Gene Scholtens both digitized a number of recordings for me. Katherine Behar, Jake Cohen, Jennifer Jones-Wilson, Zoë Sheehan Saldaña, Karen Shelby, Leonard Sussman, Susan Tenneriello, and Andrew Tomasello listened and lent support. Thanks also to Carol Berkin for advice and friendship. The graduate students I worked with at the CUNY Graduate Center in the spring of 2010 and the fall of 2011 helped with specific sections of this book; thanks especially to Aya Hayashi, Stefanie Jones, Christopher Silsby, Kalle Westerling, Emily Clark, and Kayla Yuh.

Several grants and awards have helped me research and write sections of this book: I received PSC-CUNY research awards in 2008 and 2010, a Whiting mini-grant in 2010, and a Eugene M. Lang Junior Faculty Research Fellowship in 2008.

I am lucky to have connected with other musical theater scholars who are not only brilliant and endlessly inspiring but also lots of fun to hang out with. Thanks, especially, to Ray Knapp, David Savran, Jessica Sternfeld, and Stacy Wolf for finding me and encouraging me, and for helping this book along. The attendees at the 2011 Harvard-Princeton Musical Theater Forum made excellent comments that helped me enormously at the revision stage; thanks to everyone who was there, and to Carol Oja and Stacy Wolf for organizing what is quite possibly the most rewarding conference I've ever attended. Thanks as well to Jill Dolan for advice that helped at the revision stage. Stephen Amico and Sandra Mardenfeld are good friends and fellow academics who listen and understand.

My editor, Norm Hirschy, has seen this book from its earliest stages through its completion. I could not have dreamt a wiser or more thorough editor, and I thank him for all he has done, not only for me but also for this growing scholarly field to which we are both devoted.

On the domestic front, I am grateful for a family and a community that has provided love, support, and camaraderie in the years that I've been working on this book. While I thank almost all the residents of my quirky, wonderful Brooklyn apartment building, I'm especially grateful to have Jamie and Joe Luft, Stevie Swenson, Sarah Cassidy, Amanda and Pat Clarke, and Shawn Davis and Paizhe Pressley and their families in my life; my thanks to all of them for keeping me and various members of the Wollman-Dunn clan fed and watered, for listening to me prattle on about this book and various other topics and, in short, for being good neighbors and better friends.

My family, both immediate and extended, has provided unwavering support. Thanks Mom, Dad, Jess, Dan, Nate, Gail, Jim, Jennifer, Sean, Jacob, and Henry. My children, Paulina and Philip, have helped this book, and me, in ways too vast to list. And their dad, my beloved Andrew, is not only a brilliant editor, the person who came up with the title of this book, and an enormous help with legalese, but also an extraordinary husband, companion, and friend.

# ABOUT THE COMPANION WEBSITE

**www.oup.com/us/hardtimes**

Oxford has created a website to accompany *Hard Times* so that readers may view images related to the discussion and listen to clips of songs from most of the musicals discussed. The companion can be accessed with the username Music3 and the password Book3234. To view an image or listen to an audio example, simply click on the appropriate link on the website.

Many of the musicals featured in this book are particularly obscure, and their scores were never commercially recorded. Some of the audio clips have thus been excerpted from private recordings and are not of pristine quality. Nevertheless I have chosen to include as many clips as possible so that readers can get at least some sense of what these productions sounded like.

# Hard Times

# Introduction

Look at the sensual exhibitions of the feminine form! Listen to the salacious music! See the appeals to the sensational and the pandering to the base and vulgar elements of human nature! Hear the gross innuendo and notice the foul suggestion! Who will deny that these things are immensely damaging to the public taste and terribly ruinous to the public morals?

> —Editorial in the *New York Times,* November 8, 1868, quoted in Allen,
> *Horrible Prettiness: Burlesque and American Culture*

On a chilly morning in late March 1969, nine young actors gathered for the first rehearsal of a show that they knew little about, save that it was all about sex. Having arrived at their rehearsal space—a filthy, dilapidated theater on the Lower East Side of Manhattan—the actors nervously arranged themselves on metal chairs that had been haphazardly arranged in a circle and listened intently to their rumpled, thickly mustachioed director. They stole curious glances at one another, looked away, and shyly looked again. They wore nothing but yellow cotton robes.[1]

Their shaggy, soft-spoken director bluntly informed them that they had been very carefully screened during the audition process, because in having been cast for this particular show, they ran the risk of running into all kinds of trouble—with the law, with their own careers, with their friends and relatives, with their romantic partners. They were told that rehearsals would be particularly intense: for at least six hours a day, six days a week, they would not only sing, dance, and block the show, but would also become deeply, intimately familiar with one another emotionally and physically through what the director referred to as "sensitivity exercises." The director then informed the cast members that despite the intimate nature of their rehearsal sessions, they were never, under any circumstances, to engage in sexual relations with one another outside of the rehearsal space.

Within an hour the robes had been dropped. The cast members began, tentatively at first, and then with growing enthusiasm, to gaze upon, touch, kiss, and fondle one another's naked bodies. Rehearsals for *Oh! Calcutta!* were under way.

While certainly the most famous and long running, *Oh! Calcutta!* was hardly the only musical of its kind to appear in New York City during the 1970s. Rather, a number of "adult" musicals cropped up on and especially off Broadway over the course of the decade. Adult musicals generally distinguished themselves from other types of musicals in their reliance on any or all of the following: full-frontal nudity, simulated sexual activity, sexually suggestive or explicit dialogue or musical numbers, or plotlines containing what contemporary ratings boards would label as strong sexual content.

With exceptions, representatives of the subgenre were reviled by theater critics when they were reviewed at all. Critics alternately attacked adult musicals for going too far in the direction of hard-core pornography or for not going far enough, for being too sugary and breezy about the country's rapidly changing sexual mores, or for being too preachy and heavy-handed about them. Many members of the commercial theater industry worried that the more explicit adult musicals were not terribly distinct from the live sex shows and pornographic films that had begun to proliferate in New York City, especially in the Times Square area, by the late 1960s. Nevertheless adult musicals appealed to many producers—especially young, cash-strapped up-and-comers—because they were easy to cast with eager unknowns, usually cheap to stage, and of course not terribly hard to costume. And even the ones that earned the nastiest reviews often managed to run long enough to make at least a modest amount of money. Clearly, and certainly as befitting the mood of the era, 1970s spectators were more interested in the sex that adult musicals offered than in what critics thought about their orchestrations, scenic design, or narrative flow.

Adult musicals fell out of fashion by the late 1970s as the country inched toward the more socially and politically conservative 1980s. Few scripts were published or recordings made, and virtually no scholarly work exists on this subgenre. Historians and journalists who mention adult musicals at all tend to focus on how dated they seem, with their low-budget sets; their mellow, soft-rock scores; their soft-bodied, hirsute cast members undulating earnestly under dimmed stage lights; and their cheery messages about how sex is fun and bodies are beautiful. A few have noted as well the seemingly mercenary desires of producers and directors eager to capitalize on the faddishness of stage nudity and simulated sex, spurred specifically by the commercial success of *Hair* in 1968 and more generally by the cultural tenor of the time.[2]

Yet while they have been dismissed as mere trifles that collectively amount to the musical theater equivalent of streaking—a silly fad befitting a silly decade—adult musicals represent aspects of 1970s American culture at their messiest and most confused, and thus perhaps at their most honest. Adult musicals simultaneously drew from and reflected the country's rapidly changing, often contradictory attitudes about gender and sexuality at a time when the sexual revolution had given way to the gay and women's liberation movements, New York City was teetering toward bankruptcy, hard-core pornography had become trendy, and heated debates about the relationship between art and obscenity were being waged in courts, in the media, and in communities across the country.

This book is about commercial musicals that were directly influenced by the sexual revolution, staged on or off Broadway in New York City during the 1970s and at least at some point in their production histories aimed specifically at mainstream audiences. The musicals discussed herein thus all focus on some aspect of human sexuality as it was being negotiated in the United States during the 1970s. Yet as is often the case with labels, applying the term *adult musical* to all shows that fit this general description is problematic. While many of these shows were sexually explicit, even the most risqué could not be—and were typically not, whether by spectators, critics, or members of the production itself—considered truly pornographic, at least according to Linda Williams's "minimal" and "neutral" definition of the term as "the visual (and sometimes aural) representation of living, moving bodies engaged in explicit, usually unfaked, sexual acts with a primary intent of arousing viewers."[3] Rather, adult musicals featured sexual activity that was simulated, not real, and few if any were specifically designed to cause sexual arousal among audience members. Most were meant instead to comment on the sociosexual mores of the time: to criticize them, praise them, educate audiences about them, spoof them, capitalize on them. In this respect, the term *adult* is not an ideal descriptor because of its widespread use as a euphemism for pornography.[4] And adult musicals were, even at the time, rarely perceived as pornographic, which points again to problems that many of them had in terms of reception by both critics and audiences. So many were perceived as occupying a strange middle ground—not erotic enough on the one hand, yet too risqué to be considered serious theater on the other—that describing what adult musicals are *not* is far easier than neatly defining what they *are*.[5]

Nevertheless the term *adult musicals* is the one I find myself returning to, despite its shortcomings and despite several attempts to come up with snappier, more accurate alternatives. When I first began my research, for example, I was in the habit of using the term *nudie musicals*, which I eventually abandoned since many of these musicals not only featured no nudity, but were staged by individuals who took pains to avoid it for fear that naked bodies would distract audiences from the musicals' overlying social or political messages. The term *nudie musicals* is thus inappropriate for many of the same reasons that some of the subgenre's directors chose to keep their actors clothed. While copious nudity is certainly one of the subgenre's more evocative features, it is also one of the more superficial and distracting; thus to focus overmuch on the nudity in these productions is to lose sight of their meanings. For many of the same reasons that *nudie musicals* fails as a proper descriptor, *sex musicals*—tempting because it can be condensed into the catchy term *sexicals*—seems too focused on the subgenre's overtly suggestive aspects. While aptly descriptive, the phrase *commercial musicals staged in New York City during the 1970s that were directly influenced by the sexual revolution, women's liberation, or gay liberation* is just a tad too wordy. Imperfect though it may be, then, *adult musicals* seems more suitable than any other descriptor I have been able to come up with.

The fact that the term *adult musicals* was coined by the sole individual to write previously about this subgenre, and thus automatically holds some degree of academic street cred, only contributes to my fondness for the term. *Adult musicals* was first used, at least as far as he knows, by Jonathan Ward, in his 2002 feature article "'Come in My Mouth': The Story of the Adult Musicals of the 70s," which ran in the online music magazine *Perfect Sound Forever.*[6] Along with a cassette tape of *Let My People Come* that the friend of a friend sent me as a joke when I was researching rock musicals over a decade ago, Ward's article was responsible for first piquing my curiosity about this subgenre; both the article and the author continued to be important fonts of information during the research process. In using Ward's terminology, I express my gratitude to him for laying the groundwork.

## WHY THE NEED FOR EXPOSURE?

Because of the economic and aesthetic difficulties that plagued the commercial theater in New York City during this period, the 1970s has been largely ignored by musical theater historians, many of whom tend to focus on the decade's mainstream high points— *Grease, The Wiz, A Chorus Line,* the works of Stephen Sondheim—and otherwise write the decade off as a series of forgettable flops unworthy of attention or analysis. Of course, the fact that a number of scholars ascribe the end of Broadway's so-called Golden Age to the late 1960s or very early 1970s, thereby inadvertently dismissing the past forty-plus years of Broadway musicals as inherently subpar, does not help matters much, nor does a general tendency among those writing about the musical theater to focus almost entirely on critical and commercial hits on Broadway at the expense of more modest successes, let alone abject flops.[7] By necessity, then, this book departs from the norm: precious few adult musicals became blockbusters, and many small, modestly successful adult musicals running in New York during the 1970s resonated with audiences at the time, even if they have faded largely from cultural memory in the decades since.

Those writers who have discussed musical theater in the 1970s tend to focus specifically on the works of one composer or one individual and usually critically and financially successful Broadway production. For example, in *Our Musicals, Ourselves: A Social History of the American Musical Theater*, John Bush Jones makes the musical *Grease* central to a chapter on 1970s nostalgia and its relationship to spectacle. In *The Megamusical*, Jessica Sternfeld pinpoints the birth of that subgenre in the 1970s productions of *Jesus Christ Superstar* and *Evita.*[8] And of course there is no shortage of books on the many contributions that Stephen Sondheim has made to the American musical theater.[9] While many of these studies are excellent, most focus more on the productions themselves than they do on the relationship between the musical theater and its sociocultural surroundings.

This book attempts a comprehensive study of a single musical theater subgenre that existed during a specific decade in a specific place, taking into consideration social, political, and economic contexts. With this approach, I hope to build on the many musical theater studies that focus primarily on sexuality and gender.[10] I also aim to provide a clearer picture of New York's theater scene as a whole during a particular time and to contribute to a better understanding of the social and sexual culture in which these productions were developed and staged.

As I did in my previous book, here I move beyond what I see as a tendency to compartmentalize analyses of the musical theater as it has developed in New York City.[11] Most writing about the American stage musical tends to treat Broadway as central to the genre's development. This approach is, of course, entirely appropriate when it comes to the history of the genre as it unfolded through the mid-twentieth century. But any study that focuses on the musical theater as it has developed since the 1950s must take into consideration the enormous contributions of Off and Off Off Broadway.[12]

Off and especially Off Off Broadway were the loci for influential experimentation and innovation during the 1960s and early 1970s. Although these three realms of New York theater are often treated as separate entities—with, for example, histories of Broadway more or less ignoring Off and Off Off Broadway, and vice versa—they in fact have historically exerted a great deal of influence on one another. Off Broadway, originally known as the Little Theater Movement, developed through the 1950s as a smaller, less risky, less expensive alternative to Broadway; as it became increasingly commercial through the late 1950s and early 1960s, the even-more-experimental and freewheeling Off Off Broadway movement was born.[13]

Like rock musicals, some adult musicals were created specifically for Broadway runs, but most were nurtured Off and Off Off Broadway. This is due in part to the fact that just as Broadway, plagued by financial problems and perceived as stubbornly outdated, entered something of a commercial and aesthetic rut in the late 1960s and early 1970s, the Off and especially Off Off Broadway realms experienced a heyday. Committed to making theater that challenged the social, cultural, and political perceptions of audiences, and thus to staging tiny revolutions on minuscule budgets, Off Off Broadway artisans grew invigorated by the antiwar movement, the messages of contemporary youth culture(s), the sexual revolution, and even the country's economic downturn. The movement thus exerted unprecedented stylistic influence on the theatrical mainstream. So, then, did adult musicals, which, while small and seemingly insignificant, in fact reflect the slow absorption of the sexual revolution into mainstream America through the course of the decade.

I thus intend to build on some of the excellent studies that detail the history of the Off and Off Off Broadway scenes.[14] While these studies do not necessarily focus on the slew of musicals that were written and performed Off and Off Off Broadway at the time, they nevertheless provide a great deal of information about the Caffe Cino and Judson Poets' Theater, both of which either directly or indirectly contributed to the development of the adult musical and will be discussed at length in this book.

## COMINGS AND GOINGS: THE STRUCTURAL APPROACH

This study focuses primarily on commercial adult musicals staged in New York City during the 1970s. While the structure is roughly chronological, some discussions appear out of chronological order so that relevant social, commercial, entertainment, or theater trends can be considered. To this end, while most musicals are discussed once in specific chapters, a few are examined in several different chapters in relation to specific issues. Because they enjoyed the longest commercial runs and thus stirred more than a typical share of controversies, for example, *Oh! Calcutta!* and *Let My People Come* are revisited several times in the book.

The central chapters consider legal, economic, political, aesthetic, or cultural issues that relate to adult musicals, either individually or collectively. While each chapter has its own trajectory and point of view, some of the chapters share related topics, and thus work well in tandem. Chapters 2 and 3, for example, are about gay musicals; chapters 4 and 5 are about feminist musicals; and chapters 6, 7, and 8 are about obscenity and the law. Readers interested in particular themes or topics may thus choose to read specific chapters.

Chapter 1 examines the aesthetic predecessors to the adult musical. These include relatively early forms like vaudeville and burlesque, which developed and cross-pollinated through the late nineteenth century and early twentieth. More immediate influences are also considered, in particular the Off Off Broadway scene as it developed from the mid-1950s through the 1970s. The rock musical *Hair*—which was developed Off Off Broadway in 1966, staged Off Broadway in 1967, and then reworked into an enormously successful Broadway production in 1968—is treated as an immediate and monumentally influential predecessor to the adult musical in general. The earliest of the adult musicals—*We'd Rather Switch, Oh! Calcutta!, Salvation,* and *Stag Movie*—are also discussed here.

Chapter 2 focuses on the rise of the gay rights movement, the Caffe Cino scene, the play *The Boys in the Band,* and the musical *Company,* all of which influenced depictions of gay men in adult musicals after *Oh! Calcutta!* Because Off Off Broadway was the cradle of modern gay theater long before the Stonewall riots erupted in June 1969, it became thereafter a convenient home for a number of gay rights–themed musicals, including *The Faggot, Boy Meets Boy, Lovers, Gay Company,* and *Sextet.* These musicals, which are related to the trajectory of the gay rights movement during the 1970s, are the subject of chapter 3.

While not as immediately influential, the second wave of feminism, which is the focus of chapter 4, nevertheless had a strong impact on adult musicals, especially in terms of the genre's depictions of sexual freedom and pleasure. While overtly polemical musicals like Myrna Lamb's *Mod Donna* (1970) tended not to sit well with critics or spectators, the lighter, more humorous feminist musicals from the later 1970s— Eve Merriam's *The Club* and especially Nancy Ford and Gretchen Cryer's *I'm Getting My Act Together and Taking It on the Road*—were far more commercially successful. These two musicals are the subject of chapter 5.

Chapter 6 traces the history of obscenity law, with emphasis on those rulings handed down between the mid-1950s and early 1970s that most directly impacted mass entertainment in the United States. The increased public acceptance of pornographic movies, the changing definitions of the word *obscenity*, and the blurred boundaries between art and erotica are related to the musical theater on the stage. "Porno chic" and its influence on *Let My People Come* are considered in this chapter. Chapter 7 continues to examine the impact of porno chic as the decade continued; musicals considered in this chapter include the feature film *The First Nudie Musical,* the porn-musical hybrid film *Alice in Wonderland: An X-Rated Musical Fantasy*, and the Marilyn Chambers live revue *Le Bellybutton*.

Chapter 8 considers the impact of contemporary obscenity laws on the play *Che!* and the musical *Let My People Come*. Chapter 9 examines the socioeconomic health of New York City between the mid-1960s and mid-1970s, and the impact of the financial crisis on the city's Broadway and Off Broadway theaters. The theater industry's desire to clean up an increasingly seedy Times Square—in part by setting a good example and offering wholesome family- and tourist-friendly musicals—clashed with its need to keep up with the country's rapidly changing social and sexual mores and to compete with newer, more explicit, mass-mediated forms of entertainment. The view of the sexual revolution in the 1977 hit Broadway musical *I Love My Wife* reflects the ultimate "mainstreaming" of the adult musical. The conclusion considers the influences that the adult musical of the 1970s have had on commercial musicals that have run in New York City, either on or Off Broadway, since the 1990s.

## MARKETPLACE, CANON, ARCHIVE, MEMORY: METHODOLOGY

Adult musicals constitute a subgenre that simultaneously drew from and reflected American culture at a time when "a new ethic of personal liberation trumped older notions of decency, civility, and restraint," resulting in a population that collectively decided, at least for the better part of a decade, to just "let it all hang loose."[15] Yet, with the possible exception of *Oh! Calcutta!*, which remains well known largely because of its extraordinary longevity, the entire subgenre has slipped rather rapidly from cultural memory. This is likely because adult musicals were, almost overwhelmingly, relatively small-scale productions that together did not have anywhere near the aesthetic or commercial impact of, say, Rodgers and Hammerstein or Sondheim or megamusicals. But it also has at least something to do with the fact that adult musicals existed during—and actively reflected aspects of—a time period that is, for a host of reasons, hardly revered as a glorious or memorable time in contemporary American history. Rather, as Beth Bailey and David Farber note in their introduction to *America in the Seventies*:

> The 1970s may be our strangest decade. It was an era of incoherent impulses, contradictory desires, and even a fair amount of self-flagellation. It was the decade that gave us the yellow smiley face, a sadly ironic symbol for a nation on the downswing of postwar prosperity. It was an age of limits and an age of excess: gas lines, pet rocks, and sixteen minutes of orgasmic moaning in Donna Summer's 1975 hit, "Love to Love You Baby." The 1970s were a time when "earth-tone polyester" made sense.[16]

The 1970s also had the great misfortune of coming directly after—and thus being almost immediately overshadowed by—the 1960s, which has been celebrated since it happened as "a decade of passion, grandeur, and tragedy."[17] In sharp contrast, the 1970s was painted, even as it progressed, as an era of defeat in Vietnam, political leadership that was disappointing at best and baldly corrupt at worst, endless oil crises, staggering economic problems, disenchantment, disenfranchisement, stupid fads, and ugly pants.[18] As cultural memory would have it, adult musicals, much like pet rocks and high-heeled sneakers filled with goldfish, reflect Americans at their most puerile, during the most absurd of recent decades: tucked behind cocktail tables in their leisure suits and feathered hairdos, gawking as naked actors sing, dance, and simulate sex acts for the price of admission and a two-drink minimum.

Yet cultural memory, or "the interplay of present and past in socio-cultural contexts," cannot be equated with history itself.[19] Rather, a culture collectively and perpetually decides not only how to remember itself—and thus what to preserve, to forget, to canonize, or to render to the junk piles of the past—but also how it wishes to be remembered as history unfolds. Because, as Aleida Assmann points out, "forgetting is the normality of personal and cultural life," memory is unique. It is the "exception which—especially in the cultural sphere—requires special and costly precautions."[20] Cultures choose to remember and to perpetuate themselves in specific ways, so that "in the context of cultural memory, the distinction between myth and history vanishes."[21]

Cultural artifacts, which help perpetuate cultural memory, can exist in several places: actively in the marketplace and the canon or passively in the archive. In some cases, past examples of cultural production continue to occupy all three. More than forty years after they hit their artistic peak, for example, the Beatles continue to be celebrated as musical innovators in Western collective memory. This collective memory is reinforced by the widespread availability of Beatles recordings, published writings, interviews, and written reception history, both in archives and in the marketplace. Having been canonized as one of the most important and innovative bands in popular music history, the Beatles are taught in schools, written about in books, and broadcast regularly via mass media. Constant exposure to the band, even decades after their breakup, helps perpetuate collective memory about them: they were artists; their music is important; they are worth remembering and teaching to later generations.

And yet the cultural memory of someone or something can never be mistaken for the event itself or the person himself or herself. A scholar, for example, can devote her life to the obsessive study of every cultural artifact pertaining to Mozart and still never know who, exactly, Mozart was or precisely how he was perceived in his place and time. In *Horrible Prettiness: Burlesque and American Culture*, Robert C. Allen reminds us that "objects and texts alone do not constitute culture," but that culture is instead created as "groups of people make sense, relevance, and pleasure out of the symbol systems they encounter in their daily experience."[22] As these "symbol systems" are sifted through time, their immediacy is lost, and they are either preserved as artifacts that help fuel cultural memory, or they are forgotten.

Which brings us back to adult musicals, a subgenre that American cultural memory has not treated very kindly. Not only were many adult musicals never recorded (or, if they were, then only poorly on vinyl or reel-to-reel tapes that have long since been sent to attics, basements, or dumpsters), but many of the performers, directors, and writers are either impossible to trace (due to assumed names, career changes, or self-imposed anonymity, all of which make identifying and locating them prohibitively difficult) or dead. Audience members proved similarly hard to track down. A number of people I've spoken with vaguely remember seeing the odd adult musical, but almost always the exclamation "I saw *Oh! Calcutta!*" or "I saw *Let My People Come*" is followed immediately by an apologetic statement such as "I can hardly remember it." "I was really drunk." "I was completely stoned." Or, "It was the seventies, you know." Because most of these shows were done by small theater companies on shoestring budgets, media coverage was relatively scant, and thus many adult musicals take up little or no space in archives. Although it is true that cultural artifacts and second-hand memories are not equivalent to culture itself, I often found myself longing for more in the way of tangible evidence or of stronger recollections from a larger pool of company members and spectators.

While adult musicals existed during a time that I experienced directly, I have not seen a vast majority of the musicals discussed herein. As the child of an uprooted New Yorker who never relinquished his strong ties to the city, I visited New York very frequently in my youth, before relocating here permanently in 1987. I have plenty of firsthand knowledge, as well as some crystal-clear memories, of the city in the 1970s. That said, the closest I ever came to seeing a 1970s adult musical was the afternoon I decided, while standing on the TKTS line with my parents and younger sister, that we should get tickets to see *Oh! Calcutta!* Because I was eight years old at the time, the answer was, of course, a firm no. Thus although I have read extant scripts, convinced the occasional original company member, composer, or lyricist to sing for me, listened repeatedly to several selfishly guarded if absolutely dismal bootleg recordings of performances, and tracked down original cast recordings whenever possible, many of these musicals remain frustratingly evasive. In piecing together the story of adult musicals, I have relied on those accounts that *have* made it into various archives, those recordings that remain available in the marketplace, and, most important, the memories of as many participants in adult musicals as I could find and who were willing to speak with me.

This, however, brings me to another challenge: as befitting the decade during which they existed, adult musicals are enormously embarrassing to many of the people who wrote and produced them, many of the actors who performed in them, many of the spectators who saw them, and many of the critics who deigned to review them. This embarrassment is often palpable in the writings that have been left behind by critics, many of whom were clearly made just as uneasy by the sight of naked bodies simulating sex as they were by clothed actors talking frankly about sexual freedom, gay rights, and women's liberation. Embarrassment was also customary in many of the interviews I conducted with actors, writers, producers, composers, and directors, a few of whom were reticent to speak with me at all and a larger number of whom sat for interviews but were nevertheless quick to tell me that their work in adult musicals was not their proudest moment, or something that they only did once, or something that they did because it was trendy, or something they took part in when they were young, naïve, foolish, and quite possibly perpetually stoned.

While this current of embarrassment is, as noted earlier, reflective of the ways the 1970s are preserved in cultural memory, it speaks as well to the fact that while the sexual revolution pervaded mainstream America in the 1970s, its entire citizenry did not thus suddenly, magically rise up and embrace the "new" sexuality with nary a blush. The nebulous middle ground, mentioned earlier, that many adult musicals occupied, hit home for a lot of critics and spectators, who were often just as embarrassed by human sexuality in the 1970s as most people were during any other time in American history. Further, and from a distance of several decades, the sexual openness and frequent proclamations of acceptance that were so integral to so many of these musicals clearly strikes even many of my informants as sneeringly quaint and naïve. Thus embarrassment has colored a great deal of the preserved history of this subgenre.

Any road to the past is filled with myriad pitfalls in the form of hazy memories, conflicting reports, exaggerations, revisions, omissions, and mistakes. I have tried my best to reconstruct as respectful a chronicle of this subgenre as possible, and I take responsibility for all errors, misinterpretations, and misrepresentations herein. With this book I hope to shed light on a long-ignored and thus little-known subgenre of the musical theater. My concern that what I am documenting may not always be perfectly accurate has been trumped by my desire to make sense of what continues to strike me as an oddly innocent, curiously touching subgenre—to allow it, at the very least, to take its proper place in the archive; to ease some of the collective embarrassment about it and its time; and even, perhaps, to nudge it, however gently, back into the approving embrace of collective memory.

# CHAPTER 1

# Burlesque, Off Off Broadway, and the Birth of the Adult Musical

This is the best fucking show I've ever seen!
—Buddy Hackett, on *Oh! Calcutta!*

I think it is disgusting, shameful and damaging to all things American. But if I were 22, with a great body, it would be artistic, tasteful, patriotic, and a progressive religious experience.
—Shelley Winters, on *Oh! Calcutta!*

When it opened at the Biltmore Theater on April 29, 1968, *Hair: The American Tribal Love-Rock Musical* became the first critically and commercially successful rock musical to land on Broadway. *Hair* served as a linchpin that harnessed the commercial potential of the theatrical mainstream to the experimentalism of Off Off Broadway. Featuring a book and lyrics by Open Theater members Gerome Ragni and James Rado and an innovative score by the jazz and R&B musician Galt MacDermot,[1] *Hair* was originally produced Off Broadway in 1967 as the inaugural production of Joseph Papp's Public Theater. Recast and reworked by the La MaMa director Tom O'Horgan for its leap to Broadway,[2] *Hair* retained a distinct Off Off Broadway sensibility due to its disjunct structure, frequent disregard of the traditional fourth wall, mélange of left-leaning social and political messages, and emphasis on collaboration and communal experience in both rehearsal and performance. *Hair* was celebrated as well for its catchy, contemporary-sounding score, the improvisatory feel of its loose plotline, and its disarmingly affectionate depiction of a subculture that was often misunderstood or maligned by the middle-aged mainstream that comprised a majority of the Broadway audience.

Yet none of *Hair*'s innovations had quite the immediate impact of its use of full-frontal nudity during the reenactment of a human be-in at the end of Act I. In a 1993 interview with the *New York Times*, Tom O'Horgan looked back and winced at this particular innovation. After *Hair* opened on Broadway, he remembered, it seemed that every play to open in New York "had to have an obligatory nude scene, no matter what, usually in the most tasteless possible fashion."[3]

By 1968 stage nudity was in fact being used fairly regularly in the Off Off Broadway realm, where O'Horgan had established his reputation. Yet *Hair* is frequently credited as the straw that broke the naked camel's back. The musical's extraordinary commercial success resulted in countless imitations, and thus a lot more stage nudity, not only Off Off Broadway but in the commercial mainstream, and not only in straight plays, but suddenly in musicals as well. By the end of the 1968–69 season, stage nudity had attained such faddishness that the critic Otis L. Guernsey Jr. was prompted to gripe that for all the nudity and groping happening onstage, very "little came of it except publicity, and not much of that. There was hardly even a sense of shock. Theatrically speaking, the nudity and mimed fornication accomplished so little, at the cost of so much effort, that perhaps we have got *that* notion out of the way at last, once and for all."[4] Guernsey was wrong, of course. When it came to stage nudity, the late 1960s were just the beginning.

While *Hair*'s nude scene almost single-handedly jump-started the adult musicals fad during the 1970s, the musical's impact on the subgenre went somewhat deeper. Like *Hair*, most adult musicals were topical, featured rock- and contemporary pop-based scores, and took, at the very least, a cursory stab at left-leaning social or political issues. Also like *Hair*, adult musicals were influenced by the overarching aesthetics and idealism of Off Off Broadway and, by extension, the various youth-driven social and political movements that had begun to take hold during the 1960s. *Hair*'s cocreator James Rado remembers that he and Gerome Ragni were always certain about who their ideal audience should be. "The original impulse was to write it for Broadway," Rado remembers. "We didn't want to just preach to the colored folks, to the Off Off Broadway scene. We wanted to bring the whole message and the scene uptown to a wider audience."[5] Like *Hair*, many adult musicals were ultimately used as much to educate mainstream audiences about contemporary sociosexual mores as to entertain.

While there is no question that *Hair* was an important immediate predecessor, adult musicals nevertheless also reflect the imprints of much older entertainment forms. The adult musical is probably most intimately connected with the overarching aesthetics and idealism of the Off Off Broadway experimentalism of the 1960s. But aesthetically speaking, adult musicals owe much to classic burlesque, both for its bawdy subject matter and, more often than not, its structure. In this chapter I consider both distant and immediate predecessors of the earliest adult musicals, *We'd Rather Switch* and *Oh! Calcutta!*, both of which opened within a year of *Hair*'s premiere on Broadway.

## IMMEDIATE PREDECESSORS: THE OFF OFF BROADWAY MOVEMENT

At both a physical and a philosophical distance from the Great White Way, Off Off Broadway inhabited roughly the same geographical area as its immediate predecessor, the Off Broadway realm, but was freer in terms of its organization and objectives.[6] The loose movement began in the late 1950s in reaction to Off Broadway's increasing commercialism and stretched even further than Off Broadway had in terms of scope and experimentation. Throughout the 1960s Off Off Broadway was populated by individuals and collectives devoted to developing artistically challenging work in alternative, noncommercial spaces. In New York

City during the 1960s members of the theatrical avant-garde pondered various ways that the theater might help transform a tumultuous nation. Many Off Off Broadway collectives devoted themselves to developing theater as a tool for sociopolitical change by blending political and aesthetic radicalism, pushing the boundaries of what was deemed theatrically appropriate, and encouraging audiences to engage directly with—and thereby become part of—performances.[7]

Although stage nudity would be adapted far more readily Off Off Broadway than in the commercial realm, it was relatively taboo in all of New York's theaters through the early 1960s. This would begin to change after the Royal Shakespeare Company's production of Peter Weiss's *The Persecution and Assassination of Marat as Performed by the Inmates of the Asylum of Charenton under the Direction of the Marquis de Sade* (commonly known as *Marat/Sade*) opened to critical acclaim at Broadway's Martin Beck Theater on December 27, 1965. This political morality play, directed by Peter Brook, was widely celebrated for its innovative staging, which reflected the influence of both Brecht and Artaud. *Marat/Sade* created a sensation as well not only because it featured plenty of "guillotined heads, buckets of red, white, and blue blood being poured down drains," and one "actress using her long hair as a whip," but also because it allowed audiences a glimpse of the naked backside of Ian Richardson as Marat, who at one point emerged naked from a bathtub beneath the stage.[8] Although this first flash of nudity took place on a Broadway stage, it was Off Off Broadway that would recognize Richardson's exposed *derrière* as the beginnings of a trend and run with it.

Due in large part to the influence of the sexual revolution, stage nudity became increasingly fashionable in the experimental realm through the mid- to late 1960s. The playwright Robert Patrick remembers that the trend was less inspired by a desire to shock audiences than by a genuine interest in creating honest depictions of the human condition. "When we first started putting nudity into plays, it was in situations where people would be nude in real life," he recalls. "So when people were making love in my plays, I had them nude! Who makes love in armor?"[9] As Off Off Broadway continued to exert stylistic influence on the mainstream, nudity became an increasingly familiar, if still controversial, feature on both fringe and commercial stages and arguably helped draw audiences to plays like *Scuba Duba* (Off Broadway, 1967), *The Prime of Miss Jean Brodie* (Broadway, 1968), *Sweet Eros* (Off Broadway, 1968) and *Tom Paine* (Off Off Broadway, 1968).

In the 1968 article "Theater of the Nude," which appeared in that paean to nudity, *Playboy* magazine, the journalist Howard Junker opined that stage nudity was no passing fad, but a crucial aspect of the revolution that he believed was taking place in the theater, and in the country at large. In their attempts to "knock down the barrier between art and life and make the audience part of the action," Junker wrote, radical playwrights in New York City were well on their way to transforming contemporary drama into a ritual of collectivism and collaboration, "where everybody is involved and the sound and the fury is all around." Nudity, he argued, was a central part of the contemporary theater's transformation. "It stands for freedom, for shedding old taboos, for throwing off the up-tight conventions of the older generation," he wrote. "For actors, trained to hide behind their roles, nudity can be a challenge. Actors have to work free of their own inhibitions in order to peel before an audience. Perhaps this kind of liberation will work for the audience, too. Instead of hiding behind conventional responses, it will come alive, jolted by the confrontation of naked self with naked self."[10]

Junker wasn't completely off the mark here. The increasingly copious use of stage nudity by the end of the 1960s was representative of the fringe's attempts to close the gap between audience and performer and to use theater as a tool with which to explore socially relevant subject matter, including that which, like sexuality, was traditionally considered taboo. Nevertheless Junker's argument for stage nudity as the key to revolution proved a bit overzealous, especially considering the fact that for every radical committed to using stage nudity toward social change, there were two or three entrepreneurs who were just as interested in the money that could be made by hiring young, good-looking people to show a little skin. Plenty of adult musicals were developed by companies or individuals devoted to some sort of social or political agenda, but just as many were backed by starry-eyed young producers eager to make a buck. Because adult musicals developed as the ideals of the counterculture and New Left were rapidly being absorbed into the commercial mainstream, most ended up with feet in both camps.

While adult musicals reflected some of the ideological influence of Off Off Broadway, a much older, more overtly commercial form also had a hand in shaping the subgenre. By the time adult musicals began to appear in New York City in the late 1960s, classic American burlesque had been dead for over twenty-five years. Nevertheless, the 1970s subgenre would not have existed if not for burlesque's aesthetic and structural influence.

## DISTANT PREDECESSORS: THE RISE OF BURLESQUE

Burlesque was so subversive for its time that it was eventually driven out of New York City by religious and antivice activists, Times Square business owners, and municipal officials.[11] Burlesque's demise, which took place between 1937 and 1942, was largely the result of social concerns about what it had become infamous for by the early twentieth century: scantily clad women on sexual display for audiences consisting primarily of working-class men. Yet when it first arrived in the United States a century earlier, burlesque bore little resemblance to the "filth" that Mayor Fiorello LaGuardia would eventually chase out of New York City in his quest to preside over "a clean American city" and to protect the morality of its citizens.[12]

Although burlesque shows have been documented in the United States as early as the 1840s, it was not until Lydia Thompson and her troupe of British Blondes arrived from London in 1868 to perform *Ixion* at Wood's Broadway Theater in lower Manhattan that the entertainment form became all the rage, first in New York, and then across the country. British burlesque derived from pantomime, which Thompson had performed regularly during the early years of her career ( Ex. 1.1).[13] Yet while pantomime was typically based on familiar children's stories, nineteenth-century burlesque tended instead to lampoon entertainment forms that were associated with high culture: drama, opera, and classic literature.

In burlesque spectacular staging was matched with broad physical humor and an abundance of punning and malapropism. Musical numbers were usually traditional or popular melodies outfitted with new lyrics or laden with double entendres resulting from new performance contexts. Dance numbers were similarly eclectic: individual productions parodied various folk and classical styles, and once burlesque gained a foothold in America the blackface minstrel tradition became fair game as well.

Thompson's troupe, like the many American companies that quickly formed and began to imitate it, featured female performers who wore pink tights beneath skirts that fell above the knee or dressed up like and impersonated men.[14] As Allen points out, while neither the men's clothing nor the blousy skirts revealed nearly as much of the female form as, for example, the tights and leotards of contemporaneous ballerinas, no performing art had ever attempted to represent women or femininity "as boldly or as inescapably" as Thompsonian burlesque; that it "did so not as a 'serious' dramatic treatment of the place of women in American society but rather in a form that united 'the coarsest fun with the most intoxicating forms of beauty' merely heightened its impact ( Ex. 1.2)."[15] Thus although burlesque was not initially associated with the striptease, the bump and grind, or the "hootchy-kootchy" dance—all of which would come much later—its appeal did rely from inception on female performers who transgressed conventions of sexuality, gender, and class ( Ex. 1.3).[16] Burlesque thus threatened the patriarchy through its representations of women in revealing clothing who were "dangerously impertinent in their mocking male impersonations, streetwise language, and nonsensical humor."[17]

Burlesque's subversive qualities were, of course, an enormous part of its appeal. But they also attracted the attention of noisy, persistent detractors, often in the form of religious and antivice organizations. Such groups grew increasingly focused on burlesque during the 1880s and 1890s. These decades saw the transformation of the rough-and-tumble, saloon-based variety entertainment form into middle-class family-oriented fare that was repackaged as vaudeville in the quest for a more civilized clientele. Forced into increasingly stiff competition with the newly middlebrow vaudeville circuit, the burlesque industry responded by cementing its position as the chief purveyor of "sexual titillation for the common man" by the turn of the century.[18]

Once burlesque established itself as an industry in the United States, the influence of other, contemporaneous entertainment forms like minstrelsy and vaudeville caused it to diverge sharply from the Thompsonian style in terms of content and structure over the course of several decades. Whereas in Thompson's time the centerpiece of burlesque was one long and fairly detailed sketch, late nineteenth-century burlesque had evolved into something that was structurally far more similar to vaudeville. By this point both vaudeville and burlesque typically blended short comic skits, variety acts, the occasional *tableaux vivants*, and musical numbers. What separated burlesque from vaudeville was less structural than contextual: vaudeville courted family audiences, while burlesque bluntly emphasized the raw sexuality of its female performers.

By the turn of the century the burlesque industry had developed into two circuits, known as "wheels." The central office of each wheel sent traveling burlesque companies out to participating theaters across the country. Entrepreneurs who were excluded from participating in these wheels found that they could compete on the local level by offering stock shows that were decidedly more risqué. As the wheels and stock companies locked themselves deeper and deeper into competition, burlesque's notable innovations began to center almost entirely on new ways to exploit female sexuality.

Within a few years of its introduction to American audiences at the Chicago World's Columbian Exhibition of 1893, for example, the "cooch" or "hootchy-kootchy" dance became a perennial favorite of burlesque houses. According to the autobiography of Morton Minsky, whose family ran some of the most well-known stock burlesque houses in New York during the late teens and 1920s, the addition of a runway to the stage at the Minskys' National Winter Garden in 1917 allowed audiences to get closer than ever before to the scantily clad, gyrating women they paid to watch perform onstage. Finally, and perhaps most infamously, the striptease became the centerpiece of burlesque by the mid-1920s.[19]

Burlesque began its slow decline in the early 1930s as film and live entertainment forms like cabaret, extravaganza, vaudeville, and the revue gradually began to eat away at its audience. The fact that the different factions of the burlesque industry continued to compete so fiercely with one another only hurt matters. Unable to keep up with the increasingly bawdy fare offered in the stock theaters, burlesque's wheels had all folded by 1931.[20]

Despite these setbacks, as well as the formation in 1932 of an antiburlesque campaign that would succeed in essentially destroying the entertainment form within the decade, burlesque benefited briefly from the onset of the Great Depression and the subsequent drastic toll that the stock market crash took on Broadway entertainment. While it was common for well over fifty musicals to open each season on Broadway during the roaring twenties, output after 1929 fell precipitously: the 1929–30 Broadway season offered only thirty-two new musicals, and there would be an all-time low of thirteen during the 1933–34 season.[21]

In 1931 the Minsky brothers learned that Oscar Hammerstein's grandiose Republic Theater on Forty-second Street was not only available, but also dirt cheap as a result of the ongoing, Depression-related financial difficulties of Hammerstein's heir, Arthur. Quick to seize the opportunity, the Minskys rented the Republic, thereby becoming the first outfit to transfer stock burlesque out of working-class neighborhoods like the Lower East Side, Union Square, and Harlem and bring it to Broadway. Like-minded producers followed suit, and soon burlesque had cropped up all over Times Square: down Forty-second Street from the Republic at the Eltinge and the Apollo, up at the Gaiety on Forty-sixth Street, and at the Central on Forty-seventh.[22]

The sudden prevalence of burlesque on Broadway initially gave this lowbrow entertainment form a huge boost in sales as well as a brief moment of mainstream appeal. But the jump from working-class enclaves to the Great White Way ultimately proved fatal. Burlesque's attempt to move into a neighborhood long associated with more respectable fare helped galvanize its traditional opponents, among them the

New York Society for the Suppression of Vice and an interdenominational branch of the Catholic Church's nationwide Legion of Decency campaign. These groups joined forces with the Forty-second Street Property Owners Association (POA), members of which included many Times Square corporations and businessmen, including hotels, banks, and "legitimate" producers, all of whom had money and political clout.[23]

The POA in particular grew concerned that the presence of burlesque houses in the neighborhood would lower its already precarious property values and attract a growing population of "disorderlies"—working-class and unemployed men who, it was feared, would surely spend their days loitering around the theaters, becoming at any moment and without warning violently overwhelmed by their dangerous and primitive sexual urges. The POA thus began to pressure the city's license commissioner not to renew any of the burlesque houses' annual licenses.[24] A decade-long legal battle ensued, which culminated in the Supreme Court's dismissal of the Gaiety Theater owner's petition for renewal in 1942 ( Ex. 1.4). What little was left of the burlesque industry was decimated after the lengthy, well-organized attack; short on money and facing dwindling audiences, the four burlesque houses that remained in New York City were forced to close their doors ( Ex. 1.5).[25] Burlesque as a specific entertainment style had faded significantly from public memory by the late 1960s, but the strong association of the form with scantily clad performers on sexual display had not. This is because in the decades since the entertainment style was driven out of town, the term *burlesque* was appropriated by far more explicit entertainment forms that were, like burlesque in its time, primarily associated with male, working-class audiences. By the 1960s peepshows, strip clubs, and pornographic movie theaters frequently featured some variant of the word *burlesque* on their marquees or in advertisements about their productions.

Because a vast majority of adult musicals were aimed at middle-class, mixed-gender audiences, the term *burlesque* was thus carefully avoided by producers who were eager to keep their adult musicals from risking association with "common" peepshows or strip clubs. As Allen notes in *Horrible Prettiness*, the perceived social or moral transgression of some entertainment forms is closely linked to class. As a result that which the dominant culture fears as degenerate or attacks as depraved when it emerges from the lower classes is often celebrated or at the very least blithely tolerated when it emerges from the upper or middle classes.[26]

Ziegfeld-style extravaganzas come to mind here. Flo Ziegfeld's *Follies*, which were mainstays on Broadway between 1907 and the early 1930s, borrowed heavily from the *Folies Bergère* but also from the minstrel, vaudeville, and burlesque traditions. Ziegfeld took from the burlesque an emphasis on female sexual display, but he recycled it so that mass audiences associated his *Follies* with the sophisticated cosmopolitanism of Paris instead of with American working-class sexuality.[27] The use of partial female nudity in the tableaux vivants that were regular features of Ziegfeld shows—and that were also soon featured in the Shuberts' yearly *Passing Show* and Earl Carroll's *Vanities*—were certainly daring enough for the time that citizen complaints were occasionally lodged with the police department ( Ex. 1.6). But none of these producers—successful businessmen who catered to middle- and upper-class audiences—were ultimately considered capable of causing moral corruption and were never charged with any crime.[28] Because Ziegfeld relied on lowbrow forms but offered them up to audiences as "refined" middle-class entertainment, the *Follies*, as well as the many imitations it spawned on Broadway, escaped the kind of censure and persecution that destroyed the burlesque industry.

Clearly aware that Flo Ziegfeld made many more friends on Broadway than the Minskys ever did, Kenneth Tynan, the esteemed drama critic and creator of *Oh! Calcutta!*, frequently went out of his way to distance his project from more lowbrow sexual entertainments. "It seemed to me a pity that eroticism in the theater should be confined to burlesque houses and the sleazier sort of night club," he wrote of *Oh! Calcutta!* in the *New York Times*.[29] The fact that classic burlesque had been persecuted to death decades earlier surely did little to encourage any further comparisons.

Yet it seems no accident that a majority of adult musicals, *Oh! Calcutta!* included, emulate burlesque both structurally and stylistically despite careful avoidance of the word *burlesque* itself. Like classic burlesque shows, most adult musicals featured brief comic sketches interspersed between songs and dance numbers. Also like burlesque, adult musicals relied heavily on the revue form, which is often easier to devise, cheaper to stage than book musicals, historically reliant on high-energy topicality, and long associated with the subversive.[30] A few adult musicals even featured classic burlesque sketches without ever identifying them as such. And, of course, as with burlesque, many adult musicals—at least those not focusing exclusively on gay male culture—relied heavily on displays of the female sexual body to attract audiences.

Adult musicals also emulated burlesque in more subtle ways. Like burlesque, adult musicals cropped up on Broadway only after becoming established in less commercial theatrical realms. Also like burlesque, adult musicals that were not conceived by Broadway insiders, and thus automatically assumed to be appropriate for Broadway audiences, were not made particularly welcome on Broadway, denizens of which tended to greet the occasional transfer uptown with concern or outright hostility.

Finally, like burlesque, adult musicals were an entertainment genre that benefited greatly from economic recession. As Allen reminds us in *Horrible Prettiness*, since at least the late nineteenth century, periods of economic hardship in this country tend to favor entertainment forms that serve lower social and economic groups better than they do comparatively high-class forms. Vaudeville, Allen points out, was aimed at lower-class audiences until the Panic of 1893, after which it became solidly associated with the middle class (💾 Ex. 1.7). Similarly the economic downturn of 1907 impelled the burgeoning film industry to step up its efforts to build middle-class audiences. "With less money to spend on entertainment during times of economic hardship, commercial entertainment patrons look again at cheaper forms," Allen concludes. "So it was with burlesque in the early 1930s."[31] So it was as well with adult musicals in the 1970s.

The fact that adult musicals thrived in New York City just prior to and during a particularly harrowing financial crisis, only to fall out of fashion as the crisis was resolved, is hardly insignificant. Economic pressure can take its toll on creative output, and this was certainly the case when it came to the commercial theater in 1970s New York. Weakening attendance, both on and off Broadway, combined with skyrocketing inflation, forced producers to slash the costs of production while simultaneously boosting ticket prices, thereby offering audiences much less for much more. Financially strapped as they were, many producers grew wary of anything but the most escapist, risk-free fare, which in turn resulted in Broadway theater seasons that were economically and aesthetically disappointing, and in productions Off and Off Off Broadway that relied heavily on innovation, creativity, and risk to attract audiences. Thus in some respects the adult musical, much like the Off Off Broadway movement that helped spawn it, was born of necessity. Need to produce a show on little or no budget and still hope to make a profit? No problem: just hire a group of young, good-looking actors who are willing to talk dirty, simulate myriad sexual positions, or tap-dance in the nude!

The fact that the adult musical failed to outlive the decade and thus to thrive in more prosperous times is additionally telling: It implies that the subgenre was accepted as a viable commodity during a time of increasingly severe economic downturn, but that it was never taken particularly seriously as lasting art. Adult musicals had nowhere near the cultural impact that burlesque did, nor did the genre last nearly as long. Adult musicals had a run of a mere decade at best, whereas burlesque prevailed in the United States for the better part of a century. Burlesque was a performance genre that developed its own long-hewn aesthetic, stylistic, and structural traditions, whereas the comparatively short-lived adult musical subgenre tended to emulate earlier forms rather than contribute much in the way of its own aesthetic influences. American burlesque came into its own before it died; the adult musical was never able to escape its frustrating cultural in-betweenness or to properly define itself as something other than what it was not. Yet perhaps what links burlesque and adult musicals most closely is their mutual ability to simultaneously appeal to and embarrass both the mainstream press and the middle-class public. Both forms are ultimately about sex, after all, and sex has been a private, intimate matter, regardless of the social movements that have on occasion urged the middle class *en masse* to throw off generations of cultural conditioning in order to celebrate the body beautiful unabashedly in public places.

The adult musical subgenre was no better or worse, ultimately, than any other subgenre: there were some great musicals, and some lousy ones; some with rousing musical numbers and some with forgettable scores; some with talented, dedicated actors, and some that were cast with less inspired performers who just happened to look nice naked. Yet they were all—regardless of content, form, presentational style, overall theme, or commercial and critical reception—at base, earnestly sexual. Perhaps this explains, more than anything else, why the subgenre—like much of the content of classic burlesque—has been so thoroughly lost to time.

## WORLDS COLLIDE: *WE'D RATHER SWITCH*

The first adult musical to open in New York City was unique in the sense that it had no relationship to Off Off Broadway or to the sociopolitical ideologies of the time. *We'd Rather Switch* was instead an homage to classic burlesque. Developed among the lowbrow entertainment forms that had arrived in Times Square long after burlesque had been driven away, the musical was purely an entrepreneurial venture that capitalized on the faddishness of post-*Hair* stage nudity.

*We'd Rather Switch* began its run on May 2, 1969, at the Mermaid Theater on West Forty-second Street. Subtitled *A Groovy New Revue* on its hand-written, mimeographed program, *We'd Rather Switch* was developed and produced by the son of a capo in the notorious Genovese crime family, who was simultaneously repulsed by his father's livelihood and keenly aware of the many ways that he could benefit from it (  Ex. 1.8). Mario "The Great" Manzini (born Dennis Migliore) spent much of his adolescence working as an escape artist, both in sideshows on Coney Island and in various Times Square venues. In the spring of 1969 Manzini was driving back to New York after touring the Midwest with a traveling circus when he came up with the idea for *We'd Rather Switch*. "I was driving back and this idea came to me: Burlesque. See, Minsky's burlesque was in Times Square in the '30s and early '40s, and Mayor LaGuardia chased them all out." Aware that burlesque traditionally focused on women, Manzini came up with a novel twist. "I had this idea: what if somebody opened a *male* burlesque show for women and, you know, anyone else who wants to see that? Basically, my idea was to take an old-time burlesque show, with comedy sketches and strippers, and reverse them. So the guys did the stripping—as guys, not a drag show—and the girls did all the comedy routines. They switch parts. That's how we came up with the name *We'd Rather Switch*."[32]

Diana Lynn Goble tells jokes and Wayne Clark strips in *We'd Rather Switch*. Photo by Kenn Duncan. Courtesy of the Kenn Duncan Archive, New York Public Library for the Performing Arts.

Back in New York, Manzini brought his idea to Larry Crane, a former actor and puppeteer with whom Manzini had worked at Hubert's Dime Museum in the early 1960s. Crane had since turned to film directing and scoring, and had made several sexploitation films, including *Julie Is No Angel* (1967), *Beware the Black Widow* (1968), and *All Women Are Bad* (1969). Crane agreed to help Manzini develop his idea and immediately set to work writing original music and lyrics for it. Walter Berger, a scriptwriter with whom Crane frequently collaborated, joined the team to help rework the sketches, which were "all basically standard burlesque bits—all the classics," Manzini remembers. "Except we had them in reverse, so that when things were supposed to happen to the guys, they would happen to the women, and when things were supposed to happen to the women, they would happen to the guys."[33]

Well aware of how lucrative adult entertainment was becoming by the end of the 1960s, Crane convinced Manzini that *We'd Rather Switch* should feature as much full-frontal nudity as possible. "My idea wasn't even to have nudity," Manzini remembers. "Because, traditionally, with burlesque, they just got down to g-strings and pasties. But Larry, who I hired to direct and write the whole score and the script, that was his idea. He said, 'Why don't we just go totally nude?' He said there were ways to get around [the law] and so we did it."[34]

Manzini's relationship with his well-connected father, though strained, nevertheless allowed him to pursue his creative ideas far more thoroughly than the typical Times Square dime museum escape artist might. Although he continued to hold out hopes that Manzini would abandon interest in show business and agree to join the family business, his father begrudgingly bankrolled the production and gave him free, unlimited access to the family lawyer. Manzini learned, in consultation with his father's attorney, that when it came to staged entertainment in New York City, laws were upheld "as long as you didn't have any sex onstage, or anybody naked and touching each other. Basically, all we did is have the guys strip, but nobody touched each other or nothing. It was just comedy, with music and sketches. That's all. We never had legal trouble because we didn't do anything wrong."[35]

As will be examined at greater length in chapter 6, there was in fact an awful lot of law-abiding stage nudity happening in New York City by 1969, and although *We'd Rather Switch* seems to be the first show to attempt a contemporary twist on classic burlesque, it was hardly the first show to take advantage of a number of court rulings that reflected an increasingly lenient view of obscenity. In 1957 the Supreme Court ruled in *Roth v. United States* that a performance or item could be labeled obscene only if it was judged to be "utterly without redeeming social value." In *What Wild Ecstasy: The Rise and Fall of the Sexual Revolution*, John Heidenry points out that after the ruling, because of this highly subjective terminology, "no obscenity trial was complete without a clergyman, literary critic, psychologist, or First Amendment advocate spotting at least a soupçon of redeeming social value in even the most sordid examples of hard-core."[36]

At roughly the same time that obscenity laws were being relaxed across the country, New York–based organized crime, which was already intimately connected with adult entertainment, was attempting to expand its control of coin-operated machine companies that manufactured arcade games, jukeboxes, and "peeps."[37] In 1959 Charlie "Bull" Pucciarelli, a member of the Lucchese crime family, opened the Bee See adult bookstore on West Forty-second Street and had it outfitted with a peep machine. Business was so good that within a few years Pucciarelli had opened five more bookshops in Times Square, all of which featured at least one peep.[38] Peepshows proved so overwhelmingly lucrative that the retail sex market—and with it the presence of organized crime—exploded in Times Square through the late 1960s. By the time Manzini was staging *We'd Rather Switch* there were more than thirty adult bookstores in Times Square alone; there would be sixty-eight by 1970.[39] Not at all coincidentally, considering the increasingly important role that organized crime played in Times Square, Manzini had no problem arranging to rent one of the many "sex cinemas" along Forty-second Street for the purpose of mounting *We'd Rather Switch* in spring 1969.[40]

Like most of the cinemas that Manzini could choose from, the Mermaid Theater was never meant to function as a sexploitation house. Along with a handful of other small theaters in the neighborhood, the Mermaid was built in the late 1950s and early 1960s by the West Side real estate developer Irving Maidman. Maidman had hopes that a cluster of theaters extending west on Forty-second Street from Ninth Avenue would not only help bring some of the innovative energy and intimacy of Off Broadway physically closer to Broadway, but would simultaneously help revive a particularly derelict part of Manhattan.

Maidman built his first theater, the Maidman Playhouse, in 1959. The 199-seater, at 416–18 West Forty-second Street, was by all accounts a "gorgeous little house," with plush seats, state-of-the-art lighting, and excellent sight lines.[41] After a string of shows at the Playhouse earned the admiration of critics only to flop commercially, Maidman confidently informed the press that "there was nothing wrong with 42nd Street that couldn't be fixed by opening more theaters nearby."[42] Thus in 1961 he opened two 149-seaters next to his first theater: the Midway, at 422 West Forty-second Street, and the Mermaid, right next door at 420 West Forty-second. A year later a fourth Maidman house, the Masque, opened down the block at 442 West Forty-second Street.

Yet no matter how cozy, inviting, and numerous his small theaters, Maidman failed to convince audiences that the seedy, poorly lit, eerily isolated stretch of Forty-second Street beyond Ninth Avenue was worth venturing after dark. In June 1965 the real estate developer announced that he would be renting all of his theaters for new uses rather than continue to struggle to keep them functioning as Off Broadway houses.[43] By 1968 every one of Maidman's theaters had become a venue for adult entertainment.[44]

In 1969 the Mermaid was operated by the exploitation film distributor Stan Borden, who was the head of the Times Square–based American Film Distributing Corporation. Crane and Berger had befriended Borden after his company distributed *All Women Are Bad*. With the money to bankroll *We'd Rather Switch* in place and Crane hard at work on the music and lyrics, Manzini approached Borden for help securing a theater. "Now, porn wasn't really out yet, but they had what you would call, uh, beaver films, where they would show the girl naked, but from the navel up and certain things," Manzini remembers. "Stan Borden had a bunch of these theaters and he was good friends with us, so he gave us the Mermaid, which was on 42nd Street, like at 11th Avenue."[45] Once the Mermaid was secured, Manzini and Crane placed open calls for *We'd Rather Switch* in *Back Stage* and *Show Business* magazines, cast the show, filed with Actors' Equity, started rehearsals, and were up and running within the month.

If *We'd Rather Switch* never quite established itself as proper middle-class entertainment, it nevertheless managed to set itself apart from the more sexually explicit, lowbrow fare that West Forty-second Street had become infamous for by 1969. Like a great many adult musicals that would follow it, *We'd Rather Switch*'s neither-nor status—neither raunchy enough to function as proper adult entertainment nor polished enough to please Broadway musical connoisseurs—initially helped pique curiosity about it but ultimately failed to help it connect with an audience that would sustain it.

There were several reasons for the ambiguous status of *We'd Rather Switch*, many of which apply to later productions as well. In the first place, aside from the frequent flashes of male nudity—and, Manzini remembers, one number in the second act during which a female cast member entered from the wings in the nude—the revue was firmly rooted in classic burlesque and thus decidedly more innocent than most of

Richard Schmeer, Ronnie Britton, and Phillips Cross (left to right) strike up the band in *We'd Rather Switch*. Photo by Kenn Duncan. Courtesy of the Kenn Duncan Archive, New York Public Library for the Performing Arts.

the fare that was being offered along West Forty-second Street in 1969. Here, for example, Manzini describes the opening number, which was titled "The Greatest Show on Earth / The Strangest Show on Earth":

> The opening number starts off with a guy onstage in overalls painting a sign that says "Burlesque." Some girls—two strippers—walk onstage. I can't remember the exact dialogue, but basically, the girls say, "Well, another show tonight," and the guy says, "Yeah, I'm trying to get the sign touched up for the show tonight," and then he says something like, "I'm tired of doing the same old shit," and one of the strippers says something like, "I bet I could do comedy better than you." He says, "I got an idea, why don't we switch? Why don't you girls do the comedy and I'll do the stripping?" "Oh! Okay, let's call the whole cast out!" So they all come out and go into this whole number. The lights come down and come up again, and there are four guys dressed—everything is gold—gold sandals, gold g-strings, gold bands on their chests, and they all got a hat. On the final note, they all pull off their g-strings and shock the audience. It was done in good taste and everything, it wasn't anything dirty or sexual or anything. It was a musical comedy, you know. But boy, did that pack people in.[46]

Manzini remembers that the audience for *We'd Rather Switch* consisted not only of heterosexual couples and groups of women eager to see naked men onstage, but also "a lotta gay guys."[47] The fact that *We'd Rather Switch* appealed to both straight and gay spectators at a time when far more overtly erotic entertainment of all gender affiliations had become increasingly available in the neighborhood implies that the musical was in fact quite tame. The stage nudity employed in *We'd Rather Switch*, much as it had in *Hair*, clearly functioned more to surprise—or, as Manzini remembers above, to *shock*—the audience than it did to encourage sexual arousal.

The very mixed press coverage for *We'd Rather Switch* is additionally telling. In marketing the production, Manzini and Crane initially placed advertisements in adult periodicals, such as Al Goldstein's then new weekly tabloid, *Screw*. Manzini remembers of his decision to run ads in *Screw*, "Goldstein was the same age as me, and we became friends—we had a lot in common. Everyone thought that because he was in the business, he was sick, but he was a normal guy. A nice guy. He did it for the money, you know? *I* was involved in all that stuff, and I'm a normal guy. Al was the same way. So we put ads in *Screw* because people reading it would then come to see the show, and there was nothing terrible about it."[48] Yet while reviews of *We'd Rather Switch* that appeared in *Screw* were certainly typical of the famously blunt periodical, they were also inadvertently clear that despite the copious nudity, the musical was not very erotic.

*Screw* reviewed *We'd Rather Switch* twice, once about two weeks into its run and a second time about six months later, in November 1969. The first review, unsigned but likely written by Goldstein himself,[49] struggles mightily to force the musical into an erotic, heterosexual framework, before abruptly giving up:

> Burlesque is shoddy and sad in spite of spread-eagle bodies and gyrating pussy boxes. A brave guy named Larry Crane has put on a variation of the old strip show called

"We'd Rather Switch."... The guys strip and the broads are the comedians. The whole thing isn't my cup of cunt, but the girls are interesting. Trish Sandberg is lovely and pussy-eating good and a surprisingly professional actress with solid credits. Diana Lynn Goble isn't bad as a thespian and smashing as a body. The boys in the show are slight and I understand the cats meow in homosexual happenings. They do strip to bare cocks but it's not my thing so carry on.[50]

Thereafter blurbs advertising *We'd Rather Switch* were typically listed in sections of *Screw* that were specifically designated for gay male readers.

Yet all of the mentions in *Screw*, whether they ran in the "For Straights" or "For Gays" sections, emphasize the fact that while *We'd Rather Switch* was entertaining, it was not terribly erotic for anyone. A blurb advertising the musical in the "For Gays" section of Bob Amsel's "Up and Coming" entertainment listings on October 20, 1969, notes that although the cast members' "cocks [were] used to their best advantage," the musical is merely "corny" and "lots of fun."[51] A lengthier blurb about *We'd Rather Switch*, which appeared in the "Homosexual Citizen" pages of *Screw* in early November 1969, came to much the same conclusion:

For all you "nice" folks out there in suburbia, let us be the first to tell you that there is, unfortunately, nothing perverted or sensual about WE'D RATHER SWITCH. Its [*sic*] pure old-fashioned stuff (probably the only nostalgic kickback to the old days left in these here parts). Its good-humored and lively cast will give you harmless glimpses of posteriors and unerected penises (you can blink if you have an aversion to stark reality) and will go through old-fashioned stage routines designed to remind you of the cleanliness of your youth.... Had we directed WE'D RATHER SWITCH, we'd have approached it from a somewhat different angle, with less emphasis on purely heterosexual humor and a variety of sensual males who'd work harder at *stimulating* both males and females. As it is, WE'D RATHER SWITCH is a humorous parody of the straight burlesque. As such, it's good fun for every pure and virtuous adult member of the family.[52]

Clearly *We'd Rather Switch*—which was never quite stimulating enough from either a gay or a straight perspective—was not the kind of live entertainment that *Screw*'s contributors were comfortable writing about.

The mainstream press also had a lot of trouble with *We'd Rather Switch*. While there was never any official opening date, the show was reviewed at various points between June and December 1969 by periodicals including *Back Stage*, the *Village Voice*, *Variety*, and the *New York Times*. The critics for these papers all found the show to be rather crass, but disagreed markedly about whether or not this was a bad thing.

George L. George of *Back Stage* hated *We'd Rather Switch*. He found the first act so "unfunny, tasteless and dull" that most of his paragraph-long review was devoted to the grateful description of "a providential fire in the theatre building" that began sometime during the first act of the show and "relieved him of the professional obligation of attending the second half."[53] Mel Gussow of the *New York Times* was not quite as disgusted by the production as George was, but nonetheless found it to be "depressingly tacky" and performed by an "awkward and amateurish" cast.[54]

Yet the critics for the *Village Voice* and *Variety*, while agreeing that the show was hardly the most professional they'd seen, nevertheless felt that its amateurishness lent it a certain surprising sweetness. "Sexiness is somehow lost in the translation from female to male burlesque, although the strippers go all the way and the comic innuendo is far from subtle," Marilyn Stasio noted in the *Village Voice*. But, she continued, "good humor takes its place," as does "a delightful, absurdist zaniness," which ultimately gives the musical "a dumb unpretentious friendliness not unlike that of schooldays musicals at which it's very easy to have a good time."[55] Similarly a staff writer for *Variety* acknowledged that although the musical has plenty of "tasteless and drearily obvious moments" and that Berger and Crane "can tell a dirty story or stage an unworkable scene with the worst of them," *We'd Rather Switch* nevertheless demonstrates "what off-Broadway should be like but seldom is—a place where some amateurism can be tolerated when there is a foundation of talent, a place where taste and waste can mingle without serious loss of the pulse that makes real theater."[56]

Early in its run, Manzini remembers, *We'd Rather Switch* generated enough word of mouth—and likely enough curiosity about the copious male nudity—that tickets sold briskly and that, for a time, there were "lines around the corner."[57] Nevertheless the perceived amateurishness of *We'd Rather Switch*, combined with its inability to connect solidly with middle- or lowbrow, gay or straight audiences, eventually led to trouble for the production. Like a great many adult musicals to come after it, *We'd Rather Switch* suffered from its inability to offer *enough* of any particular quality to any particular audience: it was too tame for spectators (and critics) craving erotic entertainment and was crude enough to be dismissed as a poor "excuse for a male peep show" by critics (and audiences) who were expecting a more traditional—and polished—musical.[58] By late December audiences had dropped off sharply. "The entertainment, and I use the word very loosely, has been vending its wares for nine months [*sic*] at the Mermaid Theater," Mel Gussow wrote in the *New York Times* on December 20. He continues, not bothering to disguise his condescension or preconceived notions about "proper" theater audiences: "The producer, Mario Manzini, who is a professional escape artist, must also be a magician. The other night when I attended, there were fewer than 20 people in the audience, only two of them, I think, female."[59]

By this point too the show had begun to suffer in other ways. While the original performers were all Equity actors, turnover in the cast was rapid, and Manzini began to replace outgoing cast members with professional strippers, which undoubtedly contributed to the air of amateurism that many of the theater critics noted in their reviews. The actors and strippers did not always work well together, and it didn't help matters that Manzini and his production team had little prior experience in the musical theater. After some of the actors began to complain to Equity about the lack of professionalism, Manzini grew tired of paying the union every time it fined him and decided to simply close the show and move on.[60] The Mermaid Theater quickly reverted to more overtly erotic fare; its owner divided it into two tiny rooms in early 1970 and began to screen "beaver" films in one and "male beavers" in the other.[61]

Once *We'd Rather Switch* closed, Mario Manzini opened a midtown massage parlor that he called Sultan's Harem, which proved so popular that he soon opened seven more between midtown and Wall Street. He remained in New York until his family elders—many of whom provided him much-needed protection in an illicit, increasingly competitive business—began to die off. Aware that he was becoming more vulnerable with every death in the family, especially since he had never agreed to become a "made" man, Manzini abruptly left New York City and his businesses behind in the early 1980s. He currently lives in Missouri, where he runs his own entertainment company. "I like it here," he muses. "It's peaceful."[62]

Scholars like Robert C. Allen and Andrea Friedman have written at length about the fact that the composition of an audience, especially in terms of its class and gender makeup, contributes enormously to the general public's perception of the entertainment form in question. Critics, depending on their own biases and those of the periodicals they write for, both mirror and reinforce the ideals and expectations of various types of audiences. "Legitimate" theater, for example, has been deemed legitimate in the first place largely because it attracts men and women from the middle and upper classes as well as the attention of critics who work for the publications these audiences consume.[63] *We'd Rather Switch* managed to transcend its lowbrow surroundings enough to confound lowbrow audiences and critics at *Screw* but never functioned properly as mainstream theater fare and was thus ultimately unable to resonate with any audience at all. Yet a month after *We'd Rather Switch* opened, a far more commercially successful adult musical would connect solidly with a mainstream crowd, due in large part to the efforts of its decidedly class-conscious creator and despite—or perhaps because of—the tepid reaction by mainstream critics.

## OH! CALCUTTA!

*Oh! Calcutta!* was the brainchild of the esteemed British critic and dramaturge Kenneth Tynan. An ardent free-speech advocate, Tynan was a particularly prominent force in the establishment of the Theatre Act of 1968, which abolished theater censorship in England. In anticipation of the passage of the act, Tynan approached the London theater producer Michael White with an idea for a highbrow burlesque that Tynan hoped would open in London's West End in celebration of England's newfound artistic freedom.[64]

Yet once the Theatre Act of 1968 was passed, Tynan began to have second thoughts and eventually decided to open his revue in New York first and in London thereafter. "I've been so heavily involved in the censorship fight that my name on a show right now would attract the killers, the bluenoses, who under the new law, you know, can still make trouble," he explained to Lewis Funke in the *New York Times*. "I don't want to be one of the first test cases."[65]

Tynan set about developing his erotic revue for "thinking voyeurs."[66] He began by scouting around for producers and a director and also invited a number of prominent writers he admired to "dramatize their own sexual fantasies or observations on sexuality."[67] Sketches were solicited from and eventually contributed by Samuel Beckett,

Sam Shepard, Leonard Melfi, Jules Feiffer, Dan Greenburg, Sherman Yellin, John Lennon, and Tynan himself. The sketches that were selected to be used in the production were kept anonymous in the program, in part to protect the reputations of the authors but even more so to add to the overall mystique of the production. "It's partly because I don't want them to feel that their privacy is being invaded, but mainly because I want the show to be judged as a whole," Tynan explained in the *New York Times*. "I was afraid that, if we named names, critical attention might focus on the better-known authors at the expense of the others. As it is, I think we've provided the audience with a fascinating guessing-game."[68]

Musically speaking, *Oh! Calcutta!* took a nod from *Hair's* contemporary sound. The score was composed and, with the exception of a few full-cast song-and-dance numbers, performed by a trio called the Open Window, which featured Peter Schickele, before his P. D. Q. Bach fame, and the composers Stanley Walden and Robert Dennis. All three men had had experience working in the Off or Off Off Broadway theater, and their moody, harmonically sophisticated underscoring reflected an understanding of both contemporary popular styles and a quirky, highly theatrical sensibility (🔊 Ex. 1.1).

*Oh! Calcutta!* reflected Off Off Broadway's influence not only in its score, but also in its reliance on writing by innovative playwrights like Shepard, Melfi, and Beckett, as well as in Tynan's choice of director. Jacques Levy was a clinical psychologist who, disillusioned with his career, turned in 1965 to the Off Off Broadway realm. There he directed such productions as Sam Shepard's *Red Cross* and Jean-Claude van Itallie's *America Hurrah*.[69] Levy was enlisted by Tynan not only to shape the collection of songs and sketches into an evening's entertainment, but, perhaps more important, to select a group of actors and help prepare them to be—or, at the very least, to seem—comfortable performing completely naked before a paying audience.

Aware that acting without clothes "is a problem you have to get over to get on to the normal acting problems," Levy drew both from his training in psychology and his work in the experimental realm when casting and rehearsing *Oh! Calcutta!*[70] Early in the audition process he struggled with Actors' Equity over the right to ask actors being considered for roles to disrobe during callback auditions, on the grounds that those who were unwilling would not be ideal for the production. Once Levy and Equity had agreed to the union's conditions (an Equity member had to be present during auditions, and actors had to be informed well in advance that the role they were going to be auditioning for required nudity), Levy led prospective actors through a series of improvisational exercises to gauge their comfort level.[71] One original cast member, Boni Enten, remembers the process as an entirely positive experience:

> The first thing you had to do was sing, then you had to dance, and then you read. I did that and got a callback. When they called you back, you had to—Jacques gave us an improv: you were walking through a wood, you know, green and sunny, and you had just gotten a letter that made you really happy. And you came to a stream, and it was hot, and you were feeling great, and the deal was, you would take your clothes off and skinny-dip. Now, I had never taken my clothes off in front of an audience. By this

time, you knew that you were going to have to do this. And I'm sure some people, when it got right down to it, couldn't do it. But I got to the stream, and took my clothes off, and they had a rug down where the water was supposed to be, and I just sort of got in, and it was fine. It was really okay. I did a little dancy thing, splashing water and jumping around a bit. Then I thanked them—I was sort of jumping up and down, saying, "This was *great*, thank you so much!" They put the cast together out of those last auditions.[72]

Once the show was cast, Levy led his actors through a series of "encounter group" sessions, which Enten points out were in many ways typical of Off Off Broadway companies at the time. Yet Levy's exercises were designed specifically "to enable each actor to accept the fact of his own body and to work comfortably with his fellow actors—without clothes."[73] At the first cast meeting Levy introduced two restrictions to these "sensitivity exercises," which the actors were led through three hours a day, six days a week, for the first three weeks of rehearsals. Levy's first rule was that actors were allowed to veto any activity that made them feel uncomfortable. His second rule, which was quickly dubbed the "no-fuck law" or "NFL" by the cast, was that no matter how intimate they became with one another during rehearsals, actors were not to engage in sexual intercourse with one another, for fear of inciting jealousy or feelings of exclusion in the company.[74]

Another original cast member, Nancy Tribush, describes a typical sensitivity exercise, which were almost always conducted in the nude:

> In one exercise…we all sat in a circle and made eye contact, two people at a time looking deeply into each other's eyes for a while, then each doing the same thing with somebody else. At the end of that, all but two of the ten were crying. One of the two was on the brink, and the other was just "out of it" for some personal reason. Then Jacques said, "Reach out and touch anyone you want to," and it was like a magnet—eight people reached out to touch these two people! It was as if they wanted them to join. It was a fantastic experience! Finally, the girl who was resisting most just broke down and virtually collapsed in front of us. Then everybody was on top of everybody else doing things, not obviously sexual things, but things like blowing against the skin of one's back—Boof!—like that, as you would with an infant.[75]

Raina Barrett acknowledges that although the sensitivity exercises were often both emotionally exhausting and enormously sexually frustrating, they nevertheless helped the cast develop particularly intense personal bonds. "Those of us in *Calcutta*'s original cast became aware of our deepest, most instinctive feelings in reacting to each other," she wrote. "The Sensitivity Exercises brought home the message that sex is a *good* thing, that honest passion and emotions are nothing to be ashamed of or embarrassed about. Jacques Levy knew that actors and actresses could not portray real erotica, could not depict a healthy, sensual experience, if deep in their hearts they thought such subjects were dirty. How could we expect an audience to relax and enjoy an erotic scene, if they could sense that we were inwardly cringing in distaste?"[76]

Despite its Off Off Broadway moorings, *Oh! Calcutta!* was intended from inception to be a highly commercial, widely accessible venture. The company thus frequently went out of its way to appeal to a broad, mainstream audience, all the while acknowledging the risqué subject matter. Tynan, as his show's chief spokesperson, repeatedly did so by framing *Oh! Calcutta!* as a show that would be both classy and arousing—or, as he put it in the *New York Times*, an evening of "gentle stimulation, where a fellow can take a girl he is trying to woo."[77] "Some time ago," he explained in an interview with the *Village Voice*, "it occurred to me that there was no place for a civilized man to take a civilized woman to spend an evening of civilized erotic stimulation. At one end, there's burlesque, at the other, an expensive night club, but no place in between. We're trying to fill that gap with this show."[78] The result, he hoped, would be "a few cuts above burlesque in intelligence and sophistication."[79] Note Tynan's traditional assumptions about men, women, and the theater, all of which are carefully bundled into comments he makes in some of New York's most prominent mainstream periodicals: this is, he implies, a classy show, and even an old-fashioned one. This is sexy, sure, but it's also good, clean, upmarket fun.

Tynan's interest in selling *Oh! Calcutta!* as "elegant erotica...for civilized people" is certainly evidenced in his choice of title, which derives both from a phonetic French pun and a French Surrealist painting.[80] *Oh, Calcutta! Calcutta!* was the title of a painting by the Parisian-based surrealist Clovis Trouille (1889–1975) (🖲 Ex. 1.9). The painting, which depicts the plump, decorated backside of a naked, reclining woman draped luxuriously in dark red velvet, was used, often in slightly censored form, to advertise the musical on posters and in the print media (🖲 Ex. 1.10). The title of both the painting and the musical is a pun of the French "O, quell cul t'as," or, roughly, "What a nice ass you have!" Tynan, along with Elkins and Levy, made sure to frequently and publicly emphasize the high caliber of the contributing writers, the dedication and professionalism of the actors, and the many previous accomplishments of Tynan himself.

The fact that no expense was spared on what Tynan insisted would be "an entertainment in the erotic area in the best possible taste" was also frequently—and not at all coincidentally—mentioned in the press in advance of the show's opening.[81] The creative team chose to house the production in the Phoenix, a dilapidated Yiddish theater on Twelfth Street and Second Avenue that in recent years had become a venue for live, adult entertainment. When the company first toured the theater, Elkins joked in an interview, they found "at least two beds in each dressing room."[82] Tynan and Elkins, however, were quick to make it clear that they planned on preserving only the slightest hint of association with tawdrier fare: the Phoenix was fully refurbished at enormous expense and specially renamed the Eden for the production. By the time it entered previews *Oh! Calcutta!* boasted state-of-the art lighting, scenic design, and mixed-media stage effects. All industry jokes about saving money on the costume budget notwithstanding, *Oh! Calcutta!* exceeded $100,000 in production costs, making it the most expensive show in Off Broadway history when it opened.[83]

Tynan and the *Oh! Calcutta!* company courted a mainstream audience in subtler ways as well. During the rehearsal period the show's creative team realized that an overreliance on confrontational techniques borrowed from experimental companies like the Living Theater would potentially alienate as many traditional theatergoers as the erotic subject matter itself. Thus, despite its experimental pedigree, *Oh! Calcutta!* made it to the stage with its imaginary fourth wall intact; improvisational underscoring notwithstanding, the techniques it borrowed from Off Off Broadway were largely relegated to the rehearsal process.

In a feature article for *Playboy* in October 1969, Bruce Williamson aptly noted that offstage "the performers exhibit traces of missionary zeal as a result of their participation in a sort of psychodrama conducted by Levy during casting and rehearsals." But when the actors took the stage, this "missionary zeal" came across in much subtler, more appealing ways. "Though I wasn't turned on to any degree worth mentioning," Williamson wrote, "I was decidedly tuned in to the people onstage, as well as grateful that they seemed delighted to do their thing and leave me to do mine, without any of that Living Theater I-love-you jazz about melting the barriers between art and life."[84]

Although it is unclear whether the myriad attempts to position *Oh! Calcutta!* as "well-mannered" erotica for genteel theatergoers helped sell more tickets than the simple promise of frequent nudity and simulated sex did, they do seem to have aided the audition process. "I had read about *Oh! Calcutta!* and I knew who Kenneth Tynan was, so I called my agent and said, 'I want to audition,'" remembers Boni Enten. "He said, 'are you, *crazy*?' and I said, 'no, I want to audition.' So he got me the audition. Jacques Levy, the director, had done experimental theater in New York. And the list of people involved as writers? I *knew* those people! I just had a feeling that this was going to *be* something."[85]

Tynan's unceasing interest in "elevating" *Oh! Calcutta!* above the lowbrow status of burlesque is obvious in the finished product, which featured only a single sketch that was clearly rooted in the classic burlesque tradition. "Was It Good for You Too?" is attributed to the humorist Dan Greenburg. This Masters and Johnson send-up featured a wacky, Marx Brothers–inspired medical team trying to document the mating habits of human volunteers in a laboratory. As the sketch begins, a hapless male volunteer is asked to engage in sexual intercourse with a beautiful female volunteer atop a gurney, while a team of impossibly clueless lab technicians cover them both from head to toe with electrodes in order to take scientific readings on their every move. Despite constant indignities and interruptions, the couple finally nears a noisy, clumsy climax, whereupon all hell breaks loose: the lab techs, having become aroused by the readings they are recording, attempt to join the couple on the gurney; a police officer rushes in to cite the male volunteer for double-parking and ends up affixing the parking ticket to his behind; and a random band of gypsies and their dogs burst in as the lights come down.

Greenburg's sketch was a variation on a perennial bit known in burlesque circles as "Crazy House." Once a specialty of the comedy duo Abbot and Costello, "Crazy House" was included, along with a number of chestnuts from classic burlesque, in *We'd Rather Switch*. While the details of "Crazy House" were endlessly varied depending on the performers and settings, the bit essentially focused on the comic aspects of constant, increasingly ridiculous interruption: an agitated, exhausted mental patient is desperately in need of a good night's sleep, but is repeatedly pestered by

Bill Macy introduces the hapless male volunteer (Alan Rachins) to the friendly female volunteer (Raina Barrett) at the beginning of the sketch "Was It Good for You Too?" in *Oh! Calcutta!* Photo by Friedman-Abeles. Courtesy of the Billy Rose Theater Archive, New York Public Library for the Performing Arts.

members of the hospital staff, other patients, and outside visitors, all of whom prove to be a lot crazier than the patient is. In "Was It Good for You Too?" Greenburg alters the location and shifts the desired activity from good sleep to good sex, but the basic ingredients of the original "Crazy House" bit—the broad physical comedy, the increasingly ludicrous interruptions, the slow build toward utter pandemonium—remain central to the sketch.

While all of the sketches in Manzini's *We'd Rather Switch* were lightly revised versions of classic burlesque bits, "Was It Good for You Too?" was the exception in *Oh! Calcutta!* Due largely to Tynan's eschewing of all things lowbrow, a vast majority of the sketches shied away from broad, wacky humor in an attempt at more deeply layered musings about contemporary sexuality. Topics of the sketches included swinging, fantasy and fetishism, sexual tensions between spouses, the emotional and physical brutalities of the singles' scene, and the growing generation gap. A centerpiece of the revue was a celebration of (hetero)sexual unity in the form of a nude, "funky country blues *pas de deux*."[86] Danced by George Welbes and Margo Sappington and accompanied by the Open Window's lengthy Bob Dylan–inspired number "Clarence and Mildred," this nude ballet was frequently cited as a particularly moving high point, even by the many critics who were disappointed by the revue ( Ex. 1.2).

Tynan's many careful attempts to sell *Oh! Calcutta!* as respectable middle-class erotica seemed, at least as far as critical reception was concerned, to backfire. For all its risqué subject matter and the extraordinary amount of buzz it generated in New York City during its rehearsal and preview periods, *Oh! Calcutta!* struck most critics as more quaint than progressive when it opened. Only a few critics registered any moral outrage in reviewing the show; James Davis of the *Daily News* attacked it as "hard core pornography" that was at once "dull" and "disgustingly clinical," and Emily Genauer for the *Post* called it "a bitter, mocking, outrageous, generally boring, sick but powerful social statement offering some yocks, every obscene word and gesture imaginable, an endless catalogue of impersonal sexual transactions and bottomless contempt for the human psyche, for sensibility, for sex and for life itself."[87] Bob Amsel of *Screw* magazine was morally outraged too, but for altogether different reasons; in his "Naked City" column, he sniped, "If you're a fifty-three-year old virgin from Zanesville, Ohio, you're in for a shock."[88]

In contrast with the critical divide that dogged *We'd Rather Switch,* most critics writing for mainstream presses sided this time with Amsel. Perhaps hoping to be aroused by this self-proclaimed revolution in sophisticated erotica, critics reported that *Oh! Calcutta!* was, in the end, too self-congratulatory and schoolboyishly silly to be truly sexy, or even consistently entertaining. "The [show] is a handsome revue, imaginative in its use of multi-screen visuals, which manages, for all its slickness, to be dull and somewhat smug about it," argued Gerald Weales in *Commonweal.*[89] "*Oh! Calcutta!* is likely to disappoint different people in different ways, but disappointment is the order of the right," Clive Barnes wrote in his review for the *New York Times.* "To be honest, I think I can recommend the show with any vigor only to people who are extraordinarily underprivileged, either socially, sexually, or emotionally. Now is your time to stand up and be counted."[90]

As it turned out, an awful lot of people were so underprivileged. Despite, or perhaps because of the reviews—which, after all, inadvertently pointed out to curious audiences, just as Tynan had, that this erotic show was so tame, tasteful, and urbane that there was absolutely nothing threatening about it—*Oh! Calcutta!* ran to full houses at the Eden until February 1971, when it moved uptown to Broadway's Belasco Theater for another year and a half. An even more successful revival opened at the Edison Theater on Forty-seventh Street a mere four years later. Playing to houses so packed with tourists that programs were eventually made available in nine different languages, the revival ran for thirteen years before closing in August 1989.[91]

*Oh! Calcutta!* does seem enormously conservative, especially in retrospect. The sketches, all of which were written by white men and performed by an all-white cast, depict nothing but white, heterosexual, middle-class concerns. The burgeoning women's movement clearly hadn't made much of an impact on the writers or the members of the creative team—or, as noted earlier, on Tynan's marketing of *Calcutta!* as a show that an (active, heterosexual) man might escort a (passive, heterosexual) woman to watch, as some sort of arcane courting aid. Nor did race or class issues seem to have crossed anyone's mind in creating the show. And Tynan explicitly forbade any gay subject matter, with the blunt explanation that "there's been enough of that around."[92] Tynan's unconcealed homophobia in fact apparently pervaded the production. The cast member Raina Barrett remembers that men who were openly gay or perceived by Tynan as too effeminate were immediately and unceremoniously rejected during auditions, and that as a result at least one cast member frequently referred to Tynan as a "heterosexual bigot" behind his back.[93]

Indeed the sole sketch to mention homosexuality in *Oh! Calcutta!* does so derogatorily. The sketch "Four in Hand," attributed to John Lennon, centers around four men who get together to masturbate while collectively watching a fictional device called a "telepathic thought transmitter,"[94] which transmits the sexual fantasies of all four men onto a screen that they watch as they race each other to orgasm. The three established members of the collective all fantasize about naked women, which, in classic male-gaze fashion, are projected on an upstage scrim for the audience to watch, along with the actors, who sit in chairs with their backs to the audience, gazing up at the images and pretending to masturbate. Yet the newcomer to the group, George, prefers to fantasize about the Lone Ranger, whose image, when flashed on the screen, distracts the three other men. Because these men are solely interested in heterosexual fantasies, which are clearly delineated here as "normal," George's thoughts about the Lone Ranger cause them increasing frustration, and also a rage that slowly builds as the sketch—along with the "pervert" in their midst—climaxes.[95]

It should be noted that quite a few sketches reflected Tynan's own sexual preoccupations. These included Victorian attire, sadomasochism, and the regular debasement of women by whipping, gagging, binding, and imprisoning in hanging baskets or nets. One of the sketches that Tynan contributed to the revue, and that he was especially proud of, was titled "The Empress' New Clothes" and highlighted the history of women's underwear in the Western world. The sketch was cut before previews began, not only because it was enormously expensive, wildly elaborate, and far too long, but also because no one in the company—or, it was assumed, in the audience—was quite as titillated by lacy undergarments as Tynan.[96]

While *Oh! Calcutta!* failed to win over most critics, Jack Kroll of *Newsweek* was particularly enthusiastic about the show, or at least what he felt the show represented. Kroll agreed that "many of the sketches are not very good" and that much of the "pseudo folk-rock" music underscoring the show was "indifferent" at best. Yet he alone among the critics seemed to recognize the fact that with *Oh! Calcutta*, the ideologies of the sexual revolution had actively begun to cross over into the mainstream:

> A real revolution is like a wedge: it starts with the sharp thin edge, but to be effective it has to insinuate its pyramidal heft until something breaks. With "Oh! Calcutta!" the sexual revolution reaches its middle level—middle class, middle brow, the middle of a sporadic hammering process that will certainly crack, if not break, the petrifaction of our socio-sexual lives. I do not mean to use "middle class" and "middle brow" as disparaging terms. Far from it; I liked "Oh! Calcutta!" a great deal, and in many ways it is a much more "revolutionary" theatrical event than, say, the recent eruption in our midst of the Living Theatre, which with its impacted blend of elitist and mass feeling, its relentless nagging of the audience, obscured many of the basic energies which "new" theater wants to restore to a jaded and confounded culture. "Oh! Calcutta!" has no avant-garde airs; it claims only to be, in the words of its deviser, critic

Kenneth Tynan, "just entertainment, an old-fashioned, stimulating show." But with his diabolically simple idea, and its brilliant fleshing out by director Jacques Levy, the urbane Tynan practically replaces solemn, messianic Julian Beck as the chief ideologue of the theatrical revolution.[97]

Kroll displayed a remarkable prescience here. Despite all the risks that it took, *Oh! Calcutta!* can hardly be interpreted, content-wise, as innovative. Yet because of its utterly risk-free approach to the risqué, it managed to connect with a mass audience, and this is where its real power and influence lay.

## SALVATION, STAG MOVIE, AND THE RISE OF GENDER ACTIVISM

Once *Oh! Calcutta!* proved critic-proof, more adult musicals began to appear Off and Off Off Broadway. One of the first, *Salvation*, appeared briefly at the Village Gate in concert form in the spring of 1969 before reopening in September for an open-ended run at the Jan Hus Theater. This revue, which was clearly influenced by both *Hair* and *Oh! Calcutta!*, featured music by Peter Link and book and lyrics by CC Courtney, who would pursue separate careers in the theater and music industries once their second effort, the Broadway rock musical *Earl of Ruston* (1971), closed after five performances.[98]

*Salvation* was performed by a cast of eight, including the *Oh! Calcutta!* alumnus Boni Enten, whose character, which she created, "was totally based on the *Oh! Calcutta!* experience."[99] The revue purported to critique organized religion and celebrate the various social and political messages embraced by the counterculture. There was decidedly less nudity in *Salvation* than there was in *Oh! Calcutta!* Nevertheless in reference to her work in that revue, Enten appeared topless in *Salvation*, which also featured a great deal of frank talk about contemporary sexuality.

Accompanied by a seven-piece rock band called Nobody Else, the cast of *Salvation* performed sketches and sang songs with titles like "Ballin'," "There Ain't No Flies on Jesus," "Let's Get Lost in Now," and "Tomorrow Is the First Day of the Rest of My Life" (🔊 Ex. 1.3). A modest hit when it reopened at the Jan Hus Theater, *Salvation* ran for 239 performances and spawned the top-40 hit "(If You Let Me Make Love to You Then) Why Can't I Touch You?," recorded by a *Hair* alum, Ronnie Dyson (🔊 Ex. 1.4).[100]

Because of its sparse set and loose, concert-style staging (the Jan Hus Theater was in the cavernous basement of an Upper East Side church), *Salvation* was judged almost entirely on the merits of its musical score and cast, both of which impressed most critics. Despite the fact that its budget was smaller than those of *Oh! Calcutta!* and *Hair*, comparisons to both shows were inevitable since the revue touched on similar themes, espoused similar messages, and featured a score that was heavily influenced by contemporary popular music. Also like its predecessors, however, *Salvation*'s overarching countercultural ideology and left-leaning politics concealed morals that were ultimately rather conservative and thus tailor-made for mass audiences. At the end of the show the members of the cast conclude that in "the quest for inner peace," religion—or, at the very least, spiritual reflection—"still has more to offer than the various drugs and assorted kicks so prominent in the contemporary scene."[101] Or, as an anonymous reviewer in *Time* griped, "*Salvation*...trades on the residual puritanism behind its ostensibly anti-puritan outlook. A people at ease with sexuality, and casually and thoroughly iconoclastic, would not pay good money to see an inept affirmation of a puerile paganism."[102]

These sentiments apply to most adult musicals after *Oh! Calcutta!*, often despite their creators' best intentions. Because these shows were often developed and produced by young adults, many of whom were actively involved in the Off Off Broadway scene, most were at once less opulent and self-consciously highbrow and at least somewhat more politically or socially minded than *Oh! Calcutta!* For example, many adult musicals after *Oh! Calcutta!*, inspired either directly or indirectly by gay liberation, attempted to include aspects of gay life; as the women's liberation movement gained momentum through the 1970s, several adult musicals also attempted to address feminist issues as well. Yet despite attempts to move beyond *Oh! Calcutta!*'s conservatism, most adult musicals ultimately reflected the most stubbornly traditional of gender roles, both on stage and behind the scenes.

A case in point is *Stag Movie* (1971), which opened at the Gate Theater on Tenth Street and Second Avenue, a stone's throw from the Eden, where *Oh! Calcutta!* was still playing to packed houses just prior to its move uptown. Written by David Newburge, a playwright and lyricist who subsequently turned to writing erotic stories and scripts for pornographic films, *Stag Movie* was a spoof of "the pornography vogue" in theater, according to the show's producer, Richard R. Lingeman. "But in the course of spoofing these shows," acknowledged Lingeman, *Stag Movie* "will employ plenty of nudity, simulated sex acts on stage, four-letter words and all the rest. Which means, ideally, we'll have it both ways."[103]

The plot of *Stag Movie* focuses on a group of out-of-work actors who decide to pool their resources and make a musical porn film based on the classic stag reel known as "The Grocery Boy." In a far looser variation on "Crazy House," shooting, which takes place in a seedy motel near Kennedy Airport, is repeatedly interrupted by the constant roar of airplanes overhead, the mafia, the police, and an elderly motel maid who desperately wants a part in the film. Musical numbers, which were never recorded, were composed by Jacques Urbont; they included "Get Your Rocks Off Rock," "Try a Trio," the romantic duet "We Came Together," and a wistful, waltzy ballad titled "I Want More Out of Life Than This." This last number was performed as a solo by the lead female character, who was played by a then unknown Adrienne Barbeau:

> As I do the dishes I dream of a rapist
> Who'd force me to do his desire.
> He'd grip me, he'd strip me, he might even whip me,
> He'd set my whole body on fire.
> But my handsome husband has sexual equipment
> That hasn't been used since his bris!
> I want more out of life, much more out of life,
> much more out of life than this![104]

Unlike *Oh! Calcutta!*, *Stag Movie* featured gay and lesbian characters and, as the lyrics above imply, make some attempt to ponder the possibility of female sexual desire, if not yet in anything approaching the most progressive of ways. Nevertheless because of its reliance on gender stereotypes—especially that of the swishing, effeminate gay man—*Stag Movie* became the target of the Gay Liberation Front, an activist group of gay men and lesbians that formed shortly after the 1969 Stonewall riots.

In a move that seems laughably naïve in retrospect, the producers of *Stag Movie* invited the Gay Liberation Front to a critics' preview on January 2, 1971, in hopes that the musical would catch on with gay theatergoers. Ensconced in the balcony, approximately thirty members of the Gay Liberation Front began heckling the actors almost as soon as the show began. The group objected not only to the gay stereotypes depicted onstage, but also to the fact that Barbeau's character was completely naked for most of the show, while the male characters appeared naked far more infrequently.[105] Heavy use of the word *faggot* and endless jokes about not being able to "get it up" for the film shoot didn't help matters much.[106]

The hissing, booing, chanting of "Sexist pigs!" and "Dirty old men!" and catcalls like "Raise your level of consciousness!" built to such a degree that the cast eventually had to stop performing. Some of the actors attempted to maintain order, while others simply joined the melee and began shouting back at the protesters from the stage. After about a half-hour the police arrived, removed the protesters, and allowed the musical to continue.[107]

In his review of *Stag Movie* for the *New York Times*, ominously titled "Stage: '71 Is Off to a Lamentable Start," Clive Barnes argued that while such disruptions are disrespectful and "should have no place in the theater," the presence of the Gay Liberation Front was "admittedly something of a welcome diversion from the seemingly endless tedium" of *Stag Movie*, which he called "dispiriting," "dismal," and "as erotic as cold mulligatawny soup laced with frozen porridge."[108]

Despite a near universal critical drubbing, *Stag Movie* ran for about five months due to a break on the theater rental arranged by the producer and word of mouth

Tod Miller (left) and Brad Sullivan (right) ogle Adrienne Barbeau in *Stag Movie*. Courtesy of Photofest.

about the protests.[109] The mere presence of the frequently nude Barbeau—whose ample "mammary equipment" caused many a critic to interrupt his review mid-scathe in order to blather blushingly and with something approaching genuine awe—likely also kept *Stag Movie* up and running much longer than it might have otherwise.[110]

Bad musicals often incite vitriol in the press, and in this respect *Stag Movie* is hardly atypical. Yet the fact that *Oh! Calcutta!* escaped much in the way of social criticism despite its rigid take on human sexuality, while not even two years later a small, low-budget Off Broadway spoof stocked with stale stereotypes would become the target of virulent protest, reflects the sharp increase in gender activism that occurred in New York City and across the country between the late 1960s and the early 1970s. The impact of the gay and women's liberation movements on adult musicals that opened in the 1970s will be discussed in the following chapters.

CHAPTER 2

# The Birth of Modern Gay Theater and the Subtext of *Company*

It's not like it always happens in plays, not all faggots bump themselves off at the end of the story.

—Mart Crowley, *The Boys in the Band*

The riots that erupted in and around the Stonewall Inn at 53 Christopher Street in Greenwich Village on the evening of June 28, 1969, have long been viewed as the proverbial shot heard round the world when it comes to contemporary gay activism. As Martin Duberman argues in his book *Stonewall*, the very word "resonates with images of insurgency and self-realization and occupies a central place in the iconography of lesbian and gay awareness." He adds that because the 1969 riots are often used to mark the birth of the modern gay and lesbian political movement, the decades preceding Stonewall are often dismissed as "some vast neolithic wasteland."[1]

In fact gays and lesbians had begun to organize long before the Stonewall riots. The pioneering if also deeply secretive Mattachine Society and Daughters of Bilitis were both holding regular meetings by the mid-1950s, and gay and lesbian activism and awareness progressed, slowly but surely, through the 1960s. The movement had even begun to shift in focus and momentum years before Stonewall. Rather than prioritizing personal problems and seeking to boost the self-esteem and emotional stability of disenfranchised individuals, as early Mattachine and Daughters of Bilitis incarnations had, a rising generation of activists turned their attention instead to the struggle for equal rights and an end to institutional discrimination as the 1960s progressed.[2] Duberman reminds us that resistance to oppression "takes on the confident form of political organizing only after a certain critical mass of collective awareness of oppression, and a determination to end it, has been reached."[3] In some respects, then, the Stonewall riots were less a radical new beginning than a particularly intense reaction to just another night of police harassment.

What post-Stonewall activism did possess, however, was remarkable momentum. The gay rights movement that was galvanized by the riots, and that snowballed through the 1970s, benefited enormously from the trajectory, ideologies, and practices of the New Left on which it was based. Whereas early gay activism tended toward the covert and conciliatory, Stonewall propelled a new approach to gay organization. Through the pivotal 1960s gay activists began to draw from their experiences with social and political causes and thus, by the 1970s, to employ tactics adopted from the civil rights and antiwar movements. For example, the activist group Gay Liberation Front—which, despite ideological problems that would cause its demise in 1972, was still organized enough to disrupt the preview of *Stag Movie* in 1971—was formed within weeks of the riots by several seasoned members of the New Left.[4]

Post-Stonewall gay activism quickly found a place in New York's theater fringe, largely because there had long been gay activism there in the first place. "Tired of antigay attitudes, laws, and regulations," Bruce Kirle writes of the Off Off Broadway movement, "a growing artistic community in Greenwich Village advocated sexual dissidence." Well before Stonewall, Kirle continues, "gay activists, both politically and artistically, were positing that homosexuality was an alternative lifestyle, no better or worse than straight culture. This reevaluation of the politics of the closet" was reflected in many of the plays that were developed Off Off Broadway, initially by members of the Caffe Cino scene and later in many of the like-minded theater companies that the Cino inspired.[5]

## THE CAFFE CINO

Largely credited as the cradle of modern gay theater, the enormously influential Caffe Cino scene began in December 1958, when Joe Cino opened a tiny storefront coffeehouse at 31 Cornelia Street in Greenwich Village. Born of Italian immigrants and raised in Buffalo, New York, Cino was an aspiring dancer whose constantly fluctuating weight compromised his artistic goals. Early in 1958 he began waiting tables at the Playhouse Café on MacDougal Street, where he was inspired by the play readings that frequently took place there. With the encouragement of his wide circle of friends—a group of young, mostly gay, mostly male artists—Cino opened his own café as a site for social and artistic networking. He soon began to offer poetry readings, dance performances, play readings, and art exhibits along with the cappuccino.[6]

The Caffe Cino quickly became the hub of a thriving downtown theater scene. As Stephen J. Bottoms points out, many of the artists affiliated with the Caffe Cino were actively working toward mainstream careers. In the meantime, however, they discovered that "the Cino was a space so free of commercial concerns that they could try out anything, even if this meant casually breaking rules of form and content that were sacrosanct in the professional theater."[7] The fact that many of the artists associated with the Cino were gay men had a lot to do with the scene's freewheeling quality and with the troupe's influence on queer theater in general. Sexuality was hardly the sole theme in the enormous body of work that came out of the Cino, but the scene was nevertheless unified by "an underlying awareness of difference—of being, on some basic level, *excluded* from the mainstream—that facilitated the celebratory abandon with which Cino writers embraced the bizarre, the ridiculous, and the taboo."[8]

The playwright Robert Patrick remembers that the Cino, like the Off Off Broadway scene that quickly grew around and because of it, cultivated a particularly fertile creative environment simply by encouraging followers to revel in the joy of playful, financially unfettered exploration:

> We did our plays in places that made their money in other ways: coffee houses, art galleries, churches, bars. So theater could be an individualistic, responsible art form. It was illegal to do shows anywhere that we did shows. We couldn't charge admission, so we didn't worry about an audience. We weren't reviewed, so we didn't have to worry about pleasing critics. We weren't licensed, so except when we were raided, we didn't have to worry about pandering to the police. We were scarcely noticed, so we didn't have to worry about catering to the academics. It was an unbelievable, unique revolution in theater. We could do whatever we wanted to do. We wandered into the Caffe Cino—many of us with no theatrical background or experience, or even ideas of doing theater. And Joe Cino simply showed us the floor and said, "Do what you have to do." I've always said that if Joe Cino had run a bowling alley, Lanford Wilson, Sam Shepard and I would have become champion bowlers. But that is how Off Off Broadway happened. Almost everyone—almost all the men—were gay. And gay theater grew out of that.[9]

The free-spirited atmosphere allowed for the cultivation of an impressive number of playwrights, including not only Patrick, Shepard, and Lanford Wilson, but also Doric Wilson, H. M. Koutoukas, Jean-Claude van Itallie, and William Hoffman.

Yet as the Caffe Cino scene grew in sophistication and influence through the 1960s, its commander slowly became unhinged. Joe Cino's endless schedule, which involved producing nonstop performances and operating the café six nights a week, all the while working day jobs to ensure enough money to pay the rent, resulted in physical and emotional exhaustion, as well as a growing addiction to amphetamines that soon began to cause his friends and colleagues considerable concern. The sudden death of his boyfriend, Jon Torrey, an electrician, in January 1967 seemed to push Cino over the edge. Robert Patrick remembers that as Cino deteriorated, the mood around the café became "desperate" and "baffled," and a lot of artists began to leave the scene, while others tried in vain to help their troubled friend. Yet attempts to reach out to Cino proved increasingly futile; Patrick remembers that he had become "flaccid and bleary, and had incomprehensible mood swings, cosmic mood swings, disappearances and reappearances in very bad states."[10]

In the wee hours of March 30, 1967, Cino set the lights on his café's tiny stage, turned on a record at full volume, and began hacking at himself with a collection of knives he'd amassed earlier that evening. Michael Townsend Smith, then a critic for the *Village Voice*, responded to a disturbing phone call he received from Cino at dawn by rushing to the café, where he found his bloodied, frantic, flailing friend. Cino was rushed to St. Vincent's Hospital, where he lingered in intensive care for three days while his many friends held a vigil in the waiting room, kept one another informed of his condition, and donated more blood to the hospital than at any time since World War II. Despite a brief, hopeful moment when it seemed that Cino would recover, he succumbed to his wounds on Sunday, April 2.[11]

Core members of the Cino scene resolved to keep the café open despite its founder's death. But problems quickly mounted. Robert Patrick remembers:

> There were no licenses. Joe Cino used to pay off the cops. I suppose other people did, too. After Joe died, we didn't know who to pay off. We got tens of thousands of dollars worth of summonses. Michael Smith went to court. He first showed them photos of the Cino with the tables set up like a coffee house, so that it wasn't a theater at all. Then he set it up with a proscenium stage to show that it had been running as a theater for a long time and should be allowed to. Then he showed them other photos with the chairs in the round to show that it was an avant-garde theater and therefore culturally relevant. Somehow, he got to keep it running. But it only lasted about a year after Joe died. There were a lot of shows that Joe had booked, and we did those. Wonderful people…took it over for a while.…But without Joe, after all, it was only a theater. And there were, after all, other theaters with more help and more equipment. So it just closed. It was nobody's fault.[12]

Yet by the time the Cino closed for good in March 1968, a number of like-minded troupes had sprung up in downtown Manhattan. Many of these companies—for example, the Judson Poets' Theater, the Play-House of the Ridiculous, and La Mama ETC—took up where the Cino had left off, by including in their eclectic repertories theater pieces that explored contemporary sexuality in general, and queer sensibilities, especially male ones, in particular. The Caffe Cino scene had made an indelible mark. "You understand that by 1967, there were some 300 Off Off theaters, most of them doing a new American play every few weeks, and, yeah, many of them were gay," Patrick explains. "In 1961 there was *one*. Once the Cino started doing gay plays, it became okay to do gay plays."[13]

### The Boys in the Band

Approximately one month after the Caffe Cino closed its doors, Mart Crowley's *The Boys in the Band* premiered Off Broadway. While not a musical, *The Boys in the Band* deserves special mention here because it was a particularly groundbreaking critical and commercial success in New York that generated momentum in terms of gay characterization and theatrical content. The play, which opened at Theater Four on April 15, 1968, focuses on a group of gay men in New York City who gather at their friend Michael's Upper East Side apartment to celebrate the birthday of Harold, a self-described "thirty-two year old, ugly, pock-marked Jew fairy" who nevertheless possesses enormous social and emotional insight.[14] Strong reviews and regular insistences in the press that "you do not have to be homosexual to appreciate *The Boys in the Band*" resulted in a run of a thousand performances, a London production, two national tours, and a film version directed by William Friedkin in 1970 (📖 Ex. 2.1).[15]

History has not been kind to Crowley's play, whose characters all tend toward self-loathing stereotypes. Yet for its time *The Boys in the Band* was something of a breakthrough, merely because none of the characters was a pervert, a villain, or a suicide. Sure, they drink too much, and yes, they all say things they'll probably regret the next morning. But no one dies; rather, as the curtain falls at the end of the play, the audience is given the clear sense that the characters will all simply continue to go about their lives, however complicated and unhappy they are.

The fact that *The Boys in the Band* does not end either with a death or with the "successful" transformation of a central character into heteronormativity through marriage to a woman is of a significance that should not be underestimated. As Rex Reed gleefully points out in his review of the play, the melodramatic, highly moralistic endings to plays with gay subject matter long tended to draw focus away from anything approaching honest characterization. "For years," Reed writes, "plays about homosexuality have been afraid of their own shadows. From the early Helen Menken–Basil Rathbone days of *The Captive* (a real shockeroo in the 1920s) through *The Killing of Sister George* and *Staircase* (lovable, cartoon cut-out perverts), most such plays have basically avoided the real nature of the subject. And homosexuals have always paid for their sins onstage." For Reed, *The Boys in the Band* is a near revolutionary departure. "The 'boys' in Mart Crowley's band are human beings," he notes. "They don't kill themselves or want to get married or spend the rest of their lives tortured by conscience. The only way they 'pay' is to know who they are. Then they go to bed with a hangover and start all over again the next day. Like life."[16]

Yet not everyone was as thrilled with *The Boys in the Band* as Reed was. Many members of the Cino scene, for example, greeted the commercial success of the play with mixed emotions. As Bottoms notes, the play, and especially the way it was marketed to straight audiences, was "particularly depressing for those writers who had pioneered the depiction of 'out' gay characters" and who had hopes of depictions that were not quite so self-loathing, the lack of suicides notwithstanding.[17] There was also concern about the way the play was marketed to straight audiences, who, some gay activists and playwrights felt, were being told that it allowed insights into the lives of *all* gay men, not just a few fictional prototypes. The fact that the show's producer, Richard Barr, had taken out advertisements quoting a line from the show—"Show me a happy homosexual and I'll show you a gay corpse"—which promised that the play would reveal "the inner corpses," did not help matters much (📖 Ex. 2.2).[18]

Nor did the fact that the persistent self-loathing in *The Boys in the Band* prompted so many ostensibly straight male critics to express genuine concern about Crowley's characters, and about gay men in general. In the *New York Times* Walter Kerr devoted an entire column to the pain he detected in Crowley's "remarkable" characters, who, he concluded, collectively permitted the (presumably heterosexual) audience "to inhabit and understand a world in which anguish cannot spend itself because it is condemned to seeing itself as antic, as not real, as not discussable, as something to be tied up with a tidy bow and then flung, only merrily, only maliciously, in someone else's face."[19] Similarly Clive Barnes, who raved in his review that *The Boys in the Band* was "the frankest treatment of homosexuality I have ever seen on the stage," nonetheless writes in a second review a year later, "I do hope that Mr. Crowley is wrong and that all homosexuals are not as wretchedly miserable as he paints them."[20]

They were most certainly not, argued a number of prominent gay activists. Such reviews in fact prompted Donn Teal, soon to become a cofounder of the Gay Activist Alliance, to argue in a *Times* op-ed that *The Boys in the Band* painted a distorted picture of contemporary gay life. Teal and his friends, he wrote, greeted the opening of *The Boys in the Band* with "mixed emotions," because while the play marked "our true dramatic debut in heterosexual society, it was a debasing one, as if we had arrived at our own Coming Out Party dressed in rags." While Teal and many of his fellow activists understood that "the author's attempt was not to epitomize the normal American homosexual in 'The Boys,' any more than Albee's was to apotheosize the average (childless) American marriage in 'Virginia Woolf,'" he was nevertheless incensed by the fact that such "an ugly misrepresentation has been broadcast by an excellent play." Teal thus felt compelled to set the record straight. "The average among us are appalled that the heterosexual (and maladjusted homosexual) may believe...that we store up barbiturates as Harold does for 'the long winter of his death'; that our parents have all been 'killer whales'; and that we regularly address each other as 'fairy' and 'fag,'" he wrote. "'The Boys' exude selfishness, self-absorption, and self-indulgence. Worst of all, they not only bespeak, they *proclaim*, guilt feelings through every utterance Crowley has given them.... Self-hate and a feeling of guilt are not typical of today's homosexual, though it has been a labor to shake these leftovers of a Judaeo-Christian Puritanism, and many of us are still wrestling with the inferiority complex which society has been only too glad to foist upon us."[21] The fact that the editors of the *New York Times* would recognize a need to run an op-ed serving as a primer on the Life of the Average Homosexual Man was, like *The Boys in the Band* itself, not only reflective of how far gay activism had come by 1969, but also a humbling reminder of just how far it needed to go.

### Company

The post-Stonewall musical *Company*, much like *The Boys in the Band*, deserves special consideration here. Not only is it too something of a theater landmark, but its structure, music, and characterizations exerted direct influence on several post-Stonewall gay-themed adult musicals to open in the years following its premiere. *Company*, which opened at the Alvin Theater on April 26, 1970, featured music and lyrics by Stephen Sondheim, a book by George Furth, and direction by Hal Prince, who also served as producer. The musical's disjunct narrative, frequent references to current events, and emotionally frozen, sexually ambiguous central character touched a nerve with audiences and critics, many of whom acknowledged that *Company* was both an artistic triumph and a musical that elicited deep emotional discomfort.

Famously and, for some, frustratingly fragmented, the plot of *Company* revolves around Robert, an affluent thirty-five-year-old bachelor living in Manhattan. In scene after scene, which unfold in a "timeless and dreamlike suspension of reality," Bobby visits his friends, all of whom are neurotic, upper-middle-class Manhattanites in unsatisfying heterosexual pairings.[22] Bobby dates three different women, none of whom he is willing or able to commit to emotionally. While it is never clear whether Bobby's friends know or socialize with one another, they all have in common an almost desperate desire to see their single male friend find a mate, despite (or perhaps because of) the fact that they themselves are deeply unhappy with their romantic partnerships.

Little happens in *Company*. At the climax of the musical—if his solo number "Being Alive" really is climactic at all—Bobby remains terrified of commitment and unsure that he even wants it. During this number he decides—maybe—that coupling might be, if not ideal, then better than being alone ( Ex. 2.1). Yet audiences are never told what will become of Bobby, who remains as ambiguous a character at the end of *Company* as he was when it began.

The disjointedness of *Company*'s plot, as well as the persistent neuroses of its characters, were not the only aspects of Sondheim's musical that were perceived as emotionally unsettling. Several scholars have noted as well that *Company* reflects the pessimism, uncertainty, and emotional malaise of its period.[23] The musical's cynical, anxious characters seem at once desperate to make human connections and deeply

Bobby (Larry Kert) has many friends and romantic partners but always feels curiously alone. Courtesy of Photofest.

disappointed by those they find. *Company* offers no pat resolutions for audiences seeking escapism; instead it manifests "the bitterness, rejection, and uncertainty displayed in affluent, educated, upper-middle-class New York society" and repeatedly questions such traditional values as marriage, personal freedom and responsibility, and the legitimacy of American social mores.[24]

In this respect, Raymond Knapp points out, *Company* and *Hair* share a number of parallels, despite their many overarching differences. Both, he notes, are structurally fragmented and feature a central character who remains alienated from his social group. In *Hair* Claude cannot fully commit to burning his draft card, dropping out, or even leaving his parents' home in Flushing, despite the urging of his hippie friends. Similarly in *Company* Robert cannot commit to heterosexual monogamy despite the almost ceaseless insistence of his married friends.

Further, Knapp argues, the neurotic, aging characters in *Company*, like the many spectators who recognized unflattering depictions of themselves in them, were eager to remain relevant during historically momentous, tumultuous times. Bobby's friends are older than the characters depicted in *Hair*, of course, but they nevertheless seem similarly ambivalent about traditional social and family structures, and thus attempt in a number of ways to "respond to the new, more liberating alternatives that emerged during the 1960s."[25] It is thus possible, Knapp writes, to view many of the couples in *Company* as "part of the broad audience base for *Hair*, many of them eager to submit to the liberating influence of the various revolutionary movements then on the ascendant, so long as they didn't actually have to drop out to do so."[26] This certainly helps to explain why Bobby's friends are so desperate to see him settle down in the way that they all have: in living the way that he does, Bobby "seems to operate closest to the kind of freedom the counterculture would have represented to them; getting Bobby to commit himself to a stable, partnered lifestyle would go a long way toward validating their own circumstantial compromises as both practical *and* idealistic."[27]

As the character Joanne acknowledges near the end of *Company* in the scathing number "The Ladies Who Lunch"—which, if we're focused less on the central character than on his far more engaging social circle, functions as a truer climax than Bobby's subsequent "Being Alive" does—the neurotic Manhattanites portrayed throughout the musical are merely "dinosaurs surviving the crunch." Joanne is painfully aware that she and her circle are "suddenly at an age where we find ourselves too young for the old people and too old for the young ones. We're nowhere."[28] Her knowledge of her world's impending extinction, of the fact that her kind is actively being rendered irrelevant in the seismic shifts of turbulent times, terrifies her and, likely, many of the local theatergoers who found *Company* so upsetting.

Yet while there was much about *Company* to cause discomfort, it also featured aspects that proved especially empowering. *Company* is very easy to view queerly, and when it opened—not even a year after the Stonewall riots—it quickly struck a chord with many gay men who read Robert as a coded gay or bisexual character. There are a host of reasons for this interpretation, which not only persists, but has only become more prevalent over time, even despite Sondheim's frequent insistences to the contrary.[29]

In the original Broadway production, Robert's sexual ambiguity was referenced only once, and then only in passing, by other characters. During the number "You Could Drive a Person Crazy," Robert's three girlfriends, Kathy, April, and Marta, vent their frustrations over his refusal to commit to them. At one point during the song, they wonder if perhaps his emotional distance is a sign that he is gay, singing, "I could understand a person / if it's not a person's bag. / I could understand a person / if a person was a fag (🔊 Ex. 2.2)."[30] In *Finishing the Hat* Sondheim claims that in 1970 "the word 'fag' was only faintly demeaning, perfectly appropriate for the girls' annoyance without being offensive to the audience," but that by the time it was first revived on Broadway in 1995, it seemed "not only offensive but old-fashioned, so I changed it." In this and all subsequent revivals, then, the new line is "I could understand a person if he said to go away / I could understand a person if he happened to be gay (🔊 Ex. 2.3)."[31]

Initially George Furth had also scripted a conversation between Bobby and his friend Peter that makes much more explicit the possibility that both men are gay or bisexual. The dialogue, which was cut before the musical's New York premiere and has been reinserted into the book in many productions since Sam Mendes used it in his 1996 London revival, was originally scripted for Act II, scene 3. During a private conversation that takes place on his terrace, Peter, who has recently divorced his wife, Susan, in hopes that this will improve their relationship, questions Bobby about his sexuality:

*Peter*: Robert, did you ever have a homosexual experience?
*Robert*: I beg your pardon?
*Peter*: Oh, I don't mean as a kid. I mean, since you've been adult. Have you ever?
*Robert*: Well, yes, actually, yes, I have.
*Peter*: You're not gay, are you?
*Robert*: No, no. Are you?
*Peter*: No, no, for crissake. But I've done it more than once though.
*Robert*: Is that a fact?
*Peter*: Oh, I think sometimes you meet somebody and you just love the crap out of them. Y'know?
*Robert*: Oh, absolutely, I'm sure that's true.
*Peter*: And sometimes you just want to manifest that love, that's all.
*Robert*: Yes, I understand. Absolutely.
*Peter*: I think that sometimes you can even know someone for, oh, a long, long time and then suddenly, out of nowhere, you just want to have them—I mean, even an old friend. You just, all of a sudden, desire that intimacy. That closeness.
*Robert*: Probably.
*Peter*: Oh, I'm convinced that two men really would, if it wasn't for society and all the conventions and all that crap, just go off and ball and be better for it, closer, deeper, don't you think?
*Robert*: Well, I—I don't know.
*Peter*: I mean like us, for example. Do you think that you and I could ever have anything like that?

Robert (*Looks at him for a long and uncomfortable moment. Then a big smile*): Oh, I get it. You're putting me on. Man, you really had me going there, you son of a gun.[32]

John Clum, the author of *Something for the Boys: Musical Theater and Gay Culture*, acknowledges that it is entirely possible that Furth meant for this scene to "close off the speculation that Bobby will end up with a man," but points out that the dialogue is ultimately far too ambiguous for this purpose.[33]

The scene is additionally perplexing since both Sondheim and Furth have argued repeatedly that they never intended Robert to be interpreted as anything but a heterosexual playboy. Adding to the elusive meaning of the exchange is Bobby's "long and uncomfortable" pause when Peter propositions him. Both Clum and Bruce Kirle read this pause as a particularly important part of the exchange. Why, exactly, does Bobby pause? Is the scene merely meant to add one more layer to the many demands placed on Bobby through the course of the musical? Is Bobby uncomfortable at the thought of sex with Peter? Is he wrestling with how to rebuff his friend's advances without hurting his feelings? Or is he embarrassed by the desires that Peter's proposition has stirred in him? Because the exchange is ultimately laughed off as a joke, its meaning remains impossible to interpret definitively.

Yet the widespread and persistent interpretation of Robert as gay or bisexual does not rest solely on these brief snippets of song and (once-excised) dialogue. Some of it has to do with Sondheim's general tendency to gravitate toward disenfranchised, nonconformist characters, as well as with his own admission that as a gay Jewish man, he has often felt like an outsider himself.[34] One doesn't have to make much of a leap to envision Sondheim—or Furth, for that matter—as the autobiographical inspiration for a thirty-something bachelor in the early 1970s, who loves and yet feels disenfranchised from his heterosexual circle, and who feels endless pressure to adopt a heteronormative lifestyle, despite serious and persistent doubts that he wants or would be happy in one.

Furth was gay, as is Sondheim, but as Knapp points out, they were also members of the "'silent generation' of urban professionals, born between 1924 and 1945, who were too old for the counterculture" and thus not necessarily comfortable with the more overt messages of liberation that would become increasingly prevalent in various media through the 1970s.[35] Indeed Sondheim has noted that he "was never easy with being a homosexual, which complicated things."[36] Not only were Furth and Sondheim not particularly active in the swell of gay activism that occurred after the Stonewall riots, but by most accounts neither man had come out of the closet by the time *Company* was produced.

Yet even if it had been the creative team's intent, *Company* could not have featured an openly gay leading character when it first ran. For all the strides being made in the years immediately after Stonewall, the very insinuation of Bobby's bisexuality, let alone homosexuality, would likely still have seemed threatening to many Broadway theatergoers in 1970. Despite progress after Stonewall, the journalist Don Shewey reminds us that "closet cases were still known by the psychological term 'latent homosexual,' and homosexuality was still classified as a mental illness by the American Psychiatric Association." As Sondheim himself explains, homophobia was still so socially acceptable that he thought nothing of having characters "speculate about Bobby's bachelor status by saying 'I could understand a person if a person was a fag.' That line has been revised now, but in the 1970s it reflected life so well that Truman Capote was quoted as saying, 'A fag is a homosexual gentleman who has just left the room.'"[37]

In some respects, then, there was nothing new about *Company*'s sexual ambiguity. Coded references to gay culture and sexually ambiguous characters have been integral to the musical theater since inception, but especially between the 1930s and early 1970s. During the 1910s and 1920s specific neighborhoods in New York City were particularly accepting of homosexuality. Harlem was known for its tolerance, as was the geographical space most closely associated with the commercial musical, an art form that has long served as a safe haven for the generations of gay men who cultivated and patronized it.[38] George Chauncey Jr. writes that as early as the early 1920s, a gay enclave had taken root in Times Square, largely because so many gay men lived and worked there. The theaters and other amusements in the neighborhood "attracted large numbers of gay workers, who got jobs as waiters and performers in restaurants and clubs, as busboys in hotels, and as chorus boys, actors, stagehands, costume designers, publicity people, and the like in the theater industry proper." Although Chauncey is careful to note that gay men hardly enjoyed "unalloyed acceptance in such work environments," they nevertheless found more tolerance in the theater realm, which was, after all, populated by individuals "who were themselves often marginalized because of the unconventional lives they led as theater workers."[39]

The neighborhood's acceptance notwithstanding, the relationship between gay men and the musical theater grew less obvious in the late 1920s, due largely to necessity. At this time a series of antigay laws and regulations had begun to steadily erode the civil liberties of gay men and lesbians. These laws included curfews, the outlawing of drag queens anywhere between Fourteenth and Seventy-second Streets in Manhattan, and the right to refuse service in licensed public establishments to anyone suspected of being gay. These discriminatory measures followed on the heels of the Wales Padlock Act of 1927. This law, written in language that was widely understood to denote homosexuality, instituted a ban on all "themes of 'sex degeneracy or perversion' in theater productions."[40]

In response to the institutionalized demonization of homosexuality, gay references in most forms of entertainment became more oblique, and both double entendre and coding became popular means of allowing gay men and lesbians not only to pass, but also to communicate with one another in public spaces. As Kirle notes, because "so many musicals were written, directed, choreographed, designed, and performed by gays, it was not surprising that the musical often offered both a plethora of double entendres during this period of gay repression as well as a soothing balm to gay anxieties about identity."[41]

Thus when it opened in 1970 *Company* could easily have been seen as following in a long line of musicals written by, among others, Noël Coward, Lorenz Hart, and Cole Porter, all of whom were adept at both coding and double entendre. The fact that the American musical has, in Stacy Wolf's words, "long offered personal, emotional, and cultural validation for gay men" in so many ways and for such a long time helps explain the relative ease and rapidity with which post-Stonewall gay activism influenced musicals through the 1970s, as well as the profound impact that *Company*'s themes of sexual ambiguity and fluidity had on gay men at the time.[42]

The end of *Company* was particularly moving for John Clum, as well as for many other gay men he knew. At the end of Act II Robert sings "Being Alive," and then decides not to attend a surprise birthday party that his friends may or may not have planned for him.[43] His friends wait for him in a dark, empty space that might as easily be his apartment as some undefined setting in a surreal dream; after waiting for several hours, they decide that perhaps it's time to back off a bit and leave him alone to live life on his own terms.[44] As they file off the stage, Robert steps from the shadows, sits alone before his birthday cake, "and takes a moment," before smiling, leaning forward, and blowing out the candles, ending the show.[45] Clum reads this final scene as an important transition

> from the world of compulsory heterosexuality, the usual world of the musical, to an uncharted, unseen world of homosexuality. Otherwise, why cut all ties? In 1970, coming out often meant cutting ties with one's straight friends—or we thought we did. And the society of those friends—being the third at dinner, the baby-sitter to their kids—was often a way of staving off loneliness and the feared plunge into what was still a mysterious, frightening gay possibility. Bobby, we thought, left one world to come out in another. Did Sondheim write this in? No, but come on, Robert...is thirty-five, a zombie emotionally with the women he beds, but the safe best buddy of half a dozen wives.... Gay men in 1970 and since read Bobby as gay. A few years later, an openly gay Bobby could still dish with the wives but have a romantic life of his own, or a bisexual Bobby would be sleeping unproblematically with April and Peter. But to those of us who knew how hard it was to face the Great Unknown in 1970, Company was Truth.[46]

Clum notes that he is most certainly not alone in reading the end of *Company* this way. For lots of gay men in 1970, many of whom were struggling with exciting but terrifying personal freedoms that had only just become available, Bobby's story rang true. "There I stood, in May 1970, at the back of the Alvin Theater," Clum writes of his first time seeing *Company*, "absolutely emotionally rocked by this musical, seeing myself as Bobby and, like the musical, seeing no real option for my life except a heartfelt cry for love. I was in pain at that point and *Company* seemed another cry of pain that resonated powerfully. Bobby walks off the heterosexual stage and into the unknown at the end of the show. I felt I was on the verge of doing the same thing."[47]

In recent productions many directors have recognized the importance of highlighting Bobby's sexual ambiguity. Beginning with the Mendes production in 1996, most revivals have reinserted the scene between Bobby and Peter, and otherwise play up the distance Bobby feels from his circle of friends. There has also been a bit more openness in the press about the character's sexuality. An interview in the *New York Times* with Raúl Esparza, who played Bobby in John Doyle's 2006 Broadway revival, focused almost entirely on Esparza's own complicated sexual identity and the ways it fueled his interpretation of the character he was playing.[48]

Sondheim's and Furth's insistence on the heterosexuality of their character ultimately does not matter to many spectators who love *Company* and identify with its central character. *Company* might not have featured the comparatively open sexuality of later post-Stonewall musicals, but, like *The Boys in the Band,* it did suggest that a growing number of theatregoers were slowly but surely becoming ready for increasingly honest gay characters. In the years immediately following *The Boys in the Band* and *Company*, then, more composers, book writers, producers, and directors would emerge from the closet, bringing their musicals, replete with a wider variety of gay characters, along with them.

## CHAPTER 3

# The Post-Stonewall (and Post-*Company*) Gay Musical

One of the most important events of the Broadway season was the blockbuster success off-Broadway of Mart Crowley's terrific homosexual play, *The Boys in the Band*. It would be marvelous if this success started Broadway toward a sexual freedom it has never attained. After all, the homosexual is here, and he's not going anywhere. It might be nice to know, at last, what's really on his mind.

—William Goldman, *The Season*

Many adult musicals that appeared in New York City in the years immediately following the premieres of *The Boys in the Band* and *Company* approached gay topics with increasing sensitivity. This makes sense: the times were changing rapidly, and many of these musicals were developed Off or Off Off Broadway by creative teams that included gay men who had long been active in the musical theater, grassroots gay politics, or both. Because so many of the early 1970s gay-themed adult musicals discussed herein were intended to entertain and empower gay men, but also to educate and reassure straight audiences who were new to and unfamiliar with gay culture, they were typically among the tamest of adult musicals. In most of them, emphasis was placed on the gay man's desire for love, respect, and a peaceful life, while gay male sexuality was notably downplayed in what seems a conscious attempt at extending an olive branch to the more uncomfortable members of the dominant culture. Perhaps because of the gentle, particularly inclusive way these adult musicals approached their subject matter, they were also among the most critically well received.

### THE FAGGOT

Written, composed, and directed by the Off Off Broadway denizen Al Carmines, *The Faggot* was the first commercial musical in New York City devoted entirely to contemporary gay issues. The production, which opened on April 13, 1973, at the Judson Poets' Theater at Judson Memorial Church, proved enough of a commercial and critical success to justify a move in July to the larger Truck and Warehouse Theater on East Fourth Street for an extended, commercial run of 203 performances.[1] While the musical itself was thematically groundbreaking, its trajectory was hardly atypical for a Judson show.

Most Judson productions tended to blend high and low cultures, irreverence and substance, experimental techniques and old-fashioned showmanship. Largely considered the heir to the experimental Living Theater, where the resident director Larry Kornfeld apprenticed in the 1950s, Judson strove to produce socially and aesthetically meaningful work. It subsequently earned a reputation for accessible, crowd-pleasing entertainment, and thus the productions it staged, especially through the late 1960s, quickly made the company a critical and commercial darling of the Off Off Broadway realm.[2]

Judson Poets' Theater was founded in 1961 under the auspices of the Judson Memorial Church in Greenwich Village. Like the church, which was dedicated to social activism from its inception in 1892, the theater strove to serve, but never to proselytize to, the surrounding community. "The two great doctrines of Christianity are salvation and creation," Carmines explained when asked about the church's interest in the theater. "There's been too much concern with the first. Judson wants to do more about the second."[3] In keeping with the church's philosophy, its new theater adopted only two founding principles, which the church's left-leaning congregation accepted immediately: productions were to be secular, and they could not be censored by the church. "A church should be confident enough in its faith that it is not afraid of other viewpoints and languages," Carmines explained when questioned about the second principle. "What you're really saying when you're afraid is, 'I'm afraid that what I believe isn't strong enough to combat what *you* believe.'"[4]

Fresh out of Union Theological Seminary, Alvin Carmines was hired in 1961 not only to serve as an associate minister, but also to help develop the church's theater, which originally operated out of the choir loft. Carmines quickly became invaluable to both church and theater, for which he served, at different times, as composer, performer, director, and muse. The director Larry Kornfeld credits Carmines with embodying the Judson Poets' aesthetic. "Al would have a couple of drinks and start playing the piano, and he sang beautifully," he notes, remembering the way he and Carmines became frequent collaborators.

> At some point we did a play . . . *Vaudeville Skit*, it was called.[5] It was all speech patterns, and [the actors] weren't quite getting it, so I said, "Al, would you just play some jazzy stuff on the piano so that they get used to the sound?" And so he—"dum-de-de-*dum*, de-*dum*, de-*dum* de-*dum* de-*dum*." And we rehearsed and rehearsed, and I said, "Al, let's leave it in. Let's play the music. Let's just do it." So there was this piece with the score in place. And then . . . it snowballed. He credited me with pushing him into doing musicals, but I credit him with having it in his heart![6]

Through the 1960s a combination of critical adulation and audience enthusiasm galvanized the Judson Poets' Theater, and Carmines developed a reputation for being a formidable composer and musician in his own right. The company worked nonstop through the decade, soon becoming so popular with audiences that the theater was moved out of the choir loft, which seated a hundred spectators, and into the main sanctuary, which seated four hundred. Several Judson shows did so well that they were transferred to even larger theaters for open-ended commercial runs; some of the group's best-known productions include *Promenade* (1965; inaugural production of the Promenade Theater), *In Circles* (1967; Cherry Lane and Gramercy Arts theaters), and *Peace* (1968; Astor Place Theater).

Yet as the late 1960s gave way to the early 1970s, Carmines experienced a personal awakening, and thus abruptly shifted course artistically. Newly fueled by the spirit of community activism in both his church and theater duties, Carmines turned his attention in 1969 to writing large-scale oratorios that could include far more amateur performers than the company had previously worked with.[7] While the oratorios continued to feature seasoned performers in the central roles, they were composed as well for anywhere between forty and sixty singing parts, many of which were assigned to members of the congregation. The renewed emphasis on community and the large, musically dense productions continued to prove popular with audiences, but Carmines's single-minded shift toward amateurism resulted in the resignation of several frustrated, more professional-minded senior members of Judson Poets' Theater, including Larry Kornfeld, in 1970.[8]

The collective spirit of Judson Poets' Theater was thus subsumed in the new decade by Carmines's more individualized vision. Yet his abrupt shifts in leadership and focus did not result in the immediate death of the company. Despite critics' charges that Carmines's eclectic, infectious music was consistently stronger than his directing and writing, Judson Poets' Theater offered a number of noteworthy productions through the mid- to late 1970s. Nevertheless *The Faggot* would be the last Judson Poets' Theater production to be transferred to an open-ended commercial run Off Broadway.[9]

Following the Washington, D.C., premiere of his *A Look at the Fifties* in late September 1972, Carmines turned his attention to two separate pieces: one on the life of Saint Paul and another about a New York City policeman. After struggling to write both, he decided to combine the works into a single "tribute to personal sexual liberation," which was inspired by his coming to terms with his own homosexuality and emerging from the closet.[10] Combining these two seemingly disparate ideas was not difficult, Carmines explained to the journalist Terry Gustavson, since "St. Paul was difficult to deal with because he had a strong and fearful view of sexuality, while the police acted as guardians of majority interests." In Carmines's eyes, gay men were outsiders "in terms of both tradition and law."[11]

Initially written as an oratorio for forty singers, *The Faggot* was scaled down for a cast of fifteen, revised as a revue, and redubbed a "new musical" when it transferred to the Truck and Warehouse in July 1973. Yet whether in oratorio or revue form, *The Faggot* was from the outset openly derisive of a culture that over many generations had forced individuals to deny or suppress their sexual orientation. From the start of the first act—when Carmines himself walked up to the stage, observed two male actors engaged in a covert sexual encounter, and shouted "Faggot!" at them—the songs and sketches hammered home the fact that even amid the post-Stonewall flurry of gay liberation, many gay men were still far from feeling comfortable in their own skin. More than anything else, *The Faggot* purported to examine "the odd experience of feeling normal only when you are in the midst of what society calls an abnormal act."[12] Neither the dominant culture nor the counterculture escapes condemnation: in one sketch a group of closeted hippies sings in praise of Eastern religion, macrobiotics, organic food, drugs, and meditation before announcing bluntly, "Anything's better than being a faggot."[13]

Yet one of *The Faggot*'s most forceful messages is that personal strength and security about sexual identity must come from within if society as a whole is going to change for the better. A vast majority of the songs and sketches in *The Faggot* can thus be read as short morality tales about men who lie to themselves or others, often at great personal cost. Some of the sketches make light of this message. In one, for example, two elderly women, Jenny and Sadie, chat conspiratorially on the phone about their sons, Edgar and Tom, who have grown up together. Edgar and Tom have become romantically involved and are going to elaborate lengths to hide their relationship from their mothers. This, it turns out, is futile: Jenny and Sadie are absolutely ecstatic that their sons have fallen in love with one another.

Yet other sketches on the same theme are not nearly as charming or buoyant. In many, characters are given the chance for the happiness and fulfillment that sexual

Jeff Friedman, John Harbaugh, Lawrence Eichler, and Danny Kreitzberg are convinced that "anything's better than being a faggot" in Al Carmines's revue *The Faggot*. Photo by Judith Greenberg. Courtesy of the Fales Collection, Bobst Library, New York University.

liberation allows, but instead choose to remain lonely and closeted out of fear or simple habit. In one of the saddest sketches, set twenty years in the future (thus in 1993), an aide invites the Secretary of State home to dinner after a particularly exhausting day:

*Aide:* …Why don't you come home with me for supper? My lover is a terrific cook. We could even invite someone for you.

*Secretary of State:* That's very kind of you, Hal, but I think I'd better work tonight. (Chuckles with a new ease.)

*Aide:* It's really legal now, you know. Gay liberation is a fact.

*Secretary of State:* Yes—a fact. But not necessarily a feeling—not a feeling, Hal. What you call gay liberation came just about five years too late for me.

*Aide:* Sir, it's never too late to be liberated.

*Secretary of State:* Oh yes—yes it is; it can be too late. You know, Hal, after the Emancipation Proclamation and the Civil War there were some slaves who chose to stay with their masters, who chose to stay in slavery. Well, so did I. By the time it was "legitimate" to be homosexual I was well entrenched in a kind of excitement that is only inhibited by liberation. You can become very accustomed to secrecy and furtiveness and pain. No—the sunlight of freedom is not very attractive to me. But thank you again. Good night, Hal.[14]

As the chorus launches into the number "I'll Take My Fantasy," the Secretary of State returns home, alone, to solitude and pornography (🔊 Ex. 3.1). During the song's instrumental interlude, members of the chorus heckle the lonely, furtive Secretary with homophobic epithets, and as the number ends a blackout swallows him up, alone, in darkness.

It is clear that Carmines greatly pities his closeted characters. "There are lots of reasons not to explore homosexual love," a chorister taunts the audience during the opening number. "Seventy years or so," the full chorus continues, mockingly. "Seventy years to find reasons not to do something. What a wonderful way to live."[15] The many characters in *The Faggot* who, like the Secretary of State, are not at peace with their sexual identity are similarly tormented by loneliness. This is just as true of contemporary characters—many of whom are depicted having clandestine, anonymous, joyless sex with hustlers—as it is of historic figures like Oscar Wilde, who is portrayed in *The Faggot* as being tortured by his all-consuming love for Lord Alfred Douglas, which conflicts painfully with the sense of obligation he feels toward his wife and children.

Long before the premiere of *The Faggot*, the Judson Poets' Theater had adopted Gertrude Stein as something of a guiding figure, and Carmines himself was an ardent devotee of her writings.[16] Thus by the early 1970s it would have come as no surprise for Judson audiences to see Carmines pay homage to Stein in his work. Indeed Stein and her partner, Alice B. Toklas, are the subject of a particularly disarming scene in *The Faggot*. In stark contrast with the many closeted, unhappy male characters who appear in previous sketches, Stein and Toklas are depicted midway through Act II as living in utter domestic bliss.

As this scene begins, Stein and Toklas ponder what they might prepare for dinner. Their mundane conversation, which begins simply with a list of possibilities ("Beans?" "Perhaps." "Corn?" "Corn—yes, corn"), segues into the number "Ordinary Things," which is an ecstatic declaration of love. Throughout the brief, polyphonic song, which is alternately lilting and explosively dynamic, the women trip over one another's lyrics, which vacillate between the ordinary (an evening meal, grocery shopping, daily domestic tasks) and the exceptional (the joy they experience in being devoted to one another) (  Ex. 3.2). As unofficial patron saint of the Judson Poets' Theater, Stein and her famous romantic partner are obviously heroines. For Carmines, love expressed simply and openly is clearly far more fulfilling than a life spent hiding alone in the shadows.

An original cast member, David Summers, argued that *The Faggot* was groundbreaking simply because it recognized and attempted to explore various facets of homosexuality. "Al Carmines runs the gamut from closet queens and hustlers to open love relationships," he told the press about the musical. "There are positive and negative statements, all made without tears."[17] The fact that *The Faggot* was clearly charting new territory did not go unnoticed by critics, who for the most part liked the

Alice B. Toklas (Peggy Atkinson) and Gertrude Stein (Lee Guilliatt) sing blissfully of their love for one another in Al Carmines's review *The Faggot*. Photo by Judith Greenberg. Courtesy of the Fales Collection, Bobst Library, New York University.

revue very much; the famously cranky critic John Simon, for example, concluded his enthusiastic review for *New York Magazine* by noting, "*The Faggot* is a pleasantly promising step toward a Gay Musical Liberation that could make a worthy contribution to our theater's sincerity and multiplicity."[18]

On the other hand, as Bottoms points out, Carmines's attempts to "underline the wrongs of societal oppression by stressing the consequently seedy, secretive nature of some gay lives" was often easily misinterpreted.[19] While curiously few questioned why the number "Art Song," in which Catherine the Great sang of the joys of bestiality, had any place at all in a revue about contemporary gay life, the depictions of gay men in *The Faggot* drew ire among many gay activists and generated hot debate about the overall message of the revue, the movement, and the relationship between politics and art.

Infuriated by what he saw as the mere reinforcement of pervasive gay stereotypes, Martin Duberman launched a public debate with an opinion piece in the *New York Times* in which he charged that *The Faggot* merely "pretends to a kaleidoscopic view of gay life." The revue, he argued, repeatedly treated "issues with serious implications for millions of people" by belittling them with "tinkly tunes, perky choreography and cartoon realities." In the process *The Faggot* "trivializes everything it touches—gay love or loneliness, fearful secrecies and open struggles, privatism and politics, problems of age and youth, monogamy and promiscuity, jealousy and devotion.... Seeing it, you'd have no idea that gay life in 1973 is in any way different from what it had been in the '50s—except in the absence of all authentic emotion." In sum, Duberman wrote angrily, "with friends like 'The Faggot,' the gay movement needs no enemies."[20]

Carmines's response, in a letter to the *Times* that ran a week after Duberman's op-ed appeared, maintained that politics should not influence creative vision:

> Although I agree with Mr. Duberman's political position regarding gay liberation, in the case of "The Faggot" he is not dealing with a political position paper, but rather with a personal, idiosyncratic, quirky, highly subjective theater piece. This is the crux of the disagreement between Mr. Duberman and myself. I do not believe politics is art and I believe a confusion of those two human activities is a dangerous and ultimately catastrophic misunderstanding.... As a political entity, I am committed to gay liberation and many other liberations. As an artist, I am committed only to the absolute human truth as I see it. And that truth is far more complicated than any party line, however noble, could ever be.... I do not believe that, because gays have suffered, they are perfect. I do not believe that, because we struggle, we cannot laugh at ourselves... I write of both the squalor and the glory of homosexuality, of both the confusion and the clarity; of both the ludicrousness and the holiness of the sexual life.[21]

As the first musical of its kind, *The Faggot* was bound to be subject to particularly harsh criticism, especially since the gay liberation movement was still so young and comprised so many activists struggling so intensely to make so many social and political changes at once. As letters that readers sent to the *Times* in response to the

Carmines-Duberman debate made clear, *The Faggot* meant very different things to different people. Many letter writers reflected concern over any depictions of gay men that were even remotely critical, arguing instead for representations that were solely positive and empowering. One writer, who agreed with Duberman that *The Faggot* was perpetuating stereotypes, wrote that gay artists should strive "to create a new, liberated gay culture which is both of high artistic quality and reflective of the new consciousness being created by gay liberationists." While this writer acknowledged that there was room for all kinds of perspectives, he hoped that, eventually, "more gay culture will come to embody this new gay awareness, including a sense of the social situation of homosexuals, anger at our oppression, and joyous self-affirmation."[22]

Yet a different writer sided with Carmines in arguing that Duberman was being woefully short-sighted: "What he fails to grasp is Carmines' idea that the best way of getting beyond homosexual stereotypes is not by ignoring them but by exploding them. Duberman does both the audience and the gay movement a disservice when he confuses the solemnity of gay rhetoric with gay pride, and thinks of laughter as the enemy."[23]

The Caffe Cino playwright and gay activist Doric Wilson argues that, especially in hindsight, Duberman was rather heavy-handed in criticizing *The Faggot*. Although Wilson remembers that the musical was not without its problems, it ultimately struck him as a particularly refreshing, deeply empowering piece of theater. "*The Faggot* meandered here and there and was amateur and was meant to be," he recalls. And yet, while Wilson typically came away from more overtly polemical gay theater of the time thinking "That was very nice," *The Faggot* made him feel deeply moved "and very proud that [I was] gay. And a little taller."[24]

The activist and writer Vito Russo wrote a typically insightful review of *The Faggot* for the post-Stonewall newspaper *Gay*, in which he confessed that he had been eagerly anticipating the musical for a long time and thus knew that he was bound to be disappointed by it at some point or another. Wisely, however, he refused to fault the production, concluding instead, "[At] the present time it is impossible to appraise a work dealing with homosexuality solely as a piece of theatre, especially if one is involved in gay politics. That is not to say that a particularly good show is any less successful depending on its politics, but let's say a little less satisfying personally for one who has been waiting so long to hear certain things 'said out loud.'" Russo commended *The Faggot* for its strengths and was not too critical of its weaknesses. "When it doesn't work, it's crushingly disappointing," he admitted, but "more because of the political expectations which precede it than any substantial shortcomings it might have as a work of art."[25] As Russo's comments imply, the real problem with *The Faggot* was that, at the time of its opening, it was the only musical of its kind in town.

*The Faggot* proved that while there was plenty of interest in musicals depicting contemporary gay life, one production could not single-handedly satisfy the needs of every spectator who came to see it, especially during such an intensely political time. Clearly there was room and demand for more gay musicals, and indeed within a year of the premiere of *The Faggot* New York audiences would have many other productions to choose from.

One of the first post-Stonewall—and post-*Faggot*—musicals to reflect the direct influence of contemporary gay activism was also one of the most commercially successful adult musicals to run in New York City during the 1970s. *Let My People Come: A Sexual Musical* began its run Off Broadway at the Village Gate in January 1974, moved to Broadway's Morosco Theater in June 1976, and closed the following October. Written and composed by Earl Wilson Jr., who developed the show with the producer and director Phil Oesterman, *Let My People Come* was a response to *Oh! Calcutta!*, which both men saw as distressingly out of touch.

"*Oh! Calcutta!* was a dirty show," Wilson remembers. "It was my parents' generation. It was old, old, old: let me look and have a good time looking through the binoculars. . . . It made you feel dirty when you left it."[26] Wilson and Oesterman decided to try to represent contemporary sexuality more honestly, while being as "outrageous as the law will allow, and the cast will go along with."[27] Wilson remembers that he and Oesterman also hoped to capitalize on the spirit of the times, and thus the underlying message of *Let My People Come* was, in essence, " 'Open up the closet door, come out, have fun with us, we all do it, everybody does it, it's ok.' . . . Because everybody I knew—that's how they felt! You know, this was in the seventies, and we were in the middle of all this 'if it feels good, it's great.' "[28]

Once Wilson and Oesterman came up with the general idea for their revue, they held auditions in search of young, multiracial, nonunion actors who, Wilson felt, would come across as more innocent than seasoned professionals. Of course, nonunion actors would also likely be more willing to appear naked and simulate sex acts on stage in exchange for Equity cards. Partly because this was the case, and partly because of the spirit of the times, casting the show proved remarkably easy.[29]

*Let My People Come* began its run at the Village Gate in January 1974. In a shrewd move Oesterman not only never announced an official opening, but also refused to allow critics admission to the show unless they paid for tickets themselves. Word spread fast: enough critics griped loudly about the nudie musical they'd been shut out of that *Let My People Come* soon became one of the hottest tickets Off Broadway.[30] During its run it spawned national and international tours, an original cast album, and spinoff productions in Amsterdam, London, Paris, Toronto, and elsewhere.[31]

In keeping with the Off Off Broadway ancestry of adult musicals, most of the songs and sketches for *Let My People Come* were based on conversations between the original cast and the creative team, which took place during a series of encounter sessions that preceded and then continued through the rehearsal period. Wilson remembers:

> We had auditions and we said, "We don't really have a show. We have a couple songs, we have an idea, and we're going to write it around you guys. It'll be based on what you think. I don't want you to say anything you don't believe, because that will come across. It has to be honest, or nobody's gonna come to the show." We had five months of rehearsal, five nights a week. We had encounter sessions where we would all talk.

Then I would go home and write a song for somebody, because I knew what they sounded like.[32]

As a result of this process, *Let My People Come* is reflective of a particularly broad swath of contemporary sexuality. Songs like "I Believe My Body," the spoof "The Cunnilingus Champion of Company C," the anthem "Doesn't Anybody Love Anymore?," and the title song celebrated various aspects of the sexual revolution. "And She Loved Me" and "Give It to Me," both of which are discussed at length in the following chapter, focused on contemporary women's issues. The song "Dirty Words," which consisted almost entirely of taboo sexual terms and euphemisms, paid direct homage to Lenny Bruce and served as an inadvertent tribute to *Hair*'s own taboo number, "Sodomy." And the number "Linda, Georgina, Marilyn and Me," which is also discussed later in this book, poked fun at the mainstream popularity of pornographic films.

Unlike *Oh! Calcutta!*, which Tynan devised as entirely heterosexual in both content and appeal, or *The Faggot*, which focused on gay life, Phil Oesterman insisted that *Let My People Come* be all-inclusive. Although Wilson, who is straight, agreed with his openly gay and politically active producer, he nevertheless remembers being daunted by the challenge of coming up with gay content. The cast and creative team, however, included a number of gay actors and a gay music director, all of whom contributed ideas during the encounter sessions.

*Let My People Come* featured two numbers that touched on the lives of contemporary gay men. The first, "Take Me Home with You," was set in a crowded gay bar. A torchy, languid ballad originally performed by the actor and gay activist Larry Paulette,[33] the song is comparatively understated; unlike a majority of the numbers in *Let My People Come*, "Take Me Home with You" has no explicit or even vaguely sexually suggestive lyrics. Further, the scene in which it was featured offered no simulated sex or nudity. Rather the song focuses on the singer's desire to connect with someone, not just for the night, but for the long term:

> Gee, it's getting kind of late
> Last call already is overdue
> Tommy wants to close the bar
> Won't you take me home with you?
> . . .
> The night's impossible for one
> Pretty easy, though, for two
> And tomorrow I'll be gone
> So won't you take me home with you?
>
> And when morning comes around
> We might have a lot to say
> Those feelings that we shared last night
> Might linger through the day.
>
> Tomorrow may be just the start
> Of a different point of view

And I might even hang around
If you take me home with you.

🔊 Ex. 3.3

The setting of "Take Me Home with You" rests initially on the notion of the gay bar as a site to find consequence-free sex; the line "And tomorrow I'll be gone, so won't you take me home with you?" plays on the stereotype of the sexually promiscuous gay man. The next stanzas, however, effectively explode both stereotypes, as does the gentle, lilting pace of the song. The singer clearly wants to take his time and to make a romantic connection; he longs for love, not for quick, anonymous sex. In singing openly, dreamily, of his hopes that a one night stand will result in deeper, lasting intimacy, he doubles back on his initial promise to be gone by morning.

Like "Take Me Home with You," the song "I'm Gay" is lyrically straightforward and more intent on exploding than perpetuating stereotypes. Inspired by conversations Wilson had with some of the gay cast members, "I'm Gay" was performed by two male actors who sat, center-stage and fully clothed, on barstools facing the audience. The almost samba-like "I'm Gay" was written in the style of a "coming out" letter sent home to parents:

Dear mom and pop, I'm really happy
And not ashamed at all of what I am.
Those who don't know or think it's funny
Don't pay much attention to them.

I'm hoping that you'll come to see
This is how God meant me to be.
This is my way, and I'm proud to come right out and say
I'm gay.

Dear mom and pop you know I love you
That's why you had to hear it from me
If I didn't think so much of you
I guess I could have just let it be
You'd have heard it from somebody somewhere
And that wouldn't be very fair
Maybe one day it won't be such a hard thing to say
I'm gay.

More urgently paced than "Take Me Home with You," "I'm Gay" employed a polyphonic texture in the chorus, during which one male voice hurriedly imitated each line introduced by the other, as if the young men singing the number were at once excited and terrified by the act of coming out of the closet.

The number, according to the original cast member and assistant choreographer Tobie Columbus, was always performed by "two beautiful young boys. And that was the thing—whoever was cast for the part had to be beautiful and sweet and absolute innocence." As the two young actors repeated the lyrics "I'm gay" at the very end of

Martin Duffy and Joe Jones come out to their parents in the "I'm Gay" number from *Let My People Come*. Courtesy of Photofest.

the song, they were gradually joined in solidarity by the rest of the cast, who sang offstage; as the number concluded, the entire company was singing "I'm gay" along with the two actors (🕪 Ex. 3.4). This number, Columbus recalls, was consistently one of the strongest in the show; its reflection of raw emotion and of camaraderie often brought the house down, and spectators to tears.[34]

The relative tameness of both "I'm Gay" and "Take Me Home with You"—neither of which featured nudity, simulated sex, or explicit lyrics—is reflective of the shift in direction that the gay rights movement had taken by the mid-1970s. Well under way by 1974, gay activism had evolved "into a movement that was less freewheeling, less angry, and more conventional."[35] The raw anger, idealism, and youthful energy that sparked the movement had been mitigated by the mid-1970s, along with some of "the more blatant forms of discrimination that had inspired their fury" in the first place.[36]

What replaced the call to arms that occurred immediately after the Stonewall riots was a collective realization among activists that lasting social and cultural change would result only from long-term persistence and dedication. The rallying cry that would galvanize the women's movement—"The personal is political"—applies to the gay rights movement as well. And as the nickname "the Me Decade" makes clear, much of the focus during the 1970s—not just in gay circles but in the mainstream as well—was placed on the role of the individual over the collective.

In keeping with the shift from the mass organizing of the 1960s to the more muted, self-centered introspection of the 1970s, the gay rights movement began to place new emphasis on the strength and courage of the out gay person. As Carmines implied throughout *The Faggot*, a gay person who had the courage to come out of the closet and live openly would not only no longer have to lie, but would also help prove to the dominant culture that homosexuality was neither a sickness nor something to vilify. "We did lots of community organizing, always emphasizing visibility because this was—and is—at the core of our oppression," the activist Jean O'Leary remembers of her work with the National Gay Task Force in the mid-1970s. "There's no question about it, if everybody who's gay was visible, we would probably eliminate seventy percent of the oppression. Everybody already knows gay people. They just don't know that we're gay."[37]

However simplistic the songs, the messages behind "Take Me Home with You" and especially "I'm Gay" were powerful for their time. With both numbers Wilson went out of his way to humanize gay men. In both songs sexuality is not remotely as important as the desire to be loved and respected, either by a romantic partner or by family members. The plaintive request for acceptance by and unity with the audience—composed of gay and straight spectators—who attended nightly performances of *Let My People Come* is implied as well. The gay content in *Let My People Come* ultimately attempts to strike the same deal with audience members that Al Carmines did at the conclusion of *The Faggot*, when his cast faced the audience and sang, "We will make a pact with you. Love what you want and we will too ( Ex. 3.5)."

## LOVERS

As gay activism snowballed in New York City and across the country through the 1970s, it contributed to the establishment of several not-for-profit gay theater companies, some of which featured musicals as their inaugural productions. The first gay theater company established in New York City, TOSOS (The Other Side of Silence), was founded in 1974 by a Caffe Cino alum, Doric Wilson, along with Billy Blackwell, Peter del Valle, and John McSpadden. The musical *Lovers*, with music by Steve Sterner and book and lyrics by Peter del Valle, served as TOSOS's inaugural production. Like *The Faggot* and the gay content in *Let My People Come*, *Lovers* was written to be simultaneously entertaining, empowering, and educational. Although it was initially intended specifically for gay audiences, the musical proved appealing to straight theatergoers as well and was thus moved to the Players Theater on MacDougal Street in early 1975 for a commercial run of 118 performances.

After the demise of the Caffe Cino, Doric Wilson continued to write plays but also grew increasingly active in gay politics. He remembers being inspired to form TOSOS after a concert by Alaina Reed reminded him, rather viscerally, of his outsider status. During the concert Reed changed all of the pronouns in the lyrics she sang "so that she didn't sing a single heterosexual song. They were all gay or gender non-specific. At first you didn't notice it, but she was singing standards, so soon you did." Upon leaving the show, Wilson found that a Gershwin tune was stuck in his head. "I was humming it all night. And I said to myself, 'What is this that I'm humming?' And finally the words came into my head: 'They're writing songs of love / But not for me.' And then I said, 'Holy shit!' And that was it."[38] Wilson, del Valle, Blackwell, and McSpadden quickly threw themselves into forming the company, which Wilson funded with money he'd made working as a bartender. Del Valle remembers that TOSOS was in part "a reaction to the fact that most gay theater at the time was just male nudes running around" and that the group's prime motivation, at least at first, was to offer high-quality entertainment by, for, and about gay people.[39]

With their shoestring budget, the group set up shop on Church Street in lower Manhattan, in a space appropriately named the Basement Theater. Yet finding plays to produce, let alone actors to perform in them, proved more difficult than Wilson had anticipated. "TOSOS was fairly snobby," he admits. "I wanted the plays to be good, literary plays. We turned down a lot of things that other people were quite happy to have." Further, he remembers, TOSOS met with a lot of resistance among gay playwrights and actors, many of whom were either closeted or so eager for main-stream acceptance that they were unwilling to risk being pigeonholed by working with an exclusively gay theater company.[40] The founding members of TOSOS soon realized that if they wanted to attract a following, they would have to wear many more hats than originally anticipated.

Such was the case with *Lovers*. Peter del Valle and Steve Sterner, who wrote the musical together, met while working with a children's theater company. After col-laborating on a few children's musicals, they decided to write something for TOSOS. "TOSOS started off-off-off-off-OFF Broadway, in a basement, so we had nothing," del Valle recalls. "So I told Doric I'd write a show to open TOSOS, and that's where Steve came in. And the children's theater company did too—we actually used their lights." "And one or two of the actors, too!" Sterner adds.[41] The very loosely plotted *Lovers* followed three different gay male relationships: a middle-aged couple with a fondness for leather; an upwardly mobile couple of recent college graduates who preferred matching sweater sets; and two much older men whose relationship spanned several decades. The couples sang about contemporary gay life and their own relationships.

TOSOS planned to offer *Lovers* several times over a few weekends in February 1974. Company members advertised by making occasional announcements and dis-tributing flyers in gay bars, hanging posters in gay neighborhoods, and asking friends to spread the word. The result, Sterner recalls, was houses so packed that audiences were "hanging off the rafters, with no advertising. There was such a demand for it—they kept saying, can you do it some more?"[42] TOSOS thus brought *Lovers* back by popular demand in October 1974 for an eight-week run. At this point the producers Phillip Graham-Geraci and Michael Brown offered to back the musical, which was recast and moved to the Players Theater in Greenwich Village for a commercial run that began on January 27, 1975, and lasted through mid-May.

In an interview conducted while the show was in previews at the Players Theater, del Valle explained that *Lovers* was in no way meant to be a plea for acceptance by straight people, but instead "simply a play which says very freely that gay people, like any other people, have day-to-day lives and loves, and that these experiences are really commonplace. Gay people have to be able to look at their own experience, to laugh at it, to identify with it honestly and openly. Many still must be brought to see that they need not be guilt-ridden for the rest of their lives."[43] The subtitle that del Valle and Sterner devised for their musical is particularly telling. Whereas advertisements for

The cast of *Lovers*: three committed couples. Photo by Kenn Duncan. Courtesy of the Kenn Duncan Archive, New York Public Library for the Performing Arts.

*The Boys in the Band* featured a particularly damning line of dialogue from the show—"Show me a happy homosexual and I'll show you a gay corpse"—*Lovers'* slogan, which appeared in print media and on posters, was "The Musical That Proves It's No Longer Sad to Be Gay (🔊 Ex. 3.1)."

Yet *Lovers* proved appealing to straight theatergoers as well. The broader appeal is partly due to del Valle's and Sterner's personal histories. Despite agreeing to compose *Lovers* and serve as its music director, Sterner was not only straight but also, he recalls, "a mere tyke," with very little romantic history of his own to draw from.[44] And del Valle had only recently come out of the closet. As a result, he chuckles, *Lovers* was "a little polemical because essentially it's—I had just started—I was in my first gay relationship. And so essentially it was like, 'This is what I've learned, folks, from living with ONE PERSON!'"[45] Though the opposite is almost always the case, *Lovers'* polemic tone proved advantageous, at least as far as ticket sales went. "You know, I hate to say it, but each little [song and sketch] was kind of like a lesson," del Valle admits. "So it actually turned out to be fairly universal. There were a lot of straight people that got it, because it was about relationships." Sterner agrees: "A lot of straight people said, 'I experience that in *MY* relationship!' So it showed that people are people."[46]

Yet perhaps another reason for the broader appeal of *Lovers* was the fact it was particularly tame. Of the sixteen musical numbers in the show, only one was risqué, and del Valle and Sterner were careful to infuse the lyrics and the staging with winking good humor. "The Trucks," which they wrote as a rollicking, 1950s-style rock-and-roll number, paid homage to the meatpacking district of Manhattan during the 1960s and 1970s, where gay men would frequently gather to cruise after nightfall. The number begins gently, before packing a particularly crude punch near the end of the introduction:

> There's a spot that lovers often visit
> Whether as a couple or alone
> No matter if it's hot as hell
> Or freezing to the bone
> Sex is sweet and easy there
> The smell of semen fills the air.

The song then picks up tempo and, to the accompaniment of a boogie-woogie piano and a male chorus repeating "Shut up and shove it up!" in doo-wop style, the lead singer continues to pay tribute to "the place where no one knows your name" and where "you can screw until your balls turn blue": at the trucks. As del Valle recalls:

> This was before AIDS, and the trucks down by the riverside—they left them open at night. So gays would just pack in there by the hundreds. We knew this number was going to be filthy. You see the back of this truck, and one of the leather guys, very handsome, with a great big bulge in his pants. The rest of the cast keeps going by, and looking around, and when they saw what was going on in the truck, there was always a "ding," and they climbed in. And at the end, the leather guy looked around, saw that everyone was in the truck, took a beer can out of his pants, and then climbed in, too. So it was done with a sense of humor.[47]

"The Trucks" was the sole exception to the show's emphasis on monogamy. Del Valle and Sterner made a conscious effort to represent gay men as committed partners, regardless of their background or outward appearance. Scene after scene and song after song emphasized love, devotion, and the struggle for respect, but there was very little in *Lovers* that was directly about sex. The show featured no nudity and, with the exception of what was merely implied in "The Trucks," no simulated sex, both of which might have alienated straight theatergoers. There was only one kiss in *Lovers*, and, as del Valle remembers with a shrug, it was "between the older couple. And then one of them dies. So."[48]

What *Lovers* did feature, however, was a rousing coming-out anthem, much like "I'm Gay" from *Let My People Come*. "Somehow I'm Taller" was performed by the entire cast. As the number begins, cast members take turns announcing what gay liberation means to them:

Cruisers visit "The Trucks" in the musical *Lovers*. Photo by Kenn Duncan. Courtesy of the Kenn Duncan Archive, New York Public Library for the Performing Arts.

Gay liberation is not calling your lover a roommate.

Gay liberation is not being afraid to hold hands on the street.

Gay liberation is not fixing up the guestroom like someone actually sleeps there when straight friends come to visit.

Gay liberation is not letting your parents pretend that your lover doesn't exist.

Gay liberation is not hating yourself so much that you can't love somebody else.

The sixth cast member begins with "Gay liberation is—" before suddenly breaking off to tell the audience his coming-out story:

You know, it seems like yesterday when I first marched in the Christopher Street Liberation Day Parade. I was *so* uptight. I wore a pair of dark glasses and a big floppy hat pulled down over my face. Some of my best friends didn't even recognize me. But when I saw how many of us were there—when I was suddenly surrounded by a sea of gorgeous numbers, laughing and kissing and chanting their self-pride right there in front of CBS and ABC and God and everybody, and when the whole length of Sixth Avenue, as far as the eye could see, was literally swarming with faggots! Let me tell you something, honey—something inside me snapped. Off came the hat. Off came the glasses. And I was shouting and waving at every camera pointed at my direction. Gay liberation? Oh, *God!*

He then sings the opening verses of "Somehow I'm Taller," which are repeated by the entire cast:

How can I explain this feeling that I got?
For too many years I've been fighting with my lot
Then yesterday I did something I never done before
I burned down all my bridges and walked through that closet door. Now,

Somehow I'm taller
Somehow I'm stronger
Somehow I'm bolder than yesterday.

Somehow the sun shines brighter
Somehow I'm now a better fighter
Somehow I'm younger
Somehow I'm older
Somehow I'm wiser than yesterday.

Sterner and del Valle intended the strident, march-like "Somehow I'm Taller" to be something of a centerpiece for *Lovers*; the number occurred late in the first act, about halfway through the musical. Like "I'm Gay," "Somehow I'm Taller" functioned both to educate audience members about the struggle for mutual respect and understanding, as well as to empower closeted gays and encourage them to come out of the closet. Sterner remembers, "A lot of homosexuals in the closet did come out as a direct result of the show, and I say this with all modesty, because I was told this by people who did come out, and who said to me, 'I came out because of your show.'" Del Valle adds, "One of the most moving moments for me was during the original Off Off Broadway production, when I was in the cast. This old man came to me with tears in his eyes and said, 'I am so glad I lived to see this.' That *still* gets me."[49]

The critics' reviews of *Lovers* at the Players Theater were mixed to positive, with the strongest reviews coming from some of the smaller or more alternative presses. Margaret Kry for the *Villager* argued that the musical should be seen "not because it's gay but because it's good," and Ray F. Patient argued in Columbia University's daily *Spectator* that while not terribly profound, *Lovers* was nevertheless "light, bright, and fast-paced."[50] The mainstream newspapers that covered *Lovers* tended to be at once harsher with the production and more tentative; the result, Sterner recalls, was a sense that many critics were walking on eggshells in writing their reviews, perhaps because of a general discomfort with the subject matter, however gently presented it was.

Indeed it is hard to get a clear picture of the expectations that mainstream critics had for *Lovers*. Many of them withheld much in the way of real assessment, acknowledging that since *Lovers* was one of the first shows of its kind, it was particularly hard to compare with other productions. Michael Feingold likened the musical to blaxploitation films and noted that he disliked *Lovers'* polemic undertones, which "give the show rather the air of a homosexual 'Sesame Street.'"[51] And Clive Barnes, who was often commendably quick to admit his own biases when reviewing productions that he felt uncomfortable about for one reason or another, is clear that *Lovers* was just one of these productions. His somewhat meandering review of the show, which he likens to a "musical gay lib Bill of Rights," ends with a thinly veiled confession: "It is difficult for straights to criticize the new gay theater without sounding either patronizing or foolish. However, I think 'Lovers' should appeal to the gay community, and quite a few straights might be interested in it as a sociological tourist trip. Yet they might also feel that they had stepped into a gay bar by mistake and sense themselves out of place."[52]

In response to the tentative reaction of the mainstream press, which the producers feared would stanch interest among straight theatergoers, the company of Lovers began to host free discussion sessions after Wednesday night performances, during which cast and audience members could chat informally about the musical, and gay culture in general.[53] These efforts at inclusion helped Lovers run Off Broadway for about six months. While hardly a commercial smash by New York standards, the show's staying power—and the modest profit it made before it closed—surprised and pleased the individuals involved. As del Valle recalls, Lovers' Off Broadway run was "pretty good for a non-nudie gay play" at a time when modern gay activism was still so young.

Del Valle is hardly being boastful here; John Clum reminds us that even in 1975 being involved with "a gay show in Greenwich Village" was seen as such a dangerous career move that many of the most well-established gay playwrights and composers refused to consider such projects.[54] The playwright Martin Sherman says of his play Passing By, a gay love story produced at Playwrights Horizons in 1974, "We couldn't cast it," since regardless of sexual orientation, actors were "absolutely terrified" by the prospect of appearing in the production.[55] In short, it says a lot about Lovers that it managed to run as long as it did.

Sterner and del Valle remain convinced that Lovers would have gotten even more exposure had they pushed the producers to take it on the road, especially to college campuses, where gay social and political groups were proliferating. Del Valle admits, however, "I am not a pusher. Had I been a pusher, I probably could have gotten more mileage out of it."[56] Nevertheless Lovers has enjoyed several revivals in various cities around the world. The gay theater company The Glines, based in New York City, produced the musical during its second Gay American Arts Festival in New York in 1981, and revivals of Lovers have been mounted more recently on Fire Island, in Dallas, and in Queensland, Australia. As with The Faggot, Lovers proved more widely appealing than initially expected, which resulted in the premieres of several more gay-themed musicals during the mid-1970s.

As it turned out, and despite the persistence of concerns about gay theater being a bad career move in the 1970s, 1974 turned out to be something of a banner year for small, gay-themed commercial musicals in New York. Opening quickly behind the premiere of Lovers at TOSOS in February was Sextet at the Bijou on Broadway in March, and Gay Company Off Broadway at the Little Hippodrome in November. Although Sextet and Gay Company both reflected aspects of contemporary, urban gay life, there was little else that was similar about them, structurally or stylistically, with the exception that they both reflected the lasting impact of Sondheim's Company, which had closed in January 1972 after 705 performances.

An intimate, bittersweet musical about the imperfections of romantic relationships, *Sextet* began previews on February 20, 1974, and opened on March 3 at the Bijou Theater on Forty-fifth Street.[57] *Sextet* featured a book by Harvey Perr and Lee Goldsmith, lyrics by Goldsmith, and a score by Lawrence Hurwit. The loose plot follows the thoughts and actions of three couples during a dinner party that is being held in the Manhattan apartment of David and his partner, Kenneth. Their guests include David's recently widowed mother, Fay, and Fay's new boyfriend, the twice-divorced Paul. Also present are David's old college roommate, Leonard, and Leonard's wife, Ann (played by a young and very well-received Dixie Carter).

Some of the tensions between the characters are made clear from the outset: Fay adores Kenneth but has convinced herself that he and her son are only roommates, even though, deep down, she knows better. Leonard and David have not seen one another since college, where their stint as roommates ended when David propositioned Leonard, who, in response, broke David's jaw. In town on business and eager to see his old friend, Leonard is nevertheless concerned that David will still think of him as an intolerant boor. David too is concerned about how he will feel when he sees Leonard again.

Over the course of the evening the tensions that exist within each romantic coupling become central to the plot. During the dinner party all of the characters come to doubt their choice in partners and, however briefly, their sexual preferences to boot. David, who is expecting to feel the same way he once did about Leonard, is surprised instead to find himself attracted to Ann. Leonard, a relentless womanizer, finds himself, at least for a moment, intrigued by Kenneth. Ann, reeling from the recent discovery of her husband's many infidelities, questions her role as a traditional wife and mother as she drinks herself into a tizzy. Kenneth, threatened by David's past attraction to Leonard and current one to Ann, veils his jealousy with wisecracks, biting sarcasm, and a barely concealed stash of pot. Fay, who is not used to dating after a decades-long marriage, begins to hint with increasing aggression that she'd like to remarry, while Paul, who has fallen in love with Fay, is nevertheless terrified by the thought of marrying yet again. By the end of the evening all of the characters conclude that sexuality is fluid and that they are free to define themselves as they choose. They also decide that their relationships, like all relationships, may not be perfect, but that they are worth cultivating nonetheless.[58]

*Sextet*'s lyricist and co-book-writer Lee Goldsmith fell in love with musicals as a child and wanted nothing more than to write them as an adult. After World War II, Goldsmith, who had served in the army for three and a half years, moved to Miami with his partner, Larry, and took a job at National Comics, scripting episodes of the Flash, the Green Lantern, and Wonder Woman in order to support himself while pursuing work as a lyricist. In the early 1970s a contact at a theater publishing house in New York introduced him to the composer Lawrence Hurwit, who also lived in Miami. The two quickly began to collaborate on *Sextet*.

According to Goldsmith, the book for *Sextet* was largely autobiographical. "I was writing about me and Larry, my former partner, who died after we were together 46 years," he remembers. "So it involved Larry and I, and my mother and

The couple Robert Spencer (David) and Harvey Evans (Kenneth) hold Dixie Carter (Ann), who is trying to hold on to her philandering husband, Leonard (Jerry Lanning) in *Sextet*. Courtesy of Photofest.

her then-boyfriend, whom she ultimately married and who became my stepfather, and not a college roommate, but a high school roommate of mine. It was more or less based on reality."[59] Once *Sextet* neared completion, Hurwit, whose side business in real estate gave him access to a number of wealthy potential investors, began to drum up interest in the project; Goldsmith remembers holding regular backers' auditions in Hurwit's home. Eventually Hurwit and Goldsmith secured a producer, investors, and enough money to bring *Sextet* to New York.

In the post-Stonewall years openly gay characters were featured with growing frequency on Broadway. Nevertheless these characters were often secondary, and more often than not they embraced age-old stereotypes—the evil, bitchy queen; the swishing, squealing sidekick—that were hardly new to Broadway audiences at the time, let alone reflective of any real social change.[60] *Sextet* was, in this respect, a major departure.

Goldsmith, who at eighty-six describes himself as not only "out of the closet since the day I was born," but also never uncomfortable about it, even during his stint in the army, clearly had enormous affection and respect for his central characters. As a result, their relationship is striking only in its utter ordinariness. Kenneth and David live comfortably together, share domestic duties, are steadfastly devoted to one another despite the occasional squabble or ephemeral fit of jealousy, get along with one another's families, and, in short, weather the ups and downs of their romantic lives as well as, if not far better than, the heterosexual couples around them. They do not embrace any particular stereotypes, reflect no problems or concerns with who they are, and—with the possible exception of Fay, who loves them both even as she convinces herself that they are just roommates—are readily accepted by the straight characters with whom they interact. Even Leonard, who once reacted to David's proposition with brute force, has matured in adulthood, at least insofar as his homophobia is concerned. In short, although homosexuality is central to *Sextet*, it is not remotely a big deal.

The playwright Harvey Perr, who was invited by the director Jed Barclay to help doctor the book once *Sextet* began rehearsals in New York, remembers that the relationship between David and Kenneth was particularly striking to him when he first read Goldsmith's script. "The original material was very warm towards these characters and I saw no reason to change that," he notes. "It was also helpful that I really liked the actors who were playing the parts—Robert Spencer and Harvey Evans. They weren't having a relationship, but they were definitely playing very honestly, and they were very simpatico."[61]

Goldsmith remembers feeling strongly from the start that *Sextet* was not meant for Broadway, both because it was such an intimate ensemble piece and because the unflinching, nonstereotypical approach to homosexuality struck him as too sophisticated for Broadway at the time. The composer Lawrence Hurwit and the musical's producers, however, were adamant. Goldsmith remembers at one point begging Hurwit to open the show Off Broadway, which was less risky and expensive, and thus less conservative than Broadway.

> "Mind you, this was '74—this [did] *not* belong in a Broadway theater. It was the Bijou, which was a small house, but it was still 45th Street…and the audience was *totally* different for uptown and downtown. I begged him, but he had these Broadway stars in his eyes, and so I thought, what the hell do I care? A Broadway theater is better than no theater. And so we got a whole different audience than we would have gotten downtown. It was a Broadway audience! And they expected a Broadway musical! And this was *not* a Broadway musical!"[62]

Like Goldsmith, Harvey Perr felt that *Sextet* was unprecedented in its depictions of gay men, which did not help its reception on Broadway. "We all thought we were doing something interesting in terms of putting homosexuality on the stage in a musical, certainly," he recalls. "Unfortunately, only two reviews I remember even brought up that fact as a virtuous thing. Everybody else responded to—I don't know what they responded to. They didn't like it. I have a feeling that one of the reasons they didn't like it was because they had never seen anything like it before."[63]

*Sextet* certainly caused a stir in the critical community. When it opened, the musical received reviews ranging widely from gushing raves to abject pans, and critics seemed to disagree with one another—rather hotly, at that—on just about everything. While Dick Brukenfeld argued in the *Village Voice* that the characters were all "too nonspecific and their encounters too too brief to make more than a blurred impression," Richard Watts countered in the *New York Post* that "you feel you are getting to know all six of its characters," all of whom "are played by such pleasant people."[64] While *Sextet* proved to Watts that "the theatrically troublesome subject of homosexuality can be treated with taste and effectiveness," Hobe Morrison for *Variety* revealed some of his own homophobia in panning the show, which he called a "glorification, if not outright advocacy, of homosexuality."[65] Martin Gottfried raved in *Women's Wear Daily* about *Sextet*'s "marvelous" score and "excellent" lyrics; Marilyn Stasio for *Cue* felt that the "frail musical" suffered from "the inanities of its book" and its "torpid and derivative music."[66] The mixed reviews did little to help *Sextet* attract an audience; it closed on March 10 after fourteen previews and nine performances.

Whether they loved or despised *Sextet*, virtually all of the critics agreed about one thing: the musical reminded them of *Company*. Gottfried and Watts made wholly favorable comparisons. Watts argued that *Sextet* resembled "a quieter version of 'Company'" that was "somewhat more ingratiating."[67] Gottfried referred to *Sextet* as "Son of Company" at the start of his review, but was then careful to note that *Sextet* was nevertheless a highly original, "clever and straight and musical and funny and unusual and fine show."[68]

Other critics were not nearly as kind. Clive Barnes wrote in the *New York Times* that while *Sextet* seems to attempt to depict "the New York glitter of Stephen Sondheim's *Company*," it misses: "The gloss is glassy, the diamonds are paste and the martinis are wet and warm."[69] And both Douglas Watt for the *Daily News* and the critic for *Show Business* dismissed *Sextet* as a "poor-man's *Company*."[70] Perr remembers this constant comparison as the real death knell for *Sextet*. "Let's face it, *Company* was brilliant," he chuckles. "And if you were gonna be compared to *Company*, you were gonna suffer. There was no question."[71]

Hurwit and Goldsmith both claim that Sondheim was never a major influence on their work,[72] and while a few of the songs from *Sextet*—the plaintive "Visiting Rights," for example—feature the orchestrally sparse introductions, murky dissonances, and disjunct melodies that are faintly reminiscent of songs like "Sorry/Grateful," comparisons with *Company* seem superficial ( Ex. 3.6). Hurwit tends not to stray with the regularity that Sondheim does from standard popular song form, does not shy away nearly as often from melodic repetition, and reflects less interest in metric variation.[73] Goldsmith too argues that though awed by Sondheim's brilliance as a composer, he was never influenced by—or even terribly impressed with—Sondheim's lyrics:

> Believe it or not, that never occurred to me until I saw the reviews. *Company* is about a guy who doesn't want to get married, who is involved with lots of women, and who has got these married friends who keep trying to get him married. I couldn't see the connection. I loved *Company*, but it never crossed my mind that there was any similarity. In fact, I've got a beef with Sondheim as a lyricist. What he does, which I do not approve of, and no other theater lyricist I know—you should have heard Fred Ebb on the subject of Sondheim. Sondheim put words into the mouths of his characters when they were singing that they would not have said when they were speaking. And it *drove me crazy*. Because the lyrics are brilliant beyond belief, but often too brilliant for the character who was singing. That's my main objection to Sondheim: he doesn't stay in character. It doesn't bother audiences in particular, but it bothers me as a lyricist.[74]

Indeed while Hurwit's music might occasionally suggest some Sondheim influence, Goldsmith's lyrics do not. Goldsmith avoids the many lists that Sondheim tends to make out of his lyrics and has a much more relaxed approach to rhyme and alliteration.

Sextet was likely compared with Company less because of any similarities in the score than because the musicals had similar sets and basic premises. Perr points out that not only was Company about a group of upper-middle-class couples who spend their evenings in Manhattan apartments, but also that Peter Harvey's set for Sextet was, like Boris Aronson's for Company, "that kind of bare bones, kind of steel, kind of cold...efficient set, to cover three different spaces" simultaneously: the kitchen, the living room, and the bedroom of Kenneth and David's apartment.[75]

Yet surely many comparisons with Company also resulted from the fact that both musicals were, at least subtextually, about sexual possibilities. Just as Company positively flowed with Bobby's sexual longings and misgivings, the characters in Sextet all ponder the ways that their sexual relationships contribute to their overall personae. There are no resolute answers in either musical: just as Bobby concludes, maybe, that he needs to follow his own path without constant input from his married friends, Sextet's characters decide, again maybe, that relationships do not have to be perfect to be worthwhile.

Yet while both musicals revolve around sexual identity, Sextet's characters ultimately possess far less of the pervasive sexual angst that drives Bobby's character in Company. The characters in Sextet all question, but never seem particularly bothered by, their choices in a mate, their sexual preferences, or even the failed romantic opportunities in their past. Leonard may wonder what it would be like to go to bed with another man, but the passing desire, which is treated in the script as perfectly normal, does not cause any profound changes to his character. Similarly David may find himself attracted to Ann, but this does not get in the way of his enduring love for Kenneth. Relationship woes may cause brief pangs of psychic discomfort in Sextet, but its characters differ from those in Company in that they all weather the storm of their own sexual identity, even when that identity is very much in flux.

The song "How Does It Start?," performed near the end of Act II, neatly sums up the musical's overview of romantic partnering as it relates to the individual. David sings the number to Leonard, who has just been confronted by Ann about his infidelity. Although profoundly saddened by the thought of losing Ann, Leonard is also self-aware enough to know that womanizing is a deeply embedded aspect of his character. When Leonard asks David for advice, David notes that his relationship with Kenneth is strong, but that it is something he can never take for granted. "The work it takes. The time it takes," David muses. "Five good years with Kenneth, and it's still touch and go. I admit to myself I'm gay—and someone like Ann walks through the door—I think I know who I am—and I don't know a thing."[76] David then sings Leonard the plaintive ballad "How Does It Start":

> Look at these hands
> They're a man's hands
> And so is this body and mind
> And a man loves only a woman
> Thus runs humankind
> But what if my heart leaps up at the sight of another man's face?
> And what if I find in another man's walk all that I think of as grace?

What if my thoughts are impossible thoughts
What if my heart's on my sleeve
And what if I find myself saying words that I just can't believe
And what if I lie in the arms of my love although we are both of us men
And know the first happiness deep in my heart that I've ever known—what then?

Is there a balance wheel
Is there a seesaw
Did I tip some scale
With a weight I could hardly even see?
Did I ever have a chance of being someone else
Or was I always certain to end up me?[77]

🐦 Ex. 3.7

After he finishes his quiet, contemplative song, David gently promises Leonard that reality—like relationships and personal identity—can be flexible. He shakes Leonard's hand and kisses Ann goodbye, "more than lightly...as if he's saying goodbye to something more than Ann."[78] Ann and Leonard leave together, still a couple, and decide to call their children to wish them goodnight. As *Sextet* ends, all three of the couples have resolved to work on strengthening their relationships, no matter the inevitable twists and turns.

In *Making Gay History: The Half Century Fight for Lesbian and Gay Equal Rights*, Eric Marcus notes that "the world was a dramatically different place from what it had been in 1968 [for] young gay people who were coming of age just a few years later, in the early to mid-1970s."[79] This difference is reflected in *Sextet*'s characters. *Company* ends as Bobby begins to wrestle realistically with what he wants in a romantic partner. Yet the characters in *Sextet* have already arrived at the place Bobby is only just reaching as *Company* leaves off. Whether straight, gay, or bisexual, they are all not only comfortable with who they are, but also keenly aware that, however flawed, their relationships are worth working for.

### GAY COMPANY

A few months after the demise of *Sextet*, a small, gay-themed revue premiered Off Broadway. Unlike *Sextet*, Fred Silver's *Gay Company*, which opened at the Little Hippodrome on East Fifty-sixth Street on October 29, 1974, was a sleeper hit that built an audience slowly, following promising reviews and good word of mouth.[80] Business was initially slow, Silver remembers, since the title and subject matter kept his show from topping "everyone's A-list."[81] Yet word spread quickly, and the critics, who trickled in as business began to pick up, almost all raved about the revue. *Gay Company* managed a healthy run of 244 performances, received an Obie Award nomination for best Off Broadway musical (it lost to *A Chorus Line*, which opened at the Public in the spring of the 1974–75 season), and has since been revived numerous times across the country.

Silver got the idea for the revue, which he wrote on a bet, after a particularly disappointing night at the theater. "I went with a friend to see a *horrible* gay play," he recalls. "It was so terrible that we walked out, and I said, 'This was a piece of *dreck*. In three weeks, I could write a better show than that.'" His friend bet him he couldn't and sweetened the bet by promising that if Silver wrote something especially good, he'd produce it. Silver promptly holed himself up at a friend's beach house on Fire Island and began to work on what would soon become *Gay Company*.[82] Written for four men and one woman, the completed revue featured short sketches and sixteen songs, all of which focused on some aspect of gay, male, urban life in the 1970s.

Silver remembers thinking that neither *Oh! Calcutta!* nor *Let My People Come* was worth the price of admission. "People came to see vulgarity, and they *did* see vulgarity," he says about both shows.[83] *Gay Company* was far less overtly sexual. It featured no nudity, simulated sex, or coarse language. It was in fact a direct response to the more explicit adult musicals that had become popular around town. *Gay Company* was a conscious throwback, as reflected by its classic, small-scale revue form, reliance on double entendre, and emphasis on highbrow sophistication ( Ex. 3.2).

The opening number of *Gay Company* set the tone for the evening, not only in terms of its message and bouncy Broadway sound, but also in its obvious debt to the lyrics of Cole Porter:

> Our vocabulary was far from ordinary
> When Noah Webster's book was barely complete
> Then Noah Webster's book was very discreet
> For tacky definitions met with prohibitions
>
> We've become a nation who find a fascination
> Adulterating all the language we use
> We get a bang from the slang we excuse
> We think it's necessary and so contemporary.

 Ex. 3.8

The next stanzas address the changing use of the word *gay*, the trend toward increased sexual permissiveness, and what Silver saw as the resultant decline of social decorum:

> Why is gay an old absurd cliché, now
> Why is gay a word that's so ungay, now?
> A word that's sometimes even hard to say, now?
> The very reason for this exposé, now?
>
> We took a lovely adjective and made a common noun of it
> We tortured it and trampled it and really went to town with it
>
> Once it had a meaning that was less demeaning
> We had a gleaning of the meaning of taste

But I'm afraid that has all been erased
For what was merely latent
Now's become too blatant.[84]

These lyrics, which hardly seem to embrace the concept of gay liberation, reflect Silver's ambivalence about the rapidly changing times. Silver, who came out of the closet well before Stonewall, describes himself as "gay and very proud of it." And yet, though he clearly remembers feeling thrilled by aspects of both the sexual revolution and post-Stonewall gay activism, he admits feeling simultaneously distanced from the younger generation, at least as far as their relaxed approach to decorum and increased sexual permissiveness was concerned.[85]

*Gay Company* ultimately capitalized on Silver's conflicting emotions, which resonated with the middle-aged critic corps, as well as with the aging theatergoers, both gay and straight, who made up much of *Gay Company*'s audience. Critics received the show with obvious affection, frequently applying adjectives like "nostalgic," "clever," "witty," and "charming." In contrast with more obviously polemical musicals from the period, like *The Faggot* and *Lovers*, few critics reflected discomfort with *Gay Company*'s content, likely because it did not challenge dominant cultural perceptions. Howard Thompson, for example, wrote in the *New York Times* that *Gay Company* "is obviously not for everyone. For whom, then? Most probably, for intelligent adults with a sophisticated sense of humor who are fed up with sex exploitation and some crude, shabby counterparts to this show."[86]

Silver's avoidance of obscenity and overt sexual references in *Gay Company* likely added to its appeal among theatergoers who longed for the more modest productions of yore. The only numbers that referred directly to sex played almost entirely on broad, slapstick humor or on sly double entendre, both of which were devices used liberally in the many classic musicals of which *Gay Company* was so obviously paying homage. Even the most blatantly sexual number, "A Beginner's Guide to Cruising"—in which the men in the cast assess the various public men's rooms in Manhattan—comes off as more quaintly Porteresque than as offensive or even risqué:

If you are one who is not fond of bars
And find the baths a bit expensive
Don't sit at home and bite your nails,
Or utter shrieks that sound like widow's wails
Come meet a multitude of hungry males
Not one of them the least offensive.

Where are these meccas where it's nice and quiet,
Where no one tells you their life stories?
I now refer to those utilities, those common, everyday facilities,
Where people go when they are ill-at-ease:
they're known as public lavatories!

There's a nice one at Macy's on the second floor
At Bloomingdales they perfume them throughout the store

At Cravat's and Alexander's they are now patrolled
And forget the one at Klein's because it's just too old
You could go to Sak's or Altman's and be treated regally,
But don't cruise the men's room on the BMT.[87]

*Gay Company* is similarly flippant about contemporary issues. In "There's a Fairy in the Firehouse," the revue's only number to touch on gay politics, Silver uses double entendre and punny lyrics to offset serious subject matter.

"There's a Fairy in the Firehouse" was inspired by Intro 2, a bill that forbade discrimination against homosexuals in housing, employment, or public accommodations. Introduced in 1971, the bill was soundly defeated every year that it was voted on by the New York City Council until, after a fifteen-year battle, it was finally approved in 1986.[88] Chief opponents of the bill were the Roman Catholic Archdiocese of New York and the Uniformed Fire Officer's Association.[89] Silver wrote "There's a Fairy in the Firehouse" overnight in response to the 1974 defeat.[90]

Written in the style of a jig, "There's a Fairy in the Firehouse" is scripted to be performed by the male cast members dressed as burly firefighters and singing in exaggerated Irish brogues:

> The place is so neat
> It's clean and it's swept
> The brass is polished and nicely kept!
> I think we've found a fairy in the firehouse!
>
> The hinges that squeaked all have been oiled
> This morning I found my hose uncoiled!
> I think we've found a fairy in the firehouse!
> . . .
> When we let the Italians in things went from bad to worse
> The Poles and Puerto Ricans were hard to bear
> And a black in the battalion is a fate we can't reverse
> But a faggot on the force just isn't fair!
> . . .
> If we allow a homosexual within our hallowed halls
> He'll want to attend our picnics. My god, he'd be at our balls!
> Egad, and alas, alack, aday, it's enough to make a Protestant pray.
> . . . We've got to find this fairy!
> Ship her back to Londonderry!
> No, we cannot have a fairy on the force![91]

 Ex. 3.9

As overtly political as *Gay Company* ever got, "There's a Fairy in the Firehouse" was also received as one of the production's funniest, strongest numbers. Silver remembers that "the critic from the *Times* literally fell off his chair and was rolling on the floor." The song even amused the firefighters who saw the show. Once word got around about the parody, Silver recalls, "firemen came in paying money to see the show, laughing and hooting and hollering at the fun we made of them."[92] In contrast with more polemical gay theater, the political commentary that Silver inserted into his show was perhaps not perceived as edgy or as serious enough to make anyone in the audience feel as if they were being mocked, even when, in fact, they were.

*Gay Company* did not fall prey to the constant comparisons with Sondheim's *Company* that *Sextet* was subject to. This is ironic, because while the creators of *Sextet* claim no conscious influence by Sondheim, Silver is quick to acknowledge the enormous debts he feels he owed the more established composer. "I was a Sondheim admirer—I adored the man, I think he's a genius," he gushes. "He opened the doorway to me. I mean, I always wrote like that, inside. . . . The combination of his harmonies and so forth? They were *wonderful!* This was the way *I* felt, the way *I* thought! My second fan letter—my first was to Richard Rodgers—was to Stephen Sondheim."[93]

While Silver claims that he did not consciously name his revue after Sondheim's musical, the allusion to one of his idols—as well as to the sexual subtext that he read into *Company*, which he saw five times—was nevertheless not lost on him. "I loved *Company*," Silver says, "but that is not the reason that I called it *Gay Company*. It was just that company was coming, and they're all gay!" Nevertheless Silver acknowledges that a second reason for choosing the title had to do with *Company*'s allegorical status among contemporary gay men. "Let's face it—Bobby was gay," Silver says. "And I wanted [my revue] to be a bunch of sketches and scenes about homosexuality, and my experience as a gay man coming out in the sixties and living in the seventies. And that's exactly what it was."[94] In some respects, then, *Gay Company*, like *Sextet*, may be read as the continuation of Bobby's story—or perhaps of Sondheim's and Furth's—in post-Stonewall New York. *Gay Company* was the product of an out gay composer who, a mere four years after *Company*, felt comfortable expressing himself in ways that Sondheim and Furth could not.

Silver pays direct homage to Sondheim with a number named for him. In the song "Sondheim," a woman laments a failed relationship. After she belts a slow, melodically unpredictable introduction that lays on the internal rhyming and lyrical list-making particularly thick, she launches into an underscored monologue built of Sondheim song references:

> It seems like only yesterday when we met. There you were standing in front of my apartment building waiting for the girls upstairs when a funny thing happened. I guess love was in the air that day, for when our eyes met, I was already losing my mind. . . . Soon we were walking side by side by side, together wherever we go and keeping company, remember? Right after that I was offered a job out of town, but turned it down. After all, could I leave you when for the first time in my life I knew what being alive really meant? . . . When you moved in with me shortly after that, it wasn't easy breaking the news to my folks that I'm not getting married today because some guy only wanted to marry me a little but live with me a lot. . . . I knew there was something wrong but I just couldn't put my finger on it. I thought, ah, you have an eye for pretty women, but that didn't prepare me for the awful truth. Well, as I told you when you broke the news to me at that club Reno Sweeney's, Todd, I hope you and the miller's son will be very happy together.[95]

🌐 Ex. 3.10

Despite Silver's insistence that he was more influenced by Sondheim's harmonies than by his lyrics, several of his songs, especially his romantic ballads, are both musically and lyrically suggestive. Silver references Sondheim's tendency toward lyrical list-making again in "Small Town Boy," which also acknowledges Sondheim's often complex, contrapuntal accompaniment and unconventional melodies:

> Though sometimes when the night becomes a wee bit lonely
> Life could be more meaningful to me if only
> There were someone to enjoy
> The flicker of a fire when the night gets chilly
> Someone who won't mind it if my jokes are silly
> Someone who can boost me up when my world falls down
> I want a small town boy who wants a small town boy in this great big town.[96]

🌐 Ex. 3.11

Other songs, like the wrought "If Only He'd Be Gentle," employ the Sondheim techniques Silver references in "Small Town Boy" and also mirrors the raw anxiety and desperation for connectedness evidenced in many Sondheim songs:

> All the coarseness and crudeness I've seen in men often astounds me
> Their brutality sickens the soul and it poisons the mind
> So there must be one man in this nightmarish night that surrounds me
> Who'll awaken my trust by just being gentle and kind
>
> If he'd only be gentle, him I could love and adore for as long as I live
> If he'd only be gentle there's not a thing in this world I wouldn't give
> For to live in a world where a tender word isn't permitted
> Where affection's suspected or even rejected as odd
> One must make up his mind to find someone to whom he's committed
> Someone sentimental who'd always be gentle. Oh, God!
> If he'd only be gentle, I'd never question the right, even if it were wrong
> If he'd only be gentle—If he'd only be gentle, I could be strong.

🌐 Ex. 3.12

Finally, Sondheim's use of internal rhyme followed by a repeated word (i.e., in *Company*, "It's the little things you *share* together / *swear* together / *wear* together") is reflected in Silver's wistful "Someone in My Life":

> I'm like a playground no one plays in
> A haunted house that no one stays in
> A vacant church that no one prays in
> Empty and unused.[97]

"Someone in My Life" also features accompaniment evocative of Sondheim's dark, unexpected harmonies and his tendency to stray from standard popular song form ( Ex. 3. 13 ).

While obviously in awe of Sondheim, Silver nevertheless wrote his musical as a comparatively liberated gay man. There is no need for *Company*'s is-he-or-isn't-he-gay subtext here. Further, whereas Sondheim and Furth's characters were widely interpreted as harsh reflections of the very audience flocking to see *Company* in the first place, Silver makes no enemies with his revue. Rather, in acknowledging his own conflicting feelings about the increased sexual permissiveness that came with liberation, Silver reached out to audiences, both gay and straight, whether or not they embraced the gay rights movement.

Silver's approach hardly endeared him to some gay activists. Vito Russo, for example, flatly dismissed *Gay Company* as "a 1950s closeted-chic review for pre-movement gays and well-meaning straights who like to patronize them."[98] Yet Russo's very reaction to *Gay Company* helps pinpoint the revue's crossover appeal: the show matter-of-factly acknowledges, but never judges, its audiences' feelings of nostalgia, its sense of detachment from the youth culture, and its mixed feelings about the rapidly changing times.


## BOY MEETS BOY

Though no fan of *Gay Company*, Vito Russo was delighted by *Boy Meets Boy*, Bill Solly and Donald Ward's quietly subversive take on Hollywood musicals of the 1930s, which began its run at the tiny Thirteenth Street Theater on Valentine's Day 1975. After the show's surprisingly strong seven-month run at this ramshackle Off Off Broadway theater, the producer Edith O'Hara transferred it Off Broadway, to the Actors Playhouse in Sheridan Square, where it reopened on September 17, 1975. Despite the fact that *Boy Meets Boy* was promptly panned in the *New York Times* upon reopening—usually the death-knell for productions in New York City—the musical played to full houses for 14 months, finally closing on November 14, 1976.

Born and raised in Ontario, composer Bill Solly decided as a child that he wanted to write musicals after seeing a touring production of *Oklahoma!* After moving to London as a young man, he quickly found work composing music for shows in the West End, including several for the female impersonator Danny LaRue. In 1972, Solly and the playwright Donald Ward co-wrote the book for *Boy Meets Boy*. Solly also wrote the music and lyrics.

The show, which reflects Solly's love for the plays of Noël Coward and the films of Fred Astaire, takes place at London's Savoy Hotel in December, 1936. After drinking too much at one of his notoriously wild parties, the accomplished newsman Casey O'Brien sleeps through one of the biggest stories of the decade: the abdication of King Edward VIII for the American socialite Wallis Simpson. Hoping to redeem himself to his furious editor, he agrees to cover the wedding of arrogant, selfish American millionaire Clarence Cutler to frumpy but bighearted British aristocrat Guy Rose. Rival reporters, thrilled that Casey is in trouble with his editor, tell him that Guy

Rose is the epitome of good looks, style, wit, and charm. Casey quickly becomes infatuated with Rose, having never laid eyes on him.

Rose recognizes that Clarence is not such a nice guy in the nick of time, and jilts him at the altar. Casey promptly goes in search for what he thinks is a dashing, handsome—and newly available—young bachelor. Meanwhile, the real Guy Rose, dreadfully dowdy and exceedingly shy, musters the courage to introduce himself to Casey, who refuses to believe that he is anyone but an awkward, irritating imposter. Rose finally passes himself off to Casey as a friend of Rose's, and together, they go in search of the "real" Guy Rose. Madcap confusion ensues, as does repeated meddling by the jilted, conniving Clarence. Eventually, Casey recognizes Rose for his inner beauty and realizes that he has fallen in love with him. The musical ends as Guy and Casey—like Edward and Wallis Simpson—marry and live happily ever after.[99]

Despite his footing in the West End, Solly failed to find a producer for *Boy Meets Boy* in England, and thus set his sights on New York City. Initially, however, prospects there were as slim as they were in London:

> I got an offer from a group in the Village called When We Win. They wanted to do the show, but I had never heard of them. So I said, "Okay, you can do it if I direct it." And they said fine, so they—I can't remember if they paid my airfare or not. We spent about a month trying to put the thing together, but they couldn't get it together at all. They didn't have the money, they had opposition from the block association, of all things—in the Village, in the seventies, and this was after Stonewall—because of the title, *Boy Meets Boy*. And also, they were called When We Win and they were a bit militant. Anyway, they couldn't get it on. I didn't know whether to stay or fly back. It was a big decision and I decided to stay in New York. I left everything behind in London—a magnificent apartment, a whole career. But I always wanted to live in New York. So I went to May's department store in Union Square and bought a mattress, put it on the floor of an apartment on Perry Street in the Village and lived with no possessions. It was a fascinating time. I was determined to get the show on, and eventually I got involved with the 13th Street Theater.[100]

For the next few years, Solly immersed himself in the hardscrabble world of Off Off Broadway. He wrote several children's musicals for the 13th Street Theater and, in the spirit of the movement and the time, became adept at serving, at a moment's notice, every necessary function, from usher to box-office manager to light booth operator to handyman. His efforts paid off: although initially hesitant about producing *Boy Meets Boy*, Edith O'Hara finally agreed to back it, and thus rehearsals began late in 1974.

Solly remembers that although the title might have predicted that *Boy Meets Boy* would be a hard sell, the reaction to his musical was enormously positive. "Once we got it rolling it was an instant hit. It was really wonderful. I've never seen anything like it in my life. . . . You could *watch* the word of mouth happening as people left. They couldn't wait to tell their friends. It was one of the most wonderful things."[101] Solly adds that although the audience was almost entirely gay at first, word spread about the production, which eventually caught on with straight spectators as well.

"We eventually got a mass, family audience," he remembers. "It appealed to every-body. As soon as you got them into the theater, they fell in love with the show. Because the characters are loveable—you care about Guy Rose, because he's this dowdy character who becomes beautiful because he's in love, you know? It's an old, old story, but it works if you have good jokes. And it was a very funny show."[102]

In sharp contrast with *The Faggot* and *Lovers*, *Boy Meets Boy* was intended not so much as a political or social statement as a simple expression of Solly's longing for respect and acceptance. While he is quick to acknowledge that *Boy Meets Boy* might well have benefited from the rise in gay activism in New York City during the 1970s, his desire to open the show in New York nevertheless had more to do with his lifelong dream of writing a big, splashy, Broadway production:

> We always intended for it to be a Broadway musical. I mean, it was meant for a family audience. Because it's a family show. There's nothing vulgar in it, nothing obscene. It just happens that we rewrote history. It was actually inspired by the sorts of plays that Edward Bond wrote in England. I always had the title *Boy Meets Boy*, and we just tossed the idea around for ages, and finally got the idea. The 1930s was very much in fashion then, and the show came out of wanting it to be terribly respectable. The whole idea of the chorus coming on and singing "Boy meets boy tonight!" and so on—and everything is accepted. The whole idea of acceptance, which was revolution-ary at the time. It all came from that.[103]

Solly adds that despite his Off Off Broadway pedigree, he had no desire to pursue his art in obscurity or to preach only to the converted. "I saw a lot of what I call gay ghetto theater, and I *never* wanted *Boy Meets Boy* to be part of that," he remembers. "You know, plays that really had nothing to say to anybody who was straight, and were just totally about being gay. I was only ever interested in writing for a mass audi-ence. I wanted to make some money! It's more exciting that way, because you're deal-ing with a subject that is provocative."[104] On one level an homage to a classic film genre, *Boy Meets Boy* can be easily read as breezy, apolitical, unthreatening entertain-ment. As with the vast majority of adult musicals discussed in this chapter, *Boy Meets Boy* featured no coarse language or simulated sex, nor was there much in the way of nudity, with the exception of a climactic scene in Act II.

During this scene Guy Rose, heartbroken once Clarence convinces him that Casey could never love an unattractive man, flees to Paris to stay with an aunt who is head-lining in a *Folies Bergère*–type production. Guy decides to prove his desirability by appearing in a number where the chorus boys perform a striptease. He is stopped in midstrip by Casey, who, having grown wise to Clarence's manipulations and his own love for Guy, has followed Guy to Paris ( 🔊 Ex. 3.3).

Despite the reliance here on partially nude male actors, Solly insisted that the scene function more as a plot device than as a cheap means for generating ticket sales:

> Little Guy Rose is so prim, and ends up being so brokenhearted that he'll strip on-stage. He'll degrade himself because he's so brokenhearted. It was a sexy scene, too,

but they didn't strip down completely. They stripped to a g-string. The final strip is by this character Alfonse, and he strips but he turns around at the last minute so all you see is his tush. So it was nothing. A lot of revivals have tried to put in nudity, which really offends me. That's *so* wrong, because it would definitely offend a lot of people, and you'd be cheating by doing that. So I really put my foot down.[105]

For all its perceived tameness, *Boy Meets Boy* yielded a number of strikingly different interpretations. John Clum reads nothing terribly liberating into it and points out that the musical "did not speak directly to what was going on around it in the Village or the burgeoning urban gay ghettoes across the United States." He concludes, rather cynically, that *Boy Meets Boy* might have been as appealing as it was to straight audiences merely because it kept acceptance of homosexuality squarely "in the realm of fantasy"; this, he continues, was the only place it could be at the time, since true acceptance of gays "in American society, and thus in cultural productions, was still uneasy in 1975."[106]

Yet Vito Russo offers a contrasting interpretation. Calling *Boy Meets Boy* a "delightful trap" that "lies in wait for you, pretending to be something," and then "jumps out at you, quite another," he is empowered by the musical's very premise:

For two hours we live in a world in which gay and straight relationships are equally common and interact on a breezy, captivating, and altogether mutually respectful level. The story itself is much older than Calvin Coolidge put together but in this new form it becomes expressly political. The politics emerge from the nonchalance with which the gayness becomes a "given" in the play rather than an idea fighting for respectability.... Some of the cast is gay and some of the cast is straight and they work together, men and women, with an ease and assurance that makes one proud to be around at a time when things are changing so rapidly that hits can be done on the stage and put into perspective with a sense of humor and a sense of political loyalty.[107]

Yet what is especially striking about Russo's take on *Boy Meets Boy* lies in his admission that it worked to exacerbate his own conflicts about the gay rights movement:

Of course, dealing with a play which takes straight conventions and simply translates them into rosy-world-all-is-gay-and-okay musical comedy presents some problems. There are very serious issues here as to whether or not we should be opting for such aspirations. There are those of us in the gay community who believe that instead of wanting a slice of the pie in this society, to fit in and become part of it, that the pie is basically rotten and we should be busy trying to throw it away and bake a new one. Under these circumstances, there are many gay political activists who would call a show like this one a reinforcement of the outdated concepts of heterosexual love and marriage. Then of course there are gay men and women who... maintain that there are many charming and entertaining things of this old world which would be sorely, if not fatally, missed by driving our laughter, our humor and good nature out of our hearts and minds while trying to build a perfect society for all people. Fortunately, I belong to both schools. Aren't I lucky?[108]

Like Silver, whose *Gay Company* is essentially a musical acknowledgment of the emotional conflicts experienced by an aging gay man living in rapidly changing times, Russo not only freely proffers the internal contradictions he experienced in viewing *Boy Meets Boy*, but also makes no attempt to reconcile them. He agrees with Clum that *Boy Meets Boy* is ultimately a silly fantasy. Where he departs from Clum, however, is in his recognition that sometimes, great realities result from pipedreams.

When it came to gay activism and its challenges to the representation of gay characters in entertainment media, enormous strides were made during the late 1960s and the 1970s, due in no small part to the activities of gay men on the grassroots level of American theater. Without the Caffe Cino, the efforts of TOSOS, or even such forward-thinking flops as *Sextet*, there could never have been such later commercial triumphs as *La Cage aux Folles* or *Falsettos*, and Sondheim and Furth's Bobby might just as well have found himself a wife before the final curtain. Yet while there were no specifically gay theater companies at the start of the 1970s, there were over 150 international ones by the decade's close.[109] While the few depictions of gay men adhered closely to age-old stereotypes as the 1970s began, numerous productions in New York City set about challenging dominant cultural perceptions about gay men as the decade unfolded. And when it came to musical theater, gay men began in this decade to reclaim a genre that they had for decades prior helped invent, nurture, and integrate into American popular culture, all the while ceding the spotlight.

What is striking about the adult musicals discussed in this chapter is how consciously distanced they are from gay male sexuality. This is especially noteworthy considering the decade during which they emerged. New York City in the 1970s was most certainly not a place or time that any historian would consider "quaint," especially when contemplating the trajectory of gay male culture. Rather gay life, both in New York and beyond, was all about breaking barriers, often as boisterously and as joyfully as possible: demolishing stereotypes, demanding civil rights, reclaiming public spaces. And yet at a time when both gay men and lesbians were celebrating unprecedented social, political, and sexual freedoms, the composers, book writers, and directors of the small, gay-male-themed musicals discussed herein were clearly more interested in endearing themselves to mass culture than to flying in the face of convention.

In *Place for Us: Essay on the Broadway Musical*, D. A. Miller points out that practically overnight musicals became the source simultaneously of great embarrassment and great pride for post-Stonewall gay men. "Along with very few other terms," he writes, the word "'Broadway' denominates those early pre-sexual realities of gay experience to which, in numerous lives, it became forever bound: not just the solitude, shame, secretiveness by which the impossibility of social integration was first internalized; or the excessive sentimentality that was the necessary condition of sentiments allowed no real object; but also the intense, senseless *joy* that, while identical to these destitutions, is neither extricable from them."[110] Miller concludes that for many post-Stonewall gays, the very idea of the Broadway musical became inherently contradictory: "a *living relic*: it must be granted existence...but only a shady one, tucked away in the closet, where cast albums and playbills occupy the space vacated by the recent removal of the erotic accessories to beside the bed."[111]

While Miller is speaking here specifically of the Broadway musical, his description of the weird status of musicals in the lives of post-Stonewall gay men applies as well. While gay life in the 1970s celebrated sexual liberation, the Broadway musicals to which many of these small-scale, gay-male-themed shows pay homage are not only not particularly liberated, but they are almost embarrassingly quaint: also, then, living relics. It is entirely likely that the men who created them were, consciously or not, just as intent on connecting their productions to the theatrical past as they were on linking them to the cultural present.

What unites the many diverse post-Stonewall adult musicals discussed in this chapter is the understanding among the men who wrote them that many spectators, whether gay or straight, were eager to be entertained but were not averse to also being educated about contemporary gay men. The most successful musicals of the bunch were less angrily preachy than they were gently, persuasively inclusive. Although typically small in scale, produced on shoestring budgets, and modest in their appeal, they nevertheless helped inform both gay and straight audiences in New York about what it meant to be gay and male in 1970s America. They also allowed gay men the option of "no longer [having] to read themselves into the conventions of a heterosexist musical."[112] For once, it was actively being done for them.

CHAPTER 4

# The Adult Musical Meets Second-Wave Feminism: *Mod Donna*

We are the holders
The pot and broom holders
Longing for holders
To possess us as they dress us and with
Rank and honor bless us
As they parade our thighs and breasts
Before the crowd
Their instruction tells us this should make us proud
To be thus owned and owning
Don't let them catch you moaning
That all their bull will always find you cowed.
　　　　　　—Myrna Lamb, "Liberation Song" from *Mod Donna*

Like the gay liberation movement, second-wave feminism grew from the sociopolitical movements of the 1960s and gained momentum through the 1970s.[1] While many feminists broke from the New Left due to its institutional sexism, the second wave nevertheless adopted its emphasis on "personal experience over tradition and abstract knowledge," especially because, many feminists argued, the foundations of knowledge had long relied on mores and values shaped by the very patriarchy that the movement was trying to combat in the first place.[2] Yet whereas the upsurge in gay activism rapidly helped alter the ways that gay men were depicted in musical theater productions emanating from both the fringe and the commercial mainstream, feminism made less of an initial impact in either realm during the same period and was typically not received as sympathetically.

As detailed in the previous two chapters, the relationship between gay men and musicals is long, multifaceted, and well-documented. When it comes to explorations of the relationship between women and musicals, however, less emphasis is placed on women's sociocultural connections to the musical or to its cultivation. Instead the focus is typically on the history of larger-than-life female roles that (gay) men have invented and the Broadway divas who have embodied them.[3] While the exponential rise in recent decades of female directors, designers, choreographers, composers, lyricists, and producers, as well as the increase in studies of musicals written from feminist and queer perspectives, have begun to shed light on women's and girls' relationships to the American musical, the entertainment form continues to be most closely associated, socioculturally speaking, with gay men.

A second reason for the distance between the feminist movement and the stage musical, even when the second wave was at its peak in the 1970s, has to do with activists' reactions to the theater world in general at the onset of the women's movement, as well as with critical reactions to the feminist theater that arose in response. The rise of the second wave certainly spurred an interest in theater by, about, and for women. Many second-wave pioneers viewed their work in the theater as something of a calling, which extended directly from their political activism and ideologies. To take but one example, Martha Boesing, founder of the women's theater collective At the Foot of the Mountain, based in Minneapolis, writes, "[Many of the feminists] who created these theaters came out of the radical politics of the 1960s, and I was one of them. . . . We had walked in the Civil Rights and the peace movements, 'turned on and dropped out,' lived in communes, and created theater events that flew in the face of the linear, rational thought processes of our culture and led our audiences hollering and singing into the streets. We believed that the revolution was at hand. [Yet eventually] we began to notice that we were still baking the bread, raising the children, and bringing coffee to the organizers of the institutions both inside and outside of the mainstream. So we rebelled."[4] In order to focus on woman-oriented spaces for themselves in the theater, many feminists attempted to actively separate themselves from the patriarchal, dominant culture, which proved not terribly patient or understanding in the first place.

The late 1960s and early 1970s saw the establishment of several women's theater collectives in New York, including the New Feminist Theater, the It's All Right to Be Woman Theater, and the Westbeth Playwrights' Feminist Collective. Women playwrights such as Maria Irene Fornés, Megan Terry, Rochelle Owens, and Adrianne Kennedy founded the Women's Theater Council in 1972, with the aim of increasing the presence of women in all areas of the theater.[5] Through the late 1960s many of these women worked with celebrated Off Off Broadway theater troupes like Judson Poets' (Fornés), the Open Theater (Terry), and La MaMa (Owens), some of which had women at the helm. They nonetheless felt the need at the onset of the second wave to combat perceived sexism in avant-garde circles through new organizations.[6] While the new groups all had slightly different agendas, aims, and philosophies, most of them promoted theater by and about women and also advocated the adoption of collaborative processes that encouraged communication, egalitarianism, and shared experience.[7]

What many women's theater companies also had in common was considerable pressure, both within and outside these groups, which impeded any immediate impact on the theater landscape at large. The painstakingly egalitarian, collaborative approach adopted by troupes like It's All Right to Be Woman Theater proved maddeningly cumbersome in practice, and yet companies that relied on traditional hierarchies were often soundly criticized by insiders and outsiders alike for not trying harder to demolish traditional approaches favored by the patriarchy.[8] Many women's theater groups collapsed by the early 1980s for these and a host of other reasons, including inadequate funding, a lack of professional experience, and simple burnout.[9]

External pressures often took an additional toll. Many Off Off Broadway companies were lauded by the predominantly male critic corps, who crowed about the fresh, creative approaches these troupes took in lieu of healthy budgets, professionalism, and workable, sizable performance spaces. Yet the women's theater companies that emanated from the fringe were often met with gruff impatience by the same critics, many of whom made it clear to readers that they were not supportive of the women's movement, let alone the theater companies that embraced it.

There were, of course, many exceptions: Ellen Stewart's leadership of La MaMa; playwrights like Owens, Fornés, Terry, and Kennedy; companies like the Judson Poets' Theater, which endeavored as part of its progressive approach to produce works by women.[10] Yet most Off Off Broadway troupes prioritized work written, directed, and produced by men. This was hardly difficult, since work by men constituted (and still constitutes) the vast majority of theatrical output in all sectors of the American theater.

Even the avant-garde has its sociocultural restraints. Off Off Broadway, after all, preceded both the women's and gay rights movements and took root at a time during which men, regardless of sexual orientation, were expected to be leaders, and women to embrace supporting roles. As Jill Dolan argues in discussing the postmodern avant-garde in general, and works by the Off Off Broadway denizen Richard Foreman in particular, all too often the fringe "left intact the gender dichotomies of the cultural status quo maintained by traditional theater."[11] Despite its innovations, much of Off Off Broadway's output reflected the same patriarchal mind-set inherent in the dominant culture, the New Left, and the counterculture.[12]

Second-wave feminism made even stranger bedfellows with the commercial mainstream during the 1970s. The fact that so few overtly feminist musicals were commercially produced at the time relates as much to cultural anxiety about gender and power as it does to the American musical's traditional social conservatism. During the 1960s and 1970s the stage musical struggled to retain its footing in popular culture.[13] Due to a slow and often unenthusiastic response to the entertainment preferences of a youth market that had begun to exert unprecedented power on the commercial market and thus on cultural tastes, Broadway suffered rapidly declining audiences and frequent attacks by cultural critics who declared the commercial musical dead or dying. The theater industry was forced to adapt, not only by experimenting with popular music styles with which to court young spectators, but also by following Off Off Broadway's lead in incorporating experimental techniques and topical subject matter.

In her feminist history of the stage musical, Stacy Wolf argues that the Broadway musical of the 1960s offered complex, uneasy, and even frequently contradictory depictions of gender, due in part to its need to negotiate its status as a mainstream entertainment form on the one hand and a culturally viable form on the other.[14] As a result of Broadway's internal tensions and the country's rapidly changing sexual mores, she argues that a number of 1960s musicals reflect great anxiety, ambivalence, or both about strong, single women and the heterosexual relationships they enter into. Many representations of women in 1960s musicals cut both ways, presenting central female characters as victims or fetish objects who are simultaneously emotionally empowered and physically powerful.[15] The 1960s musicals Wolf examines often manipulate musical theater's conventional elements, creating shows that adhere to "many of the structural conventions of Broadway's mid-twentieth-century integrated book musicals" while simultaneously leaning toward experimentation, resulting in shows that are not quite old but yet not new.[16]

Wolf is writing specifically of *Oliver!, Man of La Mancha, Mame, Cabaret,* and *Hello, Dolly!,* all of which were enormously commercially successful Broadway musicals. Yet the cultural anxieties that arose in response to second-wave feminism at the time can similarly be identified in both *Hair* and *Oh! Calcutta!,* as well as in the lesser known, small-scale adult musical *Mod Donna,* which ran Off Broadway in 1970. In these three musicals, all of which emanated from the fringe despite being marketed to the mainstream, cultural anxieties about women in the dawn of the second wave are palpable.

## *HAIR*'S FEMALE CHARACTERS

Despite its overwhelmingly liberal approach to the social issues it tackles, including male homosexuality, *Hair* is strikingly conservative in its depictions of women and of heterosexual relationships. Almost to a character, the women featured in *Hair* are secondary to the men, and especially to the two central male roles: Claude, the sensitive, brooding dreamer who lives with his parents in Flushing, and Berger, the high school dropout, charismatic trickster, and leader of the tribe of East Village hippies with whom Claude regularly socializes. Claude and Berger are the musical's most well-developed characters, and their relationship provides the emotional trajectory of the musical. It's no accident that *Hair* can be so easily read as a love story between them: James Rado and Gerome Ragni were romantically involved while writing the show, and they not only based Claude and Berger on themselves, respectively, but also originated the roles in the 1968 Broadway production.[17]

Rado and Ragni met while working on the Off Broadway musical *Hang Down Your Head and Die,* which opened—and closed—on October 18, 1964. Some years later, while working with Joseph Chaiken's Open Theater, they decided to write a musical about the hippie scene. They moved together into a small apartment in Hoboken, New Jersey, and between acting jobs pieced together an early draft of *Hair.* Their romantic relationship, which was an open secret for decades until Rado described Ragni as the love of his life in a 2009 interview with *The Advocate,* soon became central to the musical. *Hair,* Rado explains, was "truly about men loving each other as opposed to fighting each other";[18] in many ways, he continues, the relationship between Claude and Berger was not merely autobiographical, but representative of the hippie scene in general. "The hippie scene was very free. [There was] male-to-male

Gerome Ragni (Berger) and James Rado (Claude), in rehearsals for their own *Hair: The American Tribal Love-Rock Musical*. Photo by Dagmar.

bonding and hugging and being very affectionate. There was a wonderful warmth in the hippie atmosphere, a sense of freedom. Men would just come up to you and take you in their arms, and it was so freeing and felt so good. It's a psychological truth that had been so blocked from human behavior." *Hair* made a point of emphasizing love relationships between men, in that "there were very strong male relationships written into the play....Claude and Berger have a strong tie, but Berger has this sidekick, Woof, and Woof has his sidekick. There's a whole bunch of male relationships in addition to the traditional male-female love stories. We have the Sheila and Jeanie love stories with Claude and Berger. But we also have other things happening."[19] Yet while Rado's and Ragni's male characters, specifically Berger and Claude, were clearly drawn from the inside out, *Hair*'s female characters were just as clearly drawn from the outside in.

The women in *Hair*, despite each having slightly different character traits, are all primarily motivated by their romantic designs on men. The audience learns the least about Crissy, the naïve flower child; her solo number merely makes clear her infatuation with "a boy called Frank Mills," with whom she hopes so desperately to reunite that she spends her days sitting in front of the Waverly Theater, where they first met, awaiting his unlikely return ( Ex. 4.1). Jeanie, a pregnant acid casualty first introduced when she sings the number "Air" in Act I, is in love with Claude, who in turn pines for Sheila Franklin, a political activist and second-semester freshman at New York University. "This is the way it is," Jeanie tells the audience in Act 1. "I'm hung up on Claude. Sheila's hung up on Berger. Berger is hung up everywhere. Claude is hung up on a cross over Sheila and Berger."[20]

As the female character who is closest to Berger and Claude, Sheila is rendered more three-dimensionally than Crissy or Jeanie. She also fits Wolf's description of the "quintessential" pop culture image of a mid-1960s young woman: the Single Girl.[21] A staple in 1960s pop culture, the Single Girl was perhaps best exemplified by Ann Marie, Marlo Thomas's character in the 1966 television show *That Girl*. The

Single Girl, Wolf explains, "was sexually active and unmarried, independent and financially secure. She rejected Donna Reed's aprons and Lucy Ricardo's whining antics for her own apartment, her own paycheck, and her own birth control."[22] While Wolf identifies the Single Girl prototype in *Oliver!* (Nancy), *Sweet Charity* (Charity), and *Cabaret* (Sally), the exemplar—as well as the anxieties that surround it—applies just as well to Sheila, who is, perhaps not coincidentally, the sole representative of the New Left that Rado and Ragni feature in their hippie-heavy script.

Sheila is aware of Claude's feelings for her, but she loves Berger, with whom she has a tumultuous and obviously sexual relationship. In contrast with Berger, who views his dropout status as just another way to thumb his nose at the Man, Sheila is an active participant in the world. She is financially independent enough not only to travel to Washington, D.C., to take part in an antiwar protest, from which she returns in the middle of the first act, but also to buy Berger a yellow satin shirt while she's there. Yet for all her independence, activism, and intelligence, Sheila's main purpose in *Hair* is to complete a love triangle—a classic plot device, for all of *Hair*'s formulaic innovations—and ultimately to intensify "the central love relationship in the show," which is between Claude and Berger.[23]

Sheila's function is especially obvious in the earliest published version of the musical, which changed significantly before it reached Broadway. In the 1966 version of the script, Berger decides that before Claude goes off to war, he should get the chance to sleep with Sheila. Berger thus places Sheila under enormous pressure, as he attempts to convince her that sex with Claude is her obligation and his right, whether or not she is actually attracted to him. In scene 3 of Act I, originally titled "Sheila's Rape," Berger demonstrates his emotional control over Sheila by ritualistically raping her shortly after she enters; dressed up in experimental theater techniques, Berger's attack is ultimately treated as something he has every right to do. Sheila eventually agrees to sleep with Claude, who leaves her his freshly shorn hair as a parting gift before leaving for war.[24]

In the original script, then, Sheila becomes an object that Berger gives to Claude as a going-away present. Berger's emotional manipulation of Sheila is clear in several of their exchanges. At one point he promises Sheila, "[If] you do it tonight with Claude[,] I'll do it tomorrow night with you,"[25] and then informs her that if she refuses to give Claude "the greatest going-away gift we can give our friend," she'll ruin the farewell party and make Berger angry.[26] In describing their relationship as it was first written, Bottoms notes that *Hair* "staged a bizarre variant on the age-old patriarchal right of men to use and trade women as if they are property."[27]

The ritualistic rape is featured in the scene in which Sheila is first introduced, midway through Act I. Having just returned from the march in Washington, Sheila is greeted enthusiastically in this scene by Hud, Woof, and Claude. Although she and Berger are initially chilly to one another, she soon gives him a yellow satin shirt that she brought back with her from Washington. At first Berger mocks the gift; when Sheila asks him to stop joking, he grows "suddenly very angry" and launches into a tirade that plays on female stereotypes: "Don't tell me to stop. You always do that. You don't allow me to have any friends, you're jealous, suspicious, you use the double standard, you test me, spy on me, you nag, nag, nag, you won't allow me to be myself, you follow me, you're always picking a fight, and then you expect me to love you.... Well, I can't have sex that way.... Sex! That's the last thing I'd want."[28]

Hurt by his reaction, Sheila asks him to stop joking and try on the shirt, and this time Berger responds with violence. Here the script originally calls for Berger, while chanting a stream of gibberish, to "[grab] Woof and [have] him get on top of Sheila, screwing her": "Berger collapses onto Woof's sleeping bag, as though he has just expended himself in an orgasm.... Berger has just fucked Sheila in public. Or rather *raped* her in public. Berger has had his orgasm. She was fighting him off and reacts to his attack."[29] The stage directions describe Sheila as "in shock" moments after the rape, but the action continues all around her as if nothing out of the ordinary has happened. The scene then quickly shifts its focus from the way Berger feels about Sheila to the way that Claude feels about her.[30]

The script featuring Sheila's rape very quickly became an inaccurate gauge of the musical. *Hair* was revised significantly between its 1967 Off Broadway premiere and its Broadway run at the Biltmore. Thus while the yellow shirt remained an important part of the Broadway version of this scene, intimations of Sheila's rape were excised. Nevertheless Berger's treatment of Sheila still strongly implies that he holds all the cards in their relationship.

James Rado (Claude) and Lynn Kellogg (Sheila) exchange glances during rehearsals for *Hair: The American Tribal Love-Rock Musical*. Original tribe member Natalie Mosco is just behind Rado to the right. Photo by Dagmar.

In the Biltmore production, as in subsequent revivals of the show, Sheila enters and is greeted by Claude, Berger, Hud, and Woof midway through Act I. Claude and Berger get Sheila into an embrace "and bring HER down to the floor, ending up with each other, SHEILA apart from THEM."[31] Sheila gives Berger the shirt, and although he obviously dislikes it and delivers the "Don't tell me to stop" monologue quoted earlier, he stops short of raping her. Instead the stage directions instruct Berger to slap Sheila and rip the shirt before stalking off the stage.[32] Heartbroken, Sheila launches into the torch song "Easy to Be Hard," which allows her to expound on her frustrations with Berger (🌀 Ex. 4.2). The production script then has Berger return to embrace Sheila in apology. He holds her until he notices Claude standing nearby, whereupon he slinks back offstage, thereby saving face in front of his male friend.[33]

The resolution of the love triangle between Berger, Sheila, and Claude also changed somewhat in the move from Off Broadway to the Biltmore. Berger not only is no longer a rapist, but he also eases up considerably in encouraging Sheila to bed Claude.[34] Sheila never sleeps with Claude in the Broadway version, as she does at the end of the original script. Rather the tribe celebrates Claude's last night before induction by tripping on acid together, and Claude's edgy hallucinations make up a large section of Act II.

When the sun rises on the morning of Claude's departure, the tribe finds that Claude has disappeared. Berger and Sheila lead the tribe in a frantic search for him. He finally reenters in uniform, his long hair shorn. "I'm right here," he tells his friends, who can no longer hear or see him. "Like it or not, they got me."[35] Claude retreats from view after singing the opening lines from the final number, "The Flesh Failures (Let the Sun Shine In)." The full cast takes over, parting late in the number to reveal Claude, lying lifeless at center stage. Again according to the stage directions, as the lights fade, the tribe slowly exits the stage, leaving Berger alone to dance in a slow circle around Claude's dead body.

The changes made to the musical between the Off Broadway and Broadway productions certainly benefited its characters. Sheila is no longer treated primarily as Berger's plaything. She is empowered somewhat due to the insertion of the galvanizing number "Easy to Be Hard"; the fact that she is no longer pressured quite as frequently or as aggressively for sexual favors makes her seem more like a three-dimensional character and less like mere property. And Berger comes off less as a violent brute than as merely a petulant, self-centered child.

Nevertheless *Hair* remains without question a musical about men. While Sheila may represent the New Left and the rapidly changing woman in a way that no other character in the show does, she ultimately functions as the central love interest who either adores (Berger) or exists to be adored (by Claude). Claude's conflicts dominate the piece, while Berger—who remains "true to the hippie ethos" without wavering, as Claude does—emerges as the musical's hero at the end of the show.[36]

One of the original Broadway tribe members, Natalie Mosco, remembers that the sexism in *Hair* was the one aspect of the musical that she took issue with, even back in 1968. "Sheila was treated like the daytripper. Like she was coming in trying to be cool but she wasn't really cool... and this, by the way, is a very big problem I had with *Hair*: the treatment of women. You know: 'She's my old lady!' 'Don't be so uptight!'

'You're so hung up!' The guys could go around doing anything they wanted! And the way they talked to Sheila?" Yet Mosco was always aware that women were not at the heart of the production. "The women—it was not our culture that was being reflected," she remembers. "It was a mostly white, sometimes black, [age] 15 to 30 male lower-middle to middle-class perspective. And you see . . . it was a male point of view to some extent because they were the ones being sent [to Vietnam], and the girls weren't."[37]

To date, little in the way of oral or reception history about *Hair* makes much of its sexism. This is likely not only because *Hair* preceded the onset of the women's movement by a few years, but also because emphasis is almost always placed on the musical's many notable innovations. Yet for all its milestones, *Hair* neatly, if inadvertently, sums up the androcentrism inherent in the counterculture and New Left, and by extension much of the 1960s Off Off Broadway scene.

### OH! CALCUTTA!

Like *Hair*, the heterosexual politics in *Oh! Calcutta!* are remarkably conservative and reflect sexual assumptions inherent in both the dominant culture and the various youth movements that promoted the sexual revolution in the first place. *Oh! Calcutta!* offers a particularly rigid view of heterosexual sexuality and its emphasis on male pleasure. In sketch after sketch white women of various classes are treated as passive, emotionally stunted counterparts to the middle- to upper-middle-class men they play against and, by extension, to those in the audience for whom Tynan's "experiment in elegant erotica" was primarily designed.[38]

Nowhere is this clearer than in the sketch Tynan himself contributed to the revue. Ostensibly a polemic about the constricted roles of women in Western culture, "Who: Whom" was ultimately too bogged down in Tynan's own erotic preoccupations—spanking, bondage, Victorian garb, and the hanging of naked women in rope or mesh nets—to make much of a social statement. In the sketch a smartly dressed Victorian gentleman delivers a monologue about choice in a democratic society. As he prepares to speak, two women enter the stage. One, "Girl B," is lowered from the fly loft in a rope net. She is naked, bound, and gagged. The second woman, "Girl A," enters right. Dressed as a Victorian housemaid, she holds a birch rod, which she places on the floor before kneeling with her back to the audience and lifting her skirt and petticoat.

"Like most civilized people, I believe in democracy," the Victorian gentleman begins. "I thought I'd better make that clear right from the beginning. I don't believe that any one person is essentially more important than any other."[39] He then paraphrases Lenin in stating that the world is nevertheless "divided into the 'who' and 'whom,'" and that there are "those who do, and those to whom it is done."[40]

For the remainder of the sketch the Victorian gentleman compares Girl A, the kneeling maid, and Girl B, the bound and gagged woman struggling naked in the net. He explains that Girl B is a "pert English girl of good background, who has been captured by a tribe of savages" that will soon subject her to various unspeakable, but clearly sexual, indignities.[41] As a captive she is utterly without choice. On the other hand, Girl A "has been caught stealing bottled plums" and thus "awaits chastisement at the hands of her master."[42] The Victorian gentleman asks Girl A to prepare for her punishment. She silently pulls down her panties to midthigh and returns to a kneeling position, thereby exposing her naked buttocks to the audience. The Victorian gentleman tells the audience that unlike the woman in the net, Girl A is free to get up and leave the stage whenever she chooses.

At the end of the sketch the Victorian gentleman asks that Girl B be removed, and she is hoisted back up into the flies. He then picks up the birch rod and circles Girl A, who still kneels on the floor, all the while telling her that she is free to leave if she likes. She makes no move. The Victorian gentleman concludes, "As I was saying, I am a strict believer in democracy," as the lights come down, ending the sketch.[43]

In her memoirs Raina Barrett writes of "Who: Whom" that "as a comment on the condition of women in many societies, this wicked little playlet was both accurate and terrifying."[44] Yet while Tynan might have intended to make important social statements about the status of women in his sketch, his need to objectify and fetishize them negates any serious attempt at cultural criticism. Had he truly wanted to teach his audience a valuable lesson about the plight of women, he might have attempted to do so without relying on two mute, naked, anonymous women who flank the dashing, active male in the sketch like so many well-placed props.

It was precisely Tynan's attempt to proffer his sexual fantasies as cultural criticism that prompted Emily Genauer to cite "Who: Whom" in the *New York Post* as the very worst in a series of sketches that she found "revolting."[45] While Genauer understood Tynan's point—that neither woman is truly free—she suggested another: "Maybe his point is that [Girl A]—and all of us—submit without protest because we actually enjoy the brutal exploitation to which we are subjected."[46] Indeed "Who: Whom" was eventually dropped from *Oh! Calcutta!*, but not because anyone save Genauer seemed particularly bothered by it. Rather, once the original cast members left, "no Equity actress would agree to being cast in a role that required her to display her visible assets with no compensating lines to deliver," and Tynan was unwilling to come up with even a single word of dialogue for either woman.[47]

Although "Who: Whom" was the most overtly exploitative sketch in *Oh! Calcutta!*, it was hardly unique. Despite different authors, all of whom were male, a vast majority of the sketches depict women as subservient to men. For example, in "Will Answer All Sincere Replies," attributed to the *Bonnie and Clyde* screenwriters David Newman and Robert Benton, a young married couple named Dale and Sue Ellen Walker nervously prepare their "middle-income housing development type home in [the] suburbs of Kansas City" for a visit by a slightly older couple of experienced swingers.[48] As they tidy up and set out dishes of chips and pretzels, Sue Ellen makes it abundantly clear that she is unhappy with the arrangement, which was entirely Dale's idea.

The older couple, Monte and Cherie Jackson, arrive and quickly put the younger couple at ease. Midway through the sketch Dale ejaculates prematurely while dancing with Cherie and, mortified, slinks off to the bedroom to change. He returns to find Sue Ellen engaged in a particularly enthusiastic tryst with the older couple. He stands by limply (literally and figuratively), filled with self-doubt. In the throes of pleasure

Monte (Bill Macy) and Cherie (Margo Sappington) Jackson drive Sue Ellen Walker (Nancy Tribush) wild in the "Will Answer All Sincere Replies" sketch from *Oh! Calcutta!* Photo by Friedman-Abeles. Courtesy of the Billy Rose Theater Collection, New York Public Library for the Performing Arts.

Sue Ellen shrieks at him to hurry up and plug in a sex toy that the older couple has brought with them. He complies, watches the threesome for a moment, and then glumly begins to deal himself a hand of solitaire on the other side of the room as the lights fade.

Of course, on the one hand, this sketch allows women in the audience to identify with the character who gets the last laugh. The young wife, initially annoyed by her husband's interest in swinging, ends up deriving more sexual pleasure than she could possibly have imagined. Yet on the other hand, "Will Answer All Sincere Replies" relies on the element of surprise that occurs when traditional stereotypes—men as socially active and sexually voracious, women as emotionally and sexually passive—are subverted. The assumptions made here are typical of just about every sketch in *Oh! Calcutta!*, where female characters are regularly rendered erotic appendages to the men unless a punch line relies on undermining conventional perceptions.

Despite its groovy, art rock–inspired underscoring, its state-of-the-art stage design, and its unprecedented reliance on human sexuality as primary subject matter, *Oh! Calcutta!* was very much a throwback that paid lip service not to the burgeoning ideologies of Betty Friedan and Gloria Steinem, but to those of Hugh Hefner and Helen Gurley Brown. *Oh! Calcutta!* opened in New York about nine months after the protest at the 1968 Miss America Pageant in Atlantic City, when second-wave feminism was still in its infancy. Yet the first radical feminist musical to open in a commercial theater in New York City was just around the corner.

*Mod Donna* was written by Myrna Lamb, with music by Susan Hulsman Bingham. Produced and directed by Joe Papp at the Public Theater in 1970, the musical critiqued the ways that men and especially women are culturally conditioned to use sex as a weapon in their power struggles. Lamb, who was in her late thirties at the time that she wrote the musical, had been politically active for much of her restless, difficult life. The feminist movement, however, struck an especially personal chord with her.

Born poor in 1930 to parents who were open about the fact that they had not planned for her and were not terribly thrilled by her arrival, Lamb grew up "in a divided atmosphere of encouragement and repression."[49] Proud of her obvious intelligence, her ambition, and her passion for reading and writing, Lamb's parents nevertheless frequently reminded her that "girls don't have careers, girls get married and have children."[50] Eager to escape her parents' home, Lamb took up with an older man who had served in the navy during World War II. She sums up her late adolescence with characteristic bluntness: "I met my husband at 15, got engaged at 16, married at 17, got pregnant at 18, and had my first child at 19."[51]

Lamb and her husband settled down in a small house in suburban Nutley, New Jersey, and although she was no longer living hand-to-mouth in the slums of Newark, she still felt trapped. "I could make very complicated hors d'oeuvres, but I cried a lot," she mused about her first few years as a wife and mother. "I knew instinctively that keeping house would never totally satisfy my longings and my dreams, but housework seemed to take all my time. I began feeling trapped. So I got very angry."[52]

As her children grew older, Lamb began to pursue various passions that took her outside the home. She took college courses, became politically active, and joined a local amateur theater group. "I tried everything," she remembers. "And I kept asking myself over and over, 'What do I really want to do with all my displaced energy—with all my ideas? What can I *commit* myself to?' The answer came when I started to write seriously for hours at a time and I suddenly felt alive and in tune with myself."[53]

Because of her decades-long struggle to balance life as a homemaker with her many ambitions, Lamb was drawn to the women's movement, and much of her writing reflects both her personal experiences and her politics. Her groundbreaking one-act play, *But What Have You Done for Me Lately?*, for example, drew from the protective "mother's rage" Lamb experienced when one of her teenage daughters confessed that she thought she was pregnant.[54] In the Kafkaesque play—which tackles an antichoice culture and the patriarchal assumption that "maternity is the most beautiful thing that can happen to a woman, and is what gives her importance"—a man awakens to find that he is pregnant.[55] While Lamb's daughter turned out not to be pregnant, the man in *But What Have You Done for Me Lately?* is forced to give birth since none of the women he appeals to will permit him to have an abortion under any circumstances, no matter how desperately he pleads for one.

Although she had been writing plays in relative obscurity for several years, *But What Have You Done for Me Lately?* launched Lamb into an increasingly public realm. In 1969 she became involved as a playwright and sometime director for the New

Feminist Theater (NFT), one of the earliest second-wave feminist theater groups to form in New York City. Although the troupe disbanded soon after its formation, the work Lamb did for it culminated with *Mod Donna* at the Public Theater in 1970.

The NFT was founded by the activists Anselma Dell'Olio and Jacqui Ceballos, who had formed a play-reading committee as part of their work with the New York chapter of the National Organization for Women (NOW). When they both appeared as guests, along with Rosalyn Baxandall and Kate Millett, on a 1968 episode of *The David Susskind Show* devoted to feminism and titled "Four Angry Women," Dell'Olio mentioned the play-reading committee, and said that she was thinking of forming a women's theater group. She was subsequently so deluged with material that she resigned from her job as an Avon copywriter in order to serve as the NFT's resident director, and Ceballos signed on as publicist.[56]

Lamb, who had seen the *David Susskind* episode, quickly sent some of her plays to Dell'Olio and phoned Ceballos to introduce herself.[57] Dell'Olio, sorting through reams of submissions, recalls that she received "a lot of good material, some of it very funny," but only "one pearl: Myrna Lamb."[58] Ceballos was similarly impressed. "Myrna was fascinating in those days. Unbelievable," she remembers. "When we started the New Feminist Theater, the women and some of the men—because we had some young feminist men there—were writing little skits, and so we started a little theater to put them on. And Myrna Lamb comes in with her heavy plays. Hers were *much* heavier than the others! That's how we met."[59]

The NFT's first performance took place at a Redstockings benefit at Washington Square Church in March 1969 and featured Lamb's short plays *In the Shadow of the Crematoria, Scyklon Z,* and *But What Have You Done for Me Lately?*[60] That May the NFT performed at a larger benefit for NOW at the midtown Martinique Theater. "Betty Friedan came, and we put on a play, and Rita Mae Brown recited a poem she wrote," Ceballos remembers. "Everybody loved it because, you know, it was funny, and feminist and there was consciousness raising. And then we started getting a lot of attention in New York."[61]

The NFT, renamed the New Feminist Repertory, began to present new works with feminist themes at the Village Gate in Greenwich Village every Monday night. The pieces, which ranged from songs and short skits to full-length plays, grappled with such issues as "the polarization of male and female, the ideal norms of Masculinity and Femininity, the holiness of motherhood and the ecstasy of childbearing."[62] Soon, however, internal differences, including frequent clashes between Lamb and Dell'Olio, began to contribute to the group's demise.

Because of their strong personalities and central roles in the NFT, Lamb and Dell'Olio very quickly began to butt heads. Lamb remembers that after the two 1969 benefits, creative differences arose over what the troupe's future and mission should be. "We were going to produce, we were getting publicity, but then people said to get rid of me because my work was too serious, and that we should write for children," Lamb recalls, clearly still irritated three decades later.[63] Frustrated and eager to have her new musical, *Mod Donna*, produced in New York, Lamb set off on her own. For this project she chose to collaborate with a young composer who, though sympathetic to the women's movement, was not directly involved with it.

Newly married, newly pregnant, and nearly fifteen years younger than Lamb, Susan Hulsman Bingham, who had trained as a concert pianist, had recently composed music for a revue called *The American Sunrise* as a favor for some friends at Yale Drama School. Bingham ended up serving as accompanist for the revue, which she and her friends eventually presented at an experimental lab held at the Public Theater. After the show at the Public, Lamb, who had been in the audience, approached Bingham and invited her to write the score for *Mod Donna*.[64]

Once a draft of the musical was complete, Lamb approached Joseph Papp as a potential producer. Papp had a reputation not only for backing left-leaning, socially conscious, risky new plays, but also for showering up-and-coming playwrights with stipends, opportunities for professional growth, and enormous amounts of attention.[65] He agreed to produce *Mod Donna* at the Public and signed on as its director as well.

Subtitled *A Space-Age Musical Soap*, *Mod Donna*—much like the soap operas on which it was based—was meant to be highly melodramatic. The four main characters are Jeff, a wealthy company man; his bored, manipulative wife, Chris; his resentful, toadying employee, Charlie; and Charlie's sexually pliant wife, Donna. These characters, Lamb instructs, are to be costumed in a highly stylized manner "to further implement the non-naturalistic shading," thereby reminding audiences of the over-the-top nature of the musical.[66]

Chris (Sharon Laughlin) reminds Jeff (Larry Bryggman) who's the boss in Myrna Lamb's *Mod Donna*. Photo by Friedman-Abeles. Courtesy of the Billy Rose Theater Archive, New York Public Library for the Performing Arts.

In keeping with the soap opera theme, *Mod Donna* features eight scenes about Chris, Jeff, Donna, and Charlie; these are interspersed with "commercial breaks," during which a Greek chorus of women sings, dances, and philosophizes before retreating to the edge of the stage to watch the action unfold between the central characters.[67] Adding to the unreal quality of the musical is the dialogue, which segues frequently between conversational English and dense, almost absurdist prose. The many ways Lamb attempted to drive a wedge between the characters in the musical and the audience watching them have resulted in at least one writer comparing *Mod Donna* to Brecht-Weill pieces like *The Threepenny Opera* and *Mahagonny*.[68]

As in Brecht-Weill collaborations, class distinctions are key in *Mod Donna*. According to Lamb, Chris and Jeff should give the appearance of elegant "haves," while "Charlie is an all-American square—sensible, willing, even sweet—the kind of guy who will look very clean and proper in a Marine Corps uniform or as a cop on the beat. And yet the kind of guy that could mow them down at Mylai if he were ordered to."[69] Donna, Charlie's wife, "is a wise peasant...beautiful by unformulated standards. She is 'experienced' in the common sexual connotation of that term, but she doesn't seem to learn from it, and preserves a genuine innocence, hope, idealism."[70] Donna's blend of sexual experience and emotional naïveté are made clear in the first lines she utters: "I'm the type that goes to bed with guys because I can't bear to say no when they've asked me so politely....Because they do me the honor of wanting me...I give."[71]

Early in Act I Jeff and Chris invite Donna to move into their home and their marital bed, with the aim of improving their humdrum sex life. In return Jeff will see to it that Charlie advances at the office. The setup initially makes everyone happy, but then Charlie becomes jealous, and Chris and Jeff grow bored with their sexual plaything. They decide to rekindle their marriage in Europe, alone, and thus attempt to send Donna back to Charlie. But Donna has become pregnant and refuses to leave the wealthier couple's home. In the end Jeff and Chris leave anyway, and Charlie murders Donna. True to their role, the Greek chorus informs the audience of Donna's murder and moralizes that until class and gender inequalities are resolved, the Donnas of the world will continue to die violent, senseless deaths. *Mod Donna* ends as the chorus, facing the audience with fists raised, shouts repeatedly for liberation.

Despite the strong sexual content of *Mod Donna*, Papp chose to buck the trend and keep all of his actors clothed. "I feel it would be wrong, here," he stated, during the rehearsal period, when asked if the musical would feature nudity. "There is the nakedness of the idea, instead, a stripping away of things that are usually left unsaid."[72]

Despite its heavy themes and tragic ending, *Mod Donna* was not the bummer that its description might imply. Not only did the four central characters all deliver their share of zinging one-liners throughout the show—often in the middle of particularly intense scenes—but the chorus of women frequently broke into gleefully inane dances and enacted increasingly ludicrous commercials modeled after those featured during the afternoon soaps. In one instance a quarrel between Charlie and Donna turns physical and culminates when Charlie wrestles Donna to the couch, where he straddles her. In response, Donna looks blandly up at him and asks, "Do you want some coffee, Charlie?...You want some beer? English muffins? American cheese?"

Before he can answer, the Greek chorus swoops in and dances an exaggerated bump and grind while singing the bouncy, cheerfully forced "Food Is Love":

> He'll submit to the hand that holds a spatula
> So pick up that trusty kitchen tool
> And do your cooking thing, oh you cooking fool
> Food is love
> Baby, it won't even matter just how fat you are
> He'll submit to the hand that holds the spatula.[73]

🔊 Ex. 4.3

Just as abruptly, the chorus rushes offstage, and Donna and Charlie, calmer now, continue their dialogue.

The score of *Mod Donna*, like the dialogue and absurdist situations, does well to lighten the mood of the piece and to challenge the conventions of the traditional musical. Bingham's score tends toward jazzy dissonances and jagged rhythms; a reel-to-reel recording of the original production indicates that most of the lyrics were either chanted, loudly and bluntly, in unison by the chorus, or begun as solo pieces by principal characters who were then joined by the chorus after a verse or two.[74] The songs, all of which feature Lamb's densely poetic lyrics, are written in a variety of styles, including tango, waltz, vaudeville, striptease, and rock and roll, and the styles don't necessarily match the emotional states of the characters.

Take, for example, a scene late in the musical, when Jeff anxiously informs Donna that he and Chris plan to head off to Europe without her. Donna delivers an angry, bitter monologue in which she curses the wealthy couple, screaming the last lines before storming off. In response to the tense, ensuing silence, Jeff bursts into "Jeff's Plaint," in which he expresses his contradictory emotions not in a melancholy ballad or wistful torch song, but in a bouncy, infectiously rhythmic klezmer melody accompanied by clarinet (🔊 Ex. 4.4). The klezmer style gives way abruptly to refrains written in a 1950s rock-and-roll style, which are sung with typical maniacal glee by the chorus (🔊 Ex. 4.5). This number, like a great many in the show, functions as a tension breaker but also works against the convention that musical numbers should match the mood of the plot and should build upon and emanate from the emotional state of the characters.

*Mod Donna* went into rehearsals in the spring of 1970, and although casting went smoothly enough, problems with the production began almost immediately. This was due in no small part to Papp himself. The producer had a tendency to back the works of new playwrights a bit too ferociously and hurry them to the stage a bit too quickly when they might have benefited from more extensive revisions. Further, while highly regarded as a producer, Papp had a less strong reputation as a director. Though often viewed as innovative, he also could be gruff, impatient, disorganized, and easily distracted by his many other duties.[75]

Indeed disorganization prevailed once rehearsals began, begetting tensions among members of the production team. Bingham remembers that her input was "very minimal" once she had finished the score and that some of the women involved with *Mod Donna* "were rather flummoxed because I was both married and pregnant—how *very* unliberated!"[76] Lamb, on the other hand, was present for every rehearsal. She experienced her share of ups and downs during the rehearsal process, which she found to be emotionally taxing in ways that she did not anticipate.

Faced with criticism from many of her fellow feminists, who were annoyed that she had agreed to allow a man to produce and direct her musical,[77] Lamb often butted heads with Papp and disagreed with his choices. "It's obvious to you that the thing has to be a collaboration. Your play. His editing, his concepts," she wrote during rehearsals. And yet "you're very sensitive to every cut.... The first day is a shock. You don't want to look at the wound and you know you must work and survive."[78] The tensions between Lamb and Papp continued to rise through the rehearsal period: "[Although] I had to be [at every rehearsal] to rewrite, and do this and that, Joe was saying not to sit where he could see my face because my face disturbed him. I was to sit up above him where he couldn't see me. And I was to *never* talk to the actors."[79]

Jacqui Ceballos, whom Lamb retained as publicist for *Mod Donna*, remembers that some of the problems arose from the fact that while Papp was interested in political theater, he was not necessarily as dedicated to specific social movements as his playwrights were. The *Mod Donna* company was thus on the whole not remotely as passionate about the women's movement as Lamb, Ceballos, or the NFT had been. "The actors in the play weren't feminists," Ceballos says, "and there is always something missing when you don't have the crew and everybody aware of what was going on."[80]

In addition, though Papp was willing to work with Lamb on revisions, he ultimately expected to be fully in control of and to have the final say about the show. Ceballos remembers becoming inadvertently tangled in the power struggle between Papp and Lamb at one point. "Papp was...charming, and a very admired man, and great at what he did," she acknowledges. "But he didn't want any interference, and he was changing Myrna's play. He would want it his way, and she would argue with him, and then she would use me as a backup [because] she needed me for support." Things finally came to a head: "During rehearsal one day he came up to me in the dark, where the seats go up. And he just told me to back off, and he wasn't very nice about it. I was stunned. Because...really, it was she who was using my name, you see. She was using me because that's what she needed. It really wounded me, and no *way* was I going to interfere again!"[81] Adding to the backstage tension was the fact that Papp spent most of his time rehearsing the four major characters, while the scenes involving the Greek chorus of women were placed in the hands of the choreographer Ze'eva Cohen.

Cohen, like Ceballos, remembers Papp as enormously dynamic and impressive but also disorganized and very difficult to read. Cohen worked almost exclusively with the chorus but was never once told by Papp what she should be doing with them. "I didn't have the sense that he had an overall concept or idea of what he wanted to do with the play," she recalls. "If he did...he never shared it with me. I was given songs, [but] I had no direction from him whatsoever and I began to lose my confidence. Because I didn't know what purpose it served....Just to make movement for movement's sake with women?"[82] Cohen muddled through but remains convinced that Papp's inability to communicate led to irreparable damage. *Mod Donna* "finally shaped up but it was not a great show. It never felt like a unit." Instead, due to the distance Papp created between the chorus and the lead players, the musical always seemed to Cohen "like two plays in one."[83]

Despite its problems, *Mod Donna* received good coverage in the press during the preview period. Consciousness-raising sessions followed several performances; the cast performed at various feminist meetings, panels, and fundraisers; and Ceballos organized "Mod DonnArt," an exhibit of contemporary women artists, displayed in the hallway in front of the theater.[84] And the musical seemed to resonate with preview audiences, whom Bingham remembers as plentiful and enthusiastic."[85] "Are you kidding?" Lamb laughed when asked if she remembers whether audiences liked the musical. "They played to full houses constantly," especially because, as far as feminist theater went, *Mod Donna* was "the only game in town!"[86] Indeed at least one review describes "wild cheering" during performances, and the audience recorded on the reel-to-reel tape that was made during the preview period seems to be greatly enjoying the musical.[87]

When it opened on April 24, 1970, *Mod Donna* received several strong reviews. Clive Barnes argued that it was somewhat inconsistent but still "one of the most pertinent and stimulating offerings" the Public Theater had offered to date.[88] Dick Brukenfeld for the *Village Voice* expressed appreciation for the musical's courage and wit, and especially for Lamb's "gorgeous rage," which he found enthralling.[89] Jack Kroll raved about *Mod Donna* in *Newsweek*, where he pronounced Lamb a "tough, smart, bitter and tender" playwright with "a fine sense of how vulnerability becomes perverted power (women) and how power can be perverted vulnerability (men)." In addition, Bingham's score, Kroll wrote, was "quietly intelligent in its ability to underline the angry, cynical and hortatory language."[90] Yet Barnes, Brukenfeld, and Kroll were ultimately in the minority in praising the show. Most of the reviews for what was quickly labeled "the women's lib musical" were resolutely negative, and many critics used their reviews as platforms to mock not only Lamb and her show but the very idea of feminism itself.

Papp had obviously anticipated controversy in staging the production, as well as reactions that would extend beyond the show itself and encompass the ideologies it espoused. In his program notes he thus argued circuitously that *Mod Donna* was

> not a show about the feminist movement. Though Myrna Lamb...is an activist...and an ardent feminist, her work is much too ambiguous, too sophisticated, too comedic to satisfy the clear-cut political sloganeering required by a mass movement. However, the play digs into the very core of the matter out of which has sprung the struggle for women's liberation—frustration...the thwarting and distorting of natural aspirations. The heart of *Mod Donna* is the heart of the male-female relationship in our society: the use of sex as the ultimate weapon, the final solution....Having more options, the man finds alternatives outside the boudoir, while the wife...wields the knife of castration....Lamb has brewed a bitter, bitter medicine which we offer to you...on a sugar-coated spoon. We hope it will not be too hard to swallow.[91]

Yet many critics found *Mod Donna* unpalatable indeed.

In his review for the *Post*, for example, Jerry Tallmer lamented Lamb's inability to address "the woman question" as effectively as Strindberg, Ibsen, and Coward have, and notes that at least the female leads were attractive. "Sharon Laughlin as Chris has a beautifully modeled face and a Mona Lisa smile, which helps," he writes, "and April Shawhan as Donna is just a trifle flat as an actress though not indeed—well, Sisters, I'm not going to say it."[92] Similarly condescending of the second wave was Walter Kerr, who wrote in the *New York Times* that he was relieved to learn from Papp's program notes that *Mod Donna* "is not to be construed as a pro-feminist entertainment. I am glad because if it *were* a feminist entertainment, anything I might have to say against it would be taken as male-oriented, biased, vengeful, nearsighted, thick-headed and disloyal to that half of the population which has been making so much noise lately and to which I have hitherto been so intensely devoted. I'm off the hook, right?"[93] Like Tallmer, Kerr is clearly defensive about the idea of feminism itself and compensates by focusing his attentions on the physical characteristics of the female leads. "Sharon Laughlin is cool enough to have been carved from cold cream, with faint wisps of hair brushing her ivory cheeks," while Shawhan is "a lovely thing to look at in her pink silk and pink breasts," although "she does an increasing amount of snarling" as the play progresses.[94]

Just as telling are the few articles written by women about *Mod Donna*. In a piece that ran in the *New York Times* during rehearsals and appeared not in the entertainment but the fashion section, Marylin Bender focuses less on the musical than on Lamb's and Bingham's personal lives, physical appearance, and husbands' backgrounds.[95] And Grace Glueck's spiteful review of the show in the *New York Times*—written specifically from a "women's perspective," presumably to counter Kerr's review—serves as a particularly sharp reminder that, like their male counterparts, many women are conflicted or even threatened by feminist ideologies. "I congratulate Myrna Lamb...and Susan Hulsman Bingham...for getting this material off their—well, chests, and for getting a man to produce it," Glueck mocked, after likening the braless women's chorus to the boys from *Oliver!* "It didn't make me want to burn my bra—but it did send me back to those early women's libbers who said it all so much better: Ibsen and Shaw."[96] In general, reception of *Mod Donna* implies that New York's critics found the musical problematic and the women's movement utterly preposterous.

The nasty treatment by critics of *Mod Donna* and of the women's movement in general prompted several responses from activists, including Vivian Gornick, who, in the *Village Voice*, lamented the "patronizing and unilluminating criticism" heaped on the musical.[97] In a lengthy letter to the *New York Times*, the vice president of NOW, Lucy Komisar, wrote:

> The reactions of your reviewers to *Mod Donna* follow the predictable pattern of anti-feminist polemics. First ridicule, which Walter Kerr knows makes dandy, titillating reading and avoids confronting an issue seriously, then the almost hysterical fear expressed by Grace Glueck that women are being divested of their femininity—which seems to be embodied in the brassiere, that ultimate symbol of American womanhood.... Myrna Lamb's lyrics are vibrant and memorable—and to feminists, they are poetry that represents what we feel in our guts....Lamb is one of us and we are fiercely proud of her and of the contribution *Mod Donna* has made to the literature of our movement and to the cause of our liberation.[98]

The hotly mixed reviews, combined with a budget crunch at the Public, resulted in an abbreviated run for *Mod Donna*, which closed after six weeks.

Lamb wrote several more musicals through the 1970s, one of which, *Apple Pie*, was again produced—though not directed—by Joseph Papp at the Public in 1976. A few other Lamb plays, including *Crab Quadrille* (1976) and *Olympic Park* (1978), ran at the Women's Interart Center. Yet as the decade wore on, Lamb grew increasingly disillusioned by the cutthroat quality of the commercial theater, the infighting within the women's movement, and the frequently nasty potshots that critics took at both her feminism and her playwriting. In 2007 she waxed philosophical about her decision to withdraw from public life in the early 1980s:

> Being a feminist is a some-time thing. Maybe a one-time thing. And then...you die before you die. You disappear. You know, you don't exist if you don't make money. You don't exist if you don't keep getting produced. You don't exist if you don't keep getting published. So I existed for a while, then I died....I wanted fame, I wanted fortune, I wanted all those American things. I just want to live now, and find everything that I can find. Including my grandmother's amber beads. I want to see what [my granddaughter] April will do as long as I can, and I don't give a damn what my place in history is....I used to care. I don't anymore.[99]

Shortly after *Mod Donna* closed, Lamb wrote a letter to Joe Papp. At the time, March 1971, she was feeling discouraged, having just been rejected for a Guggenheim grant she'd applied for. In her letter she describes a conversation she'd had at a NOW fundraiser, which did little to help boost her mood:

> [Everybody] was peddling his or her ass off. Among the peddlers were a couple of women belting out an acceptable enough semi-rock, semi-show rendition of a projected women's liberation musical called *God Bless God (She Needs It)*....The enthusiastic male producer...announced that this production would be the "First Women's Liberation Musical." I...said something like, "Oh, I'm sorry...*Mod Donna* was the first women's liberation musical." To which some other vaguely connected...gentleman replied, "But this will be the first one that will run." I thought that was sweet, especially since I was a sponsor of this function and told him so. The...female composer apologized for the rude overenthusiasm of the male producer....I congratulated her on her new musical and went to extend my hand and similar congratulations to the...author of the book and lyrics....She turned on me...with a statement that, while she did not contend hers was the *first* women's liberation musical,...it was the first women's liberation musical that was *palatable*.[100]

In this case Lamb got the last laugh, since *God Bless God* never seems to have made it past the backers' audition stage. Yet its book writer's use of the term *palatable* is especially telling.

Alice Echols argues that second-wave feminism was an enormous, extraordinarily complicated movement that challenged beauty standards, domestic violence, sexual alienation, compulsory heteronormativity, the availability and safety of birth control, women's control over their own bodies, the sexual division of labor in the home and the workplace, sexual discrimination, quality child care, and gender-neutral language.[101] Because the movement was so far-reaching, because it prompted so many questions for which there were few fast or easy answers, and because it so quickly and so passionately took on so many challenges for which there were so few viable solutions, it was often dismissed by men and women alike as unpalatable, ludicrous, or unworkable, and thus generated particularly acute cultural anxiety.

This is the case not only because second-wave feminism urgently called into question countless cultural systems and assumptions that had steered Western civilization for generations, but also because "its positions were not coherent enough to offer a firm foundation to sympathizers and were various enough to provide a multiplicity of targets for opponents."[102] A result of the perceived vagueness of the women's movement, then, was a tendency within mainstream culture to react mockingly or defensively, as so many critics did upon viewing *Mod Donna*.[103] Its aesthetic and structural flaws notwithstanding, *Mod Donna* failed to connect with many critics (and, one assumes, audience members) in large part because it was perceived as the messy, angry manifestation of what was received—often with impatience, derision, or downright hostility—as a messy, angry movement.

## CHAPTER 5

# Not-So-Angry Feminist Musicals

I'm doing my strong woman number
And oh, I've got such self-esteem
I can handle any crisis
I'm so capable I could scream
    —Gretchen Cryer, *I'm Getting My Act Together and Taking It on the Road*

W hile new, increasingly varied images of women were certainly being reflected in the musical theater by the early 1970s, overt feminism, whether as an overarching theme or in representations by specific characters, remained unwelcome through the 1970s, even as the movement grew. A few notable exceptions were Eve Merriam's *The Club* (1976) and Gretchen Cryer and Nancy Ford's *I'm Getting My Act Together and Taking It on the Road* (1978), both of which managed to touch on contemporary women's issues without alienating theatergoers, largely by cultivating an especially light touch and thus the commercial palatability that *Mod Donna* lacked.[1]

## THE CLUB

*The Club* opened Off Broadway at the Circle in the Square Theater on October 14, 1976, after an initial run at the Lenox Arts Center in Massachusetts in July of the same year. The musical ran for 674 performances and won several Obie awards, including one for best musical, before closing in May 1978. Set in an exclusive men's club at the turn of the century, *The Club* featured a cast of seven women in drag, telling jokes and performing a selection of rags, cakewalks, and coon songs, all of which had been popular in the United States between 1894 and 1905.

In one of the few scholarly studies about *The Club*, Tracy C. Davis points out that the musical is "little read, rarely performed, and completely unhistoricized," despite its many innovations. *The Club* was "the first feminist play to experiment extensively with cross-gender casting" and to "ironicize the antifeminist neo-Right that was

Joanne Beretta, Julie J. Hafner, Gloria Hodes, and Carole Monderdini are members of Eve Merriam's *The Club.* Courtesy of Photofest.

burgeoning in the midst of the sexual and gender revolutions" of the 1970s. At the same time, the production, which was a commercial and critical hit, generated not so much as a sliver of the controversy that the blunter, angrier *Mod Donna* had sparked six years earlier.[2]

Long before she devised *The Club,* the poet, playwright, and activist Eve Merriam had become fascinated with gender-role reversal as a teaching tool.[3] During a writing workshop that she developed for a Minneapolis public school system, Merriam asked a group of fourth-graders to switch the sexes in their favorite fairy tales, and was thrilled by the resultant stories about "Sleeping Handsome" and "Cinderfella," among others.[4] Long after the workshop ended, Merriam kept the idea in the back of her head but "didn't know what to do with it, except maybe have a woman get up and put on a trench coat and be Humphrey Bogart . . . and that seemed boring." Every so often, Merriam remembers, she would "meet someone, and . . . say, 'Hey, isn't it strange that women don't go around impersonating men,' and people would say, 'Yes, isn't it strange,' and the conversation would go on to something else," but still, no clear ideas came. Then one evening she was listening to a radio program featuring old songs, and one of the numbers broadcast was a hit from 1919 titled "Give Me the Sultan's Harem," which gave her the inspiration she'd been seeking for so many years.[5] "When I heard that awful, awful song, I thought what a send-up it would be to have a group of women dressed as men like Fred Astaire—deadpan as can be— singing this really vicious chauvinist song. And I thought, there've got to be more songs like that—and I immediately at the same split-second thought of *Reader's Digest* jokes, because they're so vile and chauvinist, too. I thought, well, that's the way to do it."[6]

Merriam began to research songs and jokes from the 1920s before deciding to move the setting to 1903, not only because she felt that "male chauvinism had its flowering" during the late Victorian era,[7] but also because she wanted to choose popular songs that were not too familiar to audiences. "[When] you're familiar with a song you don't pay attention to the lyrics," she reasoned. "I wanted people to listen to what this sex-object stuff is doing."[8]

She settled on a number of late nineteenth- and early twentieth-century popular songs, which she strung together with jokes culled from turn-of-the-century joke books and issues of *Reader's Digest*. In contrast with the old songs, the jokes were all more familiar; Merriam was disheartened to note that many remained stubbornly rooted in contemporary popular culture, frequently cropping up in places as diverse as TV shows, magazines, and fortune cookies.[9]

*The Club* takes place in an exclusive men's social establishment, the members of which differ in age and disposition. Thrice-married Algy is the jovial, boorish club president. Freddie, a cynical bachelor and—surprise, surprise—gynecologist, chairs the membership committee. Bertie, the swaggering treasurer, is enormously defensive about having recently married for money. Young Bobby, a newlywed, is still very much a mama's boy. Musical entertainment is provided by the Maestro, who accompanies the club members on the piano and often sings as well. Henry, the club's highly stereotypical black servant, and Johnny, the white pageboy, serve drinks, run errands, and deliver messages to club members in exchange for tips.[10] The presence of these characters serves as a reminder that the brand of masculinity being enacted by the women as club members is unique to men in power. As the critic Elenore Lester observes, despite their differences in age and personality, the club members are all "members of the ruling class, keeping one eye on their stocks even while they leer over the ladies. Enhancing their sense of power are two servants—one tiny with a shiny, grinning 'Call-for-Philip-Mor-ris' face, the other black with a fixed smile and delightfully nimble tap-dancing feet."[11] In sharp contrast with the members, the servants "are demasculinized because like women they belong to the oppressed class."[12] Nevertheless these two characters regularly join the club members in their sexist joke-telling and singing. Class and race may work to divide men, *The Club* implies, but sexism is the great uniter.

Despite *The Club*'s reliance on cross-gender casting—which, when performed by men as women, is associated with camp—Merriam strove to avoid camp at all costs. Scribbled on the first page of the production script that was distributed to the entire company was an admonishment from Merriam: "This must *not* be camp, this must not be 'Nudge, nudge; wink, wink.' It will be *death* if we get women who are up there and just think they're too cute for words—'Look at us, isn't this adorable.'"[13] Because her vision of the production was so specific, Merriam was highly selective when it came to finding a director. She finally chose the young Tommy Tune, who helped the cast learn to move like men but, like Merriam, also worked to avoid camp at all costs. For example, in a "note pertaining to the back-up trio for the number 'Miranda,' a paean to a woman introduced with the quip 'To Miranda, who's nicely-reared...and not bad from the front either,' Tune scolds: 'don't do the Andrews sisters gestures—that's camp and there shall be no camp in this show.'" Director's notes for the production constantly "encourage the cast to simulate men's gestures (bold, direct, and sparing), confident bearing, and supreme enjoyment of their own jokes" as convincingly and seriously as they could.[14] The company of *The Club* thus strove to convey as straightforwardly as possible the message that, as one critic put it, "the evils that men do to women are fully capable of speaking for themselves."[15]

While ostensibly a music and dance revue, *The Club* has a loose plot: the men arrive at the club, and Henry greets them by pouring their drinks and lighting their cigars. Although occasionally interrupted by Johnny, who takes and delivers messages for them, the club patrons spend the evening singing, dancing, joking, and drinking. The focus of their songs and humor is usually women. Occasionally they discuss money as well, but even when money is mentioned, as in the medley "Ticker Tape,"[16] it is usually described as a means for power, control, and the material satisfaction of ever-demanding wives and girlfriends.

About halfway through *The Club* the men decide to rehearse for their annual Spring Frolic, which consists of more songs and jokes, an aria performed by Bertie, and a scene from Clyde Fitch's 1901 melodrama *The Climbers*. This scene focuses on a love triangle between an embezzler, Richard Sterling; his wife, Blanche; and his friend Ned Warden. During the rehearsal of this scene—which is performed by Bertie as Blanche, Freddie as Ned, and Algy as Sterling—the actress playing Bertie dons a skirt, thereby becoming a woman playing a man playing a woman. Many other aspects of the Spring Frolic rehearsal, which serves as a climax for *The Club*, begin to complicate the show's theretofore straightforward commentary on gender roles.

As Bertie, Algy, and Freddie recite their lines from *The Climbers*, it gradually becomes clear that just as Ned is involved with Blanche, so too is Freddie sleeping with Algy's wife. When Algy realizes this, he breaks character and lunges at Freddie. The lights dim as Freddie and Algy fight, while the Maestro launches into the parlor song "A Night at the Play":

> A night at the play and the drama before him
> Recalled all the pain he had borne day by day
> The husband, the home, the wife and the lover
> 'Twas his story repeated that night at the play.[17]

As Davis notes, this song reinforces the intertextuality of the play-within-a-play.[18] Yet so does what happens next.

According to the stage directions, the lights come up and "we see Freddie rubbing his neck. Bobby leaves, Freddie puts on his coat and exits, too." Algy sits at the piano, smoking his cigar "as if in a trance."[19] In the silence following the fight between Algy and Freddie, Bertie steps forward and sings the tenor aria "Vesti la giubba" from Leoncavallo's *Pagliacci*.

In the opera "Vesti la giubba" is performed at the end of Act I. Canio, who is crushed and humiliated upon learning of his wife's infidelities, nevertheless forces himself, in true "on with the show" fashion, to don his costume, take to the stage, and entertain his audience. Because the aria is performed in reaction to infidelity, and because it involves role-playing as a means to suppress deeply felt emotion, it mirrors both *The Climbers* and the *The Club* itself.

Had Merriam kept the roles straight, then "Vesti la giubba" would be sung by the cuckolded husband, Algy. But the aria in *The Club* is performed by Bertie, who sings it *to* Algy, as he sits glumly at the piano. Thus the actress playing the role of Bertie, who has just shed the skirt she donned to assume the role of Bertie playing Blanche, sings an extraordinarily famous tenor (male) aria in mezzo-soprano (female) range.

The most straightforward reason for this lack of symmetry is that the aria was not originally part of *The Club*. Rather, while rehearsing for the Massachusetts production, the cast built up detailed life histories for their characters, which often highlighted the actress's individual talents. Gloria Hodes, who originated the role of Bertie, had recently made her Metropolitan Opera debut and had jokingly sung a few bars of the aria during a photo shoot. Tommy Tune was impressed enough with her voice that he inserted the aria into *The Club*.[20] Initially, then, "Vesti la giubba" was simply assigned to the woman who could sing it.

Yet the aria—as well as the fact that Bertie performs it—drives home a series of messages about gender roles that *The Club* toys with throughout. In *Pagliacci* Canio sings the aria to himself as a means of persevering in the face of crushing despair; Davis notes that in this context the aria "wrings with pathos."[21] It does so in *The Club* as well, but assigning it to Bertie, who sings it to the cuckolded Algy after just having shifted from the role of Blanche, transforms the aria from a means to summon strength from within into a plea to reinforce stereotypical gender roles from without. In encouraging Algy, "Ridi...sul tuo amore infranto! Ridi del duol, che t'avvelena il cor" ("Laugh...at your broken love! Laugh at the grief that poisons your heart!"), Bertie is telling Algy to "man up"—that is, to conform to an acceptable mode of masculine behavior by suppressing his emotions, despite having just learned that his best friend is having sex with his wife.

It is additionally relevant that in creating Bertie, who exuded a particularly swaggering, sneering machismo, Hodes was literally driven by rage. "The key word Tommy gave me was anger," she explained when asked about her preparation for the part. "I knew I had anger to draw from, and so I took it from there and I elaborated, drawing from stereotypes I had seen, and just translated it into masculine body language."[22] By the time Bertie performs the aria, the audience has learned that he has recently married for money, that he is himself playing the role of doting husband for a wife he does not love, and that he has already grown deeply embittered by the psychic exhaustion resulting from ceaseless role-playing. Algy may be a prisoner of his sex and a victim of his own lifestyle, but Bertie is too: men, like women, suffer mightily due to the constriction of traditional gender roles.

Yet as "Vesti la giubba" dictates, the show must go on, and thus so does *The Club*. Bertie concludes his aria, and he and Algy embrace before exiting the stage. The full cast reenters as if nothing remarkable has transpired. They are all wearing floppy, flowered hats for the Spring Frolic grand finale: the American Beauty Rose Pageant, a medley comparing women to this "purest flower in the Garden of Love."[23] The pageant segues into a drinking song as some of the club members, still in their flowery hats, use an imaginary urinal. Algy returns to the piano bench and as the club members begin their drunken departures, Freddie and Algy engage in one last bit of macho posturing:

*Freddie*: . . . Algy, old sport, don't you want Johnny to call you a carriage?
*Algy*: (*At opposite end. In darkness.*) No. Think I'll stay over.
*Freddie*: Suit yourself, old sport. Sure you're all right?
*Algy*: Never felt better in all my *wife*. I mean *life*.
*Freddie*: Well, fine. Because a bit of a leg shouldn't come between two old buddies.
I mean, after all, I always did admire your taste in wines.[24]

Alone onstage Algy slowly "begins to let down his hair. With back to the audience, removes masculine makeup."[25] The actress playing Algy then turns to the audience as a woman and bids a gently lacerating adieu:

> Illusion is now at an end
> It's time our curtain must descend.
> We need no epilogue to show
> The real world, since full well we know
> That he and she do equal share
> That both our sexes are judged fair
> And there's true justice—everywhere.
> Depend on it, that you can
> *Upon my honor, as a man.*
> The curtain now, with no more pause;
> We welcome her—and his—applause.[26]

*The Club*, Davis writes, uses dated superficialities—"banal songs, misogynist jokes, limericks, and performance shticks lifted from turn-of-the-century sources"—to "challenge audiences' assurance about the correlation between appearance, sex, and gender."[27] Yet the final sequence of events, from the Spring Frolic to Algy's parting soliloquy, implies that *The Club* is also about the strictures of role-playing and power.

*The Club*, a musical in which women assume the power that men of a certain class take for granted, also demonstrates how unattractive imbalances in sexual (and class- and race-based) power can be. The fact that so many of the songs and jokes performed in *The Club* depict women as vapid, money-grubbing, overbearing twits implies—as *Mod Donna* did, albeit less subtly—that such power imbalances benefit neither sex. *The Club* comments throughout, but especially as it concludes, on the futility of adhering to social constraints that dictate what is properly masculine or feminine in the first place. "So much of that is socially imposed ridiculousness," Gloria Hodes said in an interview. "From being in the show I've learned a lot—the difference between men and women is no longer as defined for me. If we were totally honest, we would probably not manifest only those traits which are used to identify the sexes."[28]

In the press Merriam emphasized that she did not want to make audience members feel as if they were being judged or mocked by *The Club*. When asked why she chose to set her musical in 1903, for example, she explained, "A distance is achieved by that, and I think that's important. After all, I want 'The Club' to be an entertainment, not a *mea culpa*."[29] Several years later she noted that *The Club* was "disarming," but not in a way that made too many waves: "I think one reason for the popularity of the show is that you can just go to it and say, 'Wonderful songs, wonderful dancers, gorgeous looking features, terrific style,' and then underneath, you know, 'I think I'm really being made to think a little bit.' "[30] Or, it turns out, not at all: reviews and press clippings provide ample evidence that spectators reacted to the musical in a particularly wide variety of ways.

Both Davis and Alisa Solomon argue that critics' reviews of *The Club* were sharply divided between the sexes, with male critics largely rejecting the show because the cast "failed to convince the audience that they were really men," and female critics generally embracing the show.[31] Both scholars likely came to this conclusion after reading Merriam's claim, in Betsko and Koenig's *Interviews with Contemporary Women Playwrights*, that female critics, specifically Edith Oliver, Marilyn Stasio, and Erika Munk, saved the show by writing rave reviews.[32]

Yet reactions to the show were not in fact quite so black and white (or, as it were, male and female). Regardless of sex, most critics who reviewed the show liked it—or, at the very least, liked aspects of it. *The Club* easily caused as much exhilaration as discomfort among critics, and some clearly felt both at once. Critical reactions to *The Club* ultimately say as much about how complex spectator reactions can be to a specific piece and, as with *Mod Donna*, how much contentiousness surrounded the women's movement, as they do about the production itself.

Certainly some critics failed to see the cross-dressing as anything more than a gimmick, or wrote that the performers had done lackluster jobs of convincingly embodying men. "Did [Merriam] think we wouldn't notice the latent femininity under the blustering masculinity?" demanded Mel Gussow, who felt that the "very thin" musical would have worked better as a "10-minute turn in satirical revue."[33] Douglas Watt too quipped that the cross-dressing "didn't fool [him] for a minute" and that the musical on the whole did little more than provide "ample evidence why 'Pinky Panky Poo' and the other songs are totally unfamiliar today."[34] Robert Cushman for the *London Observer* argued, somewhat bizarrely, that an all-male cast would have gotten the point of the show across more forcefully.[35] And Walter Kerr seemed to miss the point entirely, noting only that *The Club* was "most entertaining" before devoting the rest of his review to an old vaudeville rope trick that was used in one scene and that he felt was poorly executed.[36] A few other critics got the point very quickly but were bored thereafter. Stanley Kauffmann for the *New Republic* agreed with Gussow that *The Club* would have made a funny enough short sketch but was monotonous at ninety minutes.[37] And Cynthia Lee Jenner of the *Villager* called *The Club* smart and stylish but argued that it made "its point about men's traditional contempt for women in the first 10 minutes" and then became frustratingly redundant.[38] Some female critics wrote that their only disappointment was that *The Club* never went quite far enough. Elenore Lester for the *Soho Weekly News*, for example, felt that the show's biggest flaw was its benignity and that ultimately "little is said that couldn't have been said in mixed company even at the turn of the century."[39]

While these critics felt that *The Club*—or, at least in Kerr's case, the rope trick therein—missed its mark, very few found the cross-dressing to be downright distasteful. The device most clearly annoyed Howard Kissel, who wrote in *Women's*

*Wear Daily,* "The idea itself is the sort of thing one would expect to find in a girls' boarding school on parent's weekend—not being any of the girls' parent, I found it hard to indulge."[40] The most ill-informed, defensive review of the production came from Rex Reed, who wrote in the *Daily News* that Merriam's script "embraces and celebrates every masculine pomposity women have been fighting since time began. To so many, vile clichés coming from the mouths of women is a gross insult. This impudent, worthless bore would be laughed out of town if performed by men. To see women impersonating the stuffiness and arrogance of male supremacy seems alarmingly like watching whites perform a minstrel show in black face. It's a gross insult to everyone."[41] Reed then resorts to a bit of masculine pomposity himself, adding that the cast is "awful" and that the show "looks more like an evening spent in a lesbian bar."[42]

Critics who disliked *The Club* thus did so for a number of reasons, ranging from boredom with the concept or material to lack of interest in the show's sociopolitical messages or revulsion at the sight of women dressed as men. What is striking, however, is that critics who liked *The Club* reflected a similarly wide spectrum of reactions. In short, many critics enjoyed the show for the very same reasons that others hated it.

Merriam herself was quick to acknowledge that *The Club*'s "hint of kinkiness" was part of its appeal for many spectators. "Certainly, there is always an erotic element in seeing one sex portray the other sex," she noted. "There is no doubt about that."[43] She adds, perhaps in a passing jab at Rex Reed, that the only people who really seem to despise the musical are those who are uncomfortable with their own sexuality.[44] Indeed plenty of spectators were drawn to *The Club* because of the erotic charge it promised. The musical earned such a strong lesbian following, for example, that the *Villager* critic Ted Hoffman credited its initial success to the many "intelligent lesbians" who flocked to the Circle in the Square Theater during the run of the production.[45]

For at least one such "intelligent lesbian," Gloria Hodes as Bertie held particular appeal. In her *Village Voice* article "Gloria Hodes Is My Cary Grant," the playwright and activist Loretta Lotman (now known as Libbe HaLevy) gushed not only about Hodes—who, she insisted, was well "on her way to being the first major sex symbol for lesbians"—but about *The Club* itself, which, she wrote, was "the best play that's ever hit New York," especially "if you're a dike."[46] For Lotman, the central thrust of *The Club* was that "the only thing that looks more ridiculous than a woman's role on a woman is that same role on a man."[47] She acknowledged, however, that her brain was not the sole organ to spark her enthusiasm. "I don't know how much of my reaction to *The Club* and this woman is tithed to closet femme, respect for a brilliantly realized play, or my overwhelming fascination with talent. I don't even know if Gloria Hodes is gay—but I can dream."[48]

Of course, one did not need to be a lesbian to derive pleasure from *The Club*. Merriam was in fact struck by the many straight women who, talking with her about having seen the show, eventually admitted "their strong sexual reactions to other women. At first, they start talking about the politics of the show; but after a while, they bring up the sex. It shocks them. They weren't prepared to respond sexually."[49]

Many men too took pleasure in the charade. The critic Ted Hoffman, writing on Hodes's appeal among lesbian audiences, concurred that she "has a great ass and a great jawbone, suitable to fantasies of every order."[50]

An acknowledgment of the erotic charge that can result from watching women in drag is only slightly less overt in the writings of other male critics. The critic for *Variety*, for example, singles out Hodes as "a very attractive young lady with a lovely operatic voice," while John Simon writes of the cast that each "achieves spectacular masculinity while retaining her fundamental feminine grace. And how deliciously they sing [and] dance!"[51]

In some respects, the erotic elements of *The Club* reflect the musical's ability to function as a deeply subversive theater piece. Jill Dolan has argued that sexual role-playing can move beyond the simply erotic to become powerfully liberating. Because heterosexuality "is naturalized by dominant ideology, it is not seen as a material choice, and is therefore compulsory." Yet in choosing to recast sexuality as a choice, thereby removing the compulsory aspect of heterosexuality, "femininity also becomes suspect as a 'natural' construct." She concludes that sexual role-play "has implications for gender-play: the way people perform their sexuality influences how they wear their gender. If desire is the subtext of narrative, sexuality and gender are equally motivating forces behind representation." At least traditionally, female bodies on display are "assumed to be heterosexual, since male desire organizes the representational system. Disrupting the assumption of heterosexuality, and replacing male desire with lesbian desire, for example, offers radical new readings of the meanings produced by representation."[52] Yet *The Club*, which functioned very successfully as breezy, beautiful entertainment, had a particularly strong mainstream appeal that often won out over its subversiveness.

By most accounts *The Club* was stunning to look at, meticulously performed by a uniformly excellent cast, and staged and choreographed by an up-and-coming young director who was heralded as nothing short of brilliant. Clearly, for a number of critics, these were pleasures enough. George Oppenheimer raved in *Newsday* about the clever staging and talented cast but seemed to have missed the point of the songs and jokes, commenting only that he enjoyed the "nostalgic tunes" and, in contrast with Kerr, the "clever" rope trick.[53] Harold Clurman too "had a good time" at the show but gave no indication that he cared about, or even grasped, its subtext; in his review he mentioned only that *The Club* pokes "harmless fun at the male chauvinism of an earlier day" before turning his attention to the talented cast and visionary director.[54]

Similarly, though many other critics got the point of the musical, they nevertheless didn't care much about it. John Simon had no trouble grasping what Merriam was trying to tell audiences; he writes that the thrust of *The Club* was "to show how male chauvinist the old songs and jokes—and mentalities—really were. By putting all this into the mouths of women impersonating men, some of the hurt is removed from the subject, distancing is achieved; at the same time, the absurdity of these patriarchal attitudes is made more laughably grotesque."[55] Yet despite the affection that Simon proceeds to lavish on the *The Club* in his rave review, he takes issue with the fact that many of the "romantic ballads, or patter songs, and even the old jokes, were not quite so anti-woman as Eve Merriam in her ardent feminism seems to think." For example, he asks, can audiences be certain "that the necessary magic of pop songs does not ineluctably depend on simplifying, romanticizing, if you will, dehumanizing their subjects? Without this, there is a total loss of romance."[56]

Still others found the central concept to be interesting, but only to a point. Martin Gottfried called *The Club* "a virtually flawless execution of an ingenious idea," yet cited the Spring Frolic sequence, which he felt was "a contrived show rehearsal for the sake of production numbers," its sole weak spot.[57] Similarly the somber soliloquy that Algy delivered at the end of the musical was not always appreciated.[58] A few spectators were so rattled by having had the illusion shattered at the end of the show that they sent letters of complaint to Merriam. One woman wrote that she was deeply moved by the illusion the cast of *The Club* created during the show, and thus she wondered "why the character lets his hair down": "[I] really have not gotten over the confusion it caused me.... Everything was a testimony of the exclusion of ... women in the 'active' world, made absolutely powerful by the acting.... Would you have Octavian step out of his role? Or roles? ... I almost plead with you to change it."[59]

Yet for others, the constant shifting between genders was precisely what made *The Club* so pleasurable. The critic Carolyn Clay described the subversive thrill she got from watching women in drag deliver an endless flow of "anti-women chestnuts, especially the wife-beating ones," to the sound of "nervous titters" from the audience:

> And hearing paeans to male camaraderie crooned in lilting soprano tones is pretty jarring. One is repeatedly lulled into near acceptance of the cast as gents, then jolted back to reality by their sweet Adeline-ish singing. And when, toward evening's end, the fellows decide to practice for their annual Spring Frolic, *The Club* gets even spookier, the lines of sexual demarcation fuzzier.... Strangely enough, by the time the "men" don elaborate flowered bonnets for the Frolic finale, we have become so confused as to their sexual identity that the headgear seems as inappropriate as it might if they were really men. Furthermore, the spectacle of the cuckolded husband, his pride dismantled and his turban in disarray, is both funny and somehow poignant. And by the time this same character lets his/her hair down to deliver the *As You Like It*–inspired epilogue, it is impossible to count the ruse's layers.[60]

Ted Hoffman agreed, arguing that *The Club*'s layered approach to gender roles is precisely what makes it so successful. "It is essentially transsexual exploration, in form and in content, as deep and puzzling and thrilling as anything in experimental theater," he wrote. "It works best not when the performers become male but when they miraculously leave their female selves, which is never total but occasional, a process of the work."[61]

Hoffman's appreciation of *The Club*, however, was tempered by his insight into its reception. Because it functioned on so many levels—aesthetic, erotic, sociopolitical, psychosexual—he worried that it veered dangerously close to signifying nothing:

> It works deceptively as pure entertainment: devilishly clever, sprightly charming, nicely crafted, down to adroitly inconsequent perfect tap routines. But that is some-

how exactly what it plays against. It is also sexy, obviously striking and capturing its audiences in ways more easily confessed superficially than personally investigated. It is the ultimate in tease, which the theatre never takes seriously, although an aesthetic of tease might define the theatre as well as any other theory. The result is most people and critics want to enjoy *and* to avoid "The Club."[62]

He concludes that for all its transgressions, "*The Club* would love 'The Club.'"[63]

Despite her enjoyment of the musical, Clay agrees with Hoffman: "What makes *The Club* so intriguing is that it works on several levels simultaneously. (It is probably possible to like it for all the wrong reasons.)" The musical "will no doubt be seen by some folks who think the sexist jokes Merriam found in old *Reader's Digests* a stitch, who still believe in the old adage that *behind* every good man there's a self-effacing, supportive little woman."[64]

Eileen Hillary, for the *East Side Express*, applied the adjective *brilliant* to so many aspects of *The Club* that her review practically glowed. Yet she, like Hoffman and Clay, was discomfited by the show's failure to take a more contemporary stand:

> The sexual clichés of the period are interesting from a historical point of view. Moreover, since much of the self-same idiotology is opined, in various forms and disguises, to this day, there are some satiric stabs of recognition. But not enough...to make this satire totally effective....Satire is...a silver-plated sword. The underlying seriousness must be sheathed in mocking humor. And that is where *The Club* too often fails. We cannot be expected to laugh at the "punch lines" of dated jokes that are being exposed for the silly, shallow, nasty, and disgusting lies they promulgate...although I did notice a few members of the audience snickering at such cocktail napkin oldies as "A toast to woman—who came into the world after man and has been after him ever since."[65]

The many levels on which *The Club* could be viewed helped ensure its commercial success. Yet its see-what-you-choose approach, as well as the careful, stylized air of emotional remove that it cultivated, also helped drive a wedge between the show and the movement it purported to support. This is perhaps why *The Club*, despite being "the first feminist drag play" and one that so completely subverts sexual and gender norms, has failed to become part of what Davis calls "the intellectual capital of feminist theater."[66]

Alisa Solomon writes that while many productions staged by feminist collectives in the 1970s featured various caricatures of men, *The Club* was the first commercial, mainstream production to mock men so openly and in such a lighthearted way. "Built of authentic period songs ('Oh, what a blissy when we kissy,' 'Come and whisper yessie, Tessie') and jokes ('What do they call a man who's lucky in love? A bachelor.' 'Do any of you chaps believe in clubs for women? If every other form of persuasion fails.'...) the...show ridiculed men by showing how absurd they are when they ridicule women. The brilliance of the play is precisely that it doesn't go to extremes."[67] Yet had *The Club* been even a touch more stringent—the performances more exaggerated, the punch lines delivered more bitterly, the songs sung less sweetly—then it surely would not have connected as solidly with mainstream audiences, nor run as long as it did. Especially in contrast with the more overtly bitter, far less successful *Mod Donna*, *The Club* serves as a reminder of just how carefully feminists had to tread to keep from alienating audiences. Whereas *Mod Donna* was reviled by critics for saying too much, *The Club* earned accolades for not seeming to say very much at all.

Deborah Siegel writes that from its "debut on the public stage of history, feminism has been blamed by opponents for going too far, and by advocates for not going far enough. The women's movement has been lambasted by dreamers for failing to transform women's lives, damned by detractors for failing to make women happy, and blamed by everyone for failing to institutionalize enough profound and lasting change."[68] Tensions between those who felt that feminists were asking for too much and those who felt they were not going far enough are just as clear in the reception history of *The Club* as they were in *Mod Donna*. Myrna Lamb's angry, topical prose was not only harshly criticized, but was also frequently used as a springboard to attack the women's movement in general. Merriam, on the other hand, wrapped ideology in stylish costumes and gentle platitudes representative of a distant—and thus perhaps too comfortable—past and ended up with a hit show. Yet it says worlds about the second wave's uphill battle that both of these musicals have been obscured by history in equal measures.

### I'M GETTING MY ACT TOGETHER AND TAKING IT ON THE ROAD

While *The Club* demonstrated the futility of socially constructed sex roles by putting women in costume, *I'm Getting My Act Together and Taking It On the Road* focused on a woman trying to drop "all the disguises" and come to terms with her own needs and expectations as she enters middle age.[69] This musical, with book and lyrics by Gretchen Cryer and music by Nancy Ford, opened at the Public Theater on May 16, 1978, and despite mixed to poor reviews, connected so strongly with audiences—especially middle-aged, female ones—that after it ran for seven months the producer Joseph Papp moved it to the Circle in the Square Theater (conveniently left empty by the recent closing of *The Club*), where it ran for three years. *I'm Getting My Act Together* subsequently spawned a national tour, productions in twenty cities across the world, and a slew of regional productions through the 1980s.[70] A more financially successful show than either *Mod Donna* or *The Club*, *I'm Getting My Act Together* was similarly pigeonholed as a "feminist" musical and demonstrated that even by the late 1970s, and despite the show's popularity, feminist ideology and the American musical still did not quite mesh.

Gretchen Cryer, born Gretchen Kiger in 1935 in rural Dunreith, Indiana, was raised with the then common belief that women who did not marry were failures and that, once betrothed, a woman was to serve as the helpmate to her husband, whose needs and career were of central importance.[71] Nancy Ford, also born in 1935 and raised in the slightly more cosmopolitan town of Kalamazoo, Michigan, met Cryer when they both began college at De Pauw University in 1953. Cryer majored in English and Ford studied music and, as was befitting the tenor of the times, both began an earnest search for a suitable husband. "My fantasy idea was to be a musical comedy star, but my reality idea was to get married," Ford acknowledged in an interview.[72]

Shortly after meeting one another, the two women decided to collaborate on a musical. Their first show, *For Reasons of Royalty*, was about a European princess who travels to America dressed as a boy to learn about woodcutting and falls in love with a lumberjack in the process. The musical was staged at De Pauw during their sophomore year.[73] In retrospect Cryer argued that their collaborative impulse was especially remarkable, since "all we were looking for was suitable men to marry."[74]

Once they graduated from college, both women, newly married, followed their husbands to New Haven, Connecticut. Their husbands entered Yale Divinity School, and Ford and Cryer took secretarial jobs to support them. Within a matter of weeks, however, both men quit school and decided instead to pursue careers in the theater. The couples thus relocated to Boston, where Ford continued working as a secretary and Cryer earned a master's degree in English at Harvard and then found work as a schoolteacher.

A few years later the Fords divorced, and Nancy followed the Cryers to New York City. Between auditions Ford worked as an accompanist and, through the 1970s, a soap opera scriptwriter. Cryer landed chorus and understudy roles in the Broadway musicals *Little Me*, *110 in the Shade*, and *1776* until the first of her two children arrived. All the while the women continued to write musicals together.

Their first professional production, *Now Is the Time for All Good Men*, opened Off Broadway at the Theater de Lys in September 1967. The musical, about a conscientious objector who teaches rural high school students about civil disobedience, received poor reviews and, despite some strong word of mouth, closed deeply in the red after four months. This disappointment was one of many for the Cryers, who had been living well below the poverty line while struggling to find work and raise their children.[75] Cryer remembers, "I was a physical wreck because I had been working all that time, I had two kids; I was trying to be the perfect wife and mother and have some kind of career....I was so exhausted I started getting sick all the time."[76] The many pressures proved too much to withstand, and the Cryers' eleven-year marriage ended in 1969.

Soon thereafter Cryer and Ford opened *The Last Sweet Days of Isaac*, which helped establish their reputation for innovative, small-scale musicals with socially conscious messages. *Isaac*, which focused on the alienating effects of technology, premiered at the Eastside Playhouse on January 26, 1970. A two-character show backed by a rock trio called the Zeitgeist, *Isaac* was divided into two playlets (⊜ Ex. 5.1). The first, "The Elevator," focuses on thirty-three-year-old Isaac, a self-described life poet who always carries a camera, tape recorder, microphone, and electric guitar. Convinced that his death is imminent, he records every moment of his life. At the start of the playlet Isaac gets trapped in an elevator with Ingrid, a secretary and aspiring poet. They decide to take advantage of their stalled moment in space and time, and thus shed their clothing (and Isaac, all of his electronic baggage), moving ever closer to one another until the power is abruptly restored. Their lovemaking and their brief respite from technology squandered, they simply go their separate ways.

In the second playlet, "I Want to Walk to San Francisco," a nineteen-year-old pro-testor named Isaac, who may or may not be the same Isaac from "The Elevator," is arrested and thrown into a jail cell next to one occupied by a woman named Alice. The two communicate with each other and the outside world via cameras in each cell that transmit to a common television screen. Alice and Isaac attempt at various times to touch each other or make love to each other's televised images, to no avail. As in Act I, sexual congress is abruptly interrupted by technology: a newscast from the outside world depicts Isaac's death at a demonstration. When the broadcast ends, Isaac and Alice, still isolated in their jail cells, are left wondering if they are in fact dead or alive.

As Judith Sebesta notes, Ford's soft-rock score "conveys a modern sound that complements the modern technological society conveyed in Cryer's book and lyrics."[77] Ford's *Isaac* score is evocative of Burt Bacharach in its frequent chord changes, irregular phrasing, loping syncopation, and backup vocals, which are sung in tight, trebly harmonies. Songs tend to reinforce the ideas present in the script. In Act I the introductory number and "A Transparent Crystal Moment" are busy pieces, with, in the first case, a thumping bass line and funky electric guitar, and, in the second, a dense polyphonic interplay between the electric piano, voices, and electric guitar (🔊 Ex. 5.1).

Yet as Isaac and Ingrid grow intimate, the music becomes less dependent on technology and more based in traditional styles. "My Most Important Moments Go By," sung by Ingrid, is a gentle waltz accompanied by electric and acoustic piano (🔊 Ex. 5.2). The urgent "Love, You Came to Me" builds on the "ecstasy" leitmotif used in Wagner's "Liebestod" from *Tristan und Isolde*, and then segues into the finale, the first half of which is a gentle refrain of "My Most Important Moments Go By," sung by Ingrid to tinkling music-box accompaniment (🔊 Ex. 5.3). The ec-stasy promised by sexual union is thwarted, and as the characters go their separate ways the finale segues into the same funky, bass-heavy music heard in the intro-duction (🔊 Ex. 5.4).

In Act II the Zeitgeist dominates. Isaac barely sings, and Alice never does. The characters' distance from the music and one another reinforces the idea that technol-ogy can isolate to the point of spiritual death. As the gospel-tinged final number, "Yes, I Know That I'm Alive," implies, Isaac and Alice are alive only if they ignore the images they see on television and instead focus on their own senses: "As long as I can hear my own sweet voice / As long as I can feel my own sweet skin / As long as I can see the flesh and blood that's me / I know, yes I know I'm alive" (🔊 Ex. 5.5).

*The Last Sweet Days of Isaac* ran for 485 performances and earned Cryer and Ford rave reviews, "the likes of which," Cryer muses, "we will never see again."[78] Their next project and only Broadway production, *Shelter*, was about a man living in a television studio and, like both Isaacs, having increasing difficulty telling the difference be-tween mediated image and reality.[79] *Shelter* opened at the Golden on February 6, 1973, and, following mixed reviews, closed a month later. Discouraged, Cryer and Ford took a hiatus from the theater to work on a cabaret act and record two albums for RCA. These activities inspired the most commercially successful musical they would write to date.

The ninety-minute *I'm Getting My Act Together and Taking It On the Road* was, like their previous shows, socially conscious in theme and intimate in scale. It was also the most overtly autobiographical show the women would write. *I'm Getting My Act Together* focuses on Heather Jones, a pop singer planning a comeback tour after having left the music scene to act in soap operas for several years. Heather is rehearsing with her band, the Liberated Men's Band Plus Two (thus inclusive of two female backup singers), for her longtime manager, Joe, on what happens to be her thirty-ninth birthday.

The action takes place in real time. The musical starts as Joe blusters in from Los Angeles to watch a rehearsal. He expects Heather to sing her old hits and perhaps to introduce a few new songs written in the same mold. Heather's new show, however, involves songs, banter, and sketches about relationships, middle age, self-actualization, and her newfound feminism. At every step Joe expresses resistance to the act: he doesn't think Heather should talk about her age, her divorce, or her emotional ups and downs, and especially not about her feminist ideology. Mired in a career that prefers artificiality and trapped in a stubbornly traditional, deeply unsatisfying marriage, Joe cannot come to terms with how much Heather, and his world in general, has changed. At the end of the show Heather, realizing for the first time that she is stronger than Joe, abruptly fires him and sends him back to LA. Although frightened

Gretchen Cryer, flanked by Margot Rose (left) and Betty Aberlin (right) is trying her best to get her act together as she enters middle age. Courtesy of Photofest.

by her actions, she is also empowered and excited for the future, as the celebratory lyrics of the rousing finale, "Happy Birthday/Natural High," make clear:

I've got these arms that can reach out
I've got these eyes that can see
I've got this voice that can sing
Celebration of me
And I don't know what's coming
But this new day feels fine
'Cause I woke up this morning
And the face in the mirror was mine ( Ex. 5.6 ).[80]

When it was less a fleshed-out musical than an elaborate idea, Cryer and Ford auditioned their show for Papp, who was not initially convinced that it had potential. "I felt it was too nice," he recalled. "It was like milk compared to the strong, powerful brew of *Mod Donna*....And it was veering toward sentimentality in certain places, which I can't stand."[81] Yet Papp liked some of the songs and was especially struck by the way that Cryer sang them during the audition. He agreed to back the musical, but only on the condition that Cryer play the role of Heather.[82]

Although it is somewhat less eclectic than her music for *Isaac*, Ford's score for *I'm Getting My Act Together* fits comfortably in the singer-songwriter subgenre made popular by musicians like Joni Mitchell, James Taylor, and Carole King. Backed by electric guitar, various acoustic strings, synthesizer, electric bass, and drums, Ford's songs for *I'm Getting My Act Together* feature boldly confessional lyrics that focus on a woman's need for time to pursue her own interests ("Natural High," "Happy Birthday"); aging in a culture that prioritizes youth and beauty ("Miss America," "Put in a Package and Sold," "Smile"); divorce ("Dear Tom"); the pitfalls that result from being a liberated woman in a man's world ("Strong Woman Number," "Feel the Love," "Lonely Lady"); and the ups and downs of heterosexual relationships ("In a Simple Way I Love You," "Old Friend") ( Ex. 5.7 ).

A particularly apt choice for this musical, the singer-songwriter genre focuses on the singer and emphasizes emotionally raw or confessional lyrics. These qualities allowed the style to become one of the few in the rock realm that was associated with both female musicians and authenticity. As early as 1970 singer-songwriters helped introduce a comparatively introspective, intimate quality into rock music. The lyrics written by such musicians were often taken as somehow soul-baringly, authentically autobiographical; critics and audiences alike often attempted to read into the meanings of the songs.[83]

Papp's insistence that Cryer star in the musical, thereby singing her own lyrics, was not only in keeping with the singer-songwriter ethos, but also proved particularly advantageous for the musical itself. Due to the common perception of the singer-songwriter as emotionally authentic, even when he or she is obviously playing a role, Cryer's performance was often loudly trumpeted as "the real deal," even by critics who were otherwise ambivalent about the production. John Simon, for example, called *I'm Getting My Act Together* "slight, schematic, and unoriginal" but fawned at great length over Cryer herself:

This is clearly an autobiographical outcry, and seldom did a more charming woman cry out more sincerely, more gracefully, more movingly....Now she has become middle-aged...and has plainly experienced her heroine's artistic, social, and sexual problems. And she puts all her disenchantment, sadness, sparkling sarcasm, and womanly wisdom into her embodiment of Heather....At one point Heather tells Joe that she stands before him naked; so does Gretchen Cryer before the world: with her battered good humor, her still not embittered rebelliousness, her no longer youthful exterior turning diaphanous to reveal a spirit full of passion, irony, and unquenchable questioning....Miss Cryer is a bundle of solace, a staged lesson in growing older and living on, and I recommend that you memorize her.[84]

Simon's caveats notwithstanding, most of the critics who reviewed the show were not nearly as enthusiastic about any aspect of it.

While almost a decade had elapsed between the premiere of *Mod Donna* in 1970 and the premiere of *I'm Getting My Act Together* in 1978, feminism remained unwelcome subject matter in the musical theater in the late 1970s, and its adherents were still perceived as fair game for derision among many critics. Thus when *I'm Getting My Act Together* opened on May 16, 1978, Cryer remembers, emphatically, that the critics in New York were "hostile. *Hostile.* Absolutely hostile."[85] Certainly the musical was not always panned; one critic even raved that it was "more consciousness-raising than *The Club* and even better theater."[86] Yet for the most part the reviews for *I'm Getting My Act Together* reflected the same discomfort with the material, and the women's movement itself, that those for *Mod Donna* had at the dawn of the decade.

"Imagine if Ibsen, instead of writing 'A Doll's House' as a conventional drama, simply had Nora stand down front and harangue the audience about her problems," wrote Howard Kissel in *Women's Wear Daily*. "That gives you a pretty good idea of the style of 'I'm Getting My Act Together and Taking It on the Road,'...the latest installment in Joe Papp's ongoing Theater of Kvetch."[87] Kissel was hardly alone in his antifeminist bent, nor was he unique in citing Ibsen as a playwright who knew and could depict contemporary American women far better than they could possibly know or depict themselves. In the *Village Voice* Julius Novick dismissed *I'm Getting My Act Together* as a series of "feminist clichés" before deciding instead that the show reminded him of "a lot of platitudinous plays and musicals that had nothing to do with feminism. 'To be a playwright is to see,' said Ibsen. Ms. Cryer has just not been able to see deeply enough."[88]

As he had with *Mod Donna* eight years earlier, Walter Kerr began his review of *I'm Getting My Act Together* in the *New York Times* by proudly confessing his own antifeminism before attacking the ideology, the musical, and Cryer herself. Despite her repeated—and to Kerr, wholly irritating—proclamations of independence, Heather is, he writes,

miserable, burdened with a permanent frown, self-righteous and—much of the time—sorry for herself. She also...looks terrible. Asked what she's done to her hair, she replies "I just let it go, this is the way it is," and the way it is is kinky-curly and, I would say, messy. Her wardrobe, if a dingy sweater covering a vest and skirt that seemed to have come from an attic last opened in 1914 can be called a wardrobe, improves nothing. She has taken her own fiat that "Nobody's dressing me" most literally, no doubt honorably. And when her manager complains that the act she plans to tour is "angry, confused and offensive," she answers with some vehemence that that's exactly what it's supposed to be. But see here now. How are we to dredge up the sympathy we're supposed to feel? No one can feel sorry for the unliberated woman *and* the liberated woman at ... the same time.[89]

Kerr concludes his review by citing at length Portia's "Dwell but I in the suburbs of your good pleasure" monologue from Shakespeare's *Julius Caesar*, after which he wonders why the women's movement "hasn't snatched it up for a slogan."[90] Clearly, for Kerr, Shakespeare trumps Ibsen when it comes to being most adept at writing dialogue for contemporary American women. Just as clearly, Kerr again proudly and stubbornly refuses to engage with the women's movement.

While some other critics were less harsh—or, at the very least, less overtly sexist—in discussing the central character of *I'm Getting My Act Together*, they were particularly put off by the character of Joe, whom they saw as being too much of a chauvinist boob to be truly believable, especially in direct contrast with the witty, engaging Heather. Some of this criticism likely results from the fact that while Heather was based closely on the lives of both Cryer and Ford, Joe was much more of an amalgam. "Joe Epstein never existed," Cryer explained in interviews, "[but] all the stuff that he says came out of the mouths of some man or other that I have known. So many men I've known are Joe Epsteins."[91] It is certainly possible, then, that to critics, Heather seemed a realer and more fully fleshed-out character than Joe.

Yet some of the difficulty critics—and later many male spectators—had with the character can just as easily be explained along cultural lines. In one lengthy complaint, for example, William Harris for the *Soho Weekly News* wrote:

> The two women creators have a firm grasp of the crippling realities of their own situations as women trying to write music for the theater, but their understanding and portrayal of men within the context of the piece is far less satisfying, sophisticated, and humorous. The central conflict revolves around ... Heather ... and her manager, Joe, who doesn't want her come-back act ... to include feminist sketches which might upset the cozy middle-class audience he expects she'll attract. The format for the show is a rehearsal of Heather's act, repeatedly interrupted by Joe's protestations. Yes, it is another backstage melodrama, and although the focal point is interesting, the arguments are far too one-sided. Joe is no match for Heather's wit or passion....Why couldn't Cryer and Ford have created a character whose intelligence equaled that of the performer?[92]

Harris's complaint can essentially be boiled down to the fact that Heather is smarter, funnier, and stronger than her hotly bombastic male counterpart.

Yet such a complaint is telling for its time. In the history of the American musical—not to mention myriad other forms of commercial entertainment—how many female characters have been depicted as dumber, less witty, morally weaker, or more emotionally fragile than their male counterparts? As Robert Kimball so presciently observed in his review of *I'm Getting My Act Together* for the *New York Post*, the musical theater has for decades "glorified women while it displayed and frequently exploited them. The touchdown pass that won the game somehow almost always led to winning the girl, the innocent Sallys, Irenes, Nanettes, and Marys of our innocent yesteryears."[93] Joe is certainly no dumber than Ado Annie (*Oklahoma!*) or Adelaide (*Guys and Dolls*); no more prejudiced than Nellie Forbush (*South Pacific*) or rigid than Sarah Brown (*Guys and Dolls*), all of whom change their behaviors or worldviews to get a man by the final curtain. Cryer and Ford's Joe doesn't change at all, nor is he expected to. And in developing and writing the show, Cryer was certainly more benevolent to Joe than many male musical theater writers have been to their prominent female characters. Joe, after all, is onstage for much of the production, gets his share of scenery-chewing monologues and tasty one-liners, and in general displays far more dynamism than, to take just one example, Liat, who, despite being the second romantic female lead in *South Pacific*, is featured in only a few scenes and never utters a word.[94]

Because of the negative reviews *I'm Getting My Act Together* received, Cryer and Ford expected Papp to close the show. Yet despite his initial misgivings, Papp had grown steadily convinced that there was an audience for the musical. He thus decided, once the reviews came out, not to immediately bow to the critics. "I got very angry at the stupidity of the reviewers," he noted. "I kept thinking: how dumb these men are! They had a preconceived idea of the show and were so deeply entrenched that they could not recognize what it was about." Papp had in fact begun to appreciate the importance of the show during the preview period. "I felt it had life. It was dealing with a major social issue—I read that there were fifty thousand women in New York City...who were either not married or whose chances of marriage were slight, for a variety of reasons including that they couldn't find a man to connect with or respect. And I thought: there's an *audience* for this play!"[95]

Thus, ignoring the lackluster reviews, Papp promptly began pouring money into advertising, which, combined with word of mouth, slowly but surely began to draw audiences. Sales began to strengthen, and by August 1978, Cryer recalls, the musical began to sell out. "Joe Papp kept extending the run at the Public—six more weeks, six more weeks—until suddenly it had run over six months there, and we had strong advance sales, so he moved it to the Circle in the Square, where it ran for three years." Papp's convictions about the show paid off; not only did it become a commercial hit in New York, but it also eventually spawned "a hundred or more companies all over the world, and cast albums in a lot of different languages. And that's so interesting," Cryer scoffs, "because the initial reviews were *so hostile*."[96]

As with many socially conscious musicals that ran in New York during the 1970s, *I'm Getting My Act Together* hosted rap sessions after certain performances. Initially devised as a means of boosting sales on Wednesday nights, which were particularly slow at the start of the run, the discussions quickly developed lives of their own. Cryer remembers that during the talks the cast would often just sit on the stage and watch "while the audience was battling it out around us." Often women in the audience would use the forum to air their feelings: "They had seen something in the play which they identified with, and having heard it talked about onstage, they felt like they, too, could talk about it, that they would have...an ally. For instance, a wife could suddenly say something which she'd been aching to say to her husband for a long time. Knowing she'd be backed up, she wouldn't have to make her little case all alone. And then he would say something, and he'd be backed up by other males in the audience. It became a public forum for very personal issues."[97]

While perhaps not the most musically or dramaturgically innovative show, *I'm Getting My Act Together* nonetheless captured the spirit of its time in a way that few musicals have. The significance of this was not lost on the producer Craig Zadan, who remembers never having seen audiences "react the way they reacted to this show. They were screaming and applauding during the show, yelling things out....The show did touch a nerve, and word got out about it very quickly." This was especially true of female audiences, Zadan recalls: "The house was packed with women and it was their show. When Gretchen would give her speeches about, 'I'd rather be alone than be with you and not be myself,' the audience went berserk."[98]

Although *I'm Getting My Act Together* made the inroads that it did, Cryer and Ford were unable to build on its success. Cryer maintains that as one of the only successful female musical writing teams, she and Ford never encountered much in the way of overt sexism, but that being labeled "feminists" after the success of *I'm Getting My Act Together* didn't help them, either:

Theater [in the 1970s] truly was dominated by men—producers, directors, and so forth. And...the feminist label would rankle men. I remember hearing some agent— he died, so I could tell you his name if I remembered it, but I can't—but he was a very high-end agent. He referred to Nancy and me as "those dykes" and...both of us are heterosexual. But there was a feeling about, I mean, who wants to work with a couple of dykes, or who wants to work with a couple of women? And you know, Nancy and I have only had one show on Broadway, and that only ran a month in 1973. As long as we were kind of relegated to the smaller arenas, and when it only took a much smaller amount of money to get a show on, we were doing okay. Our next show that we wrote, that we started way back when in the late '70s was about Eleanor Roosevelt. It's a big Broadway show. And of course, you know, "the feminists are writing about another woman, another lesbian." This kind of thing. I think that just cast a shadow. To the extent that people saw feminists as dour, serious, ball-busting people, that worked against us....And then, in the mid- to late-80s...the word "feminist" had [an even more] negative connotation. So to the extent that that label had a pejorative connotation to whoever we were dealing with, it hurt us. Also, feminists were not seen as fun-loving. You know, the musical form is supposed to have a lot of fun in it and be uplifting and so forth, and they would think, "oh, another piece written by feminists, yeah, that'll be about as much fun as going to the dentist." So it's very subtle—it wasn't anybody saying we don't want to produce your show, we don't want to work with you because you're women. We never had that. But there was just a subtle shadow.[99]

The "subtle shadow" continues at present. Ford and Cryer still collaborate, often on musicals with empowering messages for girls. They have written two musicals for the American Girl franchise, and their adaptation of the classic novel *Anne of Green Gables* ran for several months Off Broadway at the Lortel Theater in 2007. But they have yet to see a fully staged production of their Eleanor Roosevelt musical, despite many near misses, largely because the subject matter continues to be seen as much too risky for the musical theater, even more than three decades after the onset of the second wave of feminism.[100]

Of course, there have been changes for the better, as reflected in such recent feminist musicals as *Caroline, or Change*, *The Color Purple*, and *Wicked*, as well as in the slowly rising number of women playwrights, composers, directors, producers, and choreographers. Yet to be overtly feminist remains as culturally touchy now as it was three decades ago, and for every big-budget Broadway musical espousing liberated views there are many more that place emphasis on male characters—who are still widely interpreted as universal—in socially conservative, boy-wins-girl plots.

Jill Dolan begins her book *The Feminist Spectator as Critic* by noting that since "the resurgence of American feminism in the 1960s, feminist theatre makers and critics have worked to expose the gender-specific nature of theatrical representation, and to radically modify its terms. Denaturalizing the position of the ideal spectator as a representative of the dominant culture enables the feminist critic to point out that every aspect of theatrical production, from the types of plays and performances produced to the texts that are ultimately canonized, is determined to reflect and perpetuate the ideal spectator's ideology."[101] In their own ways *The Club* and *I'm Getting My Act Together and Taking It on the Road*—and, for that matter, *Mod Donna*—challenged middlebrow audiences with plots, structures, and characters that went against tradition. None of the women portrayed in these musicals wins the guy in the end: Donna is destroyed by a patriarchal culture; the women in *The Club* embody the past to expose contemporary gender imbalances, which they salute only cynically in the last act; and Heather realizes that she'd rather be alone than compromise herself for any man. It should come as no surprise that none of these musicals has been canonized. There is no way that the canon, at least as described by Dolan, could handle musicals that are so ideologically opposed to it.

As with the post-Stonewall gay male musicals examined earlier, the feminist musicals discussed in these last two chapters are not overtly sexual. While eroticism certainly comes into play—in the confidently stylish cross-dressing employed in *The Club*, the salacious partner-swapping theme dominating *Mod Donna*, the soulful groundedness of the liberated Heather in *I'm Getting My Act Together and Taking It on the Road*—the focus of these musicals is not on sexuality per se. Instead emphasis is placed on women's struggles for respect and equality. Yet running simultaneously alongside *Mod Donna*, *The Club*, and *I'm Getting My Act Together*—and often complicating the messages therein—were musicals that focused directly on female sexuality. The next chapters examine the ways several adult musicals, like so many other types of popular entertainment during the 1970s, conveniently conflated the women's movement with the sexual revolution, thereby affording audiences plenty of jiggle, gratuitous nudity, and simulated sex along with their political platitudes.

# CHAPTER 6

# Obscenity, "Porno Chic," and *Let My People Come*

Put your feet up on the sofa
Stretch out baby, close your eyes
Feel my fingers walking over part of you I idolize
Now you're here in my hand, getting stronger
So soft on my cheek, getting longer
No need to speak as I take you between my lips
> —Earl Wilson Jr., "Come in My Mouth" *from Let My People Come*

While feminist musicals failed to click with critics or audiences through much of the 1970s, ideologies related to the sexual revolution continued to reverberate strongly. This resulted, and continues to result, in enormous confusion: since the women's movement was directly influenced by the sexual revolution, feminist ideology was frequently conflated with a far more patriarchal take on sexual freedoms in the media and thus in the minds of many Americans.[1] Sexuality as related to the concept of women's liberation was especially complicated because the rise of the women's movement and the continued mainstreaming of the sexual revolution occurred at around the same time as the development of the social trend known as "porno chic," which made viewing and discussing hard-core pornographic films briefly fashionable in mainstream culture. This chapter examines the ways the women's movement, the rise of the hard-core narrative, and the overarching sexual revolution became confounded in the culture at large, as is reflected in the adult musical *Let My People Come*.

## FEMINISM AND SEXUALITY

During the 1960s and 1970s cultural attitudes about human sexuality changed significantly and very rapidly. The introduction of the birth control pill in the early 1960s allowed women to take unprecedented control of their own reproductive system and to engage more freely in sexual relationships. The many advantages of the Pill were reinforced by groundbreaking research into human sexuality, conducted by Virginia Masters and William Johnson and published as *Human Sexuality* in 1966. This study concluded that women's sexual energy was equal to if not greater than men's. More important, the study challenged the traditional distinction between vaginal and clitoral orgasm, thereby negating the long-established maxim that heterosexual intercourse was inherently superior to both homosexual sex and masturbation.[2]

By the turn of the decade these cultural shifts coincided with the rise of second-wave feminism. Through the 1970s women strove to assert control over their bodies and to embrace sexuality on their own terms. Yet as the historian Beth Bailey writes, the media wasted no time in sensationalizing feminists by alternately dehumanizing and hypersexualizing them. "Sex sells, of course, and titillating images of bra-less women and sexual freedom made for livelier stories than statistics about women's wages and the lack of affordable childcare," she writes. The media, "often for reasons no more Machiavellian than a desire to attract viewers or readers," tended to treat women's liberation interchangeably with sexual freedom. So too, she notes, did opponents of the women's movement, who "purposely conflated women's liberation with the sexual revolution to brand the women's movement as radical, immoral, and antifamily." Yet even those who "were somewhat sympathetic to the claims of the women's movement found the sexual revolution troubling, and the conflation of movements made it easier for them to draw a line between 'reasonable' demands for decent wages and (as they saw it) the sex-obliterating role reversals and illegitimate intrusions into the 'private' spheres of home, marriage, and the family demanded by 'radical' women's libbers."[3]

Jane Gerhard argues that for all the strides women made in the 1970s, celebrating sexual freedom and pleasure as the keys to liberation did not necessarily erase what many women perceived as the sexism inherent in the late 1960s sexual revolution.[4] As she saw it, the shift in sexual mores all too often resulted in the substitution of one kind of exploitation for another, especially since what was often touted as liberated sex was still largely defined by men.[5] Wanton heterosexual women were ultimately less threatening to the dominant order than women who, in demanding anything more empowering than more sexual activity and sexual pleasure, were often pigeonholed as ugly, frigid, humorless, man-hating "ball breakers." The resultant slew of mixed messages about the relationship between feminism and sexuality fueled the misperceptions that were, and still are, constantly played out in the cultural landscape.

Some of the confusion springs from the fact that the sexual revolution itself did not emanate entirely from the grassroots level of 1960s activism. Rather, much of it was encouraged, and even shaped, by the mainstream to begin with. Bailey points out that although it is now most strongly associated with the late 1960s, the term *sexual revolution* was in use in the United States by 1963 and the phenomenon is thus more correctly viewed as evolutionary than revolutionary, the result of a number of cultural trends that, despite being closely linked by the end of the 1960s, nevertheless occasionally contradicted one another.[6] These cultural trends included an increased tendency for couples to live together before marriage; the adoption on the grassroots level of sex as a tool for sociocultural revolution, even though cultural revolutionaries were unable to agree on goals or on the ideal role or meaning of sex as a tool of revolution in the first place;[7] and the growing reliance on sexuality as a tool in the marketplace.

This last trend, the broadest of the three, began to build momentum as early as the 1920s and exploded in the 1950s and 1960s. These decades, after all, saw the birth of two enormously influential national magazines that helped lay the groundwork for what became known as the 1960s sexual revolution. *Playboy*, founded by Hugh Hefner in 1953, and *Cosmopolitan*, founded by Helen Gurley Brown in 1965, both celebrated youth, style and sophistication, individual freedom, and a "new" kind of sexuality that was pleasurable and freewheeling (if entirely heterosexual). Both of these magazines offered a particular brand of sexual freedom that was heralded as new and different but was ultimately based on differentiation and deceit and that fit neatly into "a shared universe of an intensely competitive market economy."[8] Both magazines depicted the "new" sexuality as "an arena for struggle and exploitation that could be enjoined by men and women alike (though in different ways and to different ends)."[9] What is perhaps most revolutionary about these magazines is not their ideologies, but the streamlined way they linked sex to consumption and the marketplace. *Playboy* and *Cosmo* helped shape the sexual revolution by making sex "more—or less—than a rite of youth."[10]

For all the talk about the death of Puritanism, the triumph of consequence-free sex, and the resultant potential for personal and cultural empowerment, *Playboy* and *Cosmo* rely particularly heavily on traditional gender stereotypes. In the pages of the former, women, as so many mute, passive centerfolds, became shiny, airbrushed objects that were as tame and trusting as kittens and as sexually active as . . . bunnies. In the latter, women were encouraged to play the field and embrace sexual freedom, but always with the aim of eventually landing themselves a man, preferably one with oodles of cash with which to buy expensive clothing, homes, cars, and jewelry. In short, both magazines celebrated a sexual freedom that was only touted as new: the carefree sexuality of the "liberated" woman was encouraged and embraced, as long as the results were tidily circumscribed by the patriarchal order. Meanwhile, in these magazines and in the culture at large, women's claims for social, political, and economic equality continued to be mocked, rejected, or simply ignored.[11]

The mixed messages that circulated in mainstream culture regarding the relationship between female sexuality and women's demand for equality in all cultural spheres were reflected in the American theater of the time. The fact that so much feminist performance art in the 1970s featured female nudity echoed the feminist movement's preoccupation with changing attitudes about women's bodies. "Nudity in performance," Jill Dolan writes, "paralleled the impetus in women's fiction and poetry to provide a forum for women's newly heard voices, by attempting to symbolically reclaim women's subjectivity through the body." The "body art concept" stemmed as well from desire among cultural feminists "to expose women's innate differences from men, and to signify a departure from the more violent tradition of male performance art that preceded the feminist work." Performers who adhere to this ideology hold that a woman's body, "stripped to its 'essential femaleness,' communicates a universal meaning recognizable by all women. They see the nude female body as somehow outside the system of representation that objectifies women, free of the culture's imposed constructs and constrictions."[12] Dolan adds, however, that many of the artists who made a practice of performing nude had bodies that easily conformed to dominant cultural perceptions of female beauty and desirability, and that while they thus purportedly displayed their naked bodies as a sign of unity among women, "in the genderized terms of the performance space their bodies became accountable to male-defined standards for acceptable display."[13]

Dolan's description certainly applies to the adult musical. As noted, techniques that emanated from the fringe during the late 1960s and 1970s exerted particularly strong influence on the commercial musical, and many stage musicals thus incorporated nudity as a means with which to celebrate the human body and the new freedoms of contemporary sexuality. Yet more often than not, female sexuality was used to redirect—not to encourage direct confrontation with—the demands that feminist ideology made on contemporary society.

Stage musicals were hardly alone in this. The deep-seated anxieties caused by the second wave's challenges to traditional sex roles resulted in the widespread popularity on film and television of, on the one hand, wacky sex comedies like *Three's Company* (1977), which allowed audiences "to laugh at their fears while avoiding direct confrontation with the serious issues," and, on the other hand, brutal morality tales like *Looking for Mr. Goodbar* (1977), which thoroughly conflated women's liberation and the sexual revolution and which punished its main character for pursuing consequence-free sex on her own terms.[14]

The conflation between sexual liberation and women's liberation was further confounded with the rise of porno chic. Coined by Ralph Blumenthal in an article that ran in the *New York Times Magazine* in January 1973, porno chic referred to the surge in mainstream popularity of hard-core pornographic films that, beginning in the early 1970s, were briefly screened in neighborhood movie theaters, watched and discussed in mixed company, and reviewed in the popular press. Sparked by the release in 1972 of the enormously commercially successful film *Deep Throat*, porno chic was the result not only of drastically changing sexual mores across the country, but also of several groundbreaking legal decisions regarding the nature of obscenity that were handed down between the late 1950s and the early 1970s. These rulings allowed for the expansion and increased availability, especially by the late 1960s, of pornography, which was briefly legitimized by mainstream populations that were still wrestling with the trickle-down effects of the sexual revolution.

The struggle in this country between freedom of speech and information and debates regarding the ways human sexuality could and should be depicted was hardly new in the mid-twentieth century. The so-called obscenity debate has been waged in the United States from practically the moment colonization by the British began. Because New York City has long been a capital for various forms of commercial entertainment, such struggles have occurred with particular fervor there. Thus a brief synopsis of American obscenity legislation as it relates to the cultural life of New York follows and will lead into a closer examination of the rise of hard-core films, the subsequent porno chic trend, and its relationship to the adult musical in New York City.

## A BRIEF HISTORY OF AMERICAN OBSCENITY LAW

According to Andrea Friedman, prior to the Civil War anti-obscenity regulation was left to individual colonies or states and was more concerned with protecting state or church authority than with any portrayals of sexuality per se. By the early eighteenth century all American colonies had statutes that criminalized heresy or blasphemy; Massachusetts's 1711 statute, for example, prohibited the "composing, writing, printing or publishing of any filthy obscene or profane song, pamphlet, libel or mock-sermon, in imitation of preaching, or any other part of divine worship." As Friedman notes, the wording here suggests that early writings and pictures deemed obscene were those specifically containing political or religious criticism.[15]

By the outbreak of the Civil War, just as scores of men and boys were leaving their homes for the battlefront, it had become possible to produce, relatively quickly and cheaply, multiple prints of photographs. The mid-nineteenth century thus saw a sharp increase in both the volume and availability of sexually explicit material, much of which was purchased and sent through the mail. Quick to recognize a growing market, companies like G. S. Hoskins and Richards & Roche sent pamphlets and catalogues to the soldiers, offering via mail order items including photographs of Parisian prostitutes, dirty decks of cards, and miniature photographs that, when held close to the eye, revealed women and men in various sex acts.[16]

That both of these purveyors of sexually explicit material were based in New York City is no coincidence. By the mid-nineteenth century New York had become the most populous city in the United States and the site of the country's leading financial, cultural, and manufacturing organizations. It was also well on its way to becoming a formidable communications capital, especially immediately prior to the Civil War, when it eclipsed the burgeoning publishing industries in Boston and Philadelphia.[17] By the outbreak of the Civil War, then, New York had established itself as "the headquarters for an ambitious, entrepreneurial network of publishers who pioneered the production and marketing of sexual writing in the United States," a distinction that became a cause for increasing concern among antivice and religious activists as the demand for erotica grew steadily among Civil War soldiers.[18] It became nothing short of an obsession for the young Anthony Comstock, who watched his fellow soldiers' interest in pornography with concern and despair.

A man so passionately opposed to obscenity that the journalist Gay Talese described him in *Thy Neighbor's Wife* as "the most awesome censor in the history of America," Comstock was born in 1844 to an affluent, devoutly religious farm family in New Canaan, Connecticut (🖳 Ex. 6.1).[19] Having "masturbated so obsessively during his teens that he admitted in his diary that he felt it might drive him to suicide," Comstock served with a Connecticut regiment during the Civil War, where he was likely particularly unpopular; while in the army he grew increasingly vocal about the fact that many of his fellow soldiers carried and traded erotic postcards, as well as about how disappointed he was that the military was so lax about protecting the souls of its young men.[20]

Upon settling in New York City after the war, Comstock threw himself into ridding the nation of "this cursed business of obscene literature," which proliferated openly on the city streets and for which he held Satan directly responsible.[21] A grocery store clerk and dry-goods salesman by day, Comstock volunteered tirelessly at the New York City branch of the YMCA, which encouraged him to petition public officials to pass more stringent censorship laws.[22] In 1872 several prominent and moneyed members of the Y helped him found the New York Society for the Suppression of Vice;[23] in the following year he successfully lobbied Congress to pass the country's first federal anti-obscenity statute.

Known as the Comstock law, this statute stated that no "obscene, lewd, or lascivious book, pamphlet, picture, paper, print or other publication of an indecent character, or any article or thing designed or intended for the prevention of contraception or procuring of abortion, nor any article or thing intended or adapted for any indecent or immoral use or nature" was to be carried by the U.S. Postal Service.[24] Violations were punishable with fines of up to $5,000 or imprisonment with hard labor for up to ten years. Through the 1870s twenty-four states enacted "little" Comstock laws, many of which were even more draconian than the original, since they also explicitly criminalized the sale or purchase of obscene, lascivious, or lewd materials.[25]

The terms *obscene*, *lascivious*, and *lewd*, however, were never defined by the courts, which allowed Comstock—who was appointed as a special postal agent with free rein to enforce his statute as he saw fit—the power to suppress anything he deemed improper.[26] This caused Comstock to be loathed by city officials as much as if not more than he was admired. As Talese writes, while "many politicians agreed with Comstock's conclusions, there was some reluctance to support him because his corrective methods—which included the use of informers, spies, and decoys, as well as tampering with the mail—threatened constitutional freedoms."[27]

Well into the first decades of the twentieth century Comstock's excesses in fighting what he perceived as smut—basically any public reference to sex, sexual desire, sexual reproduction, or sexual practice—included raids on the esteemed Herman Knoedler Art Gallery and the city's Art Students' League, both for possessing paintings or photographs of nudes and, in the latter case, for selling catalogues containing sketches of nudes, and legal actions brought against the New York production of George Bernard Shaw's *Mrs. Warren's Profession*, which the city closed after a single performance.[28] During his reign Comstock arrested hundreds, if not thousands, of citizens for possession of questionable literature and often bragged that he drove fifteen people—including abortionists, publishers of sex manuals, prostitutes, and birth control peddlers—to suicide rather than face the embarrassment of lengthy public trials.[29]

After Comstock's death in 1915 his former assistant, John S. Sumner, assumed leadership of the New York Society for the Suppression of Vice, which he struggled to free from the shadow cast by its formidable founder. Comstock, who only got drunker with power as he aged, had become enormously unpopular by the time of his death, and the New York Society for the Suppression of Vice was often more ridiculed than feared in the early twentieth century. Sumner thus devoted himself to the nearly contradictory tasks of reiterating the Society's commitment to moral decency while simultaneously reinventing it as somehow more with-it and tolerant than it was under Comstock.[30] He failed, of course; as detailed in chapter 1, the New York Society for the Suppression of Vice shifted its attention from printed literature to the legitimate and burlesque stage but never managed to shake its reputation for being as priggish, vengeful, obstinate, and intolerant as Comstock himself.[31]

While its association with Comstock certainly did it no favors in its waning years,[32] the Society also had social change working against it. By the turn of the century the nature of the struggle over what constituted obscenity had changed significantly, and the Society failed to weather that change. As Friedman points out, during the nineteenth century anti-obscenity activism was based in moral absolutism, which preached that morality was knowable, timeless, ordained by God, and necessary for both public and private order; that social authority derived from moral hierarchy, which was determined by age, class, race, religion, and gender; and that "moral standards established by those at the top of this hierarchy should be enforced upon the larger society through public policy."[33] Very much a nineteenth-century man, Comstock held fast to the ideals of moral absolutism, but these were overshadowed by the concept of democratic moral authority in the first decades of the twentieth century.

At this point, Friedman points out, a number of New York–based activists, including social workers, members of the entertainment industry, and a collection of civil libertarians who would eventually form the ACLU-affiliated National Council on Freedom from Censorship during the 1930s, drew together to actively oppose continuing efforts to patrol obscenity under outdated, moral-absolutist terms. Instead they developed a new language of public policy, which drew on concepts of democratic moral authority and which grew steadily in acceptance through the first half of the century. Democratic moral authority provided a new means of "determining *what* representations of sexuality might be proscribed by government, and *how* they might be proscribed. Two precepts compromised its core: that whether a representation of sex was obscene ought to be judged according to the standards of the 'average person' and that regulation of that content must occur only in accordance with carefully defined democratic processes. In articulating a democratic moral authority and, finally, convincing New Yorkers of its value, opponents of censorship helped to shape a modern regime of obscenity regulation."[34]

Comstock laws remain on the books, but their fall from favor began at the turn of the twentieth century, while the man himself was still alive, kicking, and attempting to single-handedly drive smut back to the devil's lair from which he was convinced it had sprung.

Mid-twentieth-century federal actions on obscenity, all of which likely had Comstock spinning in his grave, thus placed more emphasis on community standards and social value than on the potential for obscene material to cause moral corruption. In the 1942 ruling *Chaplinsky v. New Hampshire* the court first distinguished between speech that is and is not protected under the First Amendment in deciding that libel, obscenity, lewd speech, and "fighting words" are not protected because they "are no essential part of any exposition of ideas, and are of such slight social value as a step to truth that any benefit that may be derived from them is clearly outweighed by the *social interest* in order and morality."[35]

*Chaplinsky* makes no mention of images, which have traditionally been subsumed within broader, statutory definitions of obscenity. As the legal scholar and former president of the ACLU Nadine Strossen explains, the term *pornography*, which is vague, subjective, and often politically loaded, "has no legal definition or significance."[36] Through the early to mid-twentieth century, *obscenity* was used as a legal catch-all that American law has historically relied upon to "draw the line between prohibited and permitted sexual representations."[37] Obscenity, which refers etymologically to things that are "disgusting, foul, or morally unhealthy," is thus not necessarily the same thing as pornography, which is broader in meaning and pertains specifically to "depictions of sexual lewdness or erotic behavior."[38]

In the years following World War II, however, growing concern about sexually explicit film and literature resulted in an uptick of challenges to existing obscenity statutes. Soon after taking office as mayor of New York City in 1954, Robert Wagner stepped up efforts to improve the perpetually seedy Times Square neighborhood. Strict new zoning laws were passed that prohibited the remodeling or expansion of any existing businesses on or near Forty-second Street, as well as the opening of any new "freak shows, wax museums, shooting galleries, games arcades, open-front stores, sidewalk cafes, and ground-floor auction rooms" in the area.[39] The proprietors of the fourteen grind houses in Times Square were summoned to the office of the license commissioner and informed that they would be closed down unless they collectively agreed to soften their advertising displays, which were typically violent and lurid.[40]

Wagner's rezoning plan helped rid the neighborhood of some of its dime museums and freak shows, but the resultant vacuum was quickly filled by the immediate predecessors of "adult" bookstores. These, as noted in chapter 1, had overwhelmed Times Square by the mid- to late 1960s. The first bookstores to open in the area during the 1950s seemed innocent enough, at least at first; most kept especially low profiles since they were not reliant on foot traffic and operated subject to police raids. Also, because they tended to keep illicit materials in back rooms or under the counter, they were able to attract a fairly broad, young, bohemian crowd by stocking Beat poetry and other contemporary *outré* literature on the browsing shelves.[41]

Yet in September 1954 the city closed down five bookstores on the grounds that "books, magazines and 'comics' tending to encourage crime, sex perversion, and disrespect for law and order" contributed directly to juvenile delinquency, which was a cultural preoccupation at the time.[42] All of the stores that were raided had been selling copies of *Nights of Horror*, a sixteen-volume set of sadomasochistic fetish comic books anonymously illustrated by *Superman*'s cocreator Joe Shuster, which the city held were "plainly obscene."[43] The owners of three of the bookstores simply agreed to stop selling the books, but Kingsley Books and the Times Square Book Shop both refused to comply, countering instead that the city was violating their freedoms of speech and the press.[44]

The bookstore cases eventually landed in the U.S. Supreme Court, which heard them in conjunction with a case involving Samuel Roth, a publisher and bookseller based in Greenwich Village who in 1956 had been sentenced to five years in prison for sending obscene materials through the mail.[45] In what proved a milestone ruling, *Roth v. United States* (1957), with Justice Brennan writing for the majority, upheld New York's right to prosecute on charges of obscenity but simultaneously redefined obscenity in a way that made it harder for prosecutors at any level of government to actually convict. Before *Roth*, works that were seen to "deprave and corrupt those whose minds are open to such immoral influences" could be deemed legally obscene. But Brennan's opinion allowed defense lawyers a great deal of leeway. Following *Roth* the new gauge for obscenity was "whether to the average person, applying contemporary local standards, the dominant theme of the material taken as a whole appeals to prurient interests." Further, Brennan ruled, something must be "patently offensive"— that is, offensive to community standards—and "utterly without redeeming social importance."[46] The *Roth* decision also allowed for an increase in decision making on the local rather than the state or national level.

In several Supreme Court rulings that followed, attempts were made to clarify the language used in *Roth*. For example, in *Jacobellis v. Ohio* (1964), the Court "established the principle that material dealing with sex in a manner that advocates ideas, or that has literary, scientific, or artistic value or any other form of social importance, could not be held obscene."[47] With the comparatively conservative ruling in *Miller v. California* (1973), the Court overturned the idea that material had to be "utterly without redeeming social importance," suggesting instead that something could be found obscene if "its predominant theme is prurient according to the sensibilities of an average person of the community; it depicts sexual conduct in a patently offensive way; and taken as a whole, it 'lacks serious literary, artistic, political, or scientific value.'"[48] Yet the language in these rulings remained highly subjective and the power remained with individual communities.

*Roth* and subsequent rulings, viewed collectively, allowed for the rapid growth of all forms of adult entertainment. This was especially the case in cities like Los Angeles and New York, which are traditionally inclined to "defend freedom of expression at virtually any cost."[49] In the years following the *Roth* ruling, Peter Braunstein writes, New York City metamorphosed "into an Erotic City that became both the epicenter and world marketplace of the sexual revolution."[50]

## PORNO CHIC HITS NEW YORK CITY

The advent of the hard-core feature film was roughly contemporaneous with the succession of Supreme Court rulings. By the late 1950s the Apollo, Victory, and Rialto theaters in Times Square, all of which had been functioning as grind houses, began running films that would now be categorized as soft-core porn. Some of the earliest included the 1957 nudist colony film *Garden of Eden*, as well as late 1950s pseudo-documentaries like *My Bare Lady* and *The Nude and the Prude*. By the end of the decade many filmmakers began offering movies that blended stag reel aesthetics with wacky, comic story lines, which became known as "nudie-cuties." The commercial success of Russ Meyer's *The Immoral Mr. Teas* (1959) and other pioneering nudie-cuties helped

Times Square become the fastest growing adult film market in America.[51] Films featuring copious nudity and simulated sex became increasingly explicit as local enforcement allowed, and thus as the 1960s progressed, nudie-cuties gave way to a wider variety of sexploitation films.

After *Jacobellis v. Ohio* in 1964 sex films moved relatively quickly in the direction of linear narrative despite decades of plotlessness. This rise of narrative likely "served a legitimizing function for pornographic films," the film scholar Eric Schaefer concludes, "because it was less of a stretch to argue that feature-length narratives contained social or artistic significance and therefore were not obscene under the *Jacobellis* standard."[52] Linda Williams, the author of *Hard-Core: Power, Pleasure, and the "Frenzy of the Visible,"* agrees that for lack of a plot, the film *Deep Throat* would likely have opened and closed at the New Mature World Theater in Times Square without so much as a curious glance from the mainstream audience that ended up making it a hot ticket during the summer of 1972. What made *Deep Throat* so memorable, Williams writes, was "precisely what most people disparaged about it: its 'threadbare,' 'poor excuse' for a plot. Yet in concentrating on this defect vis-à-vis other forms of narrative, critics missed the more important fact that the film had a plot at all, and a coherent one to boot, with the actions of characters more or less plausibly motivated."[53] The importance of the plot in *Deep Throat* thus should not be underestimated; for the first time a feature-length hard-core film had worked to integrate a series of sexual encounters into a full-length narrative that was screened in a legitimate theater.[54]

In the 1973 *New York Times* article where he coined the term *porno chic*, Ralph Blumenthal argued that *Deep Throat*'s plot—in which a woman discovers that her clitoris is in the back of her throat, and thus learns to achieve orgasm by performing a particularly intense brand of fellatio on the men she beds—was matched by frequent jokes and a catchy soundtrack. These factors, Blumenthal felt, helped endear *Deep Throat* to mainstream audiences. Specifically because of its sense of humor and its story line the film was a significant improvement "over the genre's ordinary offering, which all too often betrays the film maker's contempt for his audience: The sound is warped, the color thin and faded and grainy. And the story, well, there is really no story, just coupling—exhaustive, boring, mechanical, relentless minute-after-minute of poker-faced fornication in 'loops,' so-named for the splicing of the film into 10-minute repeating cycles." In comparison, Blumenthal argued, *Deep Throat* attempts to be comedic and has a surprisingly good soundtrack. These qualities, combined with the general permissiveness of the early 1970s, was "apparently enough to persuade a lot of people that there is no harm or shame in indulging their curiosity—and perhaps even their frankly prurient interest—by going to see 'Deep Throat.'"[55] The film's "legitimization" among middle-class audiences only snowballed through the summer as a result of frequent mentions in the media of the film itself and the many celebrities who began flocking to see it.

The fact that ticket prices for the film were far heftier than for typical pornographic fare at the time only increased interest.[56] When it first opened in Times Square, *Deep Throat* cost $5 per ticket. In response to the overwhelming demand for tickets, the manager at the New Mature World lowered the price to $3, figuring he'd make up in volume what he lost per person. Yet once he dropped the price of tickets, the gate slowed significantly. Clearly the more expensive it was, the more *Deep Throat* possessed an air of must-see exclusivity about it.[57]

*Deep Throat* became not only the cornerstone of the porno chic craze, but also a testament to the confusion that surrounded women's sexual pleasure at the time. Sex and sexuality were getting an enormous increase in cultural attention but continued to cause just as much confusion as they always had. This is especially the case when it came to the sexuality of women, which remained little understood through the mid-twentieth century.

Until sexologists like Alfred Kinsey and Masters and Johnson and feminist activists like Anne Koedt debunked them in studies published during the 1950s and 1960s, the most prevalent hypotheses about female sexuality were Freud's. Freud held that women were capable of both vaginal and clitoral orgasms, but that the former was superior to the latter; this reasoning allowed him to conclude that women who did not experience vaginal—or "true"—orgasms while engaging in sexual intercourse were not being fulfilled sexually, and were thus somehow not complete women.[58]

In the 2005 documentary *Inside Deep Throat* Gerard Damiano claims that he wrote and directed *Deep Throat* to show audiences that women were as capable as men of experiencing sexual pleasure, and on their own terms. His comment is quickly followed by a shot of the writer Erica Jong, who laughingly dismisses the film as a cheap male fantasy. Damiano and Jong are certainly not alone in disagreeing about the message of the film. *Deep Throat*, and the many pornographic narratives that followed it, were defended by civil libertarians, advocates of the First Amendment, and pro-pornography feminists who saw in them the reflection of a new cultural interest in women's sexual pleasure. Conversely, pornography was decried by religious groups, social conservatives, and, with increasing force in the late 1970s and early 1980s, antipornography feminists who saw in porn yet another institution founded on the debasement of women for the purpose of gratifying men.

*Deep Throat* itself is particularly complicated in its representation of sexuality and can thus be interpreted as degrading to women on the one hand and empowering on the other. As Linda Williams writes, "for all its talk about the clitoris" *Deep Throat* visually fetishizes the penis and can thus be read as a film that denies women "'natural' organic pleasure by imposing on them the perversion not merely of fellatio, but of this particular degrading, gagging, 'deep throat' variety."[59] Williams adds, however, that while she does "not question the importance for feminists to reject as inauthentic the pleasures of women portrayed in such films," *Deep Throat*'s reflection of "the new importance of the clitoris" in American culture is nevertheless profoundly important. The film's "solicitous concern for the location of the clitoris" needs "to be seen in the context of the relatively new prominence this organ has received in other forms of the *scientia sexualis*. This new knowledge views the clitoris precisely not as a diminished or absent version of the penis—as in Freud's account of the phallic economy of the one—but as a new economy not reducible to that one: an economy of the *many*, of 'diff'rent strokes for diff'rent folks.'" Although the film's focus on the phallus simultaneously "attempts to disavow difference at the moment of orgasm and to model that orgasm on a decidedly phallic model of 'bursting bombs,' and even though the woman is portrayed as dependent for her pleasure on the 'one' of the man, a contradictory subtext of plurality and difference is also registered." Finally, Williams notes, the "very fact that the expanded narrative of the new feature-length hard-core film parodically joins with the scientific, Masters and Johnson–style quest for the 'truth' of woman's difference indicates how fully the woman's invisible and unquantifiable pleasure has now been brought into frame, onto the scene of the obscene."[60]

Indeed during the trial that eventually labeled *Deep Throat* obscene in the State of New York, Judge Joel L. Tyler heard testimony from expert witnesses who, regardless of the side they represented, made the film's implied messages about female sexuality central to their arguments. In testifying for the defense, the film scholar and *Saturday Review* critic Arthur Knight argued that *Deep Throat* possessed redeeming social value because it had the potential to expand people's sexual horizons, and especially because it "showed sympathy for the idea that a woman's sexual gratification was as important as a man's."[61] Yet a psychiatrist named Max Levin argued for the prosecution that *Deep Throat* could be harmful to "normal men," who risked being blinded to "the true nature of female sexuality" upon viewing the film.

Levin elaborated that despite the insistences of contemporary "extremists, especially in women's liberation, who believe that anything other than clitoral orgasm is a male myth," he remained convinced that the "vaginal orgasm is superior to the clitoral." He believed, then, that *Deep Throat* was especially dangerous because it "might lead people to suppose that clitoral stimulation was the only way for women to reach orgasm."[62] Levin felt that *Deep Throat* was, in this respect, dangerous not only for men, but for women too, since any woman viewing the film was likely to think that "it is perfectly healthy, perfectly normal if you have a clitoral orgasm. That [it] is all the woman needs. She is wrong. She is wrong…and this film will strengthen her in her ignorance."[63] Levin's stance makes all too clear the fact that even after it had been roundly debunked, the myth of the vaginal orgasm remained deeply rooted in the culture of the time.

*Deep Throat* served as a cultural milestone because it appealed to the men *and* women of Middle America in a way that no explicit film had before. Yet its appeal also lay in the ways it reflected contemporary anxieties about women's sexual pleasure. The film, as well as the slew of hard-core films that followed fast on its heels, exerted immediate influence on many adult musicals. While this influence took both overt and subtle form, it almost always reflected the same ambivalence about female sexual pleasure exhibited in *Deep Throat*.

## LET MY PEOPLE COME (AGAIN)

In terms of the musical theater, the most overt homage to porno chic was *Let My People Come*, which began its run at the Village Gate in January 1974. Much to their credit, and in the spirit of inclusion that pervaded many aspects of this production, the all-male creative team of *Let My People Come* devised several numbers purporting to represent contemporary women's perspectives. Yet whereas the numbers "I'm Gay" and "Take Me Home with You," both of which represented aspects of contemporary gay male culture, emphasized gay men's struggles for equality and respect, those purportedly depicting the lives of contemporary women—"Give It to Me," "And She Loved Me," and "Come in My Mouth"—all prioritize sexual titillation over honest representation. These, as well as the number "Linda, Georgina, Marilyn and Me," also make at least cursory reference to the porno chic trend or to *Deep Throat* itself.

In keeping with the general approach to the writing of the revue, in which the cast held rap sessions that Earl Wilson Jr. would use to glean ideas for songs that he would later write with specific cast members in mind, the number "Give It to Me" was written for Lorraine Davidson, an aspiring opera singer who would eventually become a regular at the tiny Amato Opera house on the Lower East Side. Wilson remembers that Davidson was "very sexually liberated, sort of a women's libber. She had a certain look about her, with the dungaree jacket, open shirt, and an 'I'll take home anybody' kind of an attitude. So I came up with 'Give It To Me,' and I wrote it almost like it was a trucker kind of a song, and I gave it to her, and she was terrific with it."[64] Wilson here conflates the second wave with sexual excess; the association is reflected as well in the lyrics of the finished song.

The infectiously zippy country-western number "Give It to Me" immediately preceded "I'm Gay" in the original production of *Let My People Come*. In the song Davidson, accompanied by twangy, trebly electric guitar, voices her desire for a man who is terrific both in and out of bed. At first, the lyrics emphasize sexual pleasure:

I want a man who loves to fuck and can keep it up for days
Who's clever and smart and can make me come in a thousand different ways
I want a man who knows how to love and loves all that sex can be
And when he's driving me out of my mind, I wanna know he's fucking me

Give it to me, give it to me, give it to me, give it to me, give it to me hard and strong
Give it to me, give it to me, give it to me, give it to me, give it to me all night long
There's too many candy-assed lily-livered soft-bellied boys parading as men
Find me a man who's got some balls—I'll be happier then.[65]

🔊 Ex. 6.1

While the verses tend to focus on heterosexual lovemaking, the bridge ponders gender relationships in the midst of the second wave, albeit in the most general terms:

Let me tell you 'bout the way I am. My man has got to be my friend
I don't want somebody using me—that ain't the way it's gonna be
And if the man starts playing boss? Well, sister, that's his loss
Jack, you better just move on, 'cuz those days are dead and gone![66]

🔊 Ex. 6.2

Yet at the very end of the song the singer abruptly acknowledges that the women's movement is an exhausting uphill battle for any woman interested in more than good sex. In the final refrain a significant change is made to the very last line: "Find me a man who's got some balls—I'll be happier then" becomes "Find me a man who's got some balls—I'm tired of wearing them!" The singer thus segues, rather suddenly, from a woman whose empowerment is measured merely by how much she "loves to fuck" to a woman who is well aware that her desire for equality is all too often unfairly interpreted as "ball-busting," or emasculating. "Give It to Me" purports to offer a contemporary heterosexual woman's perspective on sexual desire and can thus certainly be read as empowering. The last line, however, can also be read as an abrupt surrender in the face of the grueling struggle for equal rights outside of the bedroom.[67]

"And She Loved Me," the sole number in *Let My People Come* to attempt to depict some aspect of contemporary lesbian culture, is similarly well-meaning, but ultimately framed to appeal specifically to the male gaze. As noted in chapter 2, Wilson conferred with several gay men before writing both "I'm Gay" and "Take Me Home with You." The cast contained several out gay men, and Wilson was working closely with the director and producer Phil Oesterman and the music director Billy Cunningham, both of whom were also gay and out. Yet as far as Wilson could glean, there were no lesbians in the cast, and so he turned instead to contemporary media representations in order to draw inspiration for "And She Loved Me." He recalls, "There was a scene in—was it *Killing of Sister George?* Some movie of the time that I had seen, that had a lesbian scene in it that I remembered. And I thought, 'I'm going to use that as my example in my head.' So I didn't talk to any lesbians, we didn't go through any of that. I saw it in my head, I thought, 'If I was writing that scene as a song, this is how I'd do it.'"[68]

Yet as Karen Hollinger points out, lesbian characters have traditionally been depicted through a highly critical heterosexual lens as "sinister villains, victims of mental illness, cultural freaks, or pornographic sexual turn-ons for a male audience."[69] The cult favorite *The Killing of Sister George* (1968) might have been noteworthy in offering numerous depictions of lesbians, but it was hardly a departure in terms of the nature of these depictions: its central character is an unhinged, alcoholic bully, and her lover is a doll-obsessed dimwit.

In *Let My People Come* the lyrics and original staging of "And She Loved Me" depicted lesbians primarily as a means to appeal to the male gaze. The number was sung by two fully clothed women flanking the stage, while two other women danced naked under soft light at center stage to give the impression of lovemaking. The fact that the women begin and end their lovemaking by gently weeping in one another's arms is indicative of Wilson's reliance on mainstream depictions of lesbian sex as forbidden and disruptive to the heteronormative order:

> And she loved me, oh
> Took me in her arms
> I softly cried
> Then she held me, oh
> Ran her fingers through my hair
> 'Til my tears had dried
> . . .

Then she woke me, oh, gently like a child
And I softly sighed
And I loved her, oh
Took her in my arms
And then we cried.[70]

The music accompanying the introductory passage and the concluding stanza reinforces the idea that the narrator has been resisting the ensuing love scene for some time, and that even when it finally commences it is not entirely free of anxiety. A soulful number performed by two alto voices that sing in tight, heavily ornamented harmonies, "And She Loved Me" begins haltingly, with long pauses between words, frequent melismas, and sparse chordal accompaniment on piano (🜋 Ex. 6.3). By the second stanza, during which the seductress kisses the narrator and "gently" touches her breast, the accompaniment speeds up significantly. The piano is joined by guitar, bass, and drums, and the women's vocal ranges widen broadly, frequently soaring into higher registers in emulation of increasingly enthusiastic lovemaking.

The piece ends somewhat ambiguously. In the last stanza the accompaniment falls away abruptly after the lyrics "And I softly sighed / And I loved her." Here, as in the introduction, the piece slows considerably, and the vocalists sing the lines "Took her in my arms / And then we cried" slowly and deliberately, with lengthy pauses between each word. The final word of the song, "cried," is sung repeatedly for almost a minute. The singers' voices climb as the accompaniment picks up again; the women sing faster and higher as "cried" shifts from a word symbolizing sorrow to one that is clearly celebratory. The song concludes a full octave higher than it began (🜋 Ex. 6.4).

In keeping with the overall message of Let My People Come, "And She Loved Me" strongly implies that consensual sex, no matter with whom, is good, wholesome fun and nothing to be ashamed of. And as the original cast member and assistant choreographer Tobie Columbus remembers, "And She Loved Me" was never intended to be anything but a reverent, "quite beautiful" commentary on the emotions that two women were experiencing while entering into a relationship that was still largely considered taboo.[71] In trying to capture the intensity of the number, Columbus attempted to make the accompanying dance less graphic than impressionistic:

The dance to "And She Loved Me" was a ballet, and there was no physical contact in that dance. It was about the women and what they felt for each other. There *was* an embrace, I think, at the very end. There *was* a moment that is a sexual illusion, but again, it was done artistically: One dancer does a full backbend and the other does what is known as a *ponche*... when one leg goes straight up in the air as your body is bending forward. So you have this moment where you have one dancer bending forward with her leg going straight up in the air, as simultaneously, the other woman does a backbend. So creating—you know, it would be like it was oral sex, but it wasn't physical in context.[72]

Nevertheless it is telling that the sole lesbian number was performed in the nude and featured women weeping, however joyfully, both before and after making love, while "I'm Gay" featured two fully clothed men who—after singing of their demand for love and respect without once baring their bodies or exhibiting concern that their sexual desires are worth fretting about, crying over, or resisting—were joined in cheery camaraderie by the full cast. In short, the staging of "And She Loved Me" emphasized naked women's bodies and implied that the women, however thrilled by their desire for one another, were also conflicted by what was ultimately treated as a transgression. In contrast, the far less complicated "I'm Gay" placed sole emphasis on the struggle for solidarity, equality, and acceptance.

The visual allusions in the choreography of "And She Loved Me" to cunnilingus were hardly unique in *Let My People Come*. The revue featured countless verbal and visual references to oral sex in sketches like the recurring "Fellatio 101"—in which the female cast members attend a workshop aimed at perfecting the technique, which they attempt on bananas, with widely mixed results—and in songs like "The Cunnilingus Champion of Company C" and the even less subtle "Come in My Mouth."

It is striking that oral sex was sung, joked, and talked about as openly and frequently as it was in *Let My People Come*, since it is mentioned only in passing, and even then usually as a transgressive kink, in *Oh! Calcutta!* a mere five years earlier. Clearly the impact of *Deep Throat* was still reverberating a full two years after the film premiered. As in *Deep Throat*, references to oral sex in *Let My People Come* initially seem, at least on the surface, to be carefree and uncomplicated.

Tobie Columbus and Daina Darzin embrace one another while Shezwae Powell and Peachena sing "And She Loved Me" from *Let My People Come*. Courtesy of Photofest.

Yet in interviews Earl Wilson Jr. acknowledged experiencing enormous anxiety in writing and staging *Let My People Come*. In an extensive discussion with Bruce David, the managing editor of *Hustler*, Wilson noted that he was frequently surprised by his own ability to write lyrics and sketches that were as "outrageous" as he felt they were, especially since he considered himself to be a very conservative man. "I wrote a show with the basic premise that sex, like anything else, should be open and honest," Wilson told David. "If the things we did with our lives were more open and honest, there'd be a lot less nonsense in this world....I don't try to inflict my conservatism on what I write because I'm writing from different points of view. Obviously, if I'm writing a show about sex, I could not possibly write from every point of view and treat it as my own. But I have to accept all the others out there because that's what the subject matter is."[73]

Later in the same interview Wilson argues that his anxieties and conservatism make him the perfect representative for his production since he relates so strongly to its mainstream audience. Most spectators, he suspects, are just as terrified of the changing sexual mores as he is. In response to a comment by David about how repressed the 1950s were and how frightened most people were of sex at the time, Wilson says, "I think that's still true, by and large, for the world today. I think we wear the guise of being sexually liberated, but the basic fears are still there." He adds, "we are all still very much like we were thousands of years ago. I think we are very repressed."[74] Indeed many of the numbers in *Let My People Come* reflect genuine unease about sexual pleasure and practices in the newly permissive world, especially as they relate to female pleasure.

To take but one example, *Let My People Come* features a showy, vaudeville-inspired musical number titled "Linda, Georgina, Marilyn and Me," which is an homage to porno chic. The character who sings it is a blithely hapless everywoman who aspires to be a porn star. Clearly more awed than she is aroused by the sexual exploits being enacted on the silver screen, the singer admits that she is not built like Linda Lovelace, Georgina Spelvin, or Marilyn Chambers. This, however, doesn't deter her; she argues that her *zaftig* figure would only be an asset:

> What have they got I haven't got more of?
> What they can take two of, I can take four of!
> It costs more money when your actors are lean
> It only takes one of me to fill up your screen![75]

Nor is her clunky given name a problem; she'll simply change it to something befitting her porn star aspirations:

> Maybe I oughta change my name
> To something more easily spoken, or sung
> Sally Strikermeyer isn't destined for fame
> How about Clitoris Leachman, or Tallulah Tongue?[76]

Yet midway through the song Sally begins to reflect some of the anxiety that Wilson describes. The lyrics even betray a touch of revulsion toward the hypersexual antics displayed in contemporary porn flicks:

I've seen every picture, I know every line
Linda Lovelace is an idol of mine
She shoulda got the Oscar, she was the best
It woulda been a little sticky, I guess.

Marilyn Chambers is really quite skilled
I tried her act and I almost got killed
I couldn't master what she does with ease
It's hard on the throat, not to mention the knees
And I kept falling off the fucking trapeze!

I've been delvin' into Georgina Spelvin
Along with everyone else I guess
. . .

There's nothin' niftier than a boa constrictior within your grasp
*The Devil in Miss Jones* shook me to my bones
But I don't wanna be just another piece of asp!

I can see it all now: Sally Strikermeyer, starring in *Sore Throat!*[77]

🔊 Ex. 6.5

Sally may be dazzled at first by the porn stars she watches on the silver screen. After all, their particular talents—elevating the art of fellatio to something approaching sword-swallowing; servicing several men while swinging on a trapeze; engaging in casual foreplay with a deadly reptile—are certainly noteworthy at a time when, Williams reminds us, oral sex was still "an exotic, even forbidden practice" in the minds of many Americans and thus representative of "the very idea of sexual exploration espoused by the then-expanding 'sexual revolution.'"[78] As Bruce David points out during his interview with Wilson, despite the popularity of *Deep Throat*, oral sex was still something of a taboo even by *Hustler* standards.[79]

For Sally—and thus for Wilson, and no doubt for a wide swath of the population—such practices, while perhaps stimulating to watch, are also potentially anxiety-provoking. Are unfamiliar, even complicated sexual antics part and parcel with liberation? Does it make us prudes if we don't instantly embrace them?

The unease Wilson admitted regarding the subject matter of his own show was shared by many members of the company of *Let My People Come*, who remember feeling pressure to prove that they were sexually liberated once they were cast in the show. While plenty of men in the original company—and in other adult musicals—have noted in interviews that they initially felt, at the very least, somewhat self-conscious about appearing naked onstage, their anxieties tended to pale in comparison with those experienced by female cast members.[80] Tobie Columbus, for example, was never comfortable performing the number "Come in My Mouth," which she remains, decades later, notably ambivalent about.

One of the most sexually explicit numbers in a show that banked its reputation on sexual explicitness, "Come in My Mouth" was written on a dare before there was a cast, or even a show. Wilson remembers:

I'm in New York, I'm still trying to be a singer. I've got some club dates, but it's rough. I don't know what I'm doing, I'm trying to write, I'm trying to sing. [Phil Oesterman] calls me on the phone, and says, "I'm coming to New York...and we're going to write a show...about sex." I said, "You want me to write a show about *sex*? I could never do that. I'm a nice, clean guy, are you kidding?" and he said, "Well I know you better than that. You're not so clean, number one, and number two, it's not gonna be dirty. It's gonna be honest." I said, "What about *Oh! Calcutta!*" which was a big hit. And he said, "*Oh! Calcutta!* is a dirty show. It makes you feel dirty when you leave it....This will not be that way. This will...have a young attitude, not an old attitude."...So I said, "What do you want me to do?" He said, "Write the most outrageous song you can think of, and call me back." So I wrote "Come in My Mouth."[81]

When Wilson played a tape of the finished song for Oesterman, he recalls, "he and I were hysterical. It was so outrageous that we could not imagine anyone actually singing the words."[82] Yet someone did: "Come in My Mouth" was crooned nightly into a microphone by Columbus, who sat center-stage, clad in a slinky red dress and bathed in the light of a single pin-spot.

Whereas much of the content of *Let My People Come* was satirical—relatively serious declarations of sexual freedom like "I'm Gay" and "And She Loved Me" notwithstanding—"Come in My Mouth" was meant to be erotic from the onset. The song, as well as the way it was performed, borrow a great deal from aural techniques that contributed to the overall aesthetic of early 1970s porn films.

In "Come in My Mouth" the singer describes the fellatio she professes to have been waiting all day to perform on her partner. Accompanied by a mechanical ostinato and the same ethereal, synthesized noodlings that are highly representative of just about every porn soundtrack ever composed, the singer softly, lavishly praises her man, all the while asserting his dominance over her:

All day long I've been planning on how I was going to love you tonight
So I could show you how I absolutely adore you. So you know I am your woman
. . .
Run your fingers through my hair as you force my mouth to open wide
Don't you just love it there as I drink you deep inside?
I can feel all your strength. What would you like me to do?
I'll take you inch by inch—just let me worship you.
Fill me up so deep, you're touching my soul.

🎵 Ex. 6.6
As the singer coaxes her partner to orgasm, the tempo of the ostinato picks up and the improvisational line on the synthesizer climbs several octaves, mimicking sexual ecstasy. The singer herself erupts in orgasmic, panted moans as the accompaniment slows and fades out and the song ends.

The primal reaction of the female singer at the end of "Come in My Mouth" is typical of much hard-core porn. This is certainly the case in *Deep Throat*, which regularly depicts the orgasms that Lovelace's character experiences during fellatio by crosscutting close-ups of her sexual handiwork with footage of fireworks exploding, bells ringing, and bombs bursting.[83] Yet *Deep Throat* is hardly unique in featuring fellatio, which Williams cites as traditionally "the most photogenic of all sexual practices" in adult films. Rather what was striking about *Deep Throat*, and what is clearly emulated in "Come in My Mouth," is the attempt to find "a visual equivalent for the invisible moments of clitoral orgasm."[84]

Whereas male arousal is visually obvious—and the "money shot," or close-up of an ejaculating penis, thus endlessly fetishized in hard-core pornography as proof of sexual satisfaction—the female orgasm is complicated to render visually. *Deep Throat*'s attempt at reflecting female sexual pleasure may be especially perverse, but it nevertheless reflects the onset of a struggle "to recognize, as the proliferating discourses of sexuality take hold, that there can no longer be any such thing as a fixed sexuality—male, female, or otherwise—that now there are proliferating sexualities."[85] As Corbett and Kapsalis point out in "Aural Sex: The Female Orgasm in Popular Sound," sound is often used to compensate for a lack of visual evidence. "Within mainstream pornography and mass culture alike," they argue, "where male sexual pleasure is accompanied by what Williams calls the 'frenzy of the visible,' female sexual pleasure is better thought of in terms of a 'frenzy of the audible.' Sound becomes the proof of female pleasure in the absence of its clear visual demonstration."[86]

The orgasmic moans elicited by the singer at the end of "Come in My Mouth" can only imply a money shot, not just because the song is performed by a woman, but because the revue it appeared in relied on simulated, and never actual, sex. Thus the orgasm the singer causes her male partner to experience is transmitted to spectators via her cries. "Come in My Mouth" ends with the female singer moaning loudly before the audience not only because she is reflecting the orgasm she has elicited from her male lover, but also, presumably, to ease the anxieties of an audience eager for some indication that she too enjoyed the sexual transaction.

Yet conveying sexual pleasure in front of an audience was in fact particularly difficult for Columbus, who viewed performing "Come in My Mouth" as "the scariest thing in the whole world. But that's why they cast me in the show....It was the first song written, the song that really got Earl started with this whole show....He told me exactly what it was supposed to be and what it was supposed to sound like....It was supposed to be every man's fantasy....What is a man's fantasy, whether he's gay or straight?" Yet Wilson's direction and regular assurances did little to make Columbus feel at ease when performing the song. "You know," she explains, "I was brought up a nice Jewish girl, and this wasn't something that I did! This was *dirty*! But I couldn't say, 'Oh, my God! I can't sing *that*! That's *dirty*!' This was the swinging seventies! You were supposed to be enlightened! You were supposed to be hip! You were not supposed to say, 'I don't do that—that's a man's fantasy...not a woman's fantasy!'" As a result, when it came to performing in the show, everything else Columbus did, including simulating sex and dancing naked, "was more comfortable" for her than singing "Come in My Mouth."[87]

While "Come in My Mouth" was Columbus's cross to bear, several female cast members recalled similar discomforts while with the show. Joanne Baron, who appeared in the revue after Columbus had left and who sang "Linda, Georgina, Marilyn and Me," remembers having "a lot of psychological trouble...being—at any point in the piece—naked. I found it frightening, confusing." The anxiety was compounded by Baron's sense of constant pressure "to loosen up, to be open to other people sexually. Not in any kind of overtly, overly aggressive way, but the tone of it was, you know, 'You have this great body, you're real sexy, don't be so scared of your sexuality.'" Her anxiety was particularly acute when friends and family members came to see her in the show. "I remember my mother came to the show," she laughs, "and I asked everyone if I could not take any of my clothing off that night because I was so horrified. The long and the short of it is, I was like a New England-kind-of-straight-A-student prude who suddenly became a well-paid...single girl who had just hit New York....I was still sort of in a state of mind that was somewhat like a good girl who had chanced upon this more free lifestyle. It wasn't a perfect psychological fit."[88]

Other women remember feeling pressured to appear naked onstage, whether or not they were willing to do so and despite the company's "nudity-optional" policy. For example, the original company member who appeared under the sole name Peachena refused to join the cast unless her contract stipulated that she would not have to remove her clothing during the run. The contract was granted, but Peachena remains convinced that her abrupt dismissal once the contract expired a year later was based solely on her refusal to disrobe and has never been given any reason to believe otherwise.[89] Tobie Columbus remembers, "If I could have stood my ground and said, look, I don't wanna be nude, I think I probably would have, but I could never voice that...because doing that would have been unhip, and I knew that I was there to be nude. And I think I would have lost my job."[90]

These experiences, which were hardly unique to *Let My People Come*, indicate that while many women during the 1970s were attempting to reject traditional values in favor of more control over their bodies, the sexual revolution's emphasis on uninhibited, detached sexuality nevertheless often resulted in widespread pressure for women to either conform to male sexual standards or appear prudish, uptight, and repressed.[91] The turmoil of the times and the barrage of conflicting social messages that adult musicals were ostensibly promoting often proved confusing for cast and company members, some of whom were simply intent on working a job. For all the messages of inclusion in *Let My People Come* and its creators' interest in depicting sexuality honestly and openly, distinctions between sexual freedom and exploitation were thus often lost behind the scenes not only of that production, but of many adult musicals.

For example, many performers, both in *Let My People Come* and in *Oh! Calcutta!*, recall ignoring or knowing others who ignored the "no sex" policy imposed by producers, some of whom openly disregarded it themselves. Raina Barrett, an original *Oh! Calcutta!* cast member, writes that some of her fellow cast members violated the production's "No Fuck Law" within hours of the very first rehearsal.[92] She also remembers that the sexual freedom *Oh! Calcutta!* supposedly celebrated did not extend to all parties; despite the company's purported disgust at Tynan's homophobia, one particularly standoffish male actor was so regularly provoked, taunted, and pigeon-holed as a "fag" by his castmates that he left the production. Meanwhile, during rehearsals, the female cast members were subject to "trust" exercises, during which they were to kiss and fondle one another and then talk at length with the male director about how they felt. These "lesbian rehearsals" were apparently deemed necessary so that female cast members would appear at ease with one another onstage, but no similar exercises were ever conducted among male cast members.[93] Clearly lesbian overtones were acceptable and even desired in *Oh! Calcutta!*, as they are in countless entertainment properties aimed primarily at straight male audiences, because they fueled heterosexual male fantasies in ways that sex between men did not.

The distinctions between liberation and exploitation seem to have been blurred not only by companies of adult musicals, but by audiences as well. Visitors to *Let My People Come*, for example, included Betty Friedan, who appreciated the show's upbeat, positive messages about sex, and Larry Flynt and Hugh Hefner, both of whom devoted ample space for pictorials of the show in their magazines and invited several female cast members to pose individually.[94] An anecdote that points especially acutely to the blurring of women's liberation and continued exploitation is offered by Barry Pearl, who joined *Let My People Come* as an understudy in 1973. As he recalls, before the show began, the cast would walk into the audience, fully clothed, and mingle with spectators. This helped break the ice and make the patrons comfortable, "because at the very end of the show, the very end, after the last number, now we're all naked, and we now go down into the audience again in a receiving line, as the audience leaves, and we shake hands, standing there, perfectly, totally, bare naked. So there was the full circle, but without clothes." Yet by the time Pearl joined the company, "most if not all of the women at that point remained on the lip of the stage, with some guys just sitting there, naked, protecting them, because they'd gotten groped too many times through the course of the run, and so they'd decided to have the ladies stay on the stage. Only men, basically, were in that receiving line."[95]

Yet despite widespread ambivalence, many female performers describe their experiences in adult musicals as generally positive ones. Boni Enten, an original cast member of *Oh! Calcutta!*, looks back fondly on her experiences with the show: "For me, it was enlightening, liberating. I was 24, and I had not really been that open about sex, or a man's body, or even my own body. So this was a real educational, growth experience. And it was really fun, and it was in a safe environment."[96] Despite her discomfort with "Come in My Mouth," Tobie Columbus's experiences with *Let My People Come* solidified her belief in "sexually being who you are, and not judging anybody else's sexuality," a message that she remains proud to have been able to convey to audiences.[97] And despite her concerns about appearing naked onstage, Joanne Baron says, "[*Let My People Come* was] a fantastic lot of fun, and a great creative experience, and I met wonderful people, so I can't say I regret it."[98]

This particular brand of uncertainty, in which women look back on their experiences in adult musicals as simultaneously exhilarating and confusing, embarrassing and liberating, freeing and exploitative, is prevalent among former female cast members of adult musicals. It implies that not even the actors advocating increased sexual freedom onstage nightly eight times a week were entirely comfortable with the changing times or with the ways contradictory messages about and for women were interpreted in such drastically different ways by different people. After all, ambivalence may be, in the end, the healthiest reaction to a production that paid young actors to cheerfully disrobe and simulate a wide variety of sex acts—while singing!— before audiences including as many Betty Friedans as Larry Flynts.

# CHAPTER 7

# Hell Freezes Over: The Hard-Core Musical on Stage and Screen

Look at all that hard-core crap. People don't need to go to the movies to see hard-core! They want something new . . . something different. They don't want to see any more licking. They've seen enough licking pictures! Genitalia? It's *boring*! But *singing* genitalia? Gentlemen, come on . . . this can revolutionize the business!
—*The First Nudie Musical*

M uch like *Let My People Come,* the 1977 films *Alice in Wonderland: An X-Rated Musical Fantasy* and *The First Nudie Musical,* as well as the 1976 Marilyn Chambers revue, *Le Bellybutton,* reflect the influence both of porno chic and of the second wave of feminism. Yet while these pieces acknowledge—and even at times manage to celebrate—the newly liberated woman, the messages they contain about feminist ideology tend to be lost to the jiggle of naked bodies that was often the real selling point for adult musicals. This chapter continues to examine the shifting lines between art and obscenity, with specific attention to the spread of the porno chic aesthetic into both mainstream film and the adult musical through the mid- to late 1970s.

Once it became legal, full length, narrative, and in vogue, Williams writes, the "new" pornographic film became

> more a genre among other genres than it was a special case. As if to insist on this fact, hard-core narratives went about imitating other Hollywood genres with a vengeance, inflicting well-known titles and genres with an X-rated difference. Films with titles such as *Sexorcist Devil* (1974), *Beach Blanket Bango* (1975), *Flesh Gordon* (1978), *Dracula Sucks* (1979), *Downstairs Upstairs* (1980), and *Urban Cowgirls* (1981) were now exhibited in movie theaters that looked—almost—like other movie theaters. Stories, too, were almost like other film stories. Audiences, though disproportionately male, were also becoming more like other film audiences.[1]

In a new quest for legitimacy hard-core films placed new emphasis on plot and genre, thereby entering what is largely considered its golden age.

The gradual transition to hard-core pornography, which derives its name from the *Roth* ruling discussed in chapter 6, was partly due to the rise in popularity and accessibility of 16mm film.[2] This was embraced by avant-garde and experimental filmmakers, and thus by the New Left and the counterculture, in the late 1960s.[3] The film scholar Eric Schaefer argues that the importance of 16mm film to the rise of the hard-core feature should not be underestimated; it became strongly associated with "freer sexual expression and social change," and thus a general social progressiveness, both among people within the film industry and among those chronicling it.[4]

Indeed quite a few actors and directors felt strongly that making hard-core films was making art; this is especially the case during an era when, the critic Richard Corliss recalls, "sexually urgent films were made for thinking adults," avant-garde and mainstream films were becoming increasingly explicit, and soft- and hard-core features were screened at celebrated film festivals like Cannes and the New York Film Festival.[5] As pornography and mainstream film edged closer to one another, a number of aspiring actors, directors, and producers became convinced that making adult films was the wave of the future, and thus their key to respectable, successful careers.

The documentary *Inside Deep Throat* features several people commenting on the artistic aspirations they brought to the hard-core scene in the early 1970s. Ron Wertheim, a writer and director who served as the production manager on *Deep Throat*, points out during his interview that hard-core pornography was "the only choice we had": "Twenty-four years old without a—what do you call it—a track record, no? And these things were so inexpensive. I meant *business*! I approached those films as if I was Luc Godard or somebody!"[6]

*Deep Throat*'s director, Gerard Damiano, had similar aspirations. After the film's success he was unwilling to do interviews with people who wanted to talk to him as a porn film director. "But if anyone wanted to speak to me because I made *films*, then I was happy to."[7] Wes Craven, who managed to cross into the Hollywood mainstream as a director of horror movies, acknowledges getting his start in hard-core films, although he remains cagey about it. "For a while there, it was kinda like the entry-level job that you would do," he says in *Inside Deep Throat*. "You would work on—on porn. I certainly worked on 'em. I'm not gonna say which ones, but I was around it."[8]

The two largest production centers for hard-core narratives in the early 1970s were San Francisco and New York City, and the films often reflected the attitudes and aesthetics of their respective towns. Corliss writes that San Francisco hard-core tended to reflect a "grainy, cinema-verite style and a behavioral openness" that seemed reminiscent of the Summer of Love and often featured performers whose attitudes were appropriately loose and freewheeling. The New York scene, on the other hand, was "slicker," "edgier," and "more professional," largely because the fashion and theater industries are also based in New York, and many models, actors, and directors sought to cross into adult films and then back again.[9] This was especially true of performers who, while struggling to support careers in the theater, realized just how lucrative work in the adult realm could be. The *Deep Throat* star Harry Reems and the *Opening of Misty Beethoven* star Jamie Gillis, for example, both began doing porn loops in the early 1970s as a means of paying rent while working for little or no pay Off Off Broadway.[10] David Newburge, the playwright and lyricist for *Stag Movie*, worked through the late 1970s as a script writer for porn films; one of his movies, *Big Thumbs* (1977), which he showed me on videocassette one afternoon in 2006, featured a veritable who's who of Off Broadway actors, including Jamie Gillis.[11] And *The Devil in Miss Jones* star Georgina Spelvin came to New York as Shelley Graham, an aspiring ballerina. She worked regularly until her midthirties, when, deemed too old to be a chorus girl, she took the title role of Justine Jones, which she remembers approaching very seriously. "I had all kinds of backstory on who she was, where she came from, everything that had happened to her," she recalls with a chuckle. "I was doing *Hedda Gabler* here . . . ! The fact that there was hard-core sex involved was incidental as far as I was concerned. . . . I was showing true life as it really was—including actual sex as it really happened—instead of the phony stuff that you got from Hollywood. That was my raison d'etre throughout the whole thing."[12]

These actors were hardly unique in their serious approach to hard-core films, which, at least for a while, were reviewed in mainstream periodicals, screened in mainstream movie theaters, and consumed by mainstream audiences. The feeling in the air, Corliss writes, "was that there might be a meeting of pornography, which had quickly established a kind of artistic pedigree, and Hollywood, which was striding toward explicit sexuality"; or, as Gerard Damiano said in 1973, "If it's left alone, within a year sex will just blend itself into film. It's inevitable."[13] Damiano turned out to be wrong, of course; soon enough the mainstream turned its back on hard-core, and many of the films that were inspired by the experimental spirit of the times seem inconceivably dated when viewed some four decades later.

## PORN-MUSICAL HYBRIDS

In an extended comparison Linda Williams traces the narrative development of 1970s pornographic film by likening it to the film musical, which she argues is the film genre most similar to hard-core, at least in structural and aesthetic terms. Both musical numbers and sex scenes can be read as expressions of desire or fulfillment. Aural and visual variety in both genres is at once hugely important and ultimately particularly formulaic: masturbation scenes in porn can be compared with solo numbers in musicals; heterosexual or lesbian couplings with duets; ménages à trois with trios; orgy scenes with big production numbers.[14] The narrative aspects of both genres, endlessly ridiculed as being secondary to the musical numbers or the sex scenes, are nonetheless intrinsic to the ways each genre resolves "the often contradictory desires of its characters."[15] While many genres deal in escapism, hard-core narratives and musicals rely on especially fantastical, utopian scenarios; just as, in the musical, characters frequently express emotion by suddenly bursting, alone or in groups, into song or dance without the slightest hint of embarrassment, hard-core films occupy a world in which characters, regardless of the scenario, would sooner tear off their clothing and go at it—again, alone or in groups—than chat, usually without embarrassment, fear of punishment or guilt, or concern for what passersby might think.[16] Finally, both genres typically rely on some variation of the classic battle of the sexes for their plots, and while the resolution often involves compromise from both sides, its terms are ultimately the man's: the guy gets the girl in the end, thereby reminding audiences of that which is "typical of women's position within a phallogocentric symbolic system."[17] Yet while her list of similarities is compelling, Williams does not take into account some of the more important ways the two genres differ from one another, almost all of which lie in the realm of audience expectation.

As noted in chapter 1, most staged adult musicals were written in revue format. Thus while adult musicals were certainly aesthetically influenced by hard-core films, their structures tend not to allow for much in the way of comparison. Yet two adult musicals, both of which involved many cast and creative team members with extensive experience in the musical theater, were released as commercial films in the mid-1970s. Although each had very different production and reception histories, *Alice in Wonderland: An X-Rated Musical Fantasy* and *The First Nudie Musical,* both of which were released in 1976, inadvertently demonstrate that for all the similarities Williams identifies, and for all the theorizing about how the mainstream and adult film worlds would inevitably merge, musicals and porn make for particularly strange bedfellows.

### Alice in Wonderland: An X-Rated Musical Fantasy

The first of what seems to be very few narrative, feature-length, pornographic adult musicals to be released as commercial films was a sexed-up conflation of Lewis Carroll's *Alice's Adventures in Wonderland* and *Through the Looking-Glass.*[18] *Alice in Wonderland: An X-Rated Musical Fantasy*, which opened nationwide in 1976, starred the Ford model and *Playboy* centerfold Kristine De Bell. Musical numbers were composed by the television writer Bucky Searles and orchestrated by Peter Matz, who was Barbra Streisand's arranger, the music director for *The Carol Burnett Show* between 1971 and 1978, and an arranger or orchestrator on dozens of Broadway shows that ran between the 1950s and the early 2000s. *Alice* was released in both soft- and hard-core versions, with X and XXX ratings, respectively; it was re-released some years later with an R rating and the subtitle *An Adult Musical Comedy.* A ceaselessly cheery paean to the swinging 1970s, *Alice in Wonderland* serves as a textbook example of how, despite their many similarities, musicals and hard-core porn don't mix. It also serves as a testament to the fact that during the second wave, female empowerment was often easily conflated with the patriarchal ideals inherent in the sexual revolution.

*Alice*'s opening song is indicative of its composer and orchestrator's work in the musical theater and in 1970s television. It begins with a loud quotation, on brass, of the first seven notes of Rodgers and Hammerstein's "Younger than Springtime." It then segues into an abbreviated AABB format that features an upbeat verse section sparsely accompanied by woodwinds and vibraphone; this gives way to an even bouncier, more densely arranged chorus that favors brass.[19] The lyrics, smoothly sung by a Paul Williams sound-alike, are descriptive of the seize-the-day potential of the self-actualized "new woman," but in only the vaguest possible sense. In this respect they are highly reminiscent of lyrics to theme songs from such 1960s and 1970s "new woman"–themed television shows as *That Girl*, *Alice*, *One Day at a Time*, and *The Mary Tyler Moore Show*:

> Where are you going, girl
> Are you looking for a rainbow in the sky?
> You keep on going, girl
> There's a chance you can catch it if you try
> So still believe in Humpty Dumptys, Tweedledee and Tweedledumdies
> They'll all be there to help you find a way
>
> There's a whole new world that's looking for you out there girl
> Get out there, girl, and give that world a chance
> You'll find that things are really cooking for you out there, girl
> It's up to you to come and join the dance.

In the case of *Alice in Wonderland*, the "whole new world" is a purely sexual one. Throughout the film Alice meets a cast of characters, almost always male, who repeatedly scoff at her refusal to conform to the ideologies of the late 1960s sexual revolution.

The first character to argue with Alice over her reluctance to "join the dance" is her beau, William. In the opening scene Alice, a librarian, is busily shelving books when William stops by to ask her out after work. She demurs: she is very busy, and furthermore, she reminds William, "I'm just not that kind of girl." William storms out, and Alice picks up a copy of *Alice in Wonderland*, which she realizes she has never read. After singing the wistful ballad "Guess I Was Too Busy Growing Up," about how much she has missed in her rush toward adulthood, she looks up to find a man dressed in a bunny suit, who informs her somewhat contradictorily that she can grow up if she wants to, and then rushes off. Alice follows him through a nearby mirror and finds herself in a house that is too small to exit from. A potion marked "Drink Me" rectifies the situation and also causes her to shrink, conveniently, out of her clothes.

She wanders into a wooded area, where most of the rest of the film takes place. As she revels in the beauty of the natural world, which serves throughout the film as a metaphor for the wholesome sanctity of sex, she falls into a stream. She is rescued by two women and a man dressed as furry woodland creatures who sing a lively verse-chorus number with a refrain on nonsense syllables and lyrics about using your imagination. Because the wide-eyed innocents, not to mention the song they sing, would fit easily into any episode of *Sesame Street*, it is somewhat jarring when, in response to Alice's request for a towel, they begin to lick her body dry. Alice tells them to stop, because "if it feels good, it must be bad." "Alice," the male woodland creature chides, "if it feels good, it *is* good. Learn to trust yourself!"

After taking leave of the woodland creatures, Alice stops to rest. Overcome by the beauty of her surroundings, she begins to masturbate, despite initial resistance because she feels that what she is doing is "not nice." To her surprise, the rock she is sitting on tells her that it *is* nice, and thus, with the encouragement of this male disembodied voice, Alice brings herself to orgasm. She soon meets the Mad Hatter, who is appalled to learn that she is a virgin. She protests, "[I'm] trying to learn, honestly, but I can't have everything shoved down my throat at once." Hatter cannot see why not, however, and thus convinces her to fellate him.

Alice, the Hatter, and the Rabbit happen upon Humpty Dumpty, who has fallen off the wall and can no longer get an erection. An ensemble number lamenting this fact, "His Dingaling Up," ends as two nurses strip and fall to the ground for the first of several "obligatory lesbian" scenes.[20] Humpty Dumpty is cured of his impotence when Alice fellates him, whereupon the characters do a celebratory hora and sing a manic refrain of "His Dingaling Up" while the lyrics appear on the screen, complete with a bouncing ball encouraging spectators to sing along.

Tweedledum and Tweedledee, here played by a man and a woman clad in blue and white tank tops and beanies, greet Alice by singing about how nice it is to meet new people. Save for the fact that both characters are naked from the waist down, they, like the woodland creatures, would not be out of place on a children's television program. Alice sits on an oversized rocking chair, clutching a Raggedy Ann doll and watching Tweedledum and Tweedledee make love. Immediately after the resultant money shot, she cheerfully joins them on their blanket and sings a song about how she too must find herself "a someone who is mine."

The Mad Hatter, Alice, and the Rabbit next happen upon a lady vigorously riding a knight beneath a tree. When confronted by the shocked Alice, the couple calmly inform her that having sex in a public place is simply wonderful. A big ensemble number to this effect, "What's a Nice Girl Like You Doing on a Knight Like This?," takes place behind, in front of, and around the copulating pair, until the knight, without missing a proverbial stroke, brings the number home with a solo sung in a particularly exaggerated, vibrato-heavy baritone.

At the royal court Alice is greeted by a group of chorines in sheer black and red body stockings whose dance number is strongly inspired by Bob Fosse. Alice meets the King, who immediately propositions her. When she informs him that she would prefer to remain a virgin until she marries, the king scoffs, "You've been listening to a lot of other people, and not hearing yourself." Here, as throughout the film, a sharp distinction is made between those who are sexually liberated and everyone else. Like all of the other (male) characters in Wonderland, the King pities Alice for not thinking as they do; the "other people" that he so witheringly refers to are those who disagree with the ideology of the sexual revolution.

The Queen arrives and demands that Alice perform cunnilingus on her ("gimme some head") or die ("off with your head"). Alice refuses and is put on trial. If she loses, she is told, she must service the Queen; if she is found innocent, she must fellate the judge. A big song-and-dance production number kicks off the trial and dissolves into an orgy as Alice is found guilty.

Alice is prepared for the Queen by two ladies-in-waiting, who initiate a ménage à trois. The Queen arrives and leads Alice away as the ladies-in-waiting continue to make love nearby. As with many lesbian scenes featured in 1970s pornographic narratives, this sequence serves not as a culmination but merely "a warm-up or rehearsal for a 'better,' more satisfying number that will follow."[21] Indeed when the Queen

The ladies-in-waiting and the court jester (Bradford Armdexter) do a Fosse-inspired number in the film *Alice in Wonderland: An X-Rated Musical Fantasy.* Courtesy of Photofest.

takes a postcoital nap, Alice flees. A chase ensues; the furry woodland creatures reappear and push Alice into the stream they fished her out of at the start of the film. Alice, now back in the library, is awakened by a concerned William, with whom she initiates sex. Although this is the only indoor scene in the film to feature sexual activity, it segues immediately into the closing sequence, which features Alice and William skinny-dipping in and frolicking along the same stream that was prominently featured in Wonderland. Alice has listened to her male Wonderland companions, and, no longer an "uptight" virgin, she is happier and freer for it.

Like many 1970s pornographic films, *Alice* was reviewed in the mainstream press. In the *New York Times* Richard Eder came up with a special subdivision of porno chic especially for the film, which he dubbed "Porno Cute."[22] Roger Ebert for the *Chicago Sun Times* was forthright about how surprised he was to like the film, which he found to be "a genuine curiosity: An X-rated musical comedy that actually has some wit and style to it."[23] Yet in a sign that porno chic was rapidly wearing out its welcome among established members of the mainstream critical corps, both Eder and Ebert noted that they enjoyed *Alice* precisely because it failed as pornography. Ebert especially emphasized that despite his low expectations, he found *Alice* to be "a pleasant surprise," largely because it was "mild, as X movies go."

When *Alice* was released on DVD in 2007 the reviews from both mainstream and adult critical camps reflected a change in sensibility. At least when it comes to pornography, many modern critics seem to have comparatively little patience for well-meaning experiments in hybridity. In a rundown of films based on the Lewis

Carroll books, Jeremy Martin for the *San Antonio Current* found the musical numbers *and* sex scenes sorely lacking. "'His Ding-a-Ling Up' is about what you'd expect for a late-'70s Wonderland-themed porn musical, but the wistful 'Guess I Was Too Busy Growing Up' gets ding-a-ling-deflatingly sentimental, and 'If You Haven't Got Dreams, You Ain't Got Nothing' sounds like a *Barney & Friends* reject," Martin gripes. "That last song…is sung by several way-too-in-character people dressed as some sort of rodent…before they lick Alice's naked body dry….The actual porn scenes, incidentally, are virtually unmasturbatable….Skip the sex scenes to get to the musical numbers. I can't believe I just said that."[24]

Similarly Casey Scott, writing for the online DVD-review site dvdrive-in.com, called the score "silly" and "unmemorable" and the hard-core scenes "a real travesty: none of the sex is erotic [and] the pacing slows to a crawl." He concluded that *Alice* functions best as "a fun, silly sexploitation film," but that those looking for something sexually titillating will be sorely disappointed.[25] Yet contemporary expectations about the aesthetics of hard-core pornography aside, some of the frustrations with *Alice* result from the ways the defining ingredients of the two genres it borrows from—musical numbers in musicals and sex scenes in porn films—are frequently placed in direct competition with one another.

As scholars like Andrea Most, Raymond Knapp, and Scott McMillin have pointed out, the American musical has long relied on the ensemble to represent inclusiveness and community.[26] This sense of inclusiveness is typically extended to the musical's audience: big ensemble numbers, and especially finales, often feature entire companies facing the audience, arms outstretched, encouraging spectators to take pleasure in the sense of community that the cast has cultivated. In musical theater happy endings—and even, in cases like *West Side Story,* sad ones—often depend on the strength of the ensemble, which literally or figuratively surrounds and supports the central characters. While there are certainly exceptions, the musical form traditionally thrives on the celebration of inclusion.[27]

In contrast, and while orgy scenes are a hard-core standard, pornography places less emphasis on inclusion, the importance of community, or, for that matter, character development. The primary purpose of pornography is to sexually stimulate spectators, and thus the pleasures being depicted are typically more intimate and individualistic, even in group scenes. Whereas in musicals a song or dance number can help add dimension and nuance to the character or characters performing,[28] the same cannot be said about porn films. Even in the pornographic golden age, devices like plot, character development, and scripted dialogue were comparatively slight, and even resisted, since the genre is primarily interested in reflecting "the visible 'truth' of sexual pleasure itself."[29]

As John H. Houchin, the author of *Censorship in the American Theater in the Twentieth Century* notes, while graphic sexual encounters depicted in films are certainly potentially viewed by a group of spectators, they are nevertheless "removed in time and space from the audience." Their impact is thus "technologically mediated" and "clearly designed to create a fantasy world in which the viewer can only participate imaginatively."[30] Indeed even when hard-core was at its closest to mainstream acceptance, its audience was hardly being encouraged to bond with the film cast in quite the same ways.

McMillin points out that in ensemble numbers of many musicals the "characters express themselves simultaneously. And the build-up of a number to a simultaneous performance is often a dramatic event in itself." Typically such a build-up takes place near the end of "each act of the book, and the act reaches its climax when that ensemble potential is realized. The earlier climaxes were sometimes called *finalettos* and the ending of the entire show the *finale ultimo*. They were important enough to need fancy names."[31] One can argue, then, that both musicals and hard-core narratives are ultimately about climax and, further, that both genres have the potential to strike spectators as subtly or even overtly erotic, but the ways climax is attained and eroticism is reflected in each genre are nevertheless radically different.[32]

The result, at least when it comes to *Alice in Wonderland*, is that the two genres coexist but never blend. Throughout the film musical numbers come out of nowhere, occasionally disrupting a sex scene; conversely, the sex scenes often seem randomly tacked on as a prelude to or at the end of musical numbers. Yet one kind of climax too often interrupts or denies the other. Hence the scene in which the Knight and Lady copulate beneath a tree makes sense from a hard-core perspective, and a big choreographed production number about the Knight and Lady makes sense from a musical perspective. Yet in the scene in question Alice and her entourage *interrupt* the sexual exchange between the Knight and Lady with the choreographed production number. When the musical number ends, so does the scene; the music has climaxed, but the Knight and Lady are no closer to orgasm than they were when the scene began. Similarly the scene in which Alice fellates a man dressed as an egg might appeal to audiences seeking sexual titillation, just as the ensuing sing-along number might appeal to musical theater lovers. But in sequence the fellatio (which does not culminate in the expected money shot) merely distracts from the ensemble number and vice versa.

Finally, *Alice* ends in a way that is typical of pornography: the title character has sex with her man, both are enormously satisfied, and all is right with the world. Yet what of the ensemble? Where did all of Alice's compatriots go, and what is to become of them? Alice, the audience learns, lives happily ever after. But the narrative, at least as far as musicals go, remains incomplete.

For all their similarities, then, porn narratives and musicals possess different senses of pacing and rhythm and different overarching ideologies that do not necessarily mesh. As Jeremy Martin wrote, "I like to think this film is the result of a director in desperate need of a script to use as an excuse to film people screwing, and a screenwriter determined to force his failed musical onscreen even if it means adding a few gratuitous blowjobs between songs."[33] Whether they liked it or hated it, most critics seemed to agree that *Alice* was a silly, if mildly diverting, experiment in genre-blending, but hardly a film worth building on or emulating.

### The First Nudie Musical

Years before *Alice in Wonderland* inadvertently proved him right, the struggling actor Bruce Kimmel often walked through Times Square chuckling at the thought of how preposterously funny it would be to make a pornographic musical film. His idea eventually developed into *The First Nudie Musical*, an R-rated feature released by Paramount Pictures in 1976. Kimmel wrote the script, music, and lyrics and also starred in and codirected the film, which, despite its decidedly innocent take on dirty movies, met with no small share of controversy when it opened.

Born and raised in Los Angeles, Kimmel became convinced upon graduating from the theater department at Los Angeles City College that he didn't have a chance of breaking into show business in Hollywood because of his unconventional looks. A lifelong devotee of musical theater, he decided to move to New York City, "thinking [he] would get work there instantly to be a huge Broadway star."[34] Though stardom evaded him, he nevertheless attended hundreds of Broadway and Off Broadway shows, went to countless auditions, took Lehman Engel's musical theater writing workshop, and, upon learning that his wife was pregnant, took a job with a survey company near the theater district.

The survey company turned out to be a haven for struggling actors, some of whom shared Kimmel's fondness for seeing nudie-cuties, which Kimmel remembers as "awful and hilarious." He and his colleagues would often take after-work trips to the local movie houses, where they "saw some classic nudies like *The Lustful Turk* and *She Came on the Bus*. We'd sit there and just howl, which didn't make the creepy men with the raincoats too happy." As an office joke Kimmel began to suggest that he and his colleagues make their own nudie-cutie, "not just an ordinary one but a musical nudie movie": "I came up with the title *Come, Come Now*, and every few days I'd come in with a new song."[35] Within the year, however, Kimmel left his job, and he and his wife returned to Los Angeles, where he found work doing bit parts on television.

By the time Kimmel began to revisit his nudie movie idea in earnest, *Deep Throat* had opened in New York. "As soon as [hard-core] porno hit, I realized that doing it the way I originally wanted to do it would never work—it was so fast when these initial hard-cores came along," he remembers. "Ultimately, by about '73, when I got really serious about [making the film] and we almost had the money, it became very apparent that the way to do it was as a film within a film."[36]

The finished project, renamed *The First Nudie Musical*, is written in the style of a 1930s-era backstage musical. The central protagonist, producer Harry Schechter (Stephen Nathan), has inherited a small, struggling film studio from his ailing father and is making porn films to make ends meet. Desperate to keep the studio out of the hands of his debtors, who are eager to build a strip mall in its place, Harry comes up with the idea for what he hopes will be a blockbuster film: a pornographic musical with a cast of thousands titled *Come, Come Now*. His debtors agree to let him make the film, with three conditions: they will front only half the budget and will loan Harry the rest; the film, which cannot go over budget or schedule, must wrap in two weeks; and the nephew of one of the debtors has to direct.

Harry and his long-suffering, good-natured assistant, Rosie (Cindy Williams), audition and hire a ridiculous cast of characters, including Juanita Juanita (Diana Canova), an over-the-top Latina stereotype whose boyfriend, Arvin, is a leather-clad greaser so obsessed with *West Side Story* that he insists on being called Riff; Joy Full, a spaced-out porn star who, when asked about her prior stage work, responds, "I've done fellatio, and straight fucking, and some minor bestiality, too," and who auditions by stripping naked, lying stiffly on the floor, and squealing; George, a hairy-chested swinger; Susie, a fresh-faced ingénue just off the bus from Indiana; and Mary LaRue, a spoiled, tantrum-throwing diva who monopolizes Harry's time and attention.

All hell threatens to break loose when the director, John Smithee, arrives on the set.[37] Young, naïve, not especially intelligent, and profoundly inexperienced when it comes to both movies and sex, Smithee shows up dressed in a 1920s-era beret and jodhpurs, spouting gibberish about filmmaking and peppering his speech with poorly placed epithets. "Shit," he announces to the bemused cast and production crew. "We can make a fucking good bitch-of-a-bastard movie if we all pull together and work as a whore-loving, cunt-penis team!" John proves so utterly inept that Harry takes to sending him out for donuts—many, many donuts—so that most of the film can be shot in his absence. *Come, Come Now* remains on schedule until Mary LaRue's child-ish, unprofessional behavior gets the best of Harry, who fires her with several days of filming left to go. Meanwhile John Smithee finally tires of combing the city for donuts.

Yet as all backstage musicals dictate, the show must go on. Harry sends John off to a local house of ill repute in search of script changes on the last day of shooting and convinces Rosie to take Mary's place for the big finale. *Come, Come Now* is saved! But, alas, one more complication arises: George, who is to be Rosie's dance partner in the big finale, is mugged and badly beaten en route to the shoot, and thus he too backs out at the last minute. Rosie and Harry partner for the film's big finale, "Let 'Em Eat Cake," a Busby Berkeley–inspired homage to oral sex featuring tuxedo-clad men and chorines who are naked save for tuxedo jackets, bowties, and white gloves, dancing into and out of enormous geometrical patterns on the rooftop of a fancy hotel.[38]

The film wraps on time and on budget and opens to critical and commercial raves. The cast members are swarmed by talent agents and producers and are all going to be big stars. Harry retains ownership of the studio and wins the heart of Rosie, who not only agrees to continue working with him but also to become his wife. The credits roll, the community triumphs, and everyone in it lives happily ever after.

Songs for *The First Nudie Musical* are varied and catchy, often very funny, and, unlike the numbers in *Alice in Wonderland*, well-placed and -paced. Harry sells his idea for a nudie musical to his debtors in the opening scene with "The First Nudie Musi-cal," a soft-shoe dream sequence that ends with a kick line of naked chorus girls in high heels, enormous flowered hats, and Mardi Gras necklaces. After learning that she has been cast in *Come, Come Now*, Susie, the shy ingénue, bursts forth with "The Lights and the Smiles," a belted declaration of empowerment and independence in which she gleefully declares—just as Mama Rose, Fanny Brice, Mame, and Sally Bowles did before her—that despite her often overwhelming insecurities, doubts, and struggles, everything's suddenly coming up roses. And before they see to John's sexual initiation, the beautiful, exceptionally lithe prostitutes who dwell at the bor-dello he visits in search of script changes perform the soulful "Honey What'cha Doing Tonight?"—a clear homage to Cy Coleman's "Big Spender" as conceived by Bob Fosse—in bright, expert harmony.

The *Come, Come Now* grand finale, "Let 'Em Eat Cake," from *The First Nudie Musical.* Courtesy of Photofest.

The musical numbers in the film-within-the-film are similarly catchy and eclectic, if a bit more over the top. A busily copulating couple is interrupted by a man in a suit and boater who wanders into their bedroom to sing "Orgasm" ("Orgasm's a short spasm of love, sweet love / Orgasm sure has 'em doing it nicely, doing it nightly / Doing it nicely, nightly") into a megaphone, à la Rudy Vallee. The number "Perversion" features Diana Canova in Carmen Miranda garb, replete with a headdress covered with phalluses in place of fruit, singing a habanera in a smoky café to an audience of goofy-looking "deviants" who sip from Crisco jars, smoke cigarettes clasped in other people's toes, sit blissfully in full bondage, or chat amicably with their tuxedoed German shepherd. The number "Lesbian Butch Dyke" ("you can call it what you like / But it's what I am and what I'll always be!") features two women dancing a jaunty tango, while "Dancing Dildoes" is a huge, *Gone With the Wind*–inspired plantation number featuring southern belles dancing with men who are dressed as vibrating sex toys. Despite the strong and unceasingly silly sexual content of the lyrics for most of the songs, Kimmel's score for *The First Nudie Musical* reflects a deep appreciation for and understanding of the classic stage and screen musicals that he grew up watching, listening to, performing in, and clearly adoring.[39]

*The First Nudie Musical* focused on the burgeoning adult film industry and its relationship to the mainstream, but also offered plenty of commentary about contemporary sex roles, which Kimmel, a struggling actor who "most certainly was not a conventional leading man type," presumably had ample time to ruminate about.[40]

Joy Full (Susan Stewart) in the *Come, Come Now* "Dancing Dildoes" number from *The First Nudie Musical*. Courtesy of Photofest.

While the trajectory of the plot does not stray from traditional backstage musicals, the male characters are notable for their confused, goofy powerlessness, while the women, all of whom are also somewhat daffy but typically more competent, end up saving the day.

Although Harry and John, as producer and director of *Come, Come Now,* occupy the most powerful positions in the film, neither one is remotely in control of his situation. John is a buffoonish pawn of circumstance, and Harry, while well-meaning and kind, is so hapless and disorganized that he is running his family business into the ground. The *Come, Come Now* leading man, George, is just as inept as John and Harry, if also somewhat less endearing. A character who represents the most aggressively chauvinistic aspects of the sexual revolution, George is a hairy-chested, open-shirted clod who uses the same tired pickup lines on every woman he meets and who seems genuinely surprised when women don't fall at his feet in response.

The film's secondary male characters fare no better. Dick Davis, the *Come, Come Now* music director, is forever slumped before the piano with a cigarette dangling from his lips. Surrounded by mountains of crumpled yellow paper that threaten to bury him, he spends most of his time desperately trying to come up with songs to teach the cast. His lyrics are always bizarre and often hilarious; a typical couplet is "I'm not deformed, I'm not a cripple / So, tell me, why won't you let me hold your nipple?" As amusing, if not quite as overt, is the fact that Dick can't play the piano very well. He thumps out a few chords here and there, but only barely, and regularly responds to his frequent errors in fingering—as well as to his own tasteless lyrics—by gruffly muttering, "Shit!" Harry, the incompetent producer of *Come, Come Now*, has hired a music director who is also inept.

So too is Juanita Juanita's *West Side Story*–obsessed boyfriend. A switchblade- and chain-toting tough guy with a vacant stare and a permanent sneer, he follows Juanita Juanita around, flashing a chain or a knife every time she so much as glances at other men. Yet she is not only not threatened by her jealous, menacing mate; she is blithely, cheerfully dismissive of him. Although he asks her repeatedly to call him Riff, she insists on referring to him by his much wimpier given name, Alvin. And while he hovers nearby at all times, she never seems bothered by him, but instead makes a practice of rolling her eyes, patting his arm, and going about her business. Alvin, like all the men in *The First Nudie Musical*, clings desperately to a traditional masculine archetype, only to fall repeatedly on his face in the process.

In marked contrast, the central female characters in *The First Nudie Musical* tend to be more grounded and competent, even though they do not occupy leadership positions. Not only does Juanita do precisely what she wants to do, but she tends to do it very well, despite Alvin's frequent interruptions. Susie, the film's ingénue, auditions so brilliantly that Harry creates a role for her on the spot. Joy Full, despite her spaced-out, bungled audition, turns out to be an excellent dancer and a consummately professional supporting actress. And Harry's secretary, Rosie, serves consistently throughout *The First Nudie Musical* as the film's level-headed voice of reason.

Bruce Kimmel created the role of Rosie for Cindy Williams, a close friend with whom he attended college. Williams was so supportive of *The First Nudie Musical* that she joined the project even though she hardly needed the work by the time filming began; she had already made *American Graffiti* and *The Conversation* and was in talks to film a television pilot for *Laverne and Shirley*. The character of Rosie reflects Kimmel's obvious gratitude, respect, and affection for Williams, but she also manifests aspects of the sexual revolution and the women's movement in several important ways.

In some respects Rosie is a traditional stereotype: the hard-working, long-suffering woman-behind-the-man who places her own aspirations aside in order to help her boss (for whom she secretly pines) realize his dreams. As is evidenced by a tap routine that she bursts into during the heated meeting between Harry and his investors in the opening scene of *The First Nudie Musical*, Rosie dreams not of serving coffee and taking minutes, but of a performing career of her own. Yet in the same scene she regularly completes Harry's sentences for him and at one point expertly mouths along with an entire motivational speech that he makes to his investors. Clearly Rosie is as devoted to Schechter Studios as Harry is, and Harry is unable to function without her. Rosie's plot trajectory is similarly traditional; her devotion to Harry pays off, since she not only helps save his studio but also lands the leading role in the film and captures Harry's heart in the process.

Yet Rosie, at least as Williams creates her, is very much a 1970s woman, especially when it comes to her embrace of both the sexual revolution and second-wave feminism. Strongly opinionated and confrontational, she suffers no fools. She is also much more Harry's equal than her status as his secretary implies: she is quick to inform him when she thinks his ideas are half-baked or unworkable; she frequently, vociferously disagrees with him on aspects of *Come, Come Now*; she keeps track of studio business far better than he does; and she regularly exhibits a level-headedness and ability to problem-solve that Harry, who becomes tongue-tied and flustered in crises, obviously lacks.

Further, Rosie, unlike the ostensibly professional men she works for and with, remains completely unruffled in even the most sexually explicit situations. During the lengthy audition scene for *Come, Come Now* she holds her own with Harry and the male backer while watching a parade of performers, in various degrees of undress, shuffle through their auditions. She bursts into maniacal giggles when George propositions her after trying out. In response to Harry's concession that despite her especially horrible audition, Joy Full's feigned orgasm "wasn't too bad," Rosie erupts in disgust. "Are you *kidding*?" she shouts. "That was the *worst* orgasm I have *ever* seen!" She regularly intervenes when the sexually inexperienced director John Smithee is rendered tongue-tied by the sight of unclothed actors on the set. And when a particularly well-endowed actor shows up to take the place of a cast member who abruptly quits the film, Rosie is the only person on the set, male or female, not to react with bug-eyed, jaw-dropping awe. Instead she glances coolly at the naked actor, taps Smithee on the shoulder, and deadpans, "Your stunt cock is here." Rosie is as comfortable in her own skin as she is with the naked bodies and the increasingly bizarre sexual situations going on around her. She is sexually liberated on her own terms.

Of course, Rosie's heated clashes with Mary LaRue, the petulant star of *Come, Come Now*, are another function not only of backstage dramas but of countless other types of narratives: "good" and "bad" women seem to be locked forever in competition over the affections of the strapping male protagonist. Yet Rosie and Mary clash because Rosie is the very model of a self-actualized, liberated, 1970s new woman, while Mary, much like George, represents the sexual revolution gone horribly wrong. An ill-tempered spoiled brat, Mary also knows that she happens to look good naked, and thus frequently relies on sexual manipulation to get her way.

Once cast, Mary quickly alienates everyone around her. She makes a point of being overly condescending to Rosie, whom she always addresses sneeringly as "honey." She is also nastily dismissive of the shy, overweight script supervisor, Eunice, and especially hostile to the naïve John Smithee, whom she regularly refers to as "twerp" or "dipshit." On the other hand, Mary cozies up to Harry, who she recognizes is in the position of power. She eventually refuses to cooperate on set unless Harry agrees to reward her with sexual favors. Out of sheer desperation, he considers complying, but when Mary then demands that he also fire Rosie, he orders Mary off the set.

Though Mary is a monster from the moment she walks onto the set, she is initially tolerated, presumably because, as Eunice muses early in the film, men find her so attractive. Yet Rosie instantly knows better: she takes an immediate dislike to Mary not necessarily because she feels threatened, but for overtly feminist reasons. "Are you kidding? She's *terrific!*" Rosie sneers sarcastically when Harry asks her early in the film why she doesn't trust Mary. "She has all the qualities I admire most in a woman. She's opportunistic, pushy, self-centered, and a bitch." The fact that Mary becomes universally detested and is ultimately fired, while Rosie saves the studio, stars in a film, and wins the devotion of a good man is certainly in keeping with the traditional backstage musical trajectory. But the story arc possesses a contemporary twist: Rosie wins because she is both sexually liberated *and* a feminist, while Mary, despite her sexual self-assurance, loses because she is decidedly antifeminist.

Yet for all its commentary on contemporary gender ideologies, *The First Nudie Musical* does what its staged counterparts tend to do: rely on broad comedy, running gags, and, especially, naked bodies and sexual situations as chief selling points. *The First Nudie Musical* featured more nudity than any film warranting an R rating had ever featured before,[41] and almost all of the characters to appear nude were women. Chorines are naked or nearly so in all the big production numbers, and Joy Full and Mary LaRue both appear onscreen more often in various stages of undress than they do clad. Only two men appear nude, however briefly, in the film: one who, with a naked female partner, performs a buck-and-wing during the audition sequence, and another who storms angrily off the *Come, Come Now* set when Mary insults him during a sex scene.

As Kimmel recalls, the original plan was to be more egalitarian when it came to the nude scenes, especially the ones involving dancers. But while he had no problems finding women who were willing to appear naked on film, casting willing men proved problematic:

> That was the funniest thing. Not only did we not have problems in casting [female chorus parts], but they kind of really wanted to do it.... They all kind of showed up and said, "yeah, it's not salacious, it's funny!" Really, is there anyone who *could* get titillated from watching this movie? They came in totally nude in that opening production number, in those costumes, those hats, which looked so *stupid*. How could you even think about anything else? They had no problems. The *guys* had problems. Not the two guys who actually [appeared nude in the film]—they were fine. It was trying to convince the male dancers, who wouldn't do the dance numbers nude.... We would have done it but we couldn't find anyone who could dance and was willing to do it nude.[42]

Kimmel's experiences with the vast discrepancy between men and women willing to appear in nude scenes points to a long history in the Western visual arts of fetishizing the female body. More specifically it indicates that in many cases, the increases in personal and sexual freedom that took place through the 1970s were often framed by heterosexual, patriarchal parameters: women were willing to do nude scenes presumably because nude scenes are typically expected of women more than they are of men.

Despite its copious nudity and strong sexual content, *The First Nudie Musical* would be difficult to pass off as the genre it spoofs. With the exception of the two flaccid penises briefly featured in as many scenes, no genitalia are shown, and the relentlessly goofy sex scenes are all obviously simulated. Yet the reception of *The First Nudie Musical* was enormously complicated and frequently pointed to the tensions that had begun to arise between the mainstream and pornographic film industries by the mid-1970s.

Paralleling his central protagonist's impossibly tight schedule and shoestring budget, Kimmel shot *The First Nudie Musical* in eighteen days for $150,000.[43] Once the film was finished, in the summer of 1975, he began showing the film at "sneak preview" screenings in southern California in order to gauge audience response, which proved consistently strong. The positive feedback convinced the producer Jack Reeves that the film had a chance for major distribution, and thus it was submitted to the MPAA for a rating.

In an early indication that even despite the porno chic trend, distributing a raunchy—if hardly pornographic—movie musical might be more difficult than anticipated, the MPAA attached an X rating to the film, citing the frequency of nudity, the use of the word *fuck* one too many times, and one scene during which (obviously) simulated sex went on for a bit too long. After a lengthy battle with the ratings board, Kimmel agreed to cut a single *fuck* and several seconds of the simulated sex scene, and the MPAA granted his film an R rating.[44] Following several more successful preview screenings, both in various parts of California and in New York City, *The First Nudie Musical* was picked up by Paramount, and a March 1976 release date was set.[45] In the ensuing months Kimmel was wined and dined by Paramount, the head of which informed him that the studio executives believed that he was "the next thing in comedy."[46]

Yet in late January 1976 *Laverne and Shirley*, which was a Paramount production, premiered after *Happy Days* on ABC during what was then known as the "family hour" and became an instant hit.[47] Kimmel thought nothing of it at first, but he soon began to notice that Cindy Williams's skyrocketing career was inversely proportionate to Paramount's enthusiasm for *The First Nudie Musical*—which, for all its charms, was hardly family friendly. The studio initially attempted to distance Williams from the film by releasing poster and ad art featuring nothing but the title of the film, the R rating, and the Paramount logo; these were halted when the *Nudie* company reminded the studio of the billing clauses included in their contracts. Meanwhile Kimmel's many calls to Paramount executives suddenly went unreturned.[48]

Paramount changed the artwork but did little else to support the film, which they refused to screen for radio, television, or newspaper critics. As Kimmel recalls, Paramount arranged only one screening, and only for the trade magazines *Hollywood Reporter* and *Variety*. "Nine o'clock in the morning, the two of them, alone, in a screening room on the Paramount lot," Kimmel scoffs. "I heard this and my head literally came off my shoulders. Unbelievable. You show a comedy, which is dependent on an audience for its effect, to two old curmudgeonly people at nine in the morning? And those reviews came out a day later, and they were devastating."[49]

Yet once the film opened in a handful of cities across the country—excluding Los Angeles and New York—critics began to rave about it, despite the lack of advertising or critics' screenings. Don Safran for the *Dallas Times Herald* began his review with the rhetorical question, "Who would have thought that something called 'The First Nudie Musical,' made with a budget that wouldn't pay for a new Japanese sports car, would turn into one of the comic surprises of the season?" The critic for the *Oregonian* compared the film with *Young Frankenstein* and said that it was funnier than *Blazing Saddles*, and the critic from the *Houston Chronicle*, similarly charmed, wrote that the "Dancing Dildos" number "is going to go right alongside 'Springtime for Hitler' from *The Producers*."[50]

Kimmel sent copies of the reviews to Paramount, which nevertheless continued to renege on its contract by refusing to open the film in Los Angeles. Finally, Cindy Williams informed the studio that she would refuse to do any publicity for *Laverne and Shirley* if *The First Nudie Musical* was not given a proper premiere. Paramount relented, but only a little: it opened the film in four theaters instead of the contractual twelve. At this point Williams, who felt responsible for Paramount's actions, sent a telegram to Paramount executives, demanding that the studio stick to its contract and threatening to leave *Laverne and Shirley* if they failed to comply.[51]

Paramount met Williams's demands, if only briefly. They provided extensive advertising and tripled the number of cinemas showing the film. *The First Nudie Musical* received good reviews in both the *New York Times* and the *Herald-Examiner*. Kimmel was thus surprised to get a phone call from a friend who worked at Mann Theaters, who informed him that the head of Paramount had called Ted Mann personally and asked him to pull the film from the theaters after two weeks because "it was an embarrassment to Paramount."[52] Enraged, Kimmel went to the *Hollywood Reporter* with the news. This, he admits, was rash: "Twenty-seven-year-old punks did not take on Paramount studios, let me tell you. And that was the end of my career. For about three years."[53]

*The First Nudie Musical* was eventually acquired by Northal Films, which opened it in New York City in 1977 to generally enthusiastic reviews.[54] For all its troubles, it was the fourth-highest grossing film in the country that year, and most of the people involved suffered no ill effects from their associations with the most explicit R-rated film to date. As Kimmel, who long ago left the film industry for a successful and less complicated career as a record producer, notes wistfully, when it came to *The First Nudie Musical,* "the only person's career that was hurt was mine."[55]

## ASPIRING PERFORMERS IN THE 1970S, BETWEEN A ROCK AND A HARD-CORE PLACE

Kimmel was hardly alone as a struggling actor and writer hoping to benefit professionally from the rise of porno chic. As noted earlier, a significant number of aspiring actors, directors, producers, and playwrights went a lot further than he did by crossing into the burgeoning adult entertainment industry as a means of getting career experience and thus, it was hoped, a foothold in the "legitimate" entertainment world. Yet as Kimmel remembers, "In those days, a lot of major filmmakers and performers were trying to push the envelope further and further. There was always talk about how major actors wanted to push and push. . . . They were talking about it a lot, but when push came to shove, they didn't do it."[56] While Kimmel's attempt at capitalizing on porno chic by merely parodying it harmed his career, there were many people who, having drawn much closer to the hard-core scene in the 1970s, learned too late that once porn had you, it tended not to let you go.

A case in point is Marilyn Chambers, who began attempting to reinvent herself as a legitimate stage performer while still at the height of her career as a porn star. Born Marilyn Briggs in 1952 and raised in Westport, Connecticut, Chambers dropped out of high school in pursuit of modeling and acting jobs.[57] After landing a few print ads, bit parts in films, and, most notoriously, a gig as the wholesome-looking model cuddling a baby on boxes of "99 and 44/100 percent pure" Ivory Snow detergent, Chambers relocated from New York to Los Angeles and then to San Francisco in the early 1970s in search of film roles.

In San Francisco Chambers auditioned for what was vaguely described as "a major motion picture." The directors, Jim and Artie Mitchell, hired her on the spot and later surprised her by granting her requests for a particularly high salary and a percentage of the film, which turned out to be *Behind the Green Door*.[58] "They called my bluff, so I had to do it," Chambers joked. "And I thought, 'God, this might be cool. Maybe I can use it as a stepping stone to legitimate movies.'"[59]

*Behind the Green Door* opened in December 1972, a few months behind *Deep Throat*. When the box office lagged in its first week in New York, the Mitchell brothers informed the press that *Behind the Green Door* starred the Ivory Snow model, and the box office promptly doubled.[60] Chambers surmised that her film would help "sell a lot more soap," but in an early indication that hard-core porn was not the "stepping stone" she hoped it would be, Ivory simply removed her image from their product and replaced her.[61] In 1973 Chambers made the film *Resurrection of Eve* (1973), which "didn't have as much success as *Green Door*," she recalls. "But that was okay because I really wanted to do legit films."[62]

In 1974 she married and turned her career over to Chuck Traynor, former husband and manager—and alleged serial abuser—of *Deep Throat*'s star Linda Lovelace.[63] "I told Chuck I didn't want to do erotic films my whole life," Chambers recalled. "I wanted to be onstage in Las Vegas. I wanted to be Ann-Margret. That's who I really wanted to be. And he was excited because he felt that I possibly could have some talent. So that's the premise we met on."[64]

Traynor and Chambers crossed the country in search of gigs that would help legitimize her. In the same year that they were married Chambers made her stage debut in the Las Vegas production of Jules Tasca's satire on censorship, *The Mind with the Dirty Man*. She kept her clothing on during the run, but her part was hardly a radical departure: she played a porn star. Following *Dirty Man* Traynor and Chambers set their sights on Broadway and, specifically, on a new musical in the *Oh! Calcutta!* mode that, it was hoped, would showcase Chambers and help boost her reputation as a cabaret performer.

Although starring in a live nudie musical as a means of getting out of the hard-core film racket might not seem like the savviest of career moves, Chambers's attempt to headline in an adult musical in New York City made good sense. Because of their association with the musical theater—and thus with a middle-class, middle-aged audience—adult musicals never carried the same stigma that hard-core film did. Appearing in adult stage musicals did not tend to destroy careers to the same degree that acting in pornography did. As a result—and often despite the impassioned warnings of friends, colleagues, and agents—a great many actors experienced no problem finding work on the legitimate stage after appearing in even the raciest of adult musicals. Graduates of such shows include Joanne Baron, Shezwae Powell, and Barry Pearl (*Let My People Come*), Bill Macy, Alan Rachins, Boni Enten, and Margo Sappington (*Oh! Calcutta!*), Reathel Bean (*Lovers*), Dixie Carter (*Sextet*), and Adrienne Barbeau (*Stag Movie*), all of whom went on to, at the very least, regular work in film, television, dance, or theater. In sharp contrast with the porn scene, adult musicals were, for most actors, indeed stepping stones. A Broadway show was thus rightly viewed by Chambers as a step in the right direction; as she noted in *Time* magazine in advance of *Le Bellybutton*'s opening, "Of course films are very lucrative . . . but this is more lucrative in the way of experience."[65]

## Le Bellybutton

Scott Mansfield, an Off Off Broadway actor active with the Judson Poets' Theater, began to branch out into playwriting, directing, composing, and producing (under the company name Jolandrea) in the early 1970s. After writing, producing, and performing in the play *Once I Saw a Boy Laughing*... in 1974, Mansfield was tapped by Chambers and Traynor to write, compose, direct, and produce *Le Bellybutton: A Sexy Musical*, which would serve as a live vehicle for Chambers. This "sexy musical" began its run at the Diplomat Cabaret Theater on April 2, 1976.

Edmund Gaynes, who performed with Mansfield in the Judson show *A Look at the Fifties*, was a coproducer on *Le Bellybutton*. While many young idealists getting their start in the business were at least partially politically motivated, Gaynes remembers that he and Mansfield were solely interested in capitalizing on current trends:

> Scott was trying to do a ripoff of *Oh! Calcutta!* basically. There was some clever stuff... a lot of nudity, a lot of jokes, a lot of music. Scott's intent was to try to make money. That's what his thinking was. There are a lot of people, as we all know, who see something that is making money and doing well, and they want to imitate it. Certainly this [show] was not something that I would have ever done, but hey, it was there, I wanted to get into producing, I was an actor, and it was like, "okay, why not?" Shows like this were trendy, and people were trying to figure out an angle to see if they could make some money.[66]

*Le Bellybutton* ran in the ballroom of the Hotel Diplomat, which, before being razed in 1994, was on Forty-third Street west of Sixth Avenue. Geographically speaking, the musical opened squarely in Broadway—not Off or Off Off Broadway—territory. Because of its location, box office listings for *Le Bellybutton* ran consistently in the "Broadway" column of the theater ABCs that appear daily in the arts section of the *New York Times*. Yet the ballroom was never outfitted to function as a traditional theater, and the semiprofessional feel of most aspects of the show would likely have confused Broadway audiences, at best. For *Le Bellybutton,* which would have likely been much more at home Off Off Broadway, straight-backed chairs were arranged on a flat dance floor surrounding a platform stage, and spectators could sip cocktails and move freely about the ballroom while watching the show, much like those spectators at *Let My People Come*. Acoustics were apparently terrible.[67]

Also like *Let My People Come* and most other adult musicals, *Le Bellybutton* was written in revue form. In this case, the sketches, songs, and dances were linked by a recurring character: throughout *Le Bellybutton* a dirty old man serving as something of a perverted emcee frequently appeared to deliver monologues, shout obscenities, lament the changing times, tell dirty jokes, and, occasionally, flash the audience. *Le Bellybutton* was never recorded, and while bootlegs of the show continue to circulate, the sound quality is mediocre at best, and usually far worse than that, not only because of poor acoustics and sound design (feedback squeals emanating from hot microphones are a regular feature of the aural landscape), but also because the bootleg has been copied so often in the more than three decades since it was made.

While everyone in the twelve-person cast appeared nude at some point or another, most sketches and musical numbers featured Chambers in a central role.[68] Much of the material in *Le Bellybutton* was contemporary, with the exception of a scene in which General Washington, about to depart for the front, asks Martha to have anal sex with him as a going-away gift. Even by adult musical standards, this revue was particularly crude.

*Le Bellybutton*'s sketches included one in which a man read an excerpt from his "favorite book," *Teenage Stewardess Nurse,* while two utterly inept actors (one of which was Chambers) simulated the scene, pausing often to question the narrator about the increasingly purple prose. A sketch parodying the Miss Subways Pageant—which was held in New York from 1941 to 1977 and which also inspired the "Miss Turnstiles" plotline and dance number in the 1944 musical *On the Town*—featured an emcee reading descriptions of each contestant. These segued abruptly from pat descriptions of hobbies and physical characteristics to sexual attributes and then back again ("She has brown hair and blue eyes. . . . She enjoys cooking, sewing, playing tennis, and sucking cock. . . . She enjoys reading *Gourmet* . . . gives a pretty good hand-job, and does needlepoint"). The television show *This Is Your Life* was spoofed in one sketch as "This Is Your Sex Life," and a fake news show featured extended dirty jokes in lieu of news stories, like the one about the man who filed a lawsuit claiming that he contracted Aer Lingus from an airport toilet seat. Musical numbers included "The S&M Polka," "Bisexual Blues," "Disco Baby/Dance for Me" (all written in the styles their titles describe), the tango-tinged "I Never Let Anyone Beat Me but You," and the vaudevillian "A Sucker's Soliloquy," in which the dirty old man sang a soft-shoe refrain between accompanied rhyming stories about various sexual scenarios gone horribly awry.

Interspersed among the copious dirty jokes, simulated sex, and naked bodies were several numbers meant to highlight Chambers's singing talents. Written, for the most part, in the style of Brill Building pop, numbers like "Gotta Get Back to You," "Let Me Make Love to You," and "Morning Light" are generic tunes accompanied by electric piano and drums. Lyrics, which offer "shelter from the rain," "kisses at the break of day," and "to be yours tonight," are, like the melodies, inoffensive, if particularly clichéd (🎵 Ex. 7.1). Most curious is the number "Jenny," which is sung midway through the show by a female cast member, not Chambers, to the accompaniment of a synthesizer.

"Jenny" traces the life of a female character whose happy childhood is disrupted when her father deserts her; she turns in young adulthood to frequent, anonymous, unfulfilling sexual encounters in search of the stability she once knew. The implication is that Jenny eventually becomes a prostitute as a result of her father's abandonment. As the number ends, the singer intones the lyrics "I'm sorry if I hurt you, daddy, but Jenny is me." Jenny's heart, which belongs to daddy, has been irreparably broken, and the male companionship she seeks as a salve has only served to make her sadder and lonelier (🎵 Ex. 7.2).

Unlike most adult musicals, which attempt a balance between broad sexual parody and comparatively serious contemporary concerns, *Le Bellybutton* tends overwhelmingly to eschew the latter for the former. As the sole number to attempt anything approximating social commentary, "Jenny" is thus somewhat jarring. Whereas most of the revue makes no bones about reveling apolitically in the cruder aspects of the sexual revolution, "Jenny" reflects concern for the contemporary woman, however unintentionally condescending that concern might seem. The fact that "Jenny" is one of the only solo numbers that Chambers herself does not sing makes its inclusion even more noteworthy. Years later Chambers would acknowledge that the sex industry "chews women up and spits them out" and that she would never want her daughter to get involved in it.[69] Yet at the time of *Le Bellybutton* it was all that she had to go on. In fact her connection to the adult film world adversely affected not only the rehearsal process but also the trajectory of the production once it opened.

An original cast member, Alan Kootsher, remembers that although *Le Bellybutton* was an Equity production, there was plenty about it that was markedly unprofessional. In the first place, he recalls, the Diplomat Hotel Ballroom, where they performed, was "literally like going to a high school play with rows of chairs."[70] Adding to the air of amateurishness was the fact that Scott Mansfield was notably inexperienced as a director. "Oh, he was real young, curly hair.... He was so gung ho on this thing. I mean, he was a nice guy, but...there really wasn't a whole lot of direction to the scenes," Kootsher recalls. "I mean, in retrospect, I was terrible. I had no direction, I was just doing what I thought I should do.... There was no specific direction, and things were not so much choreographed as—we'd just sort of move around."[71]

Further, Kootsher recalls, while Chambers was pleasant enough to work with, Chuck Traynor was so boorish and intimidating as to be detrimental to the rehearsal process:

> *She* was fine. It was her husband, or manager, Chuck Traynor, who was a—pardon my French—a real prick. He was—you know, "She's a star, and this isn't right and that isn't right." She kinda let him do all the talking and I don't know how much of it was him, but she was nice...and she didn't play the star bit with us. But he was...if you got close to her, it was "Don't you touch her, don't you go near her," you know.... He was just really protective of his property. And she was his property in every sense.... Traynor was really the kind of individual—he visualized himself as bigger and better than he was. He was a porno guy. A typical—you know, they portray people like that as stereotypes.[72]

Kootsher believes, however, that all of the behind-the-scenes antics at *Le Bellybutton* would have been less relevant if the show, and its star, had been stronger. Yet not only did he feel that the show was merely passable at best, but also that Chambers was not compelling enough to carry a musical on her own:

> Marilyn...was not an actress. I mean, if you've ever seen a movie with her in it, you can see that.... So to me, that had a lot to do with why the show closed. The surrounding cast made her look good, but she was horrible.... She was quiet, and I think that was probably why Chuck was the way he was—I think they both knew it. I think it was a vehicle for them to hopefully make money, but I think she felt very self-conscious because she knew she wasn't an actress. It's one thing in the movies where if

she can't act it doesn't matter because that's not what people are there to see, but onstage, you have to carry the show.[73]

Making matters worse was her singing voice, which is, at least as far as the bootleg recording indicates, if not unbearable, then rather thin and wooden. While she remains on pitch most of the time, Chambers displays no real grasp of timing and frequently rushes ahead or falls behind her accompaniment.

As a result, Le Bellybutton, like Alice in Wonderland: An X-Rated Musical Fantasy, failed to connect with an audience. Theatergoers hoping for a well-put-together revue headlined by solid musical talent were disappointed; fans of Marilyn Chambers's hard-core films, which were ultimately far more indicative than Le Bellybutton of what she had become famous for, would have been disappointed too. The revue, with its overly crude humor and, in the case of "Jenny," seemingly random attempts at pathos, reflected confusion as to how, exactly, to sell the "new" Marilyn Chambers at a point when she was still widely known for her work in porn films.

One interview Chambers granted in advance of Le Bellybutton is at once revealing and, considering her desire to move beyond her porn star designation, heartbreaking. A few weeks before going into rehearsals, Chambers appeared on Al Goldstein's cable television show Midnight Blue, broadcast on the old public-access Channel J in New York City, to help publicize Le Bellybutton. In response to the opening question, "What have you been up to?," Chambers eagerly lists her stage work, a jewelry line she was hoping to develop, her recently released autobiography, and Le Bellybutton, which she promised would have "very funny skits" and "sexy, wild dancing." The host, who reflects no interest in the revue save when Chambers allows that there will be nudity in it, listens distractedly before abruptly encouraging her to discuss her pornographic films. Chambers is gracious throughout the ten-minute interview, during which she answers increasingly intimate questions about her sexual preferences and fantasies and laughs gamely at the host's awkward suggestion that he tie her up and blindfold her for the camera. But clearly Midnight Blue had no interest in helping Chambers move beyond the adult film world.[74]

The mainstream press showed no interest in Chambers's project either. Although its producers advertised the show in the New York Times, New York Daily News, and Newsday, Le Bellybutton was summarily ignored by mainstream critics. This is likely, in part, because the creative team had scant budget for press relations, especially since the box office was mediocre to horrible, with show after show running at about 25 percent capacity.[75] Yet it also indicates the fact that by 1976 the door to the mainstream had closed rather decisively, not only on the hard-core narrative, but on those actors closely affiliated with it. "The pornography thing had a bad connotation and now I was seeing the consequences," Chambers acknowledged.[76] Le Bellybutton lasted twenty-eight performances and closed at a loss on April 25, 1976.

Most descriptions of porno chic pinpoint the beginning of the trend with Deep Throat and the end in the early 1980s, when the advent of home video effectively killed the hard-core feature.[77] Yet the film critic Richard Corliss argues that porno chic died long before the hard-core feature film did. "If Throat in 1972 stoked the hope that hard-core might fruitfully intersect with mainstream," he wrote, "Jaws in

1975 ended that dream, and a few others." The blockbuster success of Spielberg's shark film, and then of *Star Wars* two years later, "proved that the big-bucks audience comprised kids and teens, not adults, and it was the young who had to be pandered to. Adult films were largely marginalized, the hard-core back to the old grind houses (and later to video), the Hollywood ones to art houses and Oscar season. It's been that way for 30 years."[78]

Chambers's experience is perhaps the most sobering object lesson in the limits of sexual freedom, even at the most seemingly open and progressive of times. Like the vast majority of porn stars from her generation, Chambers was never able to leave her hard-core affiliations behind. After cutting a disco record titled *Benihana*, starring in the David Cronenberg film *Rage* (both in 1977), and making a few more attempts as a cabaret singer, she returned to adult films in the early 1980s and continued making them until her death at fifty-six in April 2009. "Back then in my naïve brain I was thinking that something like *Behind the Green Door* had never been done before and the way our sexual revolution was traveling I really thought it...would further my acting career," one of her obituaries quoted her as saying. But "there will always be a stigma on people who do adult films....That's the way society has made it."[79]

The productions discussed in this chapter imply that cultural perceptions about the nature of obscenity relaxed enough through the early 1970s for pornography to flirt briefly with the mainstream, to exert aesthetic influence on such a solidly middlebrow genre as the musical, and even to encourage such genre experimentation as the porn-musical hybrid *Alice in Wonderland: An X-Rated Musical Fantasy*. Nevertheless even at its most accepted, and no matter how hard it tried to emulate other, more established genres, pornography was always kept at least at arm's length from mainstream culture. While staged adult musicals like *Let My People Come* were free to spoof current trends without necessarily damaging the careers of the people appearing in or working on them, properties perceived to be too close to the adult film industry for mainstream comfort fared poorly. Cases in point are *The First Nudie Musical*, about which Paramount executives soured once its star, Cindy Williams, became nationally known as Shirley on the hit "family hour" TV show *Laverne and Shirley*; *Alice in Wonderland*, which was too silly to function as hard-core and too explicit to be taken seriously as a musical; and especially *Le Bellybutton*, which, like *Alice*, was too clean for Chambers's core audience and not professional enough to connect with theatergoers.

## CHAPTER 8

# Applying Contemporary Community Standards: Is It Obscene, or Merely Lewd?

Did "Che!" display any evidence of a genuinely creative mind at work? No. Was "Che!" patently the work of a pretentious amateur, a novice at language with no capacity at all for turning combinations of words into even minimally poetic images? Yes. Would I be in this theater at all, every reviewer must have asked himself, if it weren't for the "scandal" of the sexual deportment display? Would I bother to write a review, or a paragraph, or so much as a line about the event if it didn't violate, coarsely, such conventions of taste as had obtained until that time? No and no. The evening was without merit, period.

—Walter Kerr, "Would It Have Been Better to Ignore Arrabal?"

As noted in chapter 1, stage nudity was employed without incident in New York City at various points during the twentieth century, especially when the production in question was aimed at middle- to upper-class spectators. While the increasingly explicit happenings Off and Off Off Broadway during the 1960s and 1970s might have occasionally ruffled a critic or flustered the odd unprepared spectator, nudity and simulated sex in New York theaters were typically tolerated, if not blithely accepted. This is especially the case in the years after the *Roth* decision, when the city saw the explosion of businesses peddling sexuality in ways far more explicit than was typical in any realm of the legitimate theater. In summer 1969 the *New York Times* reported that a vast majority of city officials' actions on obscenity was focused on the print media, since a seemingly endless supply of explicit magazines and newspapers were being put on full display in newsstands, bookstores, delis, and corner markets all over the five boroughs.

Typically complaints about obscene materials in New York City at the time worked like this: A citizen would see something that he or she found offensive and would register a complaint about it at the local police precinct. The police would then investigate the complaint, turning over any evidence to the district attorney's office for additional investigation. If the complaint was pursued further, a judge would sign a search or arrest warrant and would typically read or view the offending material, thus acting as the final arbiter.

Because city officials were overwhelmed by obscenity complaints to local precincts, they tended not to pursue matters past the initial stages; this was just as well, in many cases, since no one was entirely clear on what was or was not in fact obscene.[1] "This is a problem the Supreme Court couldn't agree on," the exasperated deputy inspector Joseph Fink told the *New York Times* in spring 1969, "so please don't ask us to rule on what is art or how far it can go before it becomes hard-core pornography. We have no guidelines."[2] Adding to the confusion was the fact that "community standards" in New York differed drastically from neighborhood to neighborhood and venue to venue. A staff counsel with the New York Civil Liberties Union noted that, for example, a "certain movie in Parkchester would be considered obscene, but on 42nd Street nobody would give it a second thought."[3] Even individual perception varied so greatly as to make the law maddeningly "ambiguous," one prosecutor complained in the *New York Times*. "The law says a work has to be patently offensive and utterly without redeeming qualities to be obscene. Well, patently offensive to whom— adults, children, old ladies, basketball players? What offends me may not offend you."[4] In short, the sheer glut of printed, filmed, or otherwise mediated material coursing through the Erotic City—and sending all kinds of different people to police stations to lodge all kinds of different complaints—kept the vast majority of theatrical productions, no matter how graphic, from becoming a concern for most people.

Notable exceptions were the 1969 Off Off Broadway play *Che!*, which was tried in criminal court for obscenity in winter 1970, and the Off Broadway adult musical *Let My People Come*, which was pursued by the State Liquor Authority on charges of lewdness, but not obscenity, during its run at the Village Gate between 1974 and 1976. Because *Che!* and *Let My People Come* were, for all their explicitness, "legitimate" theater productions, and because they were being peddled to a mainstream, middle-class audience, their legal struggles horrified many civil libertarians, theater critics, and industry members, who argued that no matter how explicit live theater had become, especially Off and Off Off Broadway, censorship of the arts needed to be avoided at all costs. Both cases indicate just how confusing the legal terminology—and the laws about obscenity itself—had become and how difficult it was to apply "contemporary community standards" to live entertainment in New York City at a time when the sex industry had begun to run rampant, no one was sure what the rules meant, and no one was clear on how the rules should be appropriately applied and to whom.

## OBSCENITY: THE CASE OF *CHE!*

Written by a little-known Trinidadian playwright named Lennox Raphael and directed by Ed Wode at the 120-seat Free Store Theater at 14 Cooper Square in the East Village, the play *Che!* began previews on March 12, 1969, and opened on March 22. *Che!*, which envisioned the last hours of Che Guevara's life as a hallucinogenic, psychosexual nightmare, was a plotless one-act featuring characters like the President of the United States, Chilli Billy (Son of King Kong), Sister of Mercy (Viciously Delicious Angelspy), and Breakstone Fearless (Movie Director).[5] It featured dialogue built entirely of clipped non sequiturs like "Affection is despair," "God is love," "God is revolution," and "Develop a functional relationship with your ego," which were alternately shouted and intoned and were intended as a whole to convey the idea that "the relationship of a small Latin American nation to the United States was that of a victim and rapist."[6] Yet *Che!* earned notoriety less for what its performers said than for what they did: the cast, who appeared nude more often than they did clad, frequently simulated defecation and an impressively wide variety of hetero- and homosexual sex acts—alone, in pairs, and in groups—through the show.

By the time *Che!* began its run, almost a full year after the Broadway premiere of *Hair*, stage nudity and simulated sex were all the rage in the New York theater world, not only Off Off Broadway, where the trend took root, but in the more commercial realms as well. Further, most if not all of the many scatological and sexual acts depicted in *Che!* had previously been described in books, featured in films, and depicted in other stage productions. Yet even before it entered its preview period the *Che!* company made a misstep in attempting to cultivate its own reputation for being particularly sexually daring. In order to drum up publicity in advance of its opening, *Che!*'s cast and creative team began to spread rumors around town that the actors in the show would not only simulate each "sex act called for in the play, they would *do* it in reality, if they were able to at any given performance."[7]

This approach proved a double-edged sword for *Che!* On the one hand, it helped the show sell remarkably well and at inflated ticket prices; spectators eager to see if the cast would make good on its promises shelled out top Broadway prices for the privilege of viewing a work by an unknown playwright in a minuscule downtown theater.[8] On the other hand, the promise of actual, not merely simulated, sex invited much closer scrutiny than was typical of the theater, and especially the Off Off Broadway theater, at the time. It didn't help matters that the graphic depictions in *Che!* extended to homosexual sex acts, which, at the time, were still largely considered—and repeatedly described in the legalese surrounding the case—to be "deviant." Opponents of the production, many of whom formulated strong opinions about it before actually seeing it, argued that the presentation in a live setting of so many sexual and scatological acts, whether real or simulated, was the straw that broke the camel's back in transforming avant-garde theater into prurient display.[9]

After a week and a half of relatively uneventful preview performances, during which the many sex scenes were by all accounts entirely simulated, swirling rumors to the contrary, a spectator issued a formal complaint to the local precinct, citing the production as obscene due to the performers' engagement in what the complainant described as "deviate" (read: homosexual) "sexual intercourse."[10] In response to the complaint, Justice Amos S. Basel of the criminal court attended the March 24 performance. Shortly after the show and a quick discussion with Deputy Inspector Seymour Pine of the public morals squad, Basel signed arrest warrants in front of the theater.[11] Police officers promptly entered the theater and arrested five actors, Lennox Raphael, Ed Wode, the lighting designer, the wardrobe mistress, and a sixteen-year-old usher. The defendants, who were arraigned on charges of "consentual [*sic*] sodomy, public lewdness and obscenity," were each held on $500 bail. The civil rights lawyer William Kunstler was retained to represent them.[12]

When the case was heard by U.S. District Judge Dudley B. Bonsal on March 27 Kunstler argued that *Che!* "dealt with political realities in sexual terms. 'Some of it is boring, some funny, and not particularly erotic,'" but the show was by no means exclusively prurient.[13] A week later, after the producers requested a ruling that would bar the police from arresting company members should the show reopen pending trial, Federal Judge Irving Ben Cooper reserved decision on the request.[14]

After waiting for Cooper's ruling for several weeks to no avail, Wode and Raphael held a press conference at Sardi's restaurant on April 24, during which they announced that, pending the judge's decision, they would reopen *Che!* "on the premise that it's legal" and "within the bounds of what has become customary in the New York theater." The revised production, Wode elaborated, would feature as much nudity as the original production but would be less sexually specific.[15] The slightly toned-down production reopened at the Free Store Theater on the evening of April 25.

Yet on the afternoon of May 8 the cast, crew, and production team of *Che!* was again charged with "consensual sodomy, public lewdness, obscenity and conspiracy to commit such acts."[16] After that evening's performance three actors and Raphael were arrested. The company took a brief hiatus and made even further modifications, and the run of *Che!* continued undisturbed through the summer of 1969.[17] Meanwhile the obscenity case that had been brought against the production languished in the courts until January 1970.

While *Che!* awaited trial, heated and multifarious debates were waged in the press about the artistic validity of the show, the contemporary quality and health of the theater in New York City as it related to the trendiness of explicit depictions of human sexuality, censorship of the arts, the relationship between art and obscenity, and the ways assumptions about class and artistic merit influence what is or is not considered to be obscene and by whom.

These debates, however, were slow to build. Immediately following the *Che!* arrests, members of the press reacted almost unanimously by attacking the production, which was viewed as indicative of a significant lapse in sophistication, taste, and judgment in the New York theater. On April 1 the *New York Times* ran an unsigned editorial lambasting *Che!*, which, although never mentioned by name, was hardly kept anonymous. In the piece the editors referred to "a recently opened New York production that, in displaying sodomy and other sexual aberrations, reached the *reduction ad obscenum* of the theatrical art."[18] The editors extended their obvious disapproval of *Che!* to encompass particular trends in the contemporary theater in general:

> The explicit portrayal on the stage of sexual intercourse is the final step in the erosion of taste and subtlety in the theater. It reduces actors to mere exhibitionists, turns audiences into voyeurs and debases sexual relationships almost to the level of prostitution. It is difficult to see any great principle of civil liberties involved when persons indulging themselves on-stage in this kind of peep-show activity are

arrested for "public lewdness and obscenity." ... The fact that the legally enforceable standards of public decency have been interpreted away by the courts almost to the point of no return does not absolve artists, producers or publishers from all responsibility or restraint in pandering to the lowest possible public taste in quest of the largest possible monetary reward. Nor does the fact that a play, film, article or book attacks the so-called "establishment," revels in gutter language or drools over every known or unknown form of erotica justify the suspension of sophisticated critical judgment.... Far from providing a measure of cultural emancipation, such descents into degeneracy represent caricatures of art, deserving no exemption from the laws of common decency merely because they masquerade as drama or literature.[19]

The editors were certainly not alone in expressing disgust over what passed for artistic standards in New York in the late 1960s. Scapegoating *Che!* was, however, particularly easy to do, not only because it was such a small production created by relative unknowns, but also because critical reaction to it had been so resoundingly negative when it opened. For its enormous influence on the mainstream at the time, Off Off Broadway retained a strong antiestablishment bent and was thus not entirely accepted or trusted by the commercial realm; this likely made it even easier for mainstream writers to target *Che!* as an example of how Off Off Broadway had gone wrong.

Among other critics, Nat Hentoff initially wrote in the *New York Times* that *Che!* was, at its best, politically and artistically "flimsy" and that Lennox Raphael's dialogue was so obtuse that the show would have been "preferable as mime."[20] In his review for *New York* magazine, John Simon called *Che!* a "pseudoabsurdist, quasisymbolic farrago" and complained that for all the advance promise of real, unsimulated sex, the many organs he observed during the show remained "as limp as the author's inspiration."[21] And a critic for *Newsweek* wrote that the show amounted to little more than "a squalid series of loveless fornications and related sexual gymnastics, performed in the nude and reminiscent of nothing so much as the kind of peep show that used to flourish in Port Said during the reign of the late King Farouk."[22] Note that in both the *Newsweek* review and the *New York Times* op-ed piece the legitimacy and artistic worth of *Che!* is being called into question along class lines; both publications reduce the production by comparing it to a common peepshow.

Yet as the initial reaction to the *Che!* arrests died down, critics and industry members began to shift their focus from the artistic merits of the play itself to the troubling issue of arts censorship. During this wave of debate critics held fast to the collective belief that *Che!* was not an especially good production and that its reliance on writhing, naked bodies and simulated scatological and sexual acts was indicative of a larger problem in the contemporary theater in general, and the experimental realm in particular. Nonetheless much writing about the *Che!* trial eventually condemned the obscenity charge, which was seen as both patently unfair to the production and enormously dangerous to New York theater at large.

In the spring 1969 edition of *Dramatists Guild Quarterly*, the Dramatists Guild and Authors League jointly published an open letter addressed to Mayor John Lindsay and District Attorney Frank Hogan. The letter voiced serious concern about the precedent that the *Che!* obscenity trial was setting and argued that the city's decision to close the production "prior to a judicial decision amounted to censorship by intimidation and seriously endangered the freedom of expression in the theater."[23] In his overview of the spring 1969 theater season for the *Massachusetts Review*, the critic and scholar Seymour Rudin agreed. Although he made no bones about calling *Che!* "laborious," "pretentious," "incoherent," and "tedious," he argued nonetheless that the production did not deserve to be dragged through the courts. "[I] find official censorship of theatre an affront, and refuse to be concerned with irrelevancies about redeeming social importance, or whatever," he wrote. "I defend the prerogative of writer, director, and actors to go as 'far' as they and the paying customers please in the theatre, and find this an apposite time to assert that prerogative."[24]

Meanwhile in the *New York Times* Bernard Weinraub wrote a piece that pondered the distinctions between obscenity and art and attempted to home in on the double standard widely perceived to be at play when it came to official judgments on the matter. As Weinraub noted, the city's enforcement agencies and legal representatives were all quick to officially deny that any sorts of double standards were at play in governing decisions about which venues, publications, or productions were prosecuted on the grounds of obscenity and which ones were left alone. Yet off the record many of the same officials were willing to acknowledge all kinds of double standards. "Who the hell knows what's obscene anymore," a staff council with the New York Civil Liberties Union mused when questioned by Weinraub about the possibility of bias in the system. "When you judge community standards for obscenity, you get all kinds of double standards."[25] As Weinraub implied later in the article, double standards were clearly at play in the theater world, since several weeks after the *Che!* arrests, *Oh! Calcutta!* opened without incident, despite very similar advance hype.

Just as rumors preceded *Che!*, those about *Oh! Calcutta!* had begun to run rampant through the city well before that show entered its preview period. *Oh! Calcutta!*, it was being said, was going to be unprecedented in its sexual explicitness and was even going to include actual, unsimulated sexual intercourse.[26] And yet, Weinraub wrote, *Oh! Calcutta!* opened with nary a peep from city officials or concerned citizens. "Although enforcement and legal officials publicly deny that dual standards govern the decisions on what presentations remain open or closed, one official who deals in obscenity cases—and asked to remain unidentified—said: 'Oh! Calcutta!' has a roster of very important people—Tynan, Beckett, Feiffer—and the accoutrements of class are there." On the other hand, "'Che!' involves a little theater, complete unknowns and a script written by a man no one ever heard of. The official added: 'To start action against, say, "Portnoy's Complaint" would be crazy because the presumptions are all against the prosecutor. You have a respectable publisher, Random House, and an author acclaimed for other works, Philip Roth, and good critical reviews. Another book would be less difficult to prosecute.'"[27] Indeed while it might seem on the surface as if *Che!* helped save *Oh! Calcutta!* from similar censorship, a closer look at the trajectory of both shows clearly suggests that *Oh! Calcutta's* pedigree kept it from ever being in any real trouble in the first place.

This is not to imply that the producers and creative team of *Oh! Calcutta!*, which was already in rehearsals at the time of the *Che!* busts, weren't concerned. Yet unlike the *Che!* company, the *Oh! Calcutta!* team was well-established, well-known, and well-connected, and thus able to reach out to various city officials, who, in turn, willingly consulted "unofficially" with the production. A number of special favors in fact helped *Oh! Calcutta!* avoid any run-ins with the law.[28]

For example, when he grew concerned by the *Che!* arrests, the producer of *Oh! Calcutta!*, Hilliard Elkins, promptly invited various city officials to rehearsals and later to a number of early preview performances in hopes that they would help gauge audience reaction and determine what might be construed as offensive or obscene.[29] The production team also solicited advice from such artistic denizens as Rudolf Nureyev and Jerome Robbins and from such high-level politicians and public servants as Senator Jacob Javits and District Attorney Frank Hogan.[30] Of course, *Oh! Calcutta!* was ultimately able to avoid the problems that *Che!* encountered because it took such extraordinary precautions; it probably did not hurt the production, in this case, to have had Tynan insist from the outset that the content be entirely heterosexual, and thus not potentially perceived as "deviant" in nature. Then again, the creative team of *Che!*, struggling in relative obscurity, most certainly did not have the same easy access to senators, world-famous performing artists, or the district attorney as did Hilliard Elkins and Kenneth Tynan.

Like Weinraub, the theater critic Martin Gottfried expressed concern about the ways that class, race, and social status clearly exerted influence over whether or not an entertainment form could be considered obscene. Gottfried called the *Che!* trial "a disgrace to the theater," not only because it revealed how "sluggish" and predictable theater in New York City had become, but more so because it reflected a desire to censor the performing arts and to "outlaw a moral trend." Rather than attack it for being a lousy play, Gottfried openly pitied the "poor . . . tacky little production," which had become an easy scapegoat precisely because it was aesthetically unconventional, commercially disenfranchised, and had less clout than such contemporaneous, comparatively successful and marketable productions as the play *Fortune and Men's Eyes* and the musicals *Oh! Calcutta!* and *Hair*:

> The productions casting worried eyes on the "Che!" trial, far from being adventurous, are unorthodox only in their nudity. Basically, they are conventional: all are plot plays except "Calcutta," which is our old friend, the revue. This sexy theater, so shocking, so upsetting, so sensational, is middle-class theater. Its audiences are establishment audiences. But if there is a legal problem to be resolved, as in anything else, it isn't the established who get hit, it is the alienated. So it is "Che!" that is in court—"Che!," which, for all its clumsiness is the only artistically interesting show in the lot. "Che!" gets the legal hassle, being silly and ratty and politically radical and without a seemingly respectable producer or theater. Also (perhaps to its credit) because it's a bit raunchier than anything else, though nowhere as gross as some of the hits uptown. At any rate, it is the first case in anyone's memory of a New York production being challenged on such grounds, and that should concern even the most straitlaced of producers.[31]

Continued negative assessments of its artistic merit aside, *Che!* garnered a great deal of public support among critics, playwrights, and writers by the time it got to trial. Gottfried, along with fellow journalists Nat Hentoff, Ross Wetzsteon, and Clive Barnes, agreed to serve as expert witnesses for the defense; so did the playwright Israel Horovitz and the cartoonist Jules Feiffer. All of the expert witnesses discussed the play's content in light of "the liberalized mores in off-off Broadway theatre" and argued that while *Che!* was hardly a brilliant production, it nevertheless possessed redeeming social value and thus should not be labeled obscene.[32]

Of the many expert witnesses brought in to testify, only the infamously irascible Broadway producer David Merrick sided with the prosecution. Appearing in court on January 19, 1970, Merrick, never a huge fan of antiestablishment theater, told the judge that he found *Che!* to be "prurient, lewd and vulgar" and that he believed the playwright Lennox Raphael to be utterly lacking in talent and in serious need of "vocational guidance." He added that he found the show to be poorly performed and ineptly directed, and concluded that New York theater in general was "getting a bad reputation" as a result of the "public portrayal of nudity," which, in his opinion, was almost always used less as a means of advancing plot than as a way to make a quick buck.[33] When questioned about plays he had produced that featured nudity, Merrick was quick to argue that nude scenes were acceptable in the theater as long as "they advanced the telling of the story," as his nude scenes presumably always did.[34] Merrick's testimony concluded the prosecution's case.

On February 25 the so-called "*Che!* Eight" were found guilty of obscenity and public lewdness, although the criminal court failed to prove beyond a reasonable doubt that anyone in the company had committed the crime of consensual sodomy.[35] In the 2–1 decision, Judge Arthur Goldberg wrote that *Che!* was filled with "insistent and pervasive sex talk" and "vile profanity" and that the production thus "constituted 'a nadir of smut on stage.'"[36] He found the cast, playwright, producer, and lighting designer "guilty beyond a reasonable doubt of participating in an obscene performance which predominantly appealed and pandered to prurient interest and went beyond the customary limits of candor in presenting profanity, filth, defecation, masochism, sadism, masturbation, nudity, copulation, sodomy and other deviate sexual intercourse."[37]

Goldberg flatly rejected the defense's argument that *Che!* was merely reflecting Off Off Broadway's sexual frankness, as well as the argument that the show had redeeming social value because of its underlying political themes. "The stage directions permitted actual sex on stage," he wrote, but there "was no comparable testimony as to any stage direction that the political content was to be given any particular emphasis."[38] Five of the "*Che!* Eight" were given unconditional discharges, that is, sentences requiring no imprisonment or fines. The remaining three—the playwright Lennox Raphael, the producer and director Ed Wode, and Larry Bercowicz, the actor who originated the title role—were given the choice of a sixty-day prison sentence or fines ranging from $500 to $1,000.[39]

In what was likely an enormous relief to overworked city officials, outraged civil libertarians, and concerned theater industry personnel who were not David Merrick, the *Che!* case did not result in a slew of related obscenity cases, nor was there an uptick in police activity at subsequent theatrical productions. Most of the adult musicals to come after *Hair* and *Oh! Calcutta!* were not perceived as offensive enough to generate concern or official complaints; a great many, such as the vast majority of adult musicals depicting the experiences of modern gay men, were in fact self-consciously tame by contemporary standards. Nonetheless city officials continued in their Sisyphean attempt to determine what was and was not obscene at a time when definitions were vague and erotic entertainment, in its myriad forms, had run rampant in New York City. Yet while most adult musicals were blithely ignored, *Let My People Come,* which ran for a particularly long time at a particularly esteemed venue and thus garnered more attention and scrutiny than most adult musicals to run in New York, experienced its fair share of content-related legal battles.

## LEWD, PERHAPS, BUT NOT OBSCENE: *LET MY PEOPLE COME* ONCE MORE

Practically from its inception *Let My People Come* had troubles. Even before it began its Off Broadway run at the 480-seat Village Gate, where it would play in front of sold-out crowds for two years, Earl Wilson Jr. and the Village Gate proprietor Art D'Lugoff were reprimanded by Actors Equity for attempting to open a show cast entirely with non-union actors in a venue that had long functioned as an Equity house.[40] In this particular case, a different kind of double standard seems to have benefited the production: Wilson was the son of the well-known columnist "Midnight" Earl Wilson, whose syndicated gossip column focused primarily on the Broadway scene. During the exchange of memos between the production and Equity over the situation, Equity's assistant executive secretary, Vincent Donahue, wrote privately to the executive secretary, Donald Grody, voicing concerns over pursuing the infringement. "Do we want to throw up an informational picket line…and raise a bra-ha-ha??" asks Donahue. "The author…is Earl Wilson Jr. It's reasonable to believe that his father's column, and maybe the *Post* itself, would be open to espouse his cause.…Also, would we not possibly be giving publicity to a show which may die if ignored?…It got unanimously bad notice and there are just so many voyeurs available to keep it open. I'm not sure this is a battle we want."[41]

Donahue, however, vastly underestimated the number of voyeurs interested in seeing the production. Despite terrible reviews, *Let My People Come* very quickly began to outsell, by an impressively wide margin, all previous productions that had run at the Village Gate. The revue was in fact soon earning Broadway profits for the Off Broadway house.[42] Equity eventually decided to pursue the case, but due in part to the concerns voiced by Donahue, it was particularly gentle in negotiating with *Let My People Come.* The production complied with Equity: its entire cast was unionized gradually over the course of the first year of the run. Meanwhile far more serious problems would plague the production.

Some months after *Let My People Come* began its run at the Village Gate, Art D'Lugoff became embroiled in a lengthy and particularly bitter legal battle with the building's landlord, Louis Evangelista. Evangelista, who was converting the hotel directly above the Village Gate into a luxury apartment building, was not shy about making clear his desire to drive D'Lugoff out of business.[43] The feud between the two quickly grew heated enough to adversely affect the run of *Let My People Come*.

There were, for example, times when Evangelista had the venue's gas and electricity suddenly and inexplicably shut off, usually on especially cold winter days. There was the time that he had a large cinder-block wall preventing access to the club's electrical supply constructed without warning, in the dead of night. There was the evening of January 3, 1976, when the Buildings Department, citing several code violations that had been phoned in anonymously, arrived to lock the Village Gate just before show-time. On that evening Phil Oesterman, along with the general manager of *Let My People Come*, hastily secured the nearby Astor Place Theater for the 10:30 p.m. performance; as ticket holders filed out of the Village Gate en route to Astor Place, they passed Evangelista and D'Lugoff, who stood chest to chest and nose to nose in the lobby, embroiled in a red-faced screaming match over who, exactly, was to blame for the incident.[44]

Meanwhile business continued to boom for *Let My People Come*. The company released a cast recording of the show in April 1974, which sold like hotcakes but led to more legal problems. Shortly after the first pressing of the record, Earl Wilson Jr. and the music director Billy Cunningham were sued by MCA Music for copyright infringement and wrongful appropriation of the Don Raye and Hughie Prince song "Boogie Woogie Bugle Boy," which Wilson had spoofed for the show as "The Cunnilingus Champion of Company C" and which was prominently featured in both the show and cast recording. After a lengthy hearing that lasted through much of the run, the court rejected the defendants' claim that "The Cunnilingus Champion" was a clear parody of "Boogie Woogie Bugle Boy" and that any similarity between the songs was thus permissible under the doctrine of fair use. The defendants were fined for damages, and "The Cunnilingus Champion of Company C" was ordered excised from the production and all subsequent pressings of the cast recording.[45]

Yet none of these problems held a candle to the case brought against the Village Gate by the State Liquor Authority, which initiated a particularly complicated, lengthy, and costly legal investigation that aimed to determine whether or not *Let My People Come* was "lewd and indecent" enough to cost the venue its liquor license. At the time of this case, which was brought in late 1974, New York's Alcoholic Beverage Control Law stated that individuals licensed to sell alcoholic beverages were not permitted to allow their "premises to become disorderly."[46] The State Liquor Authority argued that the Village Gate was guilty of promoting disorderly conduct by exhibiting a "lewd and indecent performance," which no representatives of the State Liquor Authority had bothered to see prior to making the charge.[47]

Complicating matters was the fact that although the SLA labeled the venue "disorderly" and the production "lewd and indecent," it never directly called into question whether *Let My People Come* was "obscene," since no spectator had ever filed such a complaint with the local precinct. The chief executive officer of the SLA, in fact, went on record to insist that the musical's relationship to the venue was more important than whether or not it had any artistic merit at all. "We couldn't care less if this were done at City Hall," he told the press near the end of the hearing. "But it is performed where liquor is sold. We're not concerned with the artistic legitimacy of the show. We just want to know whether it's lewd."[48]

Yet what constituted a "lewd" or "indecent" performance, and what was the difference between "lewd and indecent" and "obscene"? What constituted an "unruly" environment? And finally, how could a theatrical production that met contemporary community standards of decency nevertheless still be deemed indecent? Was it acceptable for the SLA to exercise its own standards that differed markedly from those of the community in which it operated, especially since it purportedly protected and served that very community in the first place?

These questions, like those that arose during the *Che!* trial, touch on the imprecise nature of legal terminology, the hazy distinction between art and pornography, and the rights of both performers and ticket-buying citizens to exercise free expression. Adding to the confusion surrounding this case, which ultimately questioned whether a performance containing particularly strong sexual content belonged in a venue that sold alcohol, was the fact that there were few benchmark rulings on the matter, and thus little in the way of precedent.

The case brought against the Village Gate by the State Liquor Authority thus put the venue in a particularly frustrating and precarious position. *Let My People Come* had made business so extraordinarily good for the Village Gate that D'Lugoff had no interest in ousting the show. Yet the revocation of a liquor license at an established nightclub would be utterly devastating. Despite the fact that the case posed a clear threat to both his business and his livelihood, D'Lugoff, a left-wing activist who was particularly outspoken about civil rights and liberties, decided to fight back against the State Liquor Authority.[49]

Following the repeal of Prohibition in 1933, the 21st Amendment to the Constitution gave the states broad power to regulate the sale and consumption of alcohol, which is why rules about buying and drinking alcohol vary widely from state to state. Yet because of the country's rapidly changing socio-sexual mores through the 1960s and 1970s, the standards regarding material that was deemed permissible for the stage were thrown into a state of flux, and with them, the legal issues surrounding the relationship between alcohol and free expression. Thus, when the State Liquor Authority of New York brought the case against the Village Gate, the relationship between alcohol and freedom of expression were seen as unresolved, at best.[50] Because of the courts' reluctance to intervene with states' rights regarding the control of alcohol, there were very few rulings on the matter, and the one that most resembled the Village Gate case, *California v La Rue* (1972), left many questions unanswered.

Late in 1971, the Supreme Court agreed to decide on whether state liquor agencies could legally forbid bars and cabarets from offering particular types of erotic entertainment, including live and filmed sex acts and nude dancing, regardless of whether the entertainments in question were legally obscene.[51] The case in question, *California v. La Rue*, was brought to the Supreme Court by a group of California bar owners who took issue with regulations prohibiting certain types of sexually themed performances that the Court had decided were protected by the First Amendment, but that the California Department of Alcoholic Beverages had nevertheless separately decided were "lewd."[52] Calling California's liquor regulations unconstitutional, the bar owners sought to have them struck down, thereby allowing "bottomless" dancing and various types of live nude entertainments to take place in California venues that held liquor licenses.

The Supreme Court's 6–3 decision on *LaRue*, handed down in December 1972, "upheld the state regulation prohibiting 'bottomless' dancing and 'live' shows in bars and night clubs that sell liquor."[53] Further, according to the ruling, licensed bars and nightclubs were prohibited from displaying films or live entertainment "that partake more of gross sexuality than of communication."[54] Writing for the majority, Justice William Rehnquist argued, "We would poorly serve both the interests for which the state may validly seek vindication and the interests protected by the First and 14th Amendments were we to insist that the sort of bacchanalian revelries that the department sought to prevent by these liquor regulations were the constitutional equivalent of a performance by a scantily clad ballet troupe in a theater."[55]

In a *New York Times* article that interpreted the case in lay terms, the lawyer and political commentator Alan Dershowitz explained that the court seemed to be saying that "while you may have a right under the First Amendment to present (or view) naked dancers, you have no right to sell (or consume) liquor" while doing so, and that "in order for you to obtain the 'privilege' of selling (or consuming) liquor, you must relinquish some of your rights of free expression."[56] Dershowitz added that the *La Rue* decision was hardly definitive, but rather "a stopgap decision designed to postpone a fundamental issue now dividing the Court: whether the First Amendment protects all material of a sexually oriented nature so long as it is displayed only to willing adults." According to this theory, the Court "seized on the special power of the state to regulate liquor licenses as a way of ducking the larger issue—at least for the time being."[57]

In other words, the ruling could be read as an attempt to slow the overwhelming number of individual obscenity cases that were being heard all over the country at the time, by granting state agencies increased power to limit or censor sexually themed entertainments in indirect ways. Adding weight to Dershowitz's interpretation of the motivation behind the *La Rue* case was that in the three years between that decision and the Village Gate case, *La Rue* was most frequently applied to "problem" establishments like strip joints, peepshows, and dive bars, where violence occurred, prostitutes congregated, drugs were sold, or actual—not simulated—live sex acts were performed.[58]

While the Village Gate case was thus not technically about whether or not *Let My People Come* was obscene, it nonetheless brought into question the relationship between obscenity and art and suggested that city officials were troubled by the existence of a particularly commercially viable, especially graphic Off Broadway production that was being presented in a cabaret serving mainstream audiences, and that would thus be even more difficult than *Che!* to shutter on straightforward obscenity charges.[59] The defense, reading the State Liquor Authority's actions in these terms, took great pains to portray *Let My People Come* as a piece of legitimate theater, and thus more akin to Rehnquist's "scantily clad ballet troupe" than to any "bacchanalian revelry."

From the outset the defense repeatedly emphasized the fact that no one from the State Liquor Authority had bothered to view *Let My People Come* before bringing the

Village Gate up on charges, and described *Let My People Come* not as a mere titillating sex show, but instead as a socially relevant theater production that contained important messages about human sexuality. It was certainly no accident that when the producer Phil Oesterman took the stand in defense of his show, he was careful to describe one of the allegedly "lewd" acts cited by the SLA as a "nude ballet" and to insist repeatedly that during scenes in which sex acts were simulated, there was absolutely "no contact between the performers."[60]

During the hearings Oesterman was joined by a parade of educators, activists, critics, and actors, all of whom testified about the artistic merit of *Let My People Come* and the cultural importance of the venue that housed it. Expert witnesses for the defense included the feminist activist Betty Friedan, the writer and futurist Alvin Toffler, the playwright Garson Kanin, the theater critics Leonard Probst and Brendan Gill, and the Off Broadway producer Joseph Papp, all of whom assured the counsel for the State Liquor Authority that *Let My People Come* was neither "lewd" nor "indecent," but instead well within the parameters of contemporary theater.[61] Friedan told the court that she found *Let My People Come* to be so "joyous" and "affirmative about human sexuality" that she had seen it twice, and that she planned to return for a third viewing with her teenage daughter. Toffler testified that the Village Gate was an important cultural institution and that *Let My People Come* was, though certainly explicit, hardly lewd or indecent. "It is an affirmation of the value and virtue of sex," he said of the show. "It is not dirty, just happy and healthy."[62] An assistant professor at York College named Miriam Schneider stated that for several semesters she had taken students enrolled in her courses on human sexuality to performances of the show, since it "presents sex in a very wholesome, healthy kind of way."[63] Kanin asserted, "[There is] nothing in the show that I haven't seen in the theater in the last 10 years," and Leonard Probst scoffed, "To hold such a hearing in these times of sexual frankness is an 'anachronism.'"[64]

Probst's sentiments were echoed by a number of journalists and free-speech advocates, who reacted to this case, as many had to the *Che!* case, with anger, frustration, sarcasm, and a cynical awareness of the many types of double standards that were at play in law enforcement. "I saw *Let My People Come* last week and could find nothing disruptive in it," wrote Frederic Weiss for the *Soho Weekly News*. "If the SLA is looking for a disruptive atmosphere, maybe it should go out to Shea Stadium during the football season, or the Garden during one of the New York Rangers Sunday night games. Violence seems to stimulate disruption more than sex does."[65] As news about the hearings continued to spread, the New York Civil Liberties Union announced its intention to file a friend-of-the-court brief in the proceedings. Staff counsel Eve Cary told the *New York Times* that the actions of the SLA amounted to censorship: "The state cannot stop them from putting on the play. It should not be able to do it indirectly by removing their livelihood."[66]

When the hearings concluded on January 24, 1975, lawyers for the Village Gate made a motion to dismiss all charges against the venue, not only because the hearing officer, Herbert Rosenstein, had refused to see the performance in question, but because neither the State Liquor Authority nor anyone else involved in the case had given the cabaret prior notice as to what, precisely, was considered "disorderly," "lewd," or "indecent."[67] The lawyers argued that the language used in the *La Rue* hearings was comparatively precise in describing what was and was not forbidden in venues that sold liquor. But because the terms in question were vague and poorly defined at best, and because *Let My People Come* was not considered obscene by anyone involved in the proceedings, the Village Gate lawyers insisted that the State Liquor Authority had failed to adequately explain why the venue was under scrutiny in the first place. "We have to be told what we can't do," one of the Village Gate's lawyers stated. "It would be intolerable under our system of jurisprudence to require the licensee to guess at its peril at the type of nonobscene entertainment it could provide."[68] Despite the vagueness of the definitions, however, the motion failed in full.[69]

Although the State Liquor Authority was expected to decide on the Village Gate case within a few months of the conclusion of the hearing,[70] almost a full year went by before it reached a verdict. The 3–2 ruling was announced on December 4, 1975. "We feel that the sale of liquor and total nudity are incompatible," stated Michael Roth, chair of the SLA, in explaining the decision for a statewide ban on total nudity in venues that sold alcoholic beverages and the cancellation of the Village Gate's liquor license on the grounds that *Let My People Come* was "lewd and indecent," if decidedly not "obscene."[71]

In response to concerns that such a ruling would adversely affect commercial theaters that sold alcohol during intermission and that presented plays or musicals featuring full-frontal nudity, the SLA specified that the new rule did not apply to "performances in legitimate theaters, where the licensed premises [are] limited to the basement or a lounge."[72] Detecting yet another double standard at play— Broadway theaters, ever representative of the middle-class establishment, were neatly exempted from the ruling—Art D'Lugoff called the ruling "dastardly," announced that he would file an appeal, and declared that in the meantime he would continue to house *Let My People Come* and to serve alcohol to patrons who paid to see it.[73] The Village Gate was granted a temporary restraining order against the cancellation of its liquor license pending appeal, and the case dragged on through 1976.

When *Let My People Come* first began its run at the Village Gate in 1974, Wilson told the press that he and Oesterman had no desire to move their production to a larger, more "legitimate" venue, despite several offers. "'It needs an Off Broadway atmosphere,' Wilson said. 'It's much more relaxed at the Village Gate, and people enjoy sitting at tables, drinking, smoking and talking.'"[74] Even further, the show thrived Off Broadway, where stakes were lower, risks were expected, and a lack of rigid professionalism could be excused in the spirit of freshness and innovation. Yet after two and a half years at the Village Gate, Oesterman had grown tired of an atmosphere in which, Wilson remembers, "there was always a battle going on, legally, with somebody, that affected us. We were always being told, 'Well, you're going to be out of here in a week or two, or three.'"[75] Although Wilson remained convinced that *Let My People Come* would not work well on Broadway, Oesterman announced in early summer 1976 that the production would leave the Village Gate for Broadway's Morosco Theater in July.[76] The production closed at the Gate on July 5, 1976, and began previewing at the Morosco a mere two days later.

While the move uptown rendered the State Liquor Authority's case against the Village Gate moot, it did not end the controversy that seemed to constantly dog the production. The move uptown allowed the Village Gate to keep its liquor license and negated city officials' concerns about the strong sexual content of the musical itself. Yet it sparked a new struggle over freedom of speech and expression. As will be examined in the next chapter, *Let My People Come* found itself particularly unwelcome on Broadway at a time when the theater industry had grown so desperate in its efforts to clean up its pornography-ridden neighborhood that it had begun to resort to atypically draconian measures in hopes of rebuilding its steadily declining audiences.

## CHAPTER 9

# New York's Financial Crisis and the Adult Musical on Broadway

Ford to City: Drop Dead
Vows He'll Veto Any Bail-Out
Abe, Carey Rip Stand
                    —*Daily News* front-page headline, October 30, 1975

No one minds a little roll in the clover
If beneath it all we're purer than snow.
                    —Michael Stewart, *I Love My Wife*

The financial crisis that befell New York City in the 1970s helped sully the city's reputation internationally, compromise the quality of life of its citizens, and cause tourism to plummet perilously. Faced with empty theaters and declining revenues and surrounded by a neighborhood that typified urban decay at its most seedy and menacing, the Broadway establishment grew desperate to reassure increasingly skittish theatergoers, who began to stay home in droves by the middle of the decade. Yet in stepping up its efforts to fight back against the "smut" that was widely perceived to have taken over the neighborhood—and that some argued was slowly but surely infiltrating the commercial theater via Off Off Broadway—the industry occasionally worked to sanitize creative output.

*Let My People Come* moved to Broadway at a particularly dire time for New York City's commercial theater industry, as well as for the city itself. An understanding of the *Let My People Come* Broadway controversy thus demands some examination of the city's financial crisis, and its impact on 1970s city life in general and its commercial theaters in particular. This chapter thus considers the crisis as it affected the commercial theater industry and influenced the reception on Broadway of *Let My People Come*. With the Cy Coleman–Michael Stewart musical *I Love My Wife*, which opened a year after *Let My People Come* moved uptown, Broadway managed to both capitalize on and sanitize the adult musical in response to its own economic tensions and the country's growing conservatism at the end of the 1970s.

Nothing has come to symbolize urban decay quite like New York City between 1965 and 1977. The financial crisis itself was one thing; the impact of the crisis, which rapidly transformed the proud city from an international "standard of quality and sophistication" into the nightmarish embodiment of everything that had gone wrong in the contemporary United States, was quite another.[1] "A crisis denotes a single incident," former governor Hugh L. Carey once said in describing the era. "This was an atmosphere."[2] During the 1970s in general and the mid-decade crisis years in particular, many New Yorkers felt as if they were experiencing a particular blend of deterioration and demoralization that was "infinitely more debilitating than anything else in recent memory."[3] As the financial crisis took its toll on every aspect of city living, the collective self-esteem of the city's inhabitants sagged accordingly.

So much writing has been devoted to New York's fiscal crisis and its myriad ramifications that the many reasons for its onset will not be discussed in great detail here.[4] But in brief, the cost of city services in the 1960s, combined with a declining stock market and the onset of stagflation in the early 1970s,[5] caused the city to come dangerously close to bankruptcy in 1975, when the municipal bond market that was the city's main source of capital dried up. City officials' reactions were swift and devastating. Between June and December 1975, 20,000 civil servants from more than sixty city agencies, the transportation authority, nineteen municipal hospitals, seventeen colleges, and the public school system were furloughed or dismissed for periods ranging from a few days to a few years, or for good. Salaries for all municipal workers were frozen, as was the city's capital budget.[6] "The iceberg had hit," Jonathan Mahler writes of this exceptionally bleak time in his chronicle *Ladies and Gentlemen, the Bronx Is Burning*, "and Gotham was taking on water."[7]

Yet even before 1975 New York had been in palpable decline. Between the late 1960s and mid-1970s the city lost more than 600,000 jobs, over half of which were in manufacturing industries that had historically provided work for hundreds of thousands of low-skilled residents. This led to a rapid economic contraction, and close to a million people left New York over the course of the decade, resulting in a sharp rise in building abandonment as well as related petty crimes like arson and graffiti. While neighborhoods in all five boroughs were adversely affected, the South Bronx was decimated. And little could be done to reverse or even reduce these problems because the city's books, which had been "sagging under the weight of years of budget gimmickry, were roughly $3.3 billion in the red."[8]

As the city's industry and population shrank, its welfare rolls grew. Crime too began to rise faster in the late 1960s than it had at any point since the 1930s.[9] A host of strikes by teachers, police officers, transit workers, and sanitation workers, which took place between 1966 and the early 1970s, merely added insult to injury. New York was clearly suffering well before its bankruptcy scare.

"When I tell the neighbors that I will soon have to return to New York City, they sympathize," wrote the retired theater critic Brooks Atkinson from his home in the Catskills in late 1970. "There is nothing glamorous about New York to them today. From this secluded corner of the Catskills, New York City looks forbidding—like a monstrous heap of trouble and crime."[10] For all its problems, and though he had left it, Atkinson continued mournfully, New York remained the center of his universe in many ways: all of the newspapers he read each morning were printed there; almost all the books he owned had been published there. And then, of course, there were the stage productions that he frequently traveled south by bus to see.

Yet while fiercely proud of New York City's cultural output, Atkinson understood why so many had come to fear, mock, leave, or avoid the place by the turn of the decade; at least from where he sat, the city seemed to have been overrun by drugs, pornography, and petty crime and become burdened by financial problems that affected its schools, homes, streets, subways, workplaces, and famed entertainment venues. "New York has become a city in which the citizens hesitate to go to the theater after dark because of crime in the streets," Atkinson lamented. "This is how New York City looks from the country—irascible and barbarous." This, he wrote, was the reason people stopped visiting New York to sightsee, shop, dine, or go to the theater. "New York City," he concluded, "on which we depend for cultural energy, is in serious trouble."[11] So too was one source of the cultural energy itself: the commercial theater industry, which, like the city surrounding it, had begun to manifest signs of financial and aesthetic malaise by the mid-1960s.[12]

## THE THEATER AND TOURISM

New York City became the country's center for commercial theater at roughly the same time that it became a tourist destination. In the mid-1820s Manhattan surpassed Philadelphia and Boston as the country's center for commercial theater; this coincided with major advances in transportation, which made leisure travel easier, cheaper, faster, and more comfortable. Visitors from other parts of the country, as well as from overseas, thus only became more commonplace through the nineteenth century and early twentieth.[13]

Because the city's tourist trade and its commercial theater industry took shape at around the same time, the two have gone hand in hand more or less since inception. By the mid-twentieth century, even as Broadway began to struggle aesthetically with the changing times, roughly a third of its audience was composed of tourists who were eager to take in a glitzy production or two during their stay in New York.[14] Yet as the international image of New York City began to tarnish, tourism dropped off precipitously.

New York's many problems made national headlines through the 1960s, but tourism nevertheless remained fairly healthy through the end of the decade. Between 1967 and 1969 in fact the city enjoyed a significant boost in tourism, which came as something of a surprise following a disappointing dip that began during the World's Fair years of 1964 and 1965 and that lasted through 1966.[15] Between 1967 and 1969 some 16.5 million visitors came to New York City and generated $1.5 billion for the city annually,[16] making tourism second only to the fashion industry as an income producer.[17] As the decade drew to a close, eager representatives from the New York Convention and Visitors Bureau, armed with this information, began pushing Mayor

Lindsay to address the city's "inadequate" convention facilities in hopes that tourism could be exploited as an even greater asset to the city.[18] Yet as the saying goes, one needs to spend money to make money, and by the turn of the decade the city couldn't afford to spend money on new convention centers, let alone its schools, hospitals, housing authority, police force, transportation system, or sanitation infrastructure.

The city's economic woes and sinking reputation only intensified as the 1970s began, bringing with it a years-long period of stagflation, or mix of massive inflation and economic decline, which adversely affected the entire country.[19] Tourism suffered nationwide, and because of the myriad lurid reports of rising crime rates, drugs, prostitution, and pornography, New York City was hardly a top vacation destination for those who could afford to travel. The number of visitors took a 20 percent nose-dive between the summers of 1969 and 1970. City officials and the Convention and Visitors Bureau steeled themselves for a smaller dip—perhaps another 5 percent—between the summers of 1970 and 1971, and were horrified by yet another 20 percent drop.[20] By summer 1971 spokespeople for hotels, restaurants, and tourist attractions citywide began to complain of noticeably bad business; reports from Times Square were especially bleak. One sightseeing guide stationed in the theater district griped, "This is the worst summer I can remember since the war. They ought to burn down those porno joints on 42nd Street and those filthy movies and Broadway would come back to its own."[21]

## TIMES SQUARE AND ITS THEATERS

By the early 1970s Times Square had become the exemplar of just about everything that had gone wrong with the enormous city surrounding it. It's no accident that Martin Scorsese chose to depict Travis Bickle—the unstable, socially disaffected protagonist at the center of his 1976 "fever dream of a film," *Taxi Driver*—cruising past that neighborhood's grinders, porn-shops, pawnshops and shady-looking crowds as he sneers, in voice-over, "All the animals come out at night—whores, skunk pussies, buggers, queers, fairies, dopers, junkies. Sick. Venal. Someday a real rain will come and wash all the scum off the streets."[22] Times Square in the 1970s was largely viewed as a problem neighborhood not to be reckoned with. The two police precincts that covered it ranked first and second, city-wide, in total felony complaints.[23] More robberies and rapes were reported within Midtown South than in any other precinct in New York by a two-to-one margin in 1975, and since the police department had been forced to fire 3,000 officers in July of that year, the NYPD's constant patrols of Times Square merely aspired to "the limited objective of keeping all hell from breaking loose."[24]

In *Money Jungle: Imagining the New Times Square*, the anthropologist Benjamin Chesluk writes that for over a century, Times Square has been the site of struggle and collaboration between the performing arts, real estate, and sex industries. "Theater owners and impresarios were often one and the same," he explains, and "the performing arts industry's products often drew from or blended with those of the sex industry, and vice versa; and theater owners and real estate developers were happy to lease space to sex shops and porn entrepreneurs during lean economic times."[25] While the three industries forged a symbiotic, if not always harmonious relationship with one another and the neighborhood surrounding them, Times Square itself has long been perceived as a problem area, due to its failure to function specifically as a "respectable" locale for white, upper-middle-class sensibilities. While the neighborhood became precipitously seedy through the late 1960s and 1970s, its purported problems have thus in fact existed from inception.

New York's many entertainment venues were scattered widely across various neighborhoods until the 1870s. At this point, the city's first commercial theater district, known as the Rialto, became concentrated in and around Union Square.[26] A few theaters remain in that neighborhood, but the Rialto itself quickly became upwardly mobile in both the literal and figurative sense: as Manhattan developed northward through the late nineteenth and early twentieth centuries, the theater district moved further and further uptown into neighborhoods that were less established, and thus less expensive. Whenever theater owners collectively moved north, commercial establishments, including office buildings, restaurants, residences, and department stores, would quickly follow, as entrepreneurs attempted to take advantage of whatever increased respectability the Rialto brought to a new part of town.

Yet while the presence of such establishments helped attract audiences to the theaters, it also eventually drove up land prices and taxes. In time this would cause the theaters to become less profitable for their owners, who would simply close up shop and make another move north. Through the last decades of the nineteenth century the Rialto and the commercial ventures that relied on it leapfrogged their way up Broadway, from Union Square to Fifth Avenue at Twenty-sixth Street, to Herald Square, and then, in 1895, to Longacre Square, at the crossroads of Broadway, Seventh Avenue, and Forty-second Street.[27] Known by the late nineteenth century as a site for brothels, saloons, and street prostitution, Longacre Square, which was renamed Times Square when Adolph Ochs opened the newspaper's headquarters there in 1904, enjoyed a few decades' worth of respectability, if not quite upper-class glamour, before the 1929 stock market crash prompted its decades-long decline.[28]

Because the years prior to the Great Depression saw particularly rapid urban development in New York, the theater industry was unable to pick itself up and move north to a cheaper neighborhood in the early 1930s; by this point the city had become so densely developed that there was simply nowhere else to go to ease the blow after the stock market crash. As a result, as noted in chapter 1, Broadway theaters took quite a blow. Whereas the 1927–28 season saw the premieres of a whopping (if approximate) three hundred productions, including some fifty-one musicals, only thirty-four new musicals were produced during the 1929–30 season. By the 1933–34 season the number of new musicals had dipped to thirteen. Many of the industry's most successful producers went bankrupt; many of its actors, directors, choreographers, composers, and lyricists headed, at least temporarily, for Hollywood, which had begun to boom just as Broadway went bust.[29]

Through the early 1930s the commercial theater industry's woes affected its surrounding neighborhood. Construction on new theaters, which were being built in response to the overwhelming demand for productions during the roaring '20s,

ground to a halt in Times Square, which suddenly found itself with many more theaters than it could fill. Razing unfinished and unused theaters wasn't a realistic solution to the problem, since no one had the money needed to replace them. Theaters
thus stood empty or were converted into burlesque houses or grinders. Similarly
many of the neighborhood's upscale stores and eateries became flea circuses, arcades,
honky-tonks, cheap dance halls, automats, and penny restaurants.[30] Of the ten theaters lining Forty-second Street, only one, the grandiose New Amsterdam, was still
functioning as a Broadway house by the mid-1930s.[31] While the musical blossomed
as an art form through the 1930s, both on the silver screen and, despite the decline
in extravagance, on the stage, its cultural and economic power declined precipitously,
as did the neighborhood that helped give it life.

Although the sheer quantity of offerings would never attain pre-Depression
status, the stage musical bounced back with a vengeance through the later 1930s,
1940s, and 1950s as a thriving artistic form reaching new aesthetic heights, to the
acclaim of critics and its predominantly white, middle- to upper-middle-class audience base. Yet through these decades the neighborhood that played host to the
Broadway musical would only become more closely associated with the lowbrow. By
the end of the 1930s Times Square had grown notorious for its "honky-tonk atmosphere, its once-elegant restaurants replaced by luncheonettes, its cigar stores and
lobbies inhabited by a new element of petty hoodlums."[32]

During World War II Times Square became a mecca for countless servicemen who
drifted through the neighborhood before or after serving, or during furloughs, in
search of cheap diversions that could be procured at any time of day or night.[33] By
1944 gay cruising, for decades a well-known if historically covert feature of the neighborhood, had become so conspicuous that Mayor LaGuardia ordered the nightly closing of Bryant Park. This succeeded merely in driving cruising, and the many trysts
that resulted from it, off the streets and into the balconies and bathrooms of Times
Square's myriad grind houses.[34]

As noted in chapter 6, Mayor Wagner's 1954 attempt to clean up Times Square
resulted in a series of severe rezoning codes that killed off many of the dime museums, freak shows, and penny arcades in the area. But the amendments to the zoning
codes backfired: they restricted market demand for commercial space on Forty-
second Street, thereby giving the advantage to dirty-book dealers in search of cheap
storefronts.[35] Adult bookstores only proliferated, as did Times Square's reputation as
an urban mecca for sleaze, once the *Roth v. United States* decision was handed down
in 1957.

Chesluk points out that the widespread perception of Times Square as a "problem" neighborhood was fueled by class- and race-based "assumptions and prejudices
that radically simplified the complicated and contradictory history and culture" of
the neighborhood, which remained a thriving, crowded, and eminently profitable—if
also seedy and sexually exploitative—entertainment center through the 1960s and
1970s. The neighborhood was, after all, home to countless souvenir shops, newsstands, B-movie and porn houses, martial arts supply shops, sex stores, peepshows,
cheap restaurants, hotels, office buildings, and massage parlors, not to mention
the many Broadway theaters that, despite economic and aesthetic struggles, still

managed to draw patrons at even the very worst of times.[36] The neighborhood also boasted an impressively high degree of socioeconomic and racial diversity, which was unparalleled elsewhere in the city. At least according to some studies, even the crime statistics in the area only seemed particularly high, but were in fact quite low once population density was taken into account.[37]

What the neighborhood sorely lacked, then, especially during the beleaguered 1970s, was the kind of middle-class respectability that the increasingly anxious commercial theater industry had once enjoyed and had never stopped hoping to reclaim. Otto Guernsey, the prolific editor of the *Best Plays* theater yearbooks, noted as much when he wrote in the 1972–73 edition that although the Broadway theaters, especially during show times, were easily some of the safest places in the city, if not the world, "ballyhoo counts more than truth in matters like this."[38] Indeed as if the nation's many socioeconomic woes, the city's economic downturn, and Broadway's own aesthetic crises weren't enough, the growing fear of random street crime, which was apparently shared by locals and tourists alike, was keeping a growing number of potential spectators home, especially after dark.

Eager to appeal to as many interested, if spooked, spectators as possible, the industry found itself walking a fine line through the early 1970s: how to attract theatergoers to a sketchy, if perhaps not truly dangerous, neighborhood at a time when the musical theater was wrestling with its own economic and aesthetic demons. This was a particularly difficult problem to solve during stagflation, which had prompted producers to simultaneously slash the costs of production and increase ticket prices.[39] Contributing to this vicious cycle was the fact that many financially strapped Broadway producers grew wary of anything but the most escapist, risk-free fare, which resulted in a glut of derivative, forgettable productions on Broadway.

The theater critic Howard Kissel once quipped, "Two things are absolute certainties: the speed of light, and the imminent death of the New York theater."[40] As Kissel's crack implies, melodramatic proclamations about how the commercial theater in New York was on a fast track to hell have been sounded for almost as long as the city's theaters have existed. And while the hand-wringing over the state of Broadway leading up to and during the city's financial crisis was thus perhaps slightly alarmist, the rate of attendance at commercial theaters had in fact begun to fall dramatically as the 1960s gave way to the 1970s. While the city's smaller theaters—which drew audiences of locals more than tourists, did not have to worry quite as much about the bottom line, and could thus afford to take larger creative risks in their shows—thrived as the city around them suffered, Broadway industry people began to sweat.

Despite the commercial theater's many aesthetic concerns, Broadway theaters did fairly well, financially speaking, through the 1960s. Between 1960 and 1968, and with the exception of a disappointing 1963–64 season, annual grosses between 1960–61 and 1967–68 climbed steadily from $44 million to $59 million, and attendance increased from 7.7 million to 9.5 million. Playing weeks hovered between 1,100 and 1,250, and the number of new productions rose from forty-eight to seventy-four. But 1967–68 proved a peak year, after which new productions, attendance, and grosses began to decline steadily. New productions dropped to a dismal low of forty-three in 1973–74, attendance plummeted to 5.7 million, and annual grosses fell accordingly, to $46 million.[41]

At the end of the 1970–71 season the theater industry began a years-long scramble to appeal to larger audiences and to win back skittish tourists. Suggested remedies that were eventually enacted included a move to eliminate Monday night performances in exchange for a midweek matinee that would counter more theatergoers' concerns about being in Times Square at night, the introduction of day-of-show discount and student-rush tickets, and conversion of all Broadway box offices to accept major credit cards.[42] The League of New York Theatres approved a change in curtain time for evening performances, from 8:30 to 7:30, which would allow audiences to get home (or back to their hotels) an hour earlier and thus perhaps feel just a little safer at the prospect of venturing into Times Square.[43] Also at the behest of the League was the introduction of a new after-theater taxi line in September 1971, which directed cabbies to line up along Forty-fifth and Forty-sixth Streets to await theatergoers between the hours of 9:00 and midnight.[44] And in June 1973 TKTS, the ticket booth that distributes same-day half-price tickets, opened to great fanfare and instant success.[45]

As the 1970s continued, so did the Broadway industry's concerns about its surrounding neighborhood, the sleazy reputation of which only grew through the darkest period of the city's financial crisis. While most of the time, effort, and money went into advertising and marketing, which began to pay off in spades by the end of the decade,[46] theatrical content on Broadway occasionally became a matter for concern and heated debate as well. This was certainly the case in June 1976, when the producer Phil Oesterman announced his intention to move *Let My People Come* from its Off Broadway home at the Village Gate to Broadway's Morosco Theater.

## LET MY PEOPLE COME... TO BROADWAY

A few months prior to the Broadway premiere of *Let My People Come*, the League of New York Theatres and Producers announced "a concerted effort to ameliorate the current conditions in the Times Square area with 'respect to pornography and other sex-oriented business.'"[47] Devoted to improving the dilapidated theater district, the League issued a statement in February 1976 arguing that the "misuse of first-class film houses places a tremendous stumbling block in the path" of the effort to clean up Times Square and improve the international image of New York City.[48] Harvey Sabinson, director of the League's special projects department, dramatically informed the press that the development of Times Square into a neighborhood where tourists could more safely and comfortably find quality entertainment was absolutely crucial to the city and its economy. As "a matter of pure business, the long-range view should take precedence over immediate gain," he warned. "The League, in conjunction with other interested parties about the urban environment, will continue to keep pressure on reputable theater exhibitors who are showing pornographic films for the sake of making money.... Our fear is that once a theater turns to pornographic films, it rarely returns to quality films. It would be another battle lost for the legitimate theater area as well as for other businesses in the district."[49]

To this end the League sent letters to every first-run, "first-class" film house in Times Square, asking the owners and operators to stop booking pornographic films. A vast majority of these letters went unanswered.[50] Later in the same year the League purchased a Cushman street sweeper, which it donated to the Department of Sanitation in hopes for "a clean sweep for Broadway."[51] And in 1977 the League established its own fund, culled from a small cut of the weekly profits from all shows running on Broadway, which was used to lobby local politicians for the continued improvement of Times Square.[52] While the letters to the cinemas and the street sweeper donation were perhaps more symbolic than effective, all of the League's actions reflected the Broadway industry's exasperation with the state of Times Square and with the city's response to their complaints.

In 1972, the League had applauded the city's initiation of an intensive, long-term campaign to limit the explosion of pornography in midtown.[53] But by 1975 the League had begun to blast the city in particularly harsh language for falling so horribly short of its goals. "We in the theater community are sick and tired of hearing how difficult it is—what a threat to civil rights it is—to put a stop to this cancer," snapped the producer Alexander H. Cohen, acting as spokesperson for the League. "There is a simple choice. You can have them or you can have us, but you can't have both. For the professional theater, coexistence with whorehouses is not possible."[54]

Further indication that tensions between the Broadway and sex industries had risen considerably by the mid-1970s was the League's overwhelmingly negative reaction to news that *Let My People Come* would arrive on Broadway in summer 1976. Long a champion of civil liberties and anticensorship causes,[55] the League had nevertheless become invested by the mid-1970s in driving adult entertainment from Times Square by any means necessary. As a result, although the Off Broadway run of *Let My People Come* was an unprecedented commercial smash that had grossed $3.5 million at the time of its move, the League publicly vilified Oesterman's decision to bring the show to the Morosco.[56]

On June 28, 1976, two days after an announcement about the production's uptown transfer ran in the *New York Times*, the League's board of governors convened a special meeting. Although no formal vote was taken, the board drafted a statement deploring the booking of the production, which was viewed as "antithetical" to the "programs of the League seeking to upgrade the physical appearance of the theatrical district; to eliminate sex-related businesses such as massage parlors, peep shows, prostitution hotels, street prostitution, topless bars, and pornographic motion picture theaters from the theater district, and to generally improve the urban environment in the midtown area."[57] League members requesting anonymity told *Variety*'s drama critic Hobe Morrison that while the organization as a whole continued to oppose censorship, a growing concern about the presence of shows influenced by *Oh! Calcutta!*—the original production of which had closed by this point—had nonetheless caused a significant shift in attitude among members. As one League member explained, the organization made its statement against *Let My People Come* out of desperation about the current state of the neighborhood. "It's a matter of credibility," the unnamed source said. "We've been bringing pressure on City authorities to eradicate prostitution, massage parlors, porno films and 'adult' bookstores. The presence of a blatant sex show in one of the theatres in our own front yard tends to negate all we're trying to do to improve the quality of midtown."[58]

The League's position on *Let My People Come* clearly went so directly against the organization's own history of anticensorship activism that its president, Richard Barr, felt compelled to backpedal as soon as the official statement hit the press. Barr insisted that the League did not consider *Let My People Come* to be pornographic, and that even if it did, it "was not in the business of telling producers or theater owners what to do"—even though the League clearly just had.[59] Oesterman, quick to recognize Barr's about-face, wasted no time in attacking the League's position as hypocritical and censorious and in portraying *Let My People Come* as no tawdry sex show, but a production that paints contemporary sexuality in a wholesome, healthy, empowering way. Arguing emphatically that he, like the League, was eager to see improvements in Times Square, Oesterman was nevertheless quick to point out that his show "doesn't portray or condone any of the objectionable conditions on Eighth Ave. or West 42nd St. It isn't about prostitution or dope or vice. The ads don't mislead anyone. People know what they're coming to see. Lots of people have seen it and may be healthier for it."[60]

Several days later Oesterman mournfully told a reporter for the *Times* that the uproar over his show struck him as particularly alienating and "very strange": "I'm a theater man . . . but there are people who are trying to stop my show and reduce me to a dirty old man."[61] The scuffle between the League and Oesterman was not enough to derail the production, especially once the League chose not to take any official action.[62] *Let My People Come* began previews at the Morosco as planned on July 7, 1976, and announced an official opening three weeks later, on the 27th.

Yet late in the musical's preview period one last controversy developed, this time in the form of a bitter falling-out between Oesterman and the composer Earl Wilson Jr., who chose to side with the League on its position about the show. "How a musical is staged makes all the difference in the world," Wilson argues. "When I heard the description of how he was going to direct the show . . . firing most of the cast . . . hiring 'pretty' boys, etc., I thought he had gone crazy." Convinced that the Broadway move was a terrible mistake, Wilson "wanted to get out of the way . . . and let people know I didn't agree with his decision."[63] On July 15 Wilson requested that his name be removed from the marquee, program, and advertisements for the Broadway production of *Let My People Come*, telling the *New York Times*, "I feel that the show has become vulgar [in its new incarnation]."[64] Several days later he elaborated: "The show just doesn't convey my intentions anymore. The show I wrote was innocent and joyous, but now the subtlety of the lyrics just isn't present."[65] Oesterman fired back quickly. "What innocence?" he sneered. "The show is about sexual freedom, not innocence." Pointing out that the show was never subtle, Oesterman also did not hesitate to share with the press that for all Wilson's complaints about the vulgarization of the production, he had not been offended enough by the updated production to waive his royalties.[66] Wilson countered that were he to waive his royalties, they would go to Oesterman, which Wilson could not, in good conscience, allow.[67]

Shortly after news of the feud between Oesterman and Wilson broke, Oesterman announced that the official opening of the Broadway production would be postponed until mid-August.[68] Clearly employing the same tactic that worked so successfully during the Off Broadway run, he put off the premiere of the show twice more;[69] it never officially opened for critics. Meanwhile in mid-August Wilson went to court to stop the musical's Broadway run and to have his name removed from the marquee and all promotional materials.[70]

Wilson and the League needn't have worried about the show's appearance on Broadway. Despite never officially opening, *Let My People Come* was reviewed by several critics in the late summer and early fall of 1976, and the reviews helped kill a show that had arguably begun to run out of steam while it was still at the Village Gate. Citing the fact that for all Wilson's complaints, *Let My People Come* hadn't changed enough in trading the comparatively rough-and-tumble Off Broadway realm for the bright lights and higher stakes of Broadway, the critics, like the League, seemed to have had the sleaziness of Times Square in mind when reviewing the production. Marilyn Stasio griped less about the songs and sketches than about the show's tawdry aspects: its "gaudy Christmas tree lights" that dangled limply from the Morosco's crystal chandelier and ornate wall sconces; the "clubfooted choreography" and "Frederick's of Hollywood" costumes; the "many miles of tinsel" that substituted for a proper set.[71] Sylviane Gold, for the *Post*, agreed, sniping, "The set looks like it cost $3.89 at one of those Christmas decoration stores." Warning that "'Let My People Come' is to Broadway theater what Richard Nixon is to politics," Gold continued, "Anyone who cares about theater should be warned off this travesty," which, he concluded, is "so brazenly bad that even to pan it is to overpraise."[72] And Hobe Morrison of *Variety*, who began his review by admitting that he made it through "the mercifully short first act" before fleeing, dubbed it "cruel and unusual punishment" that was "puerile," "dull and depressing."[73]

In defense of the show, and perhaps of its alienated composer and lyricist, Ernest Leogrande argued in the *Post* that although the downtown production worked well in the relaxed, cabaret-style Village Gate, the comparatively formal Broadway milieu raised the production stakes too high, made the production seem less relaxed than simply unprofessional, and placed the audience "symbolically farther from the players," thereby making the copious nudity and simulated sex seem at once "more blatant" and "more calculating."[74] For all the controversy it caused, the Broadway production closed on October 2, 1976. When, later in October, a Broadway revival of the comparatively tame *Oh! Calcutta!* opened at the Edison Theatre on West Forty-seventh Street, the members of the League of New York Theatres and Producers simply kept their mouths shut.

The appearance of *Let My People Come* on Broadway was so rife with industry-generated controversy that no one seemed to notice that times were changing and that stage nudity and simulated sex were no longer novel. In marked contrast, the few critics who bothered to review the *Oh! Calcutta!* revival reflected indifference not only to the show, but to the cheery, positive messages about sexuality that nudie musicals in general conveyed. Clive Barnes, who made no secret about disliking *Oh! Calcutta!* the first time around, wrote of the revival, "It was a feeble show then and it is a feeble show now," and guessed correctly that it would be of little interest to locals and very successful with "our rather more diffident" tourists.[75]

A far more damning if also more telling review of the *Oh! Calcutta!* revival appeared in the June 1977 issue of *Hustler*. Frank Fortunato wrote that the production, which seemed particularly "mild in the jaded climate of the 70s...ultimately scores a zero in the titillation department." To emphasize just how jaded the sexual mores of the country seemed by the late 1970s, at least by *Hustler* standards, Fortunato argued that the sketches attempting to delve into the cast's feelings about contemporary sexuality struck him as particularly boring. "Who cares?" he sniped. "[As] a player in one skit puts it: 'For the price of this seat, I coulda' gotten a blow job!'"[76]

## BOB & CAROL & TED & ALICE AND *I LOVE MY WIFE*

The 1977 surprise success *I Love My Wife*, which opened to raves despite terrible word of mouth and rumors of a doomed out-of-town run, was never heralded for its depth or searing insight into contemporary sexuality, despite the fact that it was at least ostensibly about partner swapping among middle-class couples in Trenton, New Jersey. Nor did its rather traditional messages about sexuality, as evidenced by its title, do much to counter contemporary attacks on the Broadway musical's often old-fashioned view of the world. As far as adult musicals go, *I Love My Wife* is among the tamest. It is about partner swapping, which made it relatively risqué as far as Broadway musicals go, even by late 1970s standards. But at a time when Broadway was desperately trying to lure audiences back to the theater, *I Love My Wife* did what successful musicals do well and what very few had managed to pull off in the drama-heavy, musically sparse 1976–77 season: offer just enough provocation to draw—but not to offend or alienate—middle-aged, middle-class crowds and provide enough singing, dancing, and broad physical comedy to delight them once they got to the theater.

*I Love My Wife*, which opened at the Ethel Barrymore Theater on April 13, 1977, featured a score by Cy Coleman (*Sweet Charity, Little Me*), who had built his reputation on jazzy, strutting show-stoppers like *Sweet Charity*'s "Big Spender" and *Little Me*'s "Hey, Look Me Over." Coleman's comfort composing in a wide range of contemporary popular styles seemed to almost directly contradict his enduring fascinations with pre-bop jazz, Gershwin-era show tunes, and the classic burlesque. His ability to work with comparatively new forms while rooting himself in old ones gives much of his music the curious distinction of seeming at once freshly urbane and comfortably old-fashioned.[77]

Having recently mourned the death of Dorothy Fields, the lyricist and book writer he'd collaborated with for over a decade, Coleman teamed up for the first time with Michael Stewart (*Bye Bye Birdie, Hello, Dolly!*), who wrote *I Love My Wife*'s book and lyrics. The earliest announcements about *I Love My Wife*, made in January 1977, had Joe Layton (*George M!*) slated to serve as director and choreographer.[78] But when Layton suffered a bad fall and withdrew from the production, the choreographer Onna White (*Mame, 1776, Irma La Douce*) quickly stepped in, as did the director Gene

Saks, whose *California Suite* and *Same Time, Next Year* were already big hits on Broadway at the time.[79] Several months before *I Love My Wife* opened, Frank Sinatra released his own version of the title number, which sold well and helped build publicity and a strong advance for the musical.[80]

*I Love My Wife*'s impressive behind-the-scenes pedigree likely helped sell a musical about partner swapping to even the most straitlaced of theatergoers. Producers embraced the idea too, especially since the musical placed little to no emphasis on visual spectacle, was headlined by then unknown actors (Ilene Graff, James Naughton, Joanna Gleason, and Lenny Baker), and didn't require a cast of thousands or enormous, complicated, expensive sets. The size and simplicity of the production were clearly a bonus at a time when New York was digging itself out of financial crisis, real estate and production costs continued to rise steadily, and, in a trend that would only accelerate by the end of the decade, the commercial theater was trying to come up with ways to offer a lot less for a lot more.[81]

*I Love My Wife* was very loosely based on Luis Rego and Didier Kaminka's long-running Parisian cabaret show, *Viens chez-moi, j'habite chez une copine* (Come to My Place, I'm Living with My Girlfriend), which focused on a cheerful if morally challenged gas station attendant who sweet-talks an easygoing young couple into putting him up for a few days. Of course, the "few days" turns into a much longer time, and when the freeloader begins bringing a seemingly endless supply of girlfriends to the couple's home, they get annoyed and wackiness ensues. The rights to *Viens chez-moi* were acquired in 1976 by the producer and restaurateur Joseph Kipness, who tapped Michael Stewart to adapt a version for American audiences.[82]

Stewart took on the project but quickly found that he was less interested in *Viens chez-moi*'s storyline than in the quirky way the show employed music. Through the course of *Viens chez-moi*, whenever a song, which was always prerecorded, began, the action onstage would grind abruptly to a halt, and an actor would pick up a nearby microphone, face the audience, and sing along with the recording. When songs ended, microphones were carefully replaced, and the stage action resumed as if nothing out of the ordinary had occurred.[83]

This gimmick lent *Viens chez-moi* a cheerful anarchy that Stewart found both fascinating and very funny. Charmed by the idea of dropping songs into the middle of the action without necessarily trying to integrate, justify, or explain them, Stewart devised a script in which four onstage musicians accompanied the entire show, observed all the action, occasionally sang or spoke lines of dialogue, changed costumes according to the scene in question, and regularly interacted with the four main characters, whether or not it made sense for them to do so. The structure of *I Love My Wife* thus owes more to *Viens chez-moi* than does its plot, which, a number of critics pointed out, was remarkably similar to, if somewhat slighter than, the 1969 film *Bob & Carol & Ted & Alice*.

The first feature film by Paul Mazursky, *Bob & Carol & Ted & Alice* explored the impact of the sexual revolution on two couples at the onset of middle age. Close friends, the couples react very differently to contemporary (upper-) middle-class morality, especially as it relates to sexual freedom. Bob Sanders (Robert Culp), a documentary filmmaker, and his wife, Carol (Natalie Wood), cling as desperately to modishness and youth as Bob does to the ample collection of love beads that he never removes from around his neck. As the film opens, Bob and Carol attend an intensive weekend encounter session at a resort clearly modeled on the Esalen Institute.[84] At the start of the workshop Bob explains that he is there only because he's researching the Institute for a film project; Carol giggles shyly that she is there because Bob is her husband. Yet the weekend transforms both Bob and Carol, who decide to throw themselves into the exploration of open marriage as a means toward personal liberation and marital enlightenment. Over the course of the film Bob and Carol each embark on "purely physical" affairs, which they discuss with one another promptly, if a bit too self-consciously, using the lingo they picked up at the Institute: "The truth is always beautiful"; "You're copping out"; "I'm having insight!"; "Don't tell me what you *think*—tell me how you *feel*."

Bob and Carol's best friends, Ted Henderson (Elliott Gould), an attorney, and his wife, Alice (Dyan Cannon), are far more traditional and are at first condescendingly indulgent of their friends' purported transformation. Yet when Carol gleefully informs them of Bob's affair and of how moved she is by his honesty about it, Ted and Alice are deeply unsettled, not only because their friends' newly open but seemingly functional marriage challenges their own stalwart adherence to monogamy, but also because it forces them to acknowledge that they are not only stubbornly resistant to but also terrified by the changing times. Alice is in fact so overwhelmed by the "new" sexual freedoms that she has been rendered desensitized and can no longer bear to be touched. At the same time, however, she has become almost infantile in her need for Ted's camaraderie and reassurance. Frustrated by Alice's sexual disinterest and emotional demands, Ted begins to fantasize about sex with other women, an idea that causes him both great excitement and crippling guilt. "Alice and I have been

Bob (Robert Culp) and Carol (Natalie Wood) raise their consciousness at the beginning of *Bob & Carol & Ted & Alice*. Courtesy of Photofest.

married for twelve years," he explains to a young woman he fumblingly, apologetically approaches while on a business trip. "We feel differently about sex than your generation."

The film, which plays out less in a direct narrative than in a series of interconnected, day-in-the-life vignettes, culminates in a shared suite in Las Vegas, where Bob, Carol, Ted, and Alice have gathered to gamble, drink, and see a Tony Bennett concert. When Alice learns that her husband, like Bob and Carol, has had an affair, she reacts with a quick flash of fury. But then, just as suddenly, she removes her dress and suggests that the four of them jump into bed and do "what we came up here to do."

Aghast, Bob, Carol, and Ted resist, arguing that they are all far too close as friends to engage with one another sexually. But Alice laughingly flings their Institute lingo back at them, telling them that they're "copping out," while she alone is being "emotionally honest" and true to her feelings. When Carol insists that she has no desire to sleep with Ted, Alice reminds her that for all her talk of love, trust, and emotional clarity, her sole extramarital affair was with a man she barely knew. "*Alice*," Carol responds, "*that* was totally different—there was no *friendship* there! There was no *love!*" Yet hearing herself causes Carol to have her own moment of insight: if she and Bob are truly going to be the sexually liberated revolutionaries they've convinced themselves that they should strive to be, they need to bed their friends.

Nervously reassuring themselves with platitudes about how, in Bob's words, "we're supposed to experience everything," and, in Carol's words, "it's nice-feeling, it's something we've never done before," Bob and Carol undress and join Alice in one of the beds in the suite. Obviously terrified, Ted also joins them, after an overlong visit to the bathroom for a rinse with mouthwash and several spritzes of underarm deodorant. Yet following a few anemic kisses and a lengthy, uncomfortable pause, the two couples sheepishly get out of bed, dress in silence, and head out together to the Tony Bennett concert.

As they exit the hotel, they are followed by a long line of ethnically, racially, and gender-diverse couples of various ages, shapes, and sizes, all of whom gather in the hotel entryway. The Bacharach-David song "What the World Needs Now Is Love" begins to play in the background as all the couples begin to mingle. In a direct reference to one of the trust exercises Bob and Carol participate in during the film's opening sequence, individuals in the crowd begin to stop at random to gaze deeply into one another's eyes. In the final moments Ted and Alice, both in profile, meet one another's gaze and slowly begin to smile warmly at one another. Bob and Carol cross in front of them, also in profile, and do the same. The image of the two couples in profile, gazing deeply into one another's eyes and smiling, fades as the song swells and the credits begin to roll.

Because the four couples do not have an orgy at the end of the film, *Bob & Carol & Ted & Alice* was seen by some critics as, in its characters' words, a "cop-out" when it opened in the autumn of 1969. Vincent Canby, for example, found the film exasperatingly conventional, likened its plot to that of a passable television sitcom, and called its direction workmanlike at best.[85] Yet most critics heralded the film as a brilliant commentary that attempted, in Stephen Farber's words, to delve, without

Ted (Elliott Gould), Carol (Natalie Wood), Bob (Robert Culp), and Alice (Dyan Cannon) decide that they'd rather see a Tony Bennett concert than have an orgy at the end of *Bob & Carol & Ted & Alice*. Courtesy of Photofest.

criticizing or condescending, "into social changes that no one fully understands yet."[86] The film became one of the biggest commercial successes of 1969, grossing over $30 million and effectively launching Paul Mazursky's directorial career.[87]

As Foster Hirsch argues in *Film Quarterly*, the characters' collective "cop-out" at the end is the film's only logical conclusion, and also likely what caused it to resonate as deeply as it did with American audiences in 1969. "All four characters are basically conventional, suburban, middle-class, and rather puritanical," Hirsh writes. "The entire film insists on their conventionality and much of the comedy derives from our awareness of this."[88] As the film so carefully portrays them, Bob, Carol, Ted, and Alice are all struggling to come to terms with a lifestyle that they feel societal pressure to adopt but for which they are not prepared. To have the characters behave any differently at the end of the film would ring false.

Stephen Farber too argues that the obvious relief all four characters experience after the failed orgy is central to an understanding of the film. He acknowledges that, at the time, nothing was "easier for a mass audience movie than to put down middle class morality." But, he writes, what tended to be overlooked in films that simply bashed the establishment for the smug satisfaction of the Bobs and Carols in the audience was the fact that said morality still occasionally managed to come "closer to expressing a valid emotional response than the New Amorality." Bob, Carol, Ted, and Alice don't really want to have an orgy, which is ultimately something they all feel pressured to try only because contemporary morality says that they should. One of the central morals of the film, then, is that for all its promise of easy positives, the sexual revolution had plenty of negatives, one of which was that it put people on the defensive and made them feel obligated to experiment even when they were not particularly inclined.[89]

Todd Gitlin has pointed out that during the height of the counterculture, there were "many more weekend dope-smokers than hard-core 'heads'; many more readers of the *Oracle* than writers for it; many more co-habitors than orgiasts; many more turners-on than droppers-out."[90] *Bob & Carol & Ted & Alice* depicts the masses that Gitlin describes: they are four highly ambivalent, middle-class, almost-middle-aged people, who, like the neurotic characters in *Company*, mirror countless highly ambivalent, curiously alienated spectators. The film's brilliance, Farber concludes, lies in its depiction of people who, when presented with a culture that encourages them to say and do anything they feel like saying or doing, realize that they have no idea what it is they wish to do. *Bob & Carol & Ted & Alice* directly challenged its audiences' assumptions about contemporary mores by opining that "there is no inevitable salvation in analysis or adultery or orgy,"[91] and that in fact the teachings of the sexual revolution were ultimately just as flawed, contradictory, and easily misinterpreted—and thus as worthy of criticism, mistrust, and reproof—as many aspects of conventionalism.

Because it came out almost a decade later, and because it is not nearly as nuanced in its depictions of characters clumsily traversing "the chaos of the permissive society,"[92] *I Love My Wife* seems far more conservative than the film it was often compared with. As the title implies, the musical's characters, like their filmic counterparts, ultimately don't go through with the sexual experimentation they feel compelled to attempt. Unlike Bob, Carol, Ted, or Alice, however, they also don't wrestle terribly deeply with the "new" morality, which by 1977 was not so very new anymore after all. While the characters in the musical are comparatively two-dimensional and the humor is much broader than that in the film, both film and musical nevertheless deliver more or less the same messages and follow the same basic plot. Perhaps one of the most important differences is that *I Love My Wife* played to an American middle class whose attitudes about contemporary mores had begun to shift fairly significantly over the course of eight years.

The two central couples in *I Love My Wife* are more solidly middle class, somewhat younger, and notably less sophisticated than Bob, Carol, Ted, and Alice. They live not in southern California but in Trenton, New Jersey, where, the opening number "We're Still Friends" makes clear, they have all known one another since at least their high school years (◉ Ex. 9.1). Like Bob, Carol, Ted, and Alice, the two *I Love My Wife* couples, Wally and Monica, and Alvin and Cleo, decide to experiment with partner swapping not necessarily because they *want* to but because the new, permissive morality makes them feel as if they *should*, lest—as a phrase repeated several times throughout the show implies—they be perceived as "at least thirty years behind the times."[93] Like its filmic predecessor, then, *I Love My Wife* is less about the sexual revolution per se than about the way the sexual revolution was perceived by middle-class couples who felt drawn to but somehow excluded from it.

Despite occasional nods to the women's movement, *I Love My Wife* is a show that is overwhelmingly driven by the two central male characters. Both Wally and Alvin are somewhat better developed than Monica and Cleo, who are traditional women in the 1950s model: they are both stay-at-home wives who defer and are steadfastly devoted to their husbands, although Cleo, like Carol, is at least initially more drawn to the idea of open marriage than is Monica. The female characters' musical numbers do not help to shed much light on them: Cleo's big belter, "Love Revolution," touches on the idea of women's liberation, but only as it relates to instant sexual gratification; Monica's Act II duet with Wally, "Lovers on Christmas Eve," simply reaffirms her adoration for him. Cleo and Monica's Act I duet, "Someone Wonderful I Missed," allows the two characters to wonder what their lives might have been like had they not married Alvin and Wally, but their road not taken is simply "someone else / someone wonderful I missed." This number, too, merely reinforces the traditional roles of the female characters ( Ex. 9.2 ).

The two central male characters are somewhat more fleshed out than the women. Alvin, the shyer and more old-fashioned of the two, owns a moving company, which roots him solidly in the lower realm of the middle class and also provides justification for the four onstage musicians.[94] Introduced as members of Alvin's company, the four musicians move the props and sets around when they are not commenting on the action, singing, or accompanying the musical numbers. Their presence lends *I Love My Wife* the same air of ridiculous anarchy that Michael Stewart admired in *Viens chez-moi, j'habite chez une copine.*

*I Love My Wife* opens on Alvin and Monica, who sit in a diner waiting for their spouses after an evening of Christmas shopping. Monica pages through a magazine she purchased at the supermarket and finds a sex test that purports to let readers know how sexually liberated they are. To kill time, Alvin and Monica both take the test, and Alvin scores low enough to mark him as "repressed, frustrated, emotionally and sexually immature," and possessing attitudes about sex that "are at least thirty years behind the times." Alvin is thus established from the outset as thoroughly baffled by contemporary social mores, when he bothers to think about them at all, which is rarely.

In direct contrast with Alvin, Wally, like Bob in the film, fancies himself something of a hip, with-it sophisticate. Shortly after meeting Monica and Alvin at the diner, Wally makes it clear that he is "more exposed to the permissive society" than his peers because his job in public relations takes him to New York City "every third Thursday."[95] Wally is openly admiring of a nearby hippie commune and organic food collective that he provides PR advice for and claims to have had ample experience with such a lifestyle before settling down with Monica:

*Wally:* . . . Sometimes I think community life is the only solution for the future.
*Alvin:* You can't say that till you've actually tried it.
*Wally:* I have and it was terrific.
*Alvin:* Twenty-five people in one house, I don't think that sounds so terrific.

*Wally:* It wasn't that big a community.

*Alvin:* How many?

*Wally:* Three. Two girls and me. It worked out fine. Of course that was before I got serious with Monica.

*Alvin:* That's not a community.

*Wally:* Sure it was, we shared everything and everybody did what I decided was best for the group.

*Alvin:* But wasn't one girl always being left out?

*Wally:* No, I was with both of them. It was a strain at first, but I adjusted to it beautifully.[96]

While something of a fatuous blowhard, Wally also clearly yearns for more than he feels Trenton has to offer. Although happily married to Monica—who, "We're Still Friends" implies, was his high school sweetheart, making his "community life" claims all the more ludicrous—he covets a more thrilling life than the one he lives, and has convinced himself that he is roué enough to deserve it.

By contrast, even after failing the magazine quiz, Alvin remains comfortably traditional in his outlook and far less interested than Wally in the seismic cultural shifts that have occurred around him. Alvin responds to Wally's story about "community life" by noting that he has not only never coveted such an arrangement, but that he thinks anyone who does "would have to be some kind of sex maniac...a creep...a weirdo to go for a thing like that." When he admits to Wally that he and Cleo have always been "perfectly happy being just two,"[97] Wally scoffs that domestic happiness is overrated and attempts to influence Alvin's traditional mind-set: "Alvin, is that your only aim in life? Happiness? Well, buddy, you may be finding that happiness at the risk of being considered an oddball! Kid, I gotta tell you a few home truths. Two is out. O-U-T....And unless you want to be some kind of sociological throwback, you better start catching up while you still can."[98] In classic Broadway musical fashion, Wally wins the argument by launching into a snappy, jump-blues-inspired number, "By Threes," in which he promises Alvin the joys of "brand new positions / to meet the demands / of four pretty titties / and six busy hands," accompanied by a frantically thumping upright bass and a particularly active piano (🎵 Ex. 9.3).[99]

Because Alvin harbors a shy crush on Monica, and because Wally implies that he wouldn't mind if Monica were to engage in sex outside of their marriage, Alvin rushes home to suggest the possibility of a sexual threesome to Cleo. Again the traditional mind-set of the characters is played up: when Alvin first suggests, "The two of us ought to be three," Cleo responds joyfully, "Alvin! Darling!...We'll have a summer baby, a little Leo!"[100] Alvin quickly corrects her, and when she finally realizes what he is asking for, she throws herself down on the bed and dissolves in tears.

Yet just as Wally had no real trouble convincing Alvin, Alvin explains to Cleo that having a "multiple love experience" is the only way that they can "be part of the *today* people" and that she, specifically, can consider herself truly liberated as a woman. "All over the state, the country, the world, repressed women are breaking loose like jungle beasts!" he insists. "This is a revolt, Cleo! Get with it! Shape up or ship out."[101] Just as the pornographic incarnation of Alice was encouraged to self-actualize by submitting to the sexual desires of the men she encountered throughout *Alice in Wonderland: An X-Rated Musical Fantasy*, Cleo is encouraged to do what Alvin has framed as a civic duty, even despite his own misgivings. After his rousing speech, Cleo finds herself surrounded by the four musicians who, dressed as devils, introduce her solo number, "Love Revolution," with a lead-in during which they repeat Alvin's words about shaping up or shipping out: "Time you learned / what love today is about / Revolt! / Get yourself in shape / Or ship yourself out."[102]

Because "Love Revolution" is a declaration of female independence and empowerment—the only one in the score of *I Love My Wife*—the number situates Cleo within a large group of central female characters who find emotional strength and courage over adversity through belted song.[103] Musically speaking, "Love Revolution" is certainly comparable to numbers like Coleman's own "If My Friends Could See Me Now," among many others; its bouncing bass line and jazzy, trebly guitar chords make it sound relentlessly cheerful and upbeat and serve its repeated, anthemic declarations of strength and resolve. The melody line climbs steadily in pitch, allowing the singer's voice to build emotionally as the song builds toward an increasingly enthusiastic, virtuosic conclusion. Yet lyrically speaking, "Love Revolution" diverges sharply from previous belted liberation anthems in its rigid equation of self-actualization with sexual experience.

Throughout the number Cleo opines about the fact that in remaining committed to her husband, she is "kinda stuck in a rut," while the rest of the country is "havin' a ball." Midway through the song she resolves to "give it a try" and, perhaps inadvertently referencing gay liberation anthems, sings, "I hear the bees sweetly hummin' / as all around me they fly / if they've got love to deposit / watch out I'm comin' / out of the closet."[104] Yet Cleo's "coming out" relates solely to sleeping with men who aren't her husband:

Why
spend my life
bendin' over a pot
while there's some
other wife
doin' all that I'm not
makin' love
breakin' hearts
takin' off on a spree
while I shove
shopping carts
through the A and the P!
If there's a love revolution
show me the way, tell me how
to offer my contribution
join in the action
just lead me to it

get satisfaction
seek and pursue it…
and do it now!
And do it now!
And do it…now![105]

🎵 Ex. 9.4

By the end of "Love Revolution" Cleo has decided to honor Alvin's request and invite other people into their marital bed. This, she has determined, is somehow going to allow her to join forces with the many (heterosexual, married) women who, in merely sleeping with multiple partners, strike her as more liberated and enlightened than she is.

When her number ends, Cleo announces that she wants "to find out about the broad spectrum of the love experience before it's too late!"[106] She and Alvin enjoy about two seconds' worth of resolution on the matter before Cleo adds that she expects to extend the invitation to a man, preferably Wally, whom she finds as attractive as Alvin does Monica. Traditionalism rears its head again: the notion of any sort of homosexual encounter, between either two women or two men, is a ghastly turn-off to these staunchly heterosexual characters. Just as Alvin cannot conceive of a threesome involving Wally, Cleo responds to Alvin's suggestion that they tap Monica with comic revulsion.[107]

Finding themselves at an impasse, Cleo and Alvin talk with Wally, who promptly decides that the only logical solution would be to make the proposed threesome into a foursome so that no one feels uncomfortable or left out. He promises to discuss the plan with Monica in time for their gathering on Christmas Eve, whereupon the two couples will have a festive holiday dinner, and will then take to bed. Yet the book soon confirms what has been strongly implied all along: Wally is a smooth talker, but like the other characters, he is completely clueless about what he's promoting. As Act II opens, the four musicians fill the audience in on the fact that Wally has not yet informed Monica of the partner-swapping plan, even though Cleo and Alvin are due for Christmas Eve dinner in mere moments.

The scene leading up to Cleo and Alvin's arrival is instrumental in establishing the trajectory of the second act, which, even more than the first, contrasts contemporary mores with overt nostalgia for the good old days. After Wally and Monica give in to temptation and open one another's (ridiculous) Christmas presents a bit early, Monica waxes poetic about the holiday. In the lilting ballad "Lovers on Christmas Eve," she sits atop a piano and croons about the joys of domestic bliss during Christmastime; she is soon joined by Wally in a romantic duet. Accompanied by piano and brushy, subtle percussion, the two begin to dance ("*ballroom dancing, very 1935*,"[108] reads the stage directions) as they sing of the bliss they feel "just by being together / and married / and lovers / on Christmas Eve."[109] To this point much of the score of *I Love My Wife* is busy and upbeat, with songs evoking swing jazz and in some cases ("Monica," "By Threes") the burlesque tradition. Yet "Lovers on Christmas Eve," which pays homage to monogamy and the past, is one of the musical's most unabashedly old-fashioned, overtly sentimental numbers (🎵 Ex. 9.5).

When the number ends, Wally sits Monica down and explains his plans for a four-some with Alvin and Cleo after the holiday meal. Monica promptly retreats to the bedroom, where she begins to pack in preparation for Christmas with her mother. When Alvin and Cleo arrive, she lectures them and Wally, furiously informs them that they are all "disgusting," and marches out of the house, only to return moments later to announce sarcastically that she has changed her mind. She implies that although still angry, she is also just as curious about the sexual revolution as her friends are: "If this is the way my husband wants the wife he has promised to love and honor to spend Christmas Eve...my favorite holiday...then I'll go along with it! If you can sink to the lowest depths of degradation, then so can I!"[110] Monica stalks into the kitchen and, in yet another parallel to *Bob* & *Carol* & *Ted* & *Alice*, returns to the living room in a bra, panties, and an apron. She begins flinging around dishes and food, angrily admonishing her guests to eat quickly because "the sooner we eat, the sooner the real fun begins."[111]

Having successfully terrified her guests, Monica flings the uneaten turkey onto a nearby cabinet and clears the rest of the table by gathering all four corners of the tablecloth and yanking violently. Not willing to give up his hipster fantasy despite the agitation it has obviously caused his wife, Wally suggests that the four of them relax by smoking some hash. Although Cleo and Alvin initially react to the invitation as they did to the suggestion that they open their marriage, they eventually agree to try the drug, which Wally and Monica both profess to "smoke all the time."[112] Yet Wally again proves to be far less knowledgeable than he insists he is: the hash turns out to be modeling clay, which presumably allows the characters to retain their inherent innocence in the eyes of the audience and also conveniently sets the scene for the jug-band-inspired "Everybody Today Is Turnin' On." In this number Wally and Alvin both lament the loss of a time when "hash was fried / and tea was brewed / and someone pushing was merely rude.../ when once a week / you cut the grass / and too much acid / just gave you gas."[113] As if the old-timey music and the heavy-handed nostalgia for innocence lost is not hammered home obviously enough here, a stage note at the song's conclusion reads, "If you feel the song does not already make this point, put a tacit in here and have them say, 'It was better in the old days'" (🔊 Ex. 9.6).[114]

Cleo and Monica reenter and begin to dance with Wally and Alvin, respectively. Alvin becomes agitated when he sees Wally move his hands below Cleo's waist. His anxiety only grows when Cleo strips to her underwear as Monica opens the sofa bed. Whereas Wally hurriedly rips his clothes off when prompted by Cleo and Monica—the stage directions suggest a Velcro suit for comic effect—Alvin, like Ted in the film, resorts to myriad, endlessly protracted evening rituals as stalling tactics. After taking an agonizingly long time to undress, and then to neatly fold and stack his clothing on a nearby chair, Alvin gets gingerly into the sofa bed, only to announce that he needs something to eat before the orgy. The foursome thus devour a banana cream pie before Wally produces a how-to sex manual that they dutifully attempt to follow.

The instructions in the sex manual allow for some particularly acrobatic slapstick, as the foursome, under the blankets, attempt to engage in the "multiple love experience" they've been talking about since Act I began. After abandoning the instructions as too challenging, the four disappear under the covers to take one last stab, and the musical ends abruptly, with a literal anticlimax:

*Alvin:* (*Head appears above sheet*) Look, I don't think the Loop-the-loop is going to work. Or any of those things in the book!

*Wally:* (*Also coming into view*) Look, either we have a multiple love experience or we don't!

*Cleo:* (*Cleo and Monica appear*) Well I say we do! We've gone to all this trouble already.

*Wally:* Monica?

*Monica:* We might as well. I mean, we're this close.

*Wally:* Alvin?

*Alvin:* Well, if the girls insist. (*All go under sheet again*)

*Wally:* All right, we all put our arms around each other . . .

*Cleo:* (*As Wally gets under sheets beside her*) Oh, Wally!

*Alvin:* (*With Monica*) Monica, you're so soft!

*Monica:* (*Pulls sheets over them.*) Oh, Alvin . . . (*A moment, then*) So are you!

(*A long pause, all action stops, then slowly Alvin sticks head out from sheets.*)

*Alvin:* (*Grinning contentedly*) Yeah, I know.[115]

The four musicians then launch into the title song; they are soon joined by Alvin, and then Wally, Cleo, and Monica.

Sung gently and liltingly, accompanied by sweeping flourishes on the piano and peppered with a harmony-rich call-and-response between soloist and ensemble, "I Love My Wife" is an overtly sentimental, even schmaltzy number. Lyrically speaking, it evokes a particularly old-fashioned view of heterosexual relationships:

> But don't be cross (but don't be cross)
> or scold or cry (or scold or cry)
> he likes to stop and window shop
> but poppa's never gonna buy
> if rosy lips invite me, well, that's life (well that's life)
> but just in case you couldn't guess
> or hadn't heard
> or didn't know
> I love my wife.[116]

The number's style and its "hey, a guy can look, can't he?" approach to romance strongly evoke the 1950s. The musical may be set in the late 1970s, but the ending clearly attempts to tap into the wave of collective nostalgia for the not too distant, far more innocent (if also crushingly conservative) past ( Ex. 9.7).[117]

As the two couples slowly get out of bed, dress, and clear the stage of props and scenery, "I Love My Wife" segues into a reprise of "We're Still Friends," after which the couples exchange gifts, bid one another good night, and make plans to go shopping and have dinner together right after Christmas. As the lights dim, Cleo and Alvin reaffirm their devotion to one another, and Alvin sings a few last lines from the title song. A rousing reprise of "Hey There, Good Times" accompanies the curtain call. As with Bob, Carol, Ted, and Alice, the couples at the center of *I Love My*

Cleo (Ilene Graff), Wally (James Naughton, top), Alvin (Lenny Baker), and Monica (Joanna Gleason) would rather remain monogamous than attempt a "multiple love experience" at the end of *I Love My Wife*. Courtesy of the Billy Rose Theater Collection, New York Public Library for the Performing Arts.

*Wife* ultimately choose to remain rooted to their own traditional, even humdrum lifestyles, regardless of how outdated their choices make them seem. They are collectively relieved that their attempts at a "multiple love experience" went nowhere after all.

*I Love My Wife* opened at the tail end of the 1976–77 season, which, while commercially and artistically strong for Broadway, was so dominated by straight, and often very somber, new plays that many critics seemed genuinely astonished when this musical opened at the Barrymore. Reviews were strong, especially in the larger papers; some were even a touch overenthusiastic as a result of the notable dearth of musicals earlier that season. Both Clive Barnes and Walter Kerr for the *New York Times* received the show as ecstatically as they might have fresh water during a severe drought, and Rex Reed, for the Sunday edition of the *Daily News*, raved that *I Love My Wife* was "a total joy from beginning to end" and "the most invigorating, eye-popping musical since 'A Chorus Line.'"[118]

Though not quite as effusive, Martin Gottfried wrote in the *Post* that *I Love My Wife* was "friendly and charming, beautifully directed...engagingly performed," and "thoroughly disarming."[119] Edwin Wilson for the *Wall Street Journal* was somewhat tepid about the book, but nevertheless praised the cast, choreography, direction, and score.[120] In *Time* magazine T. E. Kalem described the musical as "twinkling," "thoroughly beguiling," and "saucily intelligent."[121] And while Hobe Morrison for *Variety* argued that *I Love My Wife* was "less than sensational," he nevertheless acknowledged its "clever lyrics, imaginative staging," and "ingenious" use of physical comedy, and concluded that for "a Broadway season that's been woefully weak on musicals, 'I Love My Wife' is a welcome arrival."[122]

Comparatively few critics panned *I Love My Wife* outright, but those who did were particularly bothered by its obvious similarities to *Bob & Carol & Ted & Alice*, as well as its conservatism. John Simon opened his review in the *New Leader* by questioning the very existence of the Luis Rego show that Stewart had adapted and guessing that instead "this is merely a strategy for deflecting our attention from how indecently the book of this musical resembles the movie." Simon detested the book, which he argued was relentlessly unfunny; he also disliked the score, which struck him as consistently uninteresting. "We have here my most loathed genre," he sniped, "the clean dirty joke, the spiritual pablum of mental eunuchs." As if he were concerned that readers would not infer by previous remarks just how much he loathed *I Love My Wife*, Simon concluded his review by noting that he found the entire cast to be both untalented and unattractive.[123] While not nearly as harsh in his review for the *Nation*, Harold Clurman found the show bland and shoddy enough to evoke "the kind of convivial fun one might enjoy in a camp for adults."[124] Howard Kissel compared *I Love My Wife* unfavorably with *Oh! Calcutta!*—which he did not like either—and noted that his favorite part of the show was the backdrop.[125]

One of the more philosophical reactions to *I Love My Wife* came from Michael Feingold. Writing for the *Village Voice* about both *I Love My Wife* and *Annie*, which opened three days later and also quickly became a hit, Feingold argued that neither musical was particularly innovative or indicative of any sort of triumph for the musical form. Although he favored *I Love My Wife* over *Annie*, he saw both as padded trifles that merely fed 1970s Broadway audiences a falsely rosy, old-fashioned outlook of the world as not such a terrible place after all. While pleased that the enormous success of both musicals implied that audiences were returning to Broadway in growing numbers very quickly postcrisis, Feingold nevertheless portrayed contemporary Broadway audiences as deeply jaded, exhausted by the upheavals of the past ten years or so, and growing increasingly conservative in their views of the world. *I Love My Wife*, he argued, was selling "not the promiscuity which has been its subject for most of the night, but sweet old one-partner marital fidelity, love-Mom-and-cherry-pie," while *Annie* struck him as irritatingly anemic and pointless. What both musicals demonstrated, he claimed, was not a triumph for the musical theater, but merely further proof that

> a few personable people and some pleasant scenery can still make a musical a hit, if the audience wants to believe in the myth the musical embodies. The attempts to give *Annie* a satirical edge, like the attempt in *I Love My Wife* to treat wife-swapping seriously, are so puerile as not to be worth discussing.... Americans, you see, are an innocent, prosperous people; millions can be made by exclusively honest means; children are innately good; husbands and wives are innately faithful; the world, barring a few mixed-up hippie criminals, is benevolent, beautiful, and just. It is quite

clear that the audience at these two shows no longer believes any of the above platitudes, but nonetheless it wants to hear them sounded again.[126]

Feingold's cynicism, if heavy-handed, is nevertheless understandable: a mere decade
after *Hair* purportedly "revolutionized" the musical theater, most Americans had
begun to tire of social and political revolution and to begin the rightward shift that
would culminate with the election in 1980 of Ronald Reagan.[127] In the theater world
the revolutionary Off Off Broadway realm had lost its force and begun a "suicidally
rapid expansion" in the early 1970s that would hasten its demise by middecade.[128]
The days in which Off Off Broadway innovations acted as fuel for an anemic Broadway were gone. All Feingold can see by the late 1970s is the triumph of the anemic.

Feingold might be dismissed for taking *I Love My Wife* so seriously. Its conservatism is easy enough to ignore since the plots of an overwhelming number of Broadway musicals—commercial enterprises, after all, aimed at large, mainstream
audiences—can be read as traditional entertainments. As Martin Gottfried pointed
out in his much cheerier review of *I Love My Wife*, a "patently commercial Broadway
musical with a warm and amiable spirit is not about to challenge our morals."[129]

But the timing of *I Love My Wife*, as well as its firm rejection of some of the precepts of the sexual revolution, lends significance to its specific brand of nostalgic
conservatism. As the historian Philip Jenkins writes, the mid-1970s saw a significant
shift in the national mood, which brought with it "a much deeper pessimism about
the state of America and its future, and a growing rejection of recent liberal ortho-
doxies," which became so palpable that Jenkins refers to "the post-1975 years as the
'anti-sixties.'"[130] Not at all coincidentally, this shift coincided with the rise in popular
entertainment of nostalgia for the 1950s.

Feingold was hardly alone in recognizing that *I Love My Wife* connected with audiences as solidly as it did in large part due to its rosy, reassuring messages about the
lasting power of monogamy. Even the critics who loved the show were not fooled into
thinking that it offered much more than reassuring platitudes aimed at increasingly
burned-out middle-class, middle-aged Americans who had tired of living through
challenging times and of attempting, or at the very least pretending, to roll with the
changes. But unlike Feingold, most critics did not take the musical's old-fashioned
qualities so deeply to heart or view its audience's reactions so cynically.

In fact most critics, like the audience they purportedly serve as the voice for, seemed
to be relieved by the outcome of the musical. "A foursome in the sofa-bed isn't what
[Monica] had in mind for Christmas Eve," wrote Martin Gottfried. "It isn't what the
show had in mind either, which I don't think gives anything away....We know these are
nice people in the orthodox sense and that no wife-swapping is going to occur with
them around. That's why we can sit back and enjoy the impossible possibility."[131] Joanna
Kyd, in the Manhattan weekly *Our Town*, was similarly charmed by the show and relieved that nothing terribly untoward occurs, despite its subject matter. Her embrace of
the traditional, even at the expense of social progress, is particularly clear:

The end can't be too near if a theatrical tribute to marital fidelity can play to pleased-
as-punch New Yorkers at the Barrymore....Marriage has been maligned for so long,

perhaps a change is overdue for audiences overdosed with dread disease, homosexuality, boredom and bitterness, failure and childlessness and great massive doses of angst.... Finally, a playwright has freed the inherent humour in the so-called "sexual revolution" that has, from the beginning, been begging to be laughed at. The new confessional writing, the truckloads of sex manuals and reports, the spectacle of Masters and Johnson on Merv Griffin, all have a serious purpose, but are at the same time absurdly funny.... If being cool is getting chilly or if the high life is getting you down, go see *I Love My Wife*. You'll be glad you did.[132]

Kyd's and Gottfried's comments serve as reminders that despite the enormous strides the country made in the 1960s and 1970s, there were sexual practices and orientations—group sex for Gottfried, homosexuality for Kyd—that remained comparatively risqué or discomfiting long after the sexual revolution took root.

In her (positive) review for the *Soho Weekly News*, Rosalyn Regelson provides some passing insight into audience reaction in noting that for many Americans, the mere suggestion of swinging, or of any nonmonogamous sexual practice, even in a musical as benign as *I Love My Wife*, would still be horrifying in 1977. "At intermission a woman who books New York theater parties for conservative southern ladies told me they'd hate this play because it's too 'explicit,'" she writes. "But just behind me another woman was burbling about the play, 'Don't you just love it, they're so *wholesome*.'"[133]

The wholesomeness of the cast was in fact one key to the success of *I Love My Wife*. In the weeks that followed the opening of the show, profiles of the actors appeared in the New York press, and many focused at least in part on the show's sexual content. Lenny Baker, who as Alvin was the unspoken star of the show, noted that he was just as flummoxed by contemporary sexuality as his character. "If people fall in love with Alvin, I'm not surprised. He's such a lovable guy; I want to take him home, too," he said in an interview with the *New York Times* a few weeks after the show had opened. "I have to admit being as baffled as he gets by the mores of society. I don't pretend to be any expert on the sexual revolution."[134] Joanna Gleason admitted bafflement too in an interview that ran in the *New York Times* a few weeks later. Unlike Baker, she argued that confusion about the times was enormously important to the success of the production. "I'm for monogamy...and I think fidelity is going to be around for a long time, regardless of what *Cosmopolitan* magazine has to say on the subject....I'm sure that's why audiences react to our show with such a mixture of relief and good humor....It's a nonthreatening treatment of a potentially threatening theme." In particular, Gleason opined, the notion of open marriage "is upsetting to a lot of people. It really would be a wholly different show if Monica and [Alvin], her best friend's husband, were actually to make it in bed together. As it is, even though both couples do wind up in bed together, all they do is eat banana cream pie."[135] While the hint at prurience might well have lured theatergoers to the Barrymore to see *I Love My Wife*, it is clearly the traditionalism of the show that helped make it such a hit with audiences, who were beginning to re-embrace conservatism in growing numbers.

# Conclusion

Each era simultaneously holds, in the personalities of its citizens, an absorption into mainstream life of previous social frontiers and an exhaustion of the energy that propelled recent breakthroughs and defiances.
> —John Updike,
> *Memories of the Ford Administration*

If history were perfectly linear and uncomplicated, the end of this story about adult musicals would go something like this: The country veered dramatically to the right under Reagan; the 1980s culture wars, as well as the AIDS crisis, significantly stanched free expression in the arts world; and, for the most part, mainstream entertainment reflected the conservative shift. As the era during which Broadway looked to the theatrical fringe for inspiration gave way to an era in which musicals became much more expensive, spectacular, global, and corporate, the adult musical—and, for that matter, many small, local, innovative musicals—fell, at the very least temporarily, out of fashion. Actors put their clothes back on; sex again became something private and, if no longer quite as taboo, then something to be wary of, to pull back from, to fear. In the cultural memory of the nation, the 1970s became a wasted decade sandwiched between the thrilling 1960s and the affluent 1980s, a long "dreary catalogue of depressing events" peppered by silly fads, the disco craze, and a lot of heavy drugs.[1] *I Love My Wife*, one of the most conservative (and popular) adult musicals to run in New York City, would also be the last.

Yet history is, of course, a lot more complicated than that, and just as this book takes pains to argue that adult musicals were not simply a stupid, forgettable fad, it cannot simply announce their abrupt death at the end of the 1970s and be done with them. Adult musicals per se did indeed fade from fashion by the late 1970s, along with theatrical trends like nudity, simulated sex, and the blunt approach to contemporary sexuality that became all the rage in the experimental theatrical realm in the mid-1960s. An exception, of course, was *Oh! Calcutta!*, which played almost exclusively to tourists until 1989, becoming something of a quaint, vaguely naughty museum piece in the process. Then again, *Oh! Calcutta!* took a remarkably conservative approach to the sexual revolution to begin with, so one might argue that it fit right in with the changing times.

But adult musicals did not simply fade away like so many pet rocks, macramé vests, or high-heeled sneakers. Rather, much like the fringe theater that helped spawn them, they continued to exert at least a small influence on live entertainment in the decades that followed. The 1980s were indeed a conservative decade, and yet some of the musicals to come out of the time reflected a new maturity about human sexuality that resulted from an odd decade's worth of serious debate about and consideration of gender issues in America. The 1970s gave rise to theater companies across the country that dedicated themselves to plays by, for, and about women, gays, and lesbians, many of which continue to operate. The decade also saw the birth of commercial musicals that attempted to portray feminist, lesbian, and especially gay male characters with increasing respect and honesty. We owe the fact that so many musicals can be queered at all, in large part, to the 1970s.

To cite but one example, William Finn's "Falsetto" trilogy—*In Trousers* (1979), *March of the Falsettos* (1981), and *Falsettoland* (1990)—takes as its subject matter the emotional and sexual evolution of the neurotic central character, Marvin. From adolescence through adulthood Marvin struggles with his own sexual identity and, as a grownup, with his relationships with his ex-wife, son, and new partner in the years prior to and during the AIDS crisis. That Finn's musicals premiered Off Broadway through the late 1970s and 1980s and were only later combined into one show, *Falsettoland*, for a Broadway run in 1992 should come as no surprise, nor should the fact that Harvey Fierstein, author of both the play *Torch Song Trilogy* (1981) and the musical *La Cage aux Folles* (1983), began his career in the Off Off Broadway realm in the early 1970s, when, he has noted, "the underground really meant something."[2] Off and Off Off Broadway may have dissipated and become increasingly commercial, but they are not dead; these realms might be harder to define, but they nevertheless remain the locus of risky, innovative productions, many of which continue to move to Broadway.

Through the 1990s and 2000s musicals featuring gay male characters—if not nearly as often lesbians—have become fully integrated both on and Off Broadway, with productions as diverse as *Kiss of the Spider Woman* (1993), *Rent* (1996), *Hedwig and the Angry Inch* (1998), *Naked Boys Singing!* (1999), *The Full Monty* (2000), *Avenue Q* (2003), *The Boy from Oz* (2003), *Yank! A World War II Love Story* (2005), *Spring Awakening* (2006), and *Priscilla Queen of the Desert* (2011) reflecting an ever-growing understanding of gay life, gay perspectives, and gay contributions to the American musical.

Although the 1970s women's movement also had a hand in encouraging major changes in the mainstream musical, the 1980s were comparatively regressive as far as depictions of women go. Although the successful 1981 Peter Stone–John Kander– Fred Ebb musical *Woman of the Year* allowed its central character to hold on to her enormously successful career *and* her man at the final curtain, and the revue *A...My Name Is Alice* enjoyed various successful runs Off Broadway and in the regional theater between 1983 and 1984, the most popular musicals of the 1980s tended, according to Stacy Wolf, to "diminish" their female characters, who were more often than not "retrograde" in their overwhelming passivity and clingy, weepy emotionalism.[3] Yet at the very least, women continued to work together to change perceptions both on the stage and behind the scenes and gradually to be featured as strong, complex, and resilient, if also sometimes fragile and flawed, in musicals like *Wings* (1993), *First Lady Suite* (1993), *Caroline, or Change* (1999), *Mamma Mia!* (1999), *Wicked* (2003), *The Color Purple* (2005), *Grey Gardens* (2006), *Next to Normal* (2008), and *Sister Act* (2011). Similarly, although the commercial theater in New York and across the country remains an overwhelmingly male-dominated industry, the number of female playwrights, composers, lyricists, directors, producers, and designers has increased significantly in recent decades, and the critical corps, while also still overwhelmingly male, has ostensibly learned enough to focus on women's work and to refrain from attacking their sexual identity, political ideologies, and physical appearance.

Whether overtly feminist, gay, or pansexual in their emphasis, the adult musicals that ran in the 1970s were no passing phase; they were instead the very roots of a modern musical that has continued to grow, change, and become ever more diverse and inclusive. At the time that they emerged, adult musicals played to commercial audiences, sometimes in tiny houses and sometimes in the city's largest venues. Like the playwrights, composers, producers, and performers themselves, the audiences who saw these productions were busily struggling—actively or passively, consciously or unconsciously—with the country's rapidly changing gender mores at a time when aspects of the sexual revolution were, despite not being fully understood or embraced, being actively absorbed into mainstream culture. Adult musicals might well have been dismissed as trivial at the time, and most remain well outside the canon at present. Yet their existence during the 1970s was no accident, nor did they merely exist as silly, entertaining fads. They also helped to educate, palliate, and ameliorate.

Their very existence otherwise makes no sense, especially at a time when there was so much other sexually steeped entertainment available. Why adult musicals, in the end, when one could go just as easily, and for a lot less money, to the local cinema for an 8 p.m. showing of *Deep Throat*? Why bother with a cheery musical meditation on sexuality when you could just as easily see a live sex show, with actual—not simulated—sex, right next door or down the block?

In his 1969 *New York Times* article about the trendiness of stage nudity, Walter Kerr wondered, rather mournfully, "Why are we, in our new visual and psychic freedoms on the stage, so dreadfully, laboriously humorless? Why are we so serious about sex and why do we dislike it so much?"[4] Kerr's gloomy question inadvertently provides the answer to the very existence of adult musicals: they helped ease collective gloom, doubt, anxiety, and ambivalence. Like *Hair*, the granddaddy of them all, adult musicals permitted audiences to revel in the simple ideas that naked bodies can be nice to look at; sexual identity doesn't need to be so very terrifying, taboo, or constricted; and sex—any kind, with anyone, in any combination—can be healthy, fun, recreational, and even, sometimes, absolutely hilarious.

Adult musicals allowed audience members—some of them questioning their own sexuality, some of them eager to learn something about the rapidly changing world, some of them comfortable in their own skins, some of them eager to experience some aspect of a sexual revolution they felt isolated from—to live vicariously without having to get in too deep. These shows, after all, espoused sex that was lighthearted and consequence-free, but there was ultimately nothing transgressive about even the most explicit of them. Attractive, young actors simulated but never actually engaged in all kinds of sexual activity that no one had previously talked about, let alone discussed positively; the overlying message of even the most risqué songs and sketches was that human bodies and their urges are no big deal, and the whole package was almost always offered in a familiar, old-fashioned format: the revue. Adult musicals allowed audience members to feel a little bit dirty, a little bit liberated, without having to brave the seediness of a peepshow or to confront the more serious ramifications of the sexual revolution and its offshoot movements.

One of the most damning adjectives critics hurled at those adult musicals they bothered to review during the 1970s was "innocent," but it is possible that deep down, they were just as relieved to apply that word as they were indignant not to have been titillated. The sexual revolution, gay liberation, and second-wave feminism were all enormously influential, complicated, interconnected movements that meant countless different things to countless different people. During the 1970s Americans began a mighty struggle over issues of sexuality and gender in ways they never had before, and it is no wonder that the result was often feelings of elation and liberation on the one hand, and confusion, frustration, and even fear on the other. In the end, then, adult musicals succeeded not so much in challenging notions about sexuality and gender as in offering cheerful, conventional, reassuring messages to audiences who more often than not were curiously comforted by the gesture.

# NOTES

## INTRODUCTION

1. Barrett 1973: 14.
2. See, for example, Reif 1983; Rich 1989; Atkinson 1990; Bordman 2001; Ward 2002.
3. Williams 1999: 30.
4. The Oxford English Dictionary notes that the word *adult* applied as a euphemism for "premises or productions ostensibly restricted to adult access" because of their sexually explicit nature was first used in an advertisement for "unusual adult photo sets" that appeared in the British periodical *New Musical Express* on June 20, 1958; the term was first used in the United States in an article about pornographic films published in *Harper's Bazaar* in July 1972.
5. Thanks to Stacy Wolf for weighing in on this.
6. Personal communication, July 10, 2008.
7. See, for example, Mast 1987; Block 1997; Bordman 2001; Grant 2004. A notable exception, of course, is Mandelbaum 1991.
8. Jessica Sternfeld, *The Megamusical* (Bloomington: Indiana University Press, 2006).
9. See, for example, Banfield 1993; Swayne 2007.
10. See, for example, Miller 1998; Clum 1999; Kirle 2005; Wolf 2002, 2011.
11. See Wollman 2006: 6–7.
12. In more recent years, the regional theater has also played an increasingly important role; this, however, is beyond the scope of my study.
13. For more on the distinctions between Broadway, Off Broadway, and Off Off Broadway, please see the introductions to Bottoms 2004 and Wollman 2006.
14. See, for example, Crespy 2003; Martin 2004; Bottoms 2004.
15. Schulman 2001: xv.
16. Bailey and Farber 2004: 1.
17. Ibid.
18. Ibid.
19. Erll 2010: 2.
20. A. Assmann 2010: 98.
21. J. Assmann 2010: 113.
22. Allen 1991: 40.

## CHAPTER 1

1. The Open Theater was an avant-garde theater troupe that was founded in New York City in 1963 and disbanded a decade later. Directed by Joseph Chaikin, who was formerly affiliated with the Living Theater, the Open Theater aimed to create works through group discussion and collaborative exercises that would intellectually challenge both actors and their audiences.
2. La MaMa is an Off Off Broadway theater that was founded in 1961 by Ellen Stewart.
3. Martin 2009.
4. Guernsey 1969: 3.
5. Personal communication, January 16, 1999.

6. Coined around 1960 in the *Village Voice*, the term *Off Off Broadway* initially denoted plays or workshops staged in small spaces anywhere in Manhattan, for which actors received little or no pay. The term, however, quickly took on more ideological associations, as many Off Off Broadway practitioners grew interested in using their art to promote social or political change. For further discussion of the term and its ideological associations, see Bottoms 2004; Crespy 2003.
7. Banham 1995: 647.
8. Drutman 1966: 1.
9. Personal communication with Robert Patrick, February 8, 2005.
10. Junker 1968: 104.
11. Friedman 1996: 203–4.
12. Friedman 2000: 82.
13. Allen 1991: 5.
14. Friedman 2000: 65.
15. Allen 1991: 137–38.
16. Friedman 2000: 65.
17. Allen 1991: 28.
18. Ibid., 179.
19. Ibid., 227–32, 243–46.
20. Ibid., 248–49.
21. Bordman 2001: 502, 534.
22. Traub 2004: 87–88.
23. Friedman 1996: 212.
24. Ibid.
25. Friedman 2000: 93.
26. Allen 1991: 92.
27. Ibid., 245.
28. Houchin 2003: 76.
29. Tynan 1969: 1.
30. McMillin 2006: 10, 145.
31. Allen 1991: 249–50.
32. Personal communication with Mario Manzini, October 21, 2008.
33. Ibid.
34. Ibid.
35. Ibid.
36. Heidenry 1997: 55.
37. Sarracino and Scott 2008: 190; Bianco 2004: 159.
38. Bianco 2004: 165–66.
39. Ibid., 169.
40. Personal communication with Mario Manzini, October 21, 2008.
41. Bianco 2004: 143.
42. Ibid., 143–44.
43. Zolotow 1965: 1.
44. Zolotow 1968: 61.
45. Personal communication with Mario Manzini, October 21, 2008.
46. Ibid.
47. Ibid.
48. Ibid.
49. In his lengthy profile of Goldstein in *Thy Neighbor's Wife*, Gay Talese notes that in *Screw*'s early years, Goldstein did most of the writing himself, while his business partner, Jim Buckley, focused on the typesetting.
50. Anonymous review in *Screw*, May 16, 1969: 18.
51. Amsel 1969a: 21.
52. Anonymous review in *Screw*, November 3, 1969: 8.
53. George 1969: 23.

54. Gussow 1969: 35.
55. Stasio, 1969: n.p.
56. Anonymous review in *Variety*, December 3, 1969.
57. Personal communication with Mario Manzini, October 21, 2008.
58. Gussow 1969: 35.
59. Ibid.
60. Personal communication with Mario Manzini, October 21, 2008.
61. Schaefer 2002: 10.
62. Personal communication with Mario Manzini, October 21, 2008.
63. Friedman 1996: 207.
64. Barber 1970: 9.
65. Funke 1968: D1.
66. Tallmer 1969: 8.
67. Tynan 1969: 1.
68. Ibid.
69. Levy and the Open Window member Stanley Walden worked together Off Off Broadway on several Open Theater productions in 1968.
70. Dunbar 1969: 40.
71. Ibid.
72. Personal communication with Boni Enten, July 3, 2005.
73. Dunbar 1969: 40.
74. Barrett 1973: 17–20.
75. Dunbar 1969: 40.
76. Barrett 1973: 22.
77. Funke 1969: 54.
78. Karpel 1969: 40.
79. Tynan 1969: 1.
80. Funke 1968: D1.
81. Rich 1989: C1.
82. Karpel 1969: 40.
83. Bunce 1969: 4.
84. Williamson 1969: 242.
85. Personal communication with Boni Enten, July 3, 2005.
86. Tynan 1969: 91.
87. Davis 1969: 74; Genauer 1969: 14.
88. Amsel 1969b: 21.
89. Weales 1969: 463.
90. Barnes 1969b: 33.
91. Reif 1983: 20.
92. Ward 2002.
93. Barrett 1973: 13.
94. Tynan 1969: 111.
95. DVD recording of *Oh! Calcutta!*, Obsession Entertainment, 1972.
96. Barrett 1973: 43–44.
97. Kroll 1969: 81.
98. Wollman 2006: 63.
99. Personal communication with Boni Enten, July 3, 2005.
100. Whitburn 2000: 205.
101. O'Connor 1969: 18.
102. "Actors and Author of 'Che!' Arrested after Performance" 1969: 78.
103. Lingeman 1971: 14.
104. Personal communication with David Newburge, July 13, 2006.
105. "Homo Libs Razz Off-B'way 'Movie,' Get the Bounce" 1971: 67.
106. Personal communication with David Newburge, July 13, 2006.

107. "Homo Libs Razz Off-B'way 'Movie,' Get the Bounce" 1971: 69.
108. Barnes 1971: 39.
109. "Off-B'way 'Stag Movie' Keeps Going" 1971: 63.
110. Lewis 1971.

## CHAPTER 2
1. Duberman 1993: xvii.
2. Marcus 2002: 74.
3. Duberman 1993: 75.
4. Valocchi 2001: 455–56.
5. Kirle 2005: 171–72.
6. Crespy 2003: 33–34.
7. Bottoms 2004: 39.
8. Ibid.
9. Personal communication with Robert Patrick, February 8, 2005.
10. Bottoms 2004: 287.
11. Crespy 2003: 63.
12. Personal communication with Robert Patrick, February 8, 2005.
13. Ibid.
14. Crowley 1968: 48.
15. Barnes 1968: 48.
16. Reed 1968: 1.
17. Bottoms 2004: 291.
18. Ibid.
19. Kerr 1968: 3.
20. Barnes 1968: 48; Barnes 1969a: 36.
21. Teal 1969: D23.
22. Lovensheimer 2002: 182.
23. See, for example, Bristow and Butler 1987; Gordon 1990; Knapp 2006a.
24. Bristow and Butler 1987: 253.
25. Knapp 2006a: 294–95.
26. Ibid.
27. Ibid.
28. Furth and Sondheim 1996: 105.
29. See, for example, Clum 1999; Rich 2000.
30. Original cast recording.
31. Sondheim 2010: 177.
32. Furth and Sondheim 1996: 102–3.
33. Clum 1999: 225.
34. Lovensheimer 2002: 182.
35. Knapp 2006a: 294.
36. Secrest 1998: 180.
37. Shewey 2007: 58.
38. See, for example, Clum 1999; Kirle 2005; Miller 1998; Wolf 2002.
39. Chauncey 1991: 317. Chauncy is writing specifically about gay men, not of lesbians.
40. Friedman 2000: 113.
41. Kirle 2005: 169.
42. Wolf 2002: 21.
43. Much has been written about the "surreal" qualities of *Company*. Sondheim himself writes, in *Finishing the Hat*, that the show was meant to take place "not over a period of time, but in an instant in Robert's mind, perhaps on a psychiatrist's couch, perhaps at the moment when he comes into his apartment on his thirty-fifth birthday. The framework is a surreal surprise party for him, which opens and closes each act" (2010: 166).
44. Ibid., 117.
45. Furth and Sondheim 1996: 118.

46. Clum 1999: 222.
47. Ibid., 226.
48. Wadler 2006: A1, 5.

**CHAPTER 3**

1. The Truck and Warehouse Theater was located at 79 East Fourth Street, in the space now occupied by the New York Theater Workshop.
2. See Bottoms 2004, especially 61–82, for a more comprehensive history of the Judson Poets' Theater.
3. Kauffmann 1966: 39.
4. Burke 1969: 7.
5. George Dennison's *Vaudeville Skit* opened at the Judson on August 24, 1962. Although Carmines had already directed one of the troupe's productions by this point, *Vaudeville Skit* marks the beginning of the collaboration between Kornfeld as a director and Carmines as a composer.
6. Personal communication with Larry Kornfeld, June 5, 2006.
7. Bottoms 2004: 274.
8. Ibid., 276.
9. Ibid., 359.
10. Ibid., 359.
11. Gustavson 1973.
12. Carmines 1973b: 28.
13. Ibid., 15.
14. Ibid., 9.
15. Ibid., 2.
16. Bottoms 2004: 147–48.
17. Gustavson 1973.
18. Simon 1973: 64.
19. Bottoms 2004: 359–60.
20. Duberman 1973: 4.
21. Carmines 1973a: D12.
22. Katz 1973: 114.
23. Grumley 1973: 114.
24. Bottoms 2004: 361.
25. Russo 1973: 12.
26. Personal communication with Earl Wilson Jr., June 22, 2005.
27. Ibid.
28. Ibid.
29. Ibid.
30. Klemesrud 1974: 3.
31. Ibid.
32. Personal communication with Earl Wilson Jr., June 22, 2005.
33. http://www.queermusicheritage.us/jan2006lp.html. Accessed September 6, 2011.
34. Personal communication with Tobie Columbus, September 14, 2006.
35. Marcus 2002: 187.
36. Ibid.
37. Ibid., 190.
38. Haagensen 2001.
39. Personal communication with Peter del Valle and Steve Sterner, July 2, 2008.
40. Haagensen 2001.
41. Personal communication with Peter del Valle and Steve Sterner, July 2, 2008.
42. Ibid.
43. Ide 1975: 5, 12.
44. Personal communication with Steve Sterner, July 2, 2008.
45. Personal communication with Peter del Valle, July 2, 2008.

46. Personal communication with Peter del Valle and Steve Sterner, July 2, 2008.
47. Ibid.
48. Ibid.
49. Ibid.
50. Kry 1975: 5; Patient 1975: 6.
51. Feingold 1975: 73.
52. Barnes 1975: 26.
53. "Lovers" 1975: 16.
54. Clum 1999: 248–49.
55. "Sex and the Theatre: Doing What Comes Naturally" 1980: 28.
56. Personal communication with Peter del Valle and Steve Sterner, July 2, 2008.
57. The Bijou was built by the Shuberts in 1917 and was razed to make room for the Marriott Hotel in 1982.
58. Goldsmith and Perr 1974.
59. Personal communication with Lee Goldsmith, June 15, 2009.
60. Kirle 2005: 186–97.
61. Personal communication with Harvey Perr, June 17, 2009.
62. Ibid.
63. Ibid.
64. Brukenfeld 1974: 67; Watts 1974: 19.
65. Watts 1974: 19; Morrison 1974: 64.
66. Gottfried 1974: 40; Stasio 1974: 17.
67. Watts 1974: 19.
68. Gottfried 1974: 40.
69. Barnes 1974: 36.
70. Watts 1974: 19; "Sextet" 1974: 11.
71. Personal communication with Harvey Perr, June 17, 2009.
72. Personal communication with Lawrence Hurwit, June 15, 2009.
73. For an analysis of the compositional techniques Sondheim used in *Company*, please see Bristow and Butler 1987.
74. Personal communication with Lee Goldsmith, June 15, 2009.
75. Personal communication with Harvey Perr, June 17, 2009.
76. Goldsmith and Perr 1974: 69.
77. Ibid., 69–70.
78. Ibid., 71.
79. Marcus 2002: 187.
80. *Gay Company* was the revue's original name. At some point during the original run, the show was retitled *In Gay Company*, which has also been the title of subsequent productions.
81. http://fredsilvermusic.com/archives.htm. Accessed June 10, 2009.
82. Personal communication with Fred Silver, October 16, 2008.
83. Ibid.
84. Cast recording, 1999.
85. Personal communication with Fred Silver, October 16, 2008.
86. Thompson 1974: 57.
87. Personal communication with Fred Silver, October 16, 2008.
88. Purnick 1986: A1.
89. Carroll 1974: 1.
90. Personal communication with Fred Silver, October 16, 2008.
91. Cast recording, 1999.
92. Personal communication with Fred Silver, October 16, 2008.
93. Ibid.
94. Ibid.
95. Cast recording, 1999. The number, like the revue itself, has been revised since its original production; the recorded version of the song includes references to Sondheim

songs that had not yet been written in 1974 and that were thus not in the original Off Broadway production of the show.

96. Cast recording, 1999.
97. Ibid.
98. Russo 1975: 12.
99. Plot synopsis courtesy of Bill Solly and of Albert Poland's liner notes on the original cast album.
100. Personal communication with Bill Solly, February 27, 2006.
101. Ibid.
102. Ibid.
103. Ibid.
104. Ibid.
105. Ibid.
106. Clum 1999: 248–49.
107. Russo 1975: 13–14.
108. Ibid., 13.
109. http://www.tosos2.org/history.htm. Accessed July 7, 2009.
110. Miller 1998: 26.
111. Ibid.
112. Clum 1999: 248.

## CHAPTER 4

1. Also like gay liberation, which is often viewed as "officially" beginning with the Stonewall riots, the women's movement gained momentum following a symbolic kickoff in the late 1960s, when the New York Radical Women staged their protest against the Miss America Pageant on the Boardwalk in Atlantic City in September 1968.
2. Canning 1993: 530–31.
3. Coleman and Sebesta 2008: 1. See in particular Wolf 2002, 2011.
4. Boesing 1996: 1012.
5. Bemis 1987: 2.
6. For more information on the formation of these troupes and organizations in relation to established Off Off Broadway companies, please see Canning 1995.
7. Rea 1972: 79–80.
8. Boesing 1996: 1021.
9. Bemis 1987: 3–4.
10. Bottoms 2004: 120.
11. Dolan 1991: 43.
12. Bottoms 2004: 120.
13. For more on the musical's marginalization in popular culture in the mid-twentieth century, please see Bordman 2001; Wollman 2006; Wolf 2011.
14. Wolf 2011: 53–58.
15. Ibid., 54–55.
16. Ibid., 57.
17. Lambert 2009.
18. Ibid.
19. Ibid.
20. Ragni and Rado n.d.: 44.
21. Wolf 2011: 58.
22. Ibid., 58–59.
23. Lambert 2009.
24. Bottoms 2004: 212.
25. Ragni and Rado 1966: 130. This exchange remains in the current production script.
26. Ibid., 127, 131.
27. Bottoms 2004: 212.
28. Ragni and Rado 1966: 77–78.

29. Ibid., 78–79.
30. Ibid., 94–95.
31. Ragni and Rado n.d.: 41.
32. Ibid., 42–43. Paulus's Broadway revival omitted the slap.
33. Ibid., 44.
34. Berger's suggestion that Sheila sleep with Claude one night in exchange for a subsequent night with him remains in the production script.
35. Horn 1991: 79.
36. Ibid., 60.
37. Personal communication with Natalie Mosco, January 3, 1999.
38. Barber 1970: 9.
39. Tynan 1969: 105.
40. Ibid., 107.
41. Ibid., 106.
42. Ibid., 107.
43. Ibid., 109.
44. Barrett 1973: 39.
45. Genauer 1969: 46.
46. Ibid.
47. Barrett 1973: 39.
48. *Oh! Calcutta!* (New York: Grove Press, 1969), 33.
49. Bosworth 1971: 12.
50. Ibid.
51. Personal communication with Myrna Lamb, January 24, 2007.
52. Bosworth 1971: 12.
53. Ibid.
54. Bender 1970: 79.
55. Regelson 1969: 5.
56. Dell'Olio 2007: 161.
57. Personal communication with Jacqui Ceballos, March 5, 2009.
58. Dell'Olio 2007: 161.
59. Personal communication with Jacqui Ceballos, March 5, 2009.
60. Rea 1972: 81.
61. Personal communication with Jacqui Ceballos, March 5, 2009.
62. Regelson 1969.
63. Personal communication with Myrna Lamb, January 24, 2007.
64. Personal communication with Susan Hulsman Bingham, January 10, 2007.
65. Epstein 1996: 223.
66. Lamb 1970: 18.
67. Ibid.
68. Sworowski 1974: 6.
69. Lamb 1970: 18.
70. Ibid.
71. Ibid., 19.
72. Bender 1970: 79.
73. Ibid., 27.
74. Thanks to Susan Hulsman Bingham for providing the reel-to-reel recording, as well as several transcriptions of songs from the score.
75. Epstein 1996: 229–30.
76. Personal communication with Susan Hulsman Bingham, January 10, 2007.
77. Report on *Mod Donna* publicity, submitted to Joseph Papp by Jacqui Ceballos, undated. Used by permission from the Billy Rose Theatre Collection and Gail Merrifield Papp.
78. Epstein 1996: 231.
79. Personal communication with Myrna Lamb, January 24, 2007.
80. Personal communication with Jacqui Ceballos, March 5, 2009.

81. Ibid.
82. Personal communication with Ze'eva Cohen, July 28, 2008.
83. Ibid.
84. Personal communication with Jacqui Ceballos, March 5, 2009.
85. Personal communication with Susan Hulsman Bingham, January 10, 2007.
86. Personal communication with Myrna Lamb, January 24, 2007.
87. Brukenfeld 1970: 53.
88. Barnes 1970: 48.
89. Brukenfeld 1970: 53.
90. Kroll 1970: 121.
91. Papp 1970.
92. Tallmer 1970: 23.
93. Kerr 1970: 1.
94. Ibid., 1–3.
95. Bender 1970: 79.
96. Glueck 1970: 24.
97. Gornick 1970: 47.
98. Komisar 1970: 28.
99. Personal communication with Myrna Lamb, January 24, 2007.
100. Letter to Joseph Papp from Myrna Lamb, March 18, 1971.
101. Echols 1994: 158–59.
102. Bailey 2004: 109.
103. Carroll 1990: 113.

## CHAPTER 5

1. Little had changed by the 1980s in terms of feminist musicals or an increased frequency of feminist characters; two exceptions were the Broadway production of *Woman of the Year* in 1981 and the Women's Project production of *A…My Name Is Alice* in 1983. Thanks to Jessica Sternfeld and Stacy Wolf, not only for pointing this out, but for confirming my suspicion that feminist characters per se have become prevalent in American musicals only since the late 1990s and early 2000s.
2. Davis 1998: 147.
3. McLaughlin 1978: 18.
4. Coburn 1980: 58.
5. "Give Me the Sultan's Harem" was written by Abner Silver with lyrics by Alex Gerber and published by Witmark and Sons. The song, recorded by the pianist and bandleader Charley Strait and the vaudevillian Eddie Cantor, focused on the peace conferences following World War II. The refrain reflected contemporary gender roles and fairly unsophisticated perceptions about the newly dismembered Ottoman Empire:

Give me the harem, the old sultan's harem
That's the only thing I crave.
The sultan's too old, for he's past eighty-three,
and his thousand wives need a fellow like me.
I'll never beat them. With kindness I'll treat them
And all that I ask is a trial.
Imagine me sitting on a carpeted floor
Telling my slave to bring me wife ninety-four.
I'll be so gallant, I'm chock full of talent.
Won't you give that harem to me?

6. McLaughlin 1978: 18.
7. "'The Club': A Shift in Perspective" 1977: 47.
8. Karr 1980: 27.
9. Coburn 1980: 58.

10. Merriam 1977: 5.
11. "Call-for-Philip-Mor-ris" is a reference to Johnny Roventini, popularly known as Johnny Philip Morris, a dwarf actor who dressed as a bellboy and voiced the cigarette company's slogan, which Philip Morris used in radio, television, and print media, from 1933 to 1974.
12. Lester 1976: 28.
13. McLaughlin 1978: 18.
14. Davis 1998: 149–50.
15. Rich 1976: 75.
16. "Ticker Tape" is a medley comprising the songs "It Makes No Diff'rence What You Do: Get the Money," by Nathan Bivins (1904); "Money," by H. B. Smith and W. H. Batchelor (1891); and "I've Just Been Down to the Bank," by M. H. Rosenfeld and F. Belasco (1885).
17. "A Night at the Play" was written by Fred J. Hamill in 1895.
18. Davis 1998: 153.
19. Merriam 1977: 32.
20. "'The Club': A Shift in Perspective" 1977: 47.
21. Davis 1998: 153.
22. Stone 1976: 19.
23. Merriam 1977: 32.
24. Ibid., 35.
25. Ibid. In the original production Joanne Beretta as Algy was the only actress who did not cut her long hair, but instead hid it under a wig.
26. Ibid. The emphasis is that of the original script.
27. Davis 1998: 148.
28. Stone 1976: 20.
29. Coburn 1980: 58.
30. Henkel 1980: 1.
31. Solomon 1993: 146; Davis 1998: 148.
32. Betsko and Koenig 1987: 310.
33. Gussow 1976: 61.
34. Watt 1976: 63.
35. Cushman 1977: 26.
36. Kerr 1977a: 13.
37. Kauffmann 1977: n.p.
38. Jenner 1976: 11.
39. Lester 1976: 28.
40. Kissel 1976: 14.
41. Reed 1976: 68.
42. Ibid.
43. Karr 1980: 27.
44. Ibid.
45. Hoffman 1977: n.p.
46. Lotman 1976: 20.
47. Ibid.
48. Ibid.
49. Stasio 1977: 43.
50. Hoffman 1977: n.p.
51. "The Club" 1977: 139; Simon 1977a: 24.
52. Dolan 1991: 63.
53. Oppenheimer 1976: 11.
54. Clurman 1976: n.p.
55. Simon 1977a: 24.
56. Ibid.
57. Gottfried 1977a: 37.

58. Davis 1998: 155.
59. Warfield quoted in ibid.
60. Clay 1977: 13.
61. Hoffman 1977: n.p.
62. Ibid., emphasis mine.
63. Ibid.
64. Clay 1977: 13.
65. Hillary 1976: 12.
66. Davis 1998: 160.
67. Solomon 1993: 147.
68. Siegel 2007: 9.
69. Fields 1978: 42.
70. Sebesta 2008: 210.
71. Christon 1980: 1.
72. Ibid.
73. Sebesta 2008: 201.
74. Christon 1980: 6.
75. Ibid.
76. Ibid., 203.
77. Ibid., 206.
78. Personal communication with Gretchen Cryer, January 25, 2007.
79. Sebesta 2008: 207.
80. Cryer 1980: 48.
81. Turan and Papp 2009: 452.
82. Ibid.
83. Brackett 2005: 238.
84. Simon 1978: 74.
85. Personal communication with Gretchen Cryer, January 25, 2007.
86. Dace 1978: 10.
87. Kissel 1978: 8.
88. Novick 1978: 70.
89. Kerr 1978: D3–4.
90. Ibid.
91. Klemesrud 1978: 48.
92. Harris 1978: 31.
93. Kimball 1978: 55.
94. Thanks to Stacy Wolf for pointing this out.
95. Epstein 1996: 352.
96. Personal communication with Gretchen Cryer, January 25, 2007.
97. Turan and Papp 2009: 456–57.
98. Ibid., 454.
99. Personal communication with Gretchen Cryer, January 25, 2007.
100. Ibid.
101. Dolan 1991: 1.

### CHAPTER 6

1. The conflation of the sexual revolution and post-Stonewall gay male activism did not take place in the same way, largely because the male gaze has historically been constructed to eroticize the female body while simultaneously disqualifying the male body as an object for eroticization. For further discussion of the male gaze and its sublimation or rejection of the erotic male body, see Stratton 2001, especially chapter 6.
2. Carroll 1990: 24.
3. Bailey 2004: 116–17.
4. Gerhard 2000: 468.
5. Carroll 1990: 25.

6. Bailey 1994: 237.
7. Ibid., 238.
8. Ibid., 249.
9. Ibid.
10. Ibid.
11. Rossi 1975: 91.
12. Dolan 1991: 62.
13. Ibid.
14. Carroll 1990: 113; Bailey 2004: 117–19.
15. Friedman 2000: 13.
16. Sarracino and Scott 2008: 6–7.
17. Dennis 2007: 47.
18. Ibid.
19. Talese 1980: 51.
20. Ibid., 53.
21. Friedman 2000: 16–17.
22. Talese 1980: 55.
23. Beisel 1997: 3.
24. Quoted in Strossen 2000: 226.
25. Friedman 2000: 17.
26. Andrist 1973: 5.
27. Talese 1980: 55.
28. Friedman 2000: 17.
29. Talese 1980: 57–58.
30. Friedman 2000: 130–31.
31. Ibid., 130–32.
32. The Society steadily lost power and influence under Sumner and was defunct by the early 1940s.
33. Friedman 2000: 4.
34. Ibid., 4–5.
35. Hall 1992: 603, emphasis mine.
36. Strossen 2000: 18.
37. Hall 1992: 603.
38. Ibid.
39. Bianco 2004: 133.
40. Ibid. "Grind houses," or "grinders," were second- or third-run movie houses that ran films—often ones with exploitative subject matter—at discounted ticket prices, often for twenty-four hours a day.
41. Ibid., 134.
42. "Sale of a Crime Book Is Blocked as City Takes 5 Sellers to Court" 1954: 19.
43. "High Court to Hear Booksellers' Cases" 1957: 18.
44. Ibid.
45. "Dealer in Obscenity Gets a 5-Year Term" 1956: 26.
46. Bianco 2004: 136.
47. Schaefer 2002: 14.
48. Hall 1992: 603.
49. Traub 2004: 193.
50. Braunstein 2004: 130.
51. Bianco 2004: 136.
52. Ibid.
53. Williams 1999: 99.
54. Ibid.
55. Blumenthal 1973: 30.
56. According to the 2005 film *Inside Deep Throat*, Blumenthal's article itself caused a significant surge in the *Deep Throat* box office.

57. Blumenthal 1973: 31.
58. Heidenry 1997: 17. For more about the history of research into the female orgasm, please see Heidenry 1997 and Gerhard 2000.
59. Williams 1999: 112.
60. Ibid., 113.
61. Montgomery 1972a: 40.
62. Montgomery 1972b: 40.
63. *Inside Deep Throat*, written and directed by Fenton Bailey and Randy Barbato, 2005.
64. Personal communication with Earl Wilson Jr., June 22, 2005.
65. Wilson 1974.
66. Ibid.
67. Thanks to my sister, Jessica Wollman, for her input on this section.
68. Personal communication with Earl Wilson Jr., June 22, 2005.
69. Hollinger 1998: 10.
70. Wilson 1974.
71. Personal communication with Tobie Columbus, September 14, 2006.
72. Ibid.
73. David 1976: 47.
74. Ibid., 46.
75. Wilson 1974.
76. Ibid.
77. Ibid.
78. Williams 1999: 150.
79. David 1976: 46.
80. Barry Pearl, for example, remembers some initial anxieties, but ultimately had no problem with the stage nudity since he is, by nature, "fairly wildly abandoned as it is, as an actor." Alan Kootsher, who appeared in *Le Bellybutton* with Marilyn Chambers, responded to my questions about appearing nude onstage with a figurative shrug. "Hey," he said, "it was the seventies."
81. Personal communication with Earl Wilson Jr., June 22, 2005.
82. David 1976: 45.
83. Williams 1999: 111.
84. Ibid., 113.
85. Ibid., 114.
86. Corbett and Kapsalis 1996: 103.
87. Personal communication with Tobie Columbus, September 14, 2006.
88. Personal communication with Joanne Baron, September 14, 2006.
89. Personal communication with Peachena, February 21, 2006.
90. Personal communication with Tobie Columbus, September 14, 2006.
91. Carroll 1990: 25.
92. Barrett 1973: 17.
93. Ibid., 23–24, 84–85.
94. "Show in 'Village' Defended by Two" 1974; personal communication with Tobie Columbus, September 14, 2006.
95. Personal communication with Barry Pearl, July 6, 2005.
96. Personal communication with Boni Enten, July 3, 2005.
97. Personal communication with Tobie Columbus, September 14, 2006.
98. Personal communication with Joanne Baron, September 14, 2005.

CHAPTER 7
1. Williams 1999: 120.
2. According to Linda Williams, the term *hard-core* was first used in the *Roth* ruling by Justice William Brennan, who wrote in his ruling of "the 'indigestible' pit of hard-core pornography," which was "'utterly without redeeming social importance'" (ibid., 88).
3. Schaefer 2002: 14.

4. Ibid., 14–15.
5. Corliss 2005: www.time.com/time/columnist/corliss/article/0,9565,1043267,00.html. Accessed August 2, 2010. Take, for example, the 1971 Melvin van Peebles film *Sweet Sweetback's Baadasssss Song*, the 1973 Nicolas Roeg film *Don't Look Now*, and the 1974 John Byrum film *Inserts*. Thanks to Ray Knapp for calling my attention to *Inserts*. The hard- or soft-core films *Behind the Green Door, Sensations, Dictionary of Sex,* and *Score* were all featured in Cannes's unofficial sidebar; also in the early 1970s the New York Film Festival featured the following films, which Corliss notes were either hard-core or, at the very least, "films with intense sexual elements": *WR: Mysteries of the Organism, Last Tango in Paris, Exhibition,* and *In the Realm of the Senses.*
6. Bailey and Barbato, *Inside Deep Throat*, 2005.
7. Corliss 2005. www.time.com/time/columnist/corliss/article/0,9565,1043267,00.html. Accessed August 2, 2010.
8. Bailey and Barbato, *Inside Deep Throat*, 2005.
9. Corliss 2005. www.time.com/time/columnist/corliss/article/0,9565,1043267,00.html. Accessed August 2, 2010.
10. Ibid., 4. *The Opening of Misty Beethoven* was based closely on both *Pygmalion* and *My Fair Lady* and thus clearly wore its legitimizing artistic aspirations on its sleeve.
11. Personal communication with David Newburge, July 13, 2006.
12. McNeil and Osborne 2005: 124.
13. Corliss 2005. www.time.com/time/columnist/corliss/article/0,9565,1043267,00.html. Accessed August 2, 2010.
14. Ibid., 133. According to Williams, while lesbian scenes aimed specifically at pleasing male viewers became more or less obligatory in 1970s hard-core, male-to-male sex scenes were—and remain—taboo.
15. Ibid., 134.
16. Ibid., 253.
17. Ibid., 138.
18. A soft-core musical film version of *Cinderella*, directed by the character actor and B-movie filmmaker Michael Pataki, was released in 1977.
19. Thanks to Ray Knapp and Jessica Sternfeld for their input on the *Alice* theme song.
20. Williams 1999: 139.
21. Ibid., 140.
22. Eder 1976: 11.
23. http://rogerebert.suntimes.com/apps/pbcs.dll/article?AID=/19761124/RE-VIEWS/611240301/1023. Accessed November 3, 2010.
24. Martin 2010.
25. Scott n.d.
26. See Most 2004; Knapp 2006a; McMillin 2006.
27. McMillin 2006: 79.
28. Ibid., 54–77.
29. Williams 1999: 50.
30. Houchin 2003: 204–5.
31. McMillin 2006: 79.
32. Thanks to Ray Knapp for his input on this section.
33. Martin 2010.
34. Interview with Bruce Kimmel, *From Dollars to Donuts: An Undressing of* The First Nudie Musical, dir. Bruce Kimmel and Mark Haggard, DVD, Image Entertainment, 2002.
35. Ibid.
36. Personal communication with Bruce Kimmel, November 13, 2007.
37. Beginning in 1968 the Directors Guild of America permitted directors to be credited via pseudonyms. Alan—or Allen—Smithee was the official pseudonym granted by the DGA to directors who were able to demonstrate that they had not been able to maintain creative control over a specific film.

38. The name of the production number itself references 1930s musicals: the Gershwins' *Let 'Em Eat Cake* was the 1933 follow-up to their 1931 *Of Thee I Sing*. Thanks to Ray Knapp for pointing this out.
39. Personal communication with Bruce Kimmel, November 13, 2007.
40. Kimmel 2010: 20.
41. Ibid., 199.
42. Personal communication with Bruce Kimmel, November 13, 2007.
43. Brantley 1977: 63.
44. Kimmel 2010: 199–200.
45. Brantley 1977: 63.
46. Kimmel 2010: 228.
47. The "family hour" or "family viewing hour" was a policy established by television network heads in 1975 in response to pressure from the FCC. According to the new policy, networks were responsible for airing family-friendly programs during the 8 to 9 p.m. primetime slot. The concept was abandoned with the start of the fall 1977 season, following a ruling handed down in 1976, which argued that the FCC had overstepped its bounds and declared the networks free to control their own programming. Nonetheless the term has stuck, especially since many networks continue to offer family-friendly programs in the earlier primetime hours.
48. Kimmel 2010: 232.
49. Interview with Bruce Kimmel, *From Dollars to Donuts: An Undressing of* The First Nudie Musical.
50. All quoted in Kimmel 2010: 236–38.
51. Ibid., 239–40.
52. Interview with Bruce Kimmel, *From Dollars to Donuts: An Undressing of* The First Nudie Musical.
53. Ibid.
54. Brantley 1977: 63.
55. Personal communication with Bruce Kimmel, November 13, 2007.
56. Ibid.
57. Glover 1976: H11.
58. Ibid., 83–86.
59. Ibid., 86.
60. Ibid., 95–96.
61. Weber 2009: 1.
62. McNeil and Osborne 2005: 98.
63. Williams 1999: 156.
64. McNeil and Osborne 2005: 117.
65. Untitled, unsigned clipping about *Le Bellybutton* in *Time* magazine. http://time-demo.newscred.com/article/868564f1ce66b53e9f8949139b20156b.html/edit. Accessed May 3, 2012.
66. Personal communication with Edmund Gaynes, February 27, 2007.
67. Ibid.
68. Personal communication with Alan Kootsher, July 1, 2008.
69. "All Cleaned Up" 2007:12.
70. Personal communication with Alan Kootsher, July 1, 2008.
71. Ibid.
72. Ibid.
73. Ibid.
74. http://www.youtube.com/watch?v=m5iLYeCD-V4. Accessed January 20, 2011, but no longer available.
75. Box office information on *Le Bellybutton* is housed in the Fales Library and Special Collections at Bobst Library, New York University.
76. McNeil and Osborne 2005: 119.
77. Ibid., 369.

78. Corliss 2005, www.time.com/time/columnist/corliss/article/0,9565,1043267,00.html. Accessed August 2, 2010.
79. Rogers 2009: 2.

## CHAPTER 8

1. Weinraub 1969: 26.
2. Raymont 1969: 56.
3. Weinraub 1969: 26.
4. Ibid.
5. Houchin 2003: 215.
6. Raymont 1969: 56; Houchin 2003: 215.
7. Guernsey 1969: 37.
8. Schroeder 1969: 39.
9. Houchin 2003: 216.
10. Kaplan 1969: 37.
11. Houchin 2003: 216.
12. Kaplan 1969: 37.
13. "Bid to Reopen 'Che' Fails in US Court" 1969.
14. "Decision Is Reserved as Judge Hears Plea for Reopening 'Che!'" 1969.
15. "'Che!' Is Scheduled to Reopen Tonight" 1969.
16. "Actors and Author of 'Che!' Arrested after Performance" 1969.
17. Rudin 1969: 583.
18. "Beyond the (Garbage) Pale" 1969.
19. Ibid.
20. Hentoff 1969: 12.
21. Simon 1969.
22. Quoted in Houchin 2003: 216–17.
23. Ibid., 217.
24. Rudin 1969: 583–84.
25. Weinraub 1969: 26.
26. Raymont 1969: 56.
27. Ibid.
28. Funke 1969: 27.
29. Ibid.
30. Houchin 2003: 220.
31. Gottfried 1970: 1–5.
32. Black 1970: 1; Houchin 2003: 218.
33. Kaplan 1970: 46.
34. Ibid.
35. Oelsner 1970: 31.
36. Black 1970: 1.
37. Cited in Houchin 2003: 218.
38. Oelsner 1970: 31.
39. Ibid.
40. Letters from Equity Executive Secretary Donald Grody to D'Lugoff and Wilson, January 28, 1974, Tamiment Archives, Bobst Library, New York University. According to Wilson, the creative team had always promised the cast their Equity cards had *Let My People Come* been a success.
41. Letter from Equity Assistant Executive Secretary Vincent Donahue to Executive Secretary Donald Grody, January 22, 1974, Tamiment Archives, Bobst Library, New York University.
42. Guernsey 1987: 300. At the end of the 1974–75 season *Let My People Come* reported having grossed over $1,500,000 and returning $350,000 on its $10,000 investment. On Broadway during the same season, the long-running *Pippin* reported a $2,500,000

net profit on a $500,000 investment; *A Little Night Music*, a more modest commercial hit, closed in the black and reported a $100,000 profit on a $650,000 investment.
43. McFadden 1976a: 36.
44. Slattery 1976: 5.
45. *MCA Music v. Earl Wilson*, 425 F. Supp 443 (1976), http://cip.law.ucla.edu/cases/1970-1979/Pages/mcawilson.aspx. Accessed May 5, 2011.
46. Goldstein 1975a: 22.
47. Ibid.
48. Goldstein 1975a: 22.
49. Robbins 2009: 1.
50. Goldstein 1975a: 22.
51. "Supreme Court Actions" 1971: 25.
52. Dershowitz 1972: E7.
53. Ibid.
54. Goldstein 1975a: 22.
55. Ibid.
56. Dershowitz 1972: E7.
57. Ibid.
58. Goldstein 1975a: 22.
59. Wilson remembers that the New York production was not alone in being pursued by the State Liquor Authority. "There were attempts to close the show in other cities usually based on local liquor laws. The show was constantly cited in Philadelphia but never lost a decision." Personal communication with Earl Wilson Jr., February 8 2012.
60. "Producer Denies Play Has Sex Acts" 1975: 21.
61. "S.L.A. Challenges Village Gate" 1975: 32.
62. "Show in 'Village' Defended by Two" 1974: 12.
63. Ibid.
64. "Producer Denies Play Has Sex Acts" 1975: 21; "S.L.A. Challenges Village Gate" 1975: 32.
65. Weiss 1976: 4.
66. Goldstein 1975a: 22.
67. "Producer Denies Play Has Sex Acts" 1975: 21.
68. Goldstein 1975a: 21.
69. Ibid.
70. Ibid.
71. Goldstein 1975b: 81.
72. Goldstein 1975a: 22; Goldstein 1975b: 81.
73. Ibid.
74. Klemesrud 1974: 3.
75. Personal communication with Earl Wilson Jr., June 22, 2005.
76. "'Let My People Come' to Go to Broadway" 1976: 13.

## CHAPTER 9
1. Cannato 2001: xii.
2. Gottlieb 1985a: 1.
3. Cannato 2001: xii.
4. See, for example, Glassberg 1981; Spear 2002; Mahler 2005; Moody 2007; Lachman and Polner 2010.
5. "The 'Wolf' Cry Is Real" 1971. Stagflation occurs when rising costs and declining revenues result from a period of simultaneous inflation and recession.
6. Gottlieb 1985a: 32.
7. Mahler 2005: 7.
8. Gottlieb 1985a: 32.
9. Mahler 2005: 12.
10. Atkinson 1970: 115.

11. Ibid.
12. Bordman 2001: 699.
13. Jackson 1995: 1193.
14. Atkinson 1990: 432. The musical theater's aesthetic problems through the 1960s and 1970s are well documented; see, for example, Atkinson 1990; Bordman 2001; Kirle 2005; Knapp 2005, 2006a; Wollman 2006; Wolf 2011.
15. Adams 1969: 30.
16. Ibid.
17. Hicks 1969: 48; Adams 1969: 30.
18. Hicks 1969: 48.
19. Bailey and Farber 2004: 2.
20. Schumach 1971: 29.
21. Ibid.
22. Quoted in Bianco 2004: 180.
23. Traub 2004: 122.
24. Bianco 2004: 177.
25. Chesluk 2008: 24.
26. Traub 2004: 8.
27. Chesluk 2008: 26.
28. Ibid.
29. Jones 2003: 66, 83.
30. Traub 2004: 88–89. Penny restaurants were established in the late nineteenth century and served small but wholesome, if somewhat uninteresting, meals to patrons who could pay a penny for a small portion, five cents for a somewhat larger one, and a dime for a jumbo portion. Founded initially for newsboys and bootblacks, the restaurants were intended to serve a working-class clientele.
31. Ibid., 91.
32. Senelick 1991: 338.
33. Bianco 2004: 118.
34. Senelick 1991: 338–39.
35. Bianco 2004: 134.
36. Chesluk 2008: 40.
37. Ibid., 40–41.
38. Guernsey 1973: 27.
39. Guernsey 1972: 29.
40. Kissel 1993: 52.
41. All Broadway season statistics supplied by the Broadway League.
42. Kissel 1993: 48.
43. Guernsey 1971: 31. The League of New York Theatres, currently the Broadway League, is the commercial theater industry's trade organization. Founded in 1930, it has been renamed three times. It became the League of New York Theatres and Producers in 1973, the League of American Theatres and Producers in 1985, and the Broadway League in 2007. Members of the League include theater owners and operators, producers, entrepreneurs, general managers, and suppliers of goods and services to the commercial theater industry, both in New York City and across North America. When discussed herein, the League will be referred to according to its name at the time.
44. Prial 1972: 85.
45. Guernsey 1974: 34.
46. New York's financial rehabilitation in the late 1970s was the result of an uptick in tourism. In 1976 the Democratic National Convention, combined with a number of large, well-publicized celebrations in New York honoring the country's bicentennial, resulted in the city's biggest tourist boom since the late 1960s. The boom generated roughly $4.5 billion in a single year and convinced city officials to focus on tourism as a fast, cheap way to strengthen the economy, hence the birth of the "I Love New York" campaign in 1977, among similar advertising efforts through the early 1980s. By 1979

New York City was setting records, both for the number of tourists and for the amount of money that they were spending. As the city rebounded, so did the commercial theater district.

47. Calta 1976: 34.
48. Ibid.
49. Ibid.
50. Ibid.
51. "Theater Unit Gives City New Sweepers" 1976: 25.
52. Joe 1977: 17.
53. Phillips 1972: 26.
54. Fowler 1975: 45.
55. The League fought state censorship laws very shortly after its inception, boycotted segregated theaters beginning in the late 1940s, and was adamantly opposed to McCarthyism during the 1950s.
56. "'Let My People Come' to Go to Broadway" 1976: 13.
57. Guernsey 1987: 362.
58. Morrison 1976a: 65.
59. Corry 1976a: 46.
60. Morrison 1976a: 65.
61. Corry 1976a: 46.
62. Leogrande 1976a: 16.
63. Personal communication with Earl Wilson Jr., February 8, 2012.
64. "Wilson Objects to New 'People'" 1976: 54.
65. Corry 1976b: 44.
66. Ibid.
67. Morrison 1976b: 91.
68. "'Let My People' Postponed" 1976: 29.
69. Morrison 1976b: 91.
70. "Wilson Jr. Says 'People' Turned to Porn" 1976: n.p.
71. Stasio 1976: 9.
72. Gold 1976: 22.
73. Morrison 1976b: 91.
74. Leogrande 1976b: 13.
75. Barnes 1976: 46.
76. Fortunato 1977: 19.
77. Mast 1987: 296.
78. Corry 1977a: 39.
79. Corry 1977b: 48.
80. Corry 1977a: 39.
81. Wollman 2006: 119–21.
82. "Marginalia" 1976: 48.
83. Wilson 1977: 3.
84. Esalen is a retreat center in Big Sur, California, that was founded in the early 1960s as a site dedicated to the exploration of humanist alternative education.
85. Canby 1969: 50.
86. Farber 1970: 103.
87. http://www.focusfeatures.com/article/all_four_one. Accessed on June 23, 2011.
88. Hirsch 1969–70: 62.
89. Farber 1970: 107–8.
90. Gitlin 1987: 214.
91. Farber 1970: 108.
92. Ibid., 106.
93. Stewart 1978: 11.
94. Quindlen 1977: C17.
95. Stewart 1978: 17.

96. Ibid., 16–17.
97. Ibid.
98. Ibid., 17.
99. Ibid., 19.
100. Ibid., 27.
101. Ibid., 28.
102. Ibid.
103. See Wolf 2011: chapter 2.
104. Stewart 1978: 29.
105. Ibid., 29–30.
106. Ibid., 30.
107. Ibid.
108. Ibid., 49.
109. Original cast recording, *I Love My Wife*. The line "and married" is not in the published script.
110. Stewart 1978: 51.
111. Ibid.
112. Ibid., 54.
113. Ibid., 58.
114. Ibid.
115. Ibid., 67.
116. Ibid., 68.
117. The 1950s was concurrently being revisited nightly on Broadway through the 1970s. *Grease*, which opened in 1972, was the longest running show on Broadway for its time. For more on Broadway's response to and capitalization on its audience's nostalgia for the 1950s, please see Jones 2003: chapter 9; Wollman and Sternfeld 2011. For more on 1970s nostalgia in general, please see Jenkins 2006: 68–70.
118. Barnes 1977: 47; Kerr 1977b: D5; Reed 1977: L13.
119. Gottfried 1977b: 17.
120. Wilson 1977: 22.
121. Kalem 1977: 87.
122. Morrison 1977: 120.
123. Simon 1977b: 29.
124. Clurman 1977: n.p.
125. Kissel 1977: 34.
126. Feingold 1977: 89.
127. Jenkins 2006: 75.
128. Bottoms 2004: 344.
129. Gottfried 1977b: 17.
130. Jenkins 2006: 75.
131. Gottfried, 1977b: 17.
132. Kyd 1977: 16.
133. Regelson 1977: 34.
134. Quindlen 1977: C17.
135. Berkvist 1977: 44.

## CONCLUSION
1. Schulman 2001: xii.
2. Kakutani 1982: C17.
3. Wolf 2011: 129.
4. Kerr 1969: 26B.

# BIBLIOGRAPHY

"Actors and Author of 'Che!' Arrested after Performance." 1969. *New York Times*, May 8.

Adams, Val. 1969. "Boom Year for Tourism." *New York Times*, April 9.

"All Cleaned Up." 2007. *New York Post,* August 3.

Allen, Robert C. 1991. *Horrible Prettiness: Burlesque and American Culture.* Chapel Hill: University of North Carolina Press.

Als, Hilton. 2009. "Not So Free Love: Breaking Out in *Hair* and *Reasons to Be Pretty*." *New Yorker*, April 12, http://www.newyorker.com/arts/critics/theatre/2009/04/13/090413 crth_theatre_als.

Amsel, Bob. 1969a. "Up and Coming: For Gays—*We'd Rather Switch.*" *Screw*, October 20.

Amsel, Bob. 1969b. "Naked City." *Screw*, November 3.

Andrist, Ralph K. 1973. "Paladin of Purity." *American Heritage* 24, no. 6: 1–8.

Assmann, Aleida. 2010. "Canon and Archive." In *A Companion to Cultural Memory Studies,* ed. Astrid Erll and Ansgar Nünning. Berlin: Gruyter, 97–107.

Assmann, Jan. 2010. "Communicative and Cultural Memory." In *A Companion to Cultural Memory Studies*, ed. Astrid Erll and Ansgar Nünning. Berlin: Gruyter, 109–18.

Atkinson, Brooks. 1970. "A Rustic Life in City's Shadow." *New York Times*, December 6.

Atkinson, Brooks. 1990. *Broadway*. Revised ed. New York: Limelight.

Bailey, Beth. 1994. "Sexual Revolution(s)." In *The Sixties: From Memory to History*, ed. David Farber. Chapel Hill: University of North Carolina Press, 235–61.

Bailey, Beth. 2004. "She 'Can Bring Home the Bacon': Negotiating Gender in Seventies America." In *America in the Seventies*, ed. Beth Bailey and David Farber. Lawrence: University Press of Kansas, 107–28.

Bailey, Beth, and David Farber. 2004. Introduction to *America in the Seventies*, ed. Beth Bailey and David Farber. Lawrence: University Press of Kansas, 1–8.

Banfield, Stephen. 1993. *Sondheim's Broadway Musicals*. Ann Arbor: University of Michigan Press.

Banham, Martin, ed. 1995. *The Cambridge Guide to Theatre*. Cambridge: Cambridge University Press.

Barber, John. 1970. "Human Wholeness on the Stage." *Daily Telegraph,* February 16.

Barnes, Clive. 1967a. "Theatre: Social Significance to Music—'Now Is the Time for All Good Men' at de Lys." *New York Times*, September 27.

Barnes, Clive. 1967b. "Theater: Reappraisal." *New York Times*, October 27.

Barnes, Clive. 1968. "Theater: 'Boys in the Band' Opens Off Broadway." *New York Times*, April 15.

Barnes, Clive. 1969a. " 'The Boys in the Band' Is Still a Sad Gay Romp." *New York Times*, February 18.

Barnes, Clive. 1969b. "Theater: 'Oh, Calcutta!' A Most Innocent Dirty Show." *New York Times*, June 18.

Barnes, Clive. 1970. "The Stage: 'Mod Donna.' " *New York Times*, May 4.

Barnes, Clive. 1971. "Stage: '71 Is Off to a Lamentable Start—'Stag Movie,' a Musical, Opens at the Gate" *New York Times*, January 4.

Barnes, Clive. 1973a. "Theatre: 'Shelter,' Musical, Arrives" *New York Times*, February 7.

Barnes, Clive. 1973b. "Theater: 'The Faggot,' an Ecumenical View of Love." *New York Times*, June 19.

Barnes, Clive. 1974. "Theater: Musical 'Sextet' at the Bijou." *New York Times*, March 4.

Barnes, Clive. 1975. "'Lovers,' a New Homosexual Musical." *New York Times*, January 28.

Barnes, Clive. 1976. "Theater: 'Oh! Calcutta' Returns—7-Year-Old, Silly Revue About Pseudo-Eroticism at Edison." *New York Times*, October 26.

Barnes, Clive. 1977. "Stage: Tuneful 'I Love My Wife.'" *New York Times*, April 18.

Barrett, Raina. 1973. *First Your Money, Then Your Clothes: My Life and* Oh! Calcutta! New York: Signet.

Beisel, Nicola. 1997. *Imperiled Innocents: Anthony Comstock and Family Reproduction in Victorian America.* Princeton, N.J.: Princeton University Press.

Bemis, Sandra. 1987. "The Difficulties Facing Feminist Theater: The Survival of At the Foot of the Mountain." *North Dakota Journal of Speech and Theatre*, vol. 1: 1–6.

Bender, Marilyn. 1970. "Women's Liberation Taking to the Stage." *New York Times*, March 26.

Berkvist, Robert. 1977. "New Face: Joanna Gleason, High on Fidelity." *New York Times*, May 27.

Berkvist, Robert. 2004. "Cy Coleman, Composer Whose Jazz-Fired Musicals Blazed on Broadway, Dies at 75." *New York Times*, November 20.

Betsko, Kathleen, and Rachel Koenig. 1987. *Interviews with Contemporary Women Playwrights.* New York: William Morrow.

"Beyond the (Garbage) Pale." 1969. *New York Times*, April 1.

Bianco, Anthony. 2004. *Ghosts of 42nd Street: A History of America's Most Infamous Block.* New York: Harper Perennial.

"Bid to Reopen 'Che' Fails in U.S. Court." 1969. *New York Times*, March 28.

Bigsby, C. W. E. 1985. *A Critical Introduction to Twentieth-Century American Drama.* Vol. 3: *Beyond Broadway.* New York: Cambridge University Press.

Black, Jonathan. 1970. "'Che!' Eight Judged Guilty of Obscenity." *Village Voice*, March 5.

Block, Geoffrey. 1997. *Enchanted Evenings: The Broadway Musical from* Show Boat *to* Sondheim. New York: Oxford University Press.

Blumenthal, Ralph. 1973. "Porno Chic: 'Hard-Core' Grows Fashionable—and Very Profitable." *New York Times*, January 21.

Boesing, Martha. 1996. "Rushing Headlong into the Fire at the Foot of the Mountain." *Signs* 21, no. 4: 1011–23.

Bordman, Gerald. 2001. *American Musical Theatre: A Chronicle.* 3rd ed. New York: Oxford University Press.

Bosworth, Patricia. 1971. "New Life Plan for the Frustrated Housewife: Myrna Lamb—Wife-Mother-Playwright." *New Woman*, July, 12–13.

Bottoms, Stephen J. 2004. *Playing Underground: A Critical History of the 1960s Off-Off-Broadway Movement.* Ann Arbor: University of Michigan Press.

Brackett, David. 2005. *The Pop, Rock, and Soul Reader: Histories and Debates.* New York: Oxford University Press.

Brantley, Robin. 1977. "New Face: Bruce Kimmel, Bare-Faced Father of 'Nudie Musical.'" *New York Times*, September 16.

Braunstein, Peter. 2004. "'Adults Only': The Construction of an Erotic City in New York During the 1970s." In *America in the Seventies,* ed. Beth Bailey and David Farber. Lawrence: University Press of Kansas, 129–56.

Bristow, Eugene K., and J. Kevin Butler. 1987. "*Company*, About Face! The Show That Revolutionized the American Musical." *American Music* 5, no. 3: 241–54.

Brukenfeld, Dick. 1970. "Off-Off: *Mod Donna.*" *Village Voice*, May 7.

Brukenfeld, Dick. 1974. "Impressionistic but Not Impressive." *Village Voice*, March 14.

Bunce, Alan. 1969. "Stage: Erotic and Otherwise." *Christian Science Monitor*, June 20.

Burke, Tom. 1969. "And I Call *That* God." *New York Times*, February 23.

Calta, Louis. 1976. "Theatre League Bids Cinemas Refrain from Using Sex Films." *New York Times*, February 25.

Canby, Vincent. 1969. "'Bob and Carol and Ted and Alice' Twits 'New Morality.'" *New York Times*, September 17.

Cannato, Vincent J. 2001. *The Ungovernable City: John Lindsay and His Struggle to Save New York*. New York: Basic Books.

Canning, Charlotte. 1993. "Constructing Experience: Theorizing a Feminist Theatre History." *Theatre Journal* 45, no. 4: 529–40.

Canning, Charlotte. 1995. *Feminist Theatres in the USA: Staging Feminist Experience.* New York: Routledge.

Carmines, Al. 1973a. "Drama Mailbag: Politics Is Not Art." *New York Times*, July 29.

Carmines, Al. 1973b. *The Faggot*. Unpublished manuscript.

Carroll, Maurice. 1974. "Council Defeats Homosexual Bill by 22-to-19 Vote." *New York Times*, May 24.

Carroll, Peter. 1990. *It Seemed Like Nothing Happened: America in the 1970s*. New Brunswick, N.J.: Rutgers University Press.

"Challenge to Nudity Ban Planned." 1975. *The New York Times*, December 8.

Chauncey, George, Jr. 1991. "The Policed: Gay Men's Strategies of Everyday Resistance." In *Inventing Times Square: Commerce and Culture at the Crossroads of the World*, ed. William R. Taylor. New York: Russell Sage Foundation, 315–98.

"'Che!' Is Scheduled to Reopen Tonight." 1969. *New York Times*, April 25.

Chesluk, Benjamin. 2008. *Money Jungle: Imagining the New Times Square*. New Brunswick, N.J.: Rutgers University Press.

Christon, Lawrence. 1980. "No Yellow Brick Road for Cryer." *Los Angeles Times*, November 4.

Clay, Carolyn. 1977. "The Agony and the Irony: *Colored Girls* and *The Club* Bring Two Feminist Poets to the Stage." *Boston After Dark Arts and Entertainment*, November 22, 1, 13.

"The Club." 1977. *Variety*, February 9.

"'The Club': A Shift in Perspective." 1977. *New York Times*, February 17.

Clum, John. 1999. *Something for the Boys: Musical Theater and Gay Culture*. New York: Palgrave.

Clurman, Harold. 1976. Review of *The Club*. *The Nation*, November 6.

Clurman, Harold. 1977. Review of *I Love My Wife*. *The Nation*, May 7.

Coburn, Marcia Froelke. 1980. "A Playwright Blends Feminist Values and Entertainment." *Chicago Sun-Times*, May 29.

Coleman, Bud, and Judith Sebesta, eds. 2008. *Women in American Musical Theatre: Essays on Composers, Lyricists, Librettists, Arrangers, Choreographers, Designers, Directors, Producers and Performance Artists*. Jefferson, NC: McFarland and Company.

Congressional Budget Office. 1975–76. "The Causes of New York City's Fiscal Crisis." *Political Science Quarterly* 90, no. 4: 659–74.

Corbett, John, and Terri Kapsalis. 1996. "Aural Sex: The Female Orgasm in Popular Sound." *Drama Review* 40, no. 3: 102–11.

Corliss, Richard. 2005. "That Old Feeling: When Porno Was Chic." *Time*, March 29, www.time.com/time/columnist/corliss/article/0,9565,1043267,00.html. Accessed August 2, 2010.

Corry, John. 1976a. "Broadway." *New York Times*, July 2.

Corry, John. 1976b. "Broadway." *New York Times*, July 23.

Corry, John. 1977a. "Broadway." *New York Times*, January 7.

Corry, John. 1977b. "Broadway." *New York Times*, March 4.

Corry, John. 1977c. "Broadway." *New York Times*, May 6.

Crespy, David A. 2003. *Off-Off Broadway Explosion: How Provocative Playwrights of the 1960s Ignited a New American Theater*. New York: Back Stage Books, 2003.

Crowley, Mart. 1968. *The Boys in the Band*. New York: Samuel French.

Cryer, Gretchen. 1980. *I'm Getting My Act Together and Taking It on the Road*. New York: Samuel French.

Cushman, Robert. 1977. Review of *The Club*. *London Observer*, July 3.

Dace, Tish. 1978. "Cryer: Affirming a Way of Life." *West Side Express*, August 19.

David, Bruce. 1976. "Earl Wilson, Jr.: Jacking Off-Broadway." *Hustler*, June, 44–50.

Davis, James. 1969. "Stag Stage Show Opens to the General Public." *Daily News*, June 18.

Davis, Tracy C. 1998. "A Feminist Boomerang: Eve Merriam's *The Club* (1976)." In *Staging Resistance: Essays on Political Theater*, ed. Jeanne Colleran and Jenny S. Spencer. Ann Arbor: University of Michigan Press, 146–65.

"Dealer in Obscenity Gets a 5-Year Term." 1956. *New York Times*, February 8.

"Decision Is Reserved as Judge Hears Plea for Reopening 'Che!'" 1969. *New York Times*, April 2.

Dell'Olio, Anselma. 2007. "Home before Sundown." In *The Feminist Memoir Project: Voices from Women's Liberation*, ed. Rachel Blau DuPlessis and Ann Snitow. New Brunswick, N.J.: Rutgers University Press, 149–70.

Dennis, Donna I. 2007. "Obscenity Law and Its Consequences in Mid-Nineteenth-Century America." *Columbia Journal of Gender and Law* 16, no. 1: 43–95.

Dershowitz, Alan M. 1972. "Sex Shows: The Court Says Nudes and Liquor Don't Mix." *New York Times*, December 10.

Dolan, Jill. 1991. *The Feminist Spectator as Critic*. Ann Arbor: University of Michigan Press.

Dowd, Maureen. 1985. "The Middle Class Pitched In to Help Bay Ridge Get By." *New York Times*, July 4.

Drutman, Irving. 1966. ". . . Was Peter Brook Its Brain?" *New York Times*, January 9.

Duberman, Martin. 1973. "The Gay Life: Cartoon vs. Reality?" *New York Times*, July 22.

Duberman, Martin. 1993. *Stonewall*. New York: Dutton.

Dunbar, Ernest. 1969. "Levy of 'Oh! Calcutta!' A Dropout Makes It As a Sex Revolutionary." *Look*, August, 38–40.

Ebert, Roger. 1976. "Alice in Wonderland." *Chicago Sun Times*, November 24.

Echols, Alice. 1994. "Nothing Distant About It: Women's Liberation and Sixties Radicalism." In *The Sixties: From Memory to History*, ed. David Farber. Chapel Hill: University of North Carolina Press, 149–74.

Echols, Alice. 2010. *Hot Stuff: Disco and the Remaking of American Culture*. New York: Norton, 2010.

Eder, Richard. 1976. "Film: Alice in Pornland—Lewd Rock and Other Skillful Silliness." *New York Times*, August 28.

Epstein, Helen. 1996. *Joe Papp: An American Life*. Cambridge, Mass.: Da Capo Press.

Erll, Astrid. 2010. "Cultural Memory Studies: An Introduction." In *A Companion to Cultural Memory Studies*, ed. Astrid Erll and Ansgar Nünning. Berlin: Gruyter.

Farber, Stephen. 1970. "Couples." *Hudson Review* 23, no. 1: 103–9.

Feingold, Michael. 1975. "The Gay Escape." *Village Voice*, February 24.

Feingold, Michael. 1977. "The Musical Is Alive and Ailing." *Village Voice*, May 2.

Fields, Sidney. 1978. "Only Human: Always Getting Their Act Together." *Daily News*, June 13.

Ford, Luke. 1999. *A History of X: 100 Years of Sex in Film*. Amherst, N.Y.: Prometheus Books.

Fortunato, Frank. 1977. "Oh! Calcutta! Again!" *Hustler*, June, 19.

Fowler, Glenn. 1975. "A Proposal to Zone 'Massage Parlors' Is Supported Here." *New York Times*, November 20.

Friedman, Andrea. 1996. "The Habitats of Sex-Crazed Perverts: Campaigns against Burlesque in Depression-Era New York City." *Journal of the History of Sexuality* 7, no. 2: 203–38.

Friedman, Andrea. 2000. *Prurient Interests: Gender, Democracy, and Obscenity in New York City, 1909–1945*. New York: Columbia University Press.

Funke, Lewis. 1968. "Tynan's Elegant Erotica." *New York Times*, October 20.

Funke, Lewis. 1969. "Tynan Plans a Stage Tribute to Eros." *New York Times*, April 9.

Furth, George, and Stephen Sondheim. 1996. *Company*. New York: Theatre Communications Group.

Genauer, Emily. 1969. "Art and the Artist." *New York Post*, June 21.

George, George L. 1969. "We'd Rather Switch." *Back Stage*, November 21.

Gerhard, Jane. 2000. "Revisiting 'The Myth of the Vaginal Orgasm': The Female Orgasm in American Sexual Thought and Second Wave Feminism." *Feminist Studies* 26, no. 2: 449–76.

Gitlin, Todd. 1987. *The Sixties: Years of Hope, Days of Rage*. Toronto: Bantam.

Glassberg, Andrew. 1981. "The Urban Fiscal Crisis Becomes Routine." *Public Administration Review* 41: 165–72.

Glover, William. 1976. "Marilyn Chambers, Live." *Louisville Courier-Journal*, April 11.

Glueck, Grace. 1970. "I Didn't Burn My Bra." *New York Times*, May 10.

Gold, Sylviane. 1976. "Let the People Beware." *New York Post*, August 13.

Goldsmith, Lee, and Harvey Perr. 1974. *Sextet*. Unpublished manuscript.

Goldstein, Tom. 1975a. "'Obscenity' and Liquor: License Case Raises Constitutional Issue." *New York Times*, January 23.

Goldstein, Tom. 1975b. "S.L.A. Imposes Ban on Total Nudity: Also Cancels Liquor License of 'Village' Club Showing 'Let My People Come.'" *New York Times*, December 5.

Goldstein, Tom. 1976. "Village Gate Shut Down by Buildings Department." *New York Times*, January 3.

Gordon, Joanne. 1990. *Art Isn't Easy: The Achievement of Stephen Sondheim*. Carbondale: Southern Illinois University Press.

Gornick, Vivian. 1970. "Who Is Fairest of Them All?" *Village Voice*, May 28.

Gottfried, Martin. 1970. "Why Is 'Che!' on Trial?" *New York Times*, January 18.

Gottfried, Martin. 1974. "Sextet." *Women's Wear Daily*, March 4.

Gottfried, Martin. 1977a. "'Hold Me' and 'The Club' Bring Life to Off'B'way." *New York Post*, April 2.

Gottfried, Martin. 1977b. "A Thoroughly Disarming 'Wife'" *New York Post*, April 18.

Gottlieb, Martin. 1985a. "A Decade after the Cutbacks, New York Is a Different City." *New York Times*, June 30.

Gottlieb, Martin. 1985b. "New York's Rescue: The Offstage Dramas." *New York Times*, July 2.

Gould, Lois. 1977. "Hers." *New York Times*, May 19.

Grant, Mark N. 2004. *The Rise and Fall of the Broadway Musical*. Lebanon, N.H.: University Press of New England.

Grumley, Michael. 1973. "Shortsighted." *New York Times*, August 12.

Guernsey, Otis L., Jr., ed. 1969. *The Best Plays of 1968–69*. New York: Dodd, Mead.

Guernsey, Otis L., Jr., ed. 1971. *The Best Plays of 1970–71*. New York: Dodd, Mead.

Guernsey, Otis L., Jr., ed. 1972. *The Best Plays of 1971–72*. New York: Dodd, Mead.

Guernsey, Otis L., Jr., ed. 1973. *The Best Plays of 1972–73*. New York: Dodd, Mead.

Guernsey, Otis L., Jr., ed. 1974. *The Best Plays of 1973–74*. New York: Dodd, Mead.

Guernsey, Otis L., Jr. 1987. *Curtain Times: The New York Theatre: 1965–87*. New York: Dodd, Mead.

Gussow, Mel. 1969. "In 'We'd Rather Switch' at the Mermaid, Most of Stripping Is Done by Men." *New York Times*, December 20.

Gussow, Mel. 1974. "Stage: More Success Than Just Blurbs—*Let My People Come*, a Sexual Musical." *New York Times*, May 7.

Gussow, Mel. 1976. "Stage: Eve Merriam's 'Club.'" *New York Times*, October 15.

Gustavson, Terry. 1973. "The Author Speaks." Unidentified clipping, Bobst Library, New York University.

Haagensen, Erik. 2001. "America's Lesbian and Gay Theater Companies—Then and Now." *On the Purple Circuit*, June, http://www.buddybuddy.com/pc-f-04.html. Accessed June 2, 2009.

Hall, Kermit L., ed. 1992. *The Oxford Companion to the Supreme Court of the United States*. New York: Oxford University Press.

Harris, William. 1978. Review of *I'm Getting My Act Together and Taking It on the Road*. *Soho Weekly News*, July 6.

Heidenry, John. 1997. *What Wild Ecstasy: The Rise and Fall of the Sexual Revolution*. New York: Simon and Schuster.

Henkel, Gretchen. 1980. "Feminist Viewpoint: All about Eve Merriam's 'Club.'" *Drama-Logue*, October 9, 1, 13.

Hentoff, Nat. 1969. "Where Do We Go from 'Che!'?" *New York Times*, May 4.

Hicks, Nancy. 1969. "Boom in Tourism Is Noted by City: A Record Total of Visitors Reported for Last Year." *New York Times*, January 19.

"High Court to Hear Booksellers' Cases." 1957. *New York Times*, January 15.

Hillary, Eileen. 1976. "Diverting Show at 'The Club.'" *East Side Express*, November 11.

Hirsch, Foster. 1969–70. "Short Notices: Bob and Carol and Ted and Alice." *Film Quarterly* 23, no. 2: 62.

Hoffman, Ted. 1977. "On Theatre: The Transsexual Experimental Hit!" *Villager*, July 7.

Hollinger, Karen. 1998. "Theorizing Mainstream Female Spectatorship: The Case of the Popular Lesbian Film." *Cinema Journal* 37, no. 2: 3–17.

"Homo Libs Razz Off-B'way 'Movie,' Get the Bounce." 1971. *Variety*, January 13.

"Homosexual Citizen: *We'd Rather Switch*." 1969. *Screw*, November 8.

Horn, Barbara Lee. 1991. *The Age of Hair: Evolution and Impact of Broadway's First Rock Musical*. Westport, Conn.: Greenwood Press.

Houchin, John H. 2003. *Censorship of the American Theatre in the Twentieth Century*. New York: Cambridge University Press.

Ide, Reed. 1975. "*Lovers* Was Born in a Basement." *Villager*, January 30.

Jackson, Kenneth T., ed. 1995. *The Encyclopedia of New York City*. New Haven, Conn.: Yale University Press.

Jenkins, Philip. 2006. *Decade of Nightmares: The End of the Sixties and the Making of Eighties America*. New York: Oxford University Press.

Jenner, Cynthia Lee. 1976. "Taps for Everyone." *Villager*, October 21.

Joe, Radcliffe. 1977. "Goal: To Make Times Square Inviting Musicals Join N.Y. Cleanup." *Billboard*, April 30.

Jones, John Bush. 2003. *Our Musicals, Ourselves: A Social History of the American Musical Theatre*. Lebanon, N.H.: Brandeis University Press.

Junker, Howard. 1968. "Theater of the Nude: Eclipsing Even Hollywood, the New York Stage Is Taking It Off—Taking It *All* Off—And the Reactions Range from Outrage to Accolades." *Playboy*, November.

Kaiser, Charles. 1997. *The Gay Metropolis, 1940–1996*. Boston: Houghton Mifflin.

Kakutani, Michico. 1982. "Fierstein and 'Torch Song': A Daring Climb from Obscurity." *New York Times*, July 14.

Kalem, T. E. 1977. "Unrequited Sin in Trenton." *Time*, May 2.

Kaplan, Morris. 1969. "Actors and Author of 'Che' Are Charged with Obscenity." *New York Times*, March 26.

Kaplan, Morris. 1970. "David Merrick, at Cast's Trial, Assails 'Che!' as Without Value." *New York Times*, January 20.

Karpel, Craig. 1969. "*Oh, Calcutta*: No Penetration in Eden." *Village Voice*, May 15.

Karr, M. A. 1980. "Eve Merriam Welcomes You to 'The Club.'" *The Advocate*, September 18.

Katz, Jonathan. 1973. "Furor over *The Faggot*." *New York Times*, August 12.

Kauffmann, Stanley. 1966. "Music by Al Carmines." *New York Times*. July 3.

Kauffmann, Stanley. 1977. Review of *The Club*. *New Republic*, February 5.

Kauffmann, Stanley. 1979. "New York: The City and the Theatre." *Theatre Quarterly* 32, no. 8: 34–40.

Kerr, Walter. 1968. "To Laugh at Oneself—or Cry." *New York Times*, April 28.

Kerr, Walter. 1969. "What Can They Do for an Encore?" *New York Times*, February 2.

Kerr, Walter. 1970. "Is It True—Women Hate Women?" *New York Times*, May 10.

Kerr, Walter. 1970a. "Would It Have Been Better to Ignore Arrabal?" *New York Times*, September 20.

Kerr, Walter. 1977a. Review of *The Club*. *New York Times*, January 15.

Kerr, Walter. 1977b. "Broadway Is Alive with the Sound of Music." *New York Times*, May 1.

Kerr, Walter. 1978. "Two Women, Both Alone, Two Moods." *New York Times*, July 9.

Kihss, Peter. 1976. "Beame Scores Court Stay Keeping Village Gate Open: Presses to Reinstate a Vacate Order—Cabaret Owners Deny Hazards, Charge Harassment by City." *New York Times*, January 5.

Kimball, Robert. 1978. "Gretchen Cryer Gets Her Act Together." *New York Post*, June 15.

Kimmel, Bruce. 2010. *"There's Mel, There's Woody, and There's You": My Life in the Slow Lane.* Bloomington, Ind.: AuthorHouse.

Kirle, Bruce. 2005. *Unfinished Show Business: Broadway Musicals as Works-in-Process.* Carbondale: Southern Illinois University Press.

Kissel, Howard. 1976. "The Club." *Women's Wear Daily*, October 15.

Kissel, Howard. 1977. "I Love My Wife." *Women's Wear Daily*, April 19.

Kissel, Howard. 1978. "I'm Getting My Act Together..." *Women's Wear Daily*, June 16.

Kissel, Howard. 1993. *David Merrick: The Abominable Showman—The Unauthorized Biography.* New York: Applause.

Klemesrud, Judy. 1974. "How to Succeed in Show Business without Really Opening." *New York Times*, September 15.

Klemesrud, Judy. 1978. "She's Got Her Act Together Again." *New York Times*, December 16.

Knapp, Raymond. 2006a. *The American Musical and the Performance of National Identity.* Princeton, N.J.: Princeton University Press.

Knapp, Raymond. 2006b. *The American Musical and the Performance of Personal Identity.* Princeton, N.J.: Princeton University Press.

Komisar, Lucy. 1970. "Drama Mailbag: Women Are the Victims." *New York Times*, May 31.

Kroll, Jack. 1969. "Eros Goes Public." *Newsweek*, June 30.

Kroll, Jack. 1970. "Guys and Dolls." *Newsweek*, May 18.

Kry, Margaret. 1975. Review of *Lovers. Villager*, January 30.

Kyd, Joanna. 1977. "*I Love My Wife*: Good News for the Happy Hearth." *Our Town*, May 20.

Lachman, Seymour P., and Robert Polner. 2010. *The Man Who Saved New York: Hugh Carey and the Fiscal Crisis of 1975.* New York: Excelsior.

Lamb, Myrna. 1970. "Mod Donna." *International Socialist Review* 31, no. 5: 18–40.

Lamb, Myrna. 1971. *Plays of Women's Liberation:* The Mod Donna *and* Scyklon Z. New York: Pathfinder Press.

Lambert, Sheela. 2009. "The Man Behind the *Hair*." *The Advocate*, online exclusive, March 12, http://www.advocate.com/arts-entertainment/theater/2008/08/13/man-behind-hair. Accessed March 31, 2010.

Leogrande, Ernest. 1976a. "'Let My People Come'—Without Earl Jr." *Daily News*, July 26.

Leogrande, Ernest. 1976b. "Skin for Skin's Sake." *Daily News*, October 9.

Lester, Elenore. 1976. "On Theatre: Ebb Tide in the Feminist Bloodstream." *Soho Weekly News*, October 28.

"'Let My People Come' to Go to Broadway." 1976. *New York Times*, June 26.

"'Let My People' Postponed." 1976. *New York Times*, July 26.

Lewis, Emory. 1971. "'Stag Movie' Is Just an Ambling Vignette." *The Record*, January 4.

Lingeman, Richard R. 1971. "I Was an Angel for 'Stag Movie.'" *New York Times*, February 14.

Lotman, Loretta. 1976. "Gloria Hodes Is My Cary Grant." *Village Voice*, November 29.

Loughery, John. 1998. *The Other Side of Silence: Men's Lives and Gay Identities—A Twentieth-Century History.* New York: Henry Holt.

Lovensheimer, Jim. 2002. "Stephen Sondheim and the Musical of the Outsider." In *The Cambridge Companion to the Musical*, ed. William A. Everett and Paul R. Laird. Cambridge: Cambridge University Press, 181–96.

"Lovers." 1975. *Gay Scene.* Clipping, date not given.

Mahler, Jonathan. 2005. *Ladies and Gentlemen, the Bronx Is Burning: 1977, Baseball, Politics, and the Battle for the Soul of a City.* New York: Farrar, Straus and Giroux.

Mandelbaum, Ken. 1991. *Not Since* Carrie: *40 Years of Broadway Musical Flops.* New York: St. Martin's Press.

Marcus, Eric. 2002. *Making Gay History: The Half Century Fight for Lesbian and Gay Equal Rights.* New York: Harper Paperbacks.

"Marginalia: Bloom, Pinter Set for Play." 1976. *New York Times*, May 5.

Martin, Bradford D. 2004. *The Theater Is in the Street: Politics and Public Performance in Sixties America.* Amherst: University of Massachusetts Press.

Martin, Douglas. 2009. "Tom O'Horgan, 84, Creator of 'Hair' Is Dead." *New York Times*, January 13.

Martin, Jeremy. 2010. "Go Ask Alice: Why Do We Keep Returning to Wonderland?" *San Antonio Current*, March 3.

Mast, Gerald. 1987. *Can't Help Singin': The American Musical on Stage and Screen*. New York: Overlook Press.

McFadden, Robert D. 1976a. "Village Gate Obtains a Court Order and Shows Go On." *New York Times*, January 4.

McFadden, Robert D. 1976b. "Settlement Set on Village Gate." *New York Times* January 6.

McLaughlin, Patricia. 1978. "Found: Eve Merriam." *Pennsylvania Gazette*, April.

McMillin, Scott. 2006. *The Musical as Drama*. Princeton, N.J.: Princeton University Press.

McNeil, Legs, and Jennifer Osborne. 2005. *The Other Hollywood: The Uncensored Oral History of the Porn Film Industry*. New York: HarperCollins.

Merriam, Eve. 1977. *The Club: A Musical Diversion*. New York: Samuel French.

"Metropolitan Briefs: Village Gate Gets Stay." 1975. *New York Times*, December 13.

Miller, D. A. 1998. *Place for Us: Essay on the Broadway Musical*. Cambridge, Mass.: Harvard University Press.

Montgomery, Paul L. 1972a. "Film Critic Says 'Deep Throat' Could Expand Sexual Horizons." *New York Times*, December 21.

Montgomery, Paul L. 1972b. "Psychiatrist Testifies That 'Deep Throat' Could Be Harmful to a Normal Man by Clouding Female Sexuality." *New York Times*, December 27.

Moody, Kim. 2007. *From Welfare State to Real Estate: Regime Change in New York City, 1974 to the Present*. New York: New Press.

Morrison, Hobe. 1974. "Sextet." *Variety*, March 6.

Morrison, Hobe. 1976a. "'People' Gonna Come to B'way: Theatre League Deplores It." *Variety*, June 30.

Morrison, Hobe. 1976b. *"Let My People Come." Variety*, September 8.

Morrison, Hobe. 1977. *"I Love My Wife." Variety*, April 20.

Most, Andrea. 2004. *Making Americans: Jews and the Broadway Musical*. Cambridge, Mass.: Harvard University Press.

Murphy, Mary. 2009. "R.I.-Born Porn Star, 56, Found Dead." *Providence Journal*, April 16.

Novick, Julius. 1978. "Heather and Wan." *Village Voice*, June 26.

"The N.Y. Theater As of Now: Hardly Anything Succeeds Like the 'Successful Thing' on Broadway or Off, at 7:30 or 8, With or Without Aid." 1971. *Dramatists Guild Quarterly* 8, no. 3: 46–49.

O'Connor, John J. 1969. "Old Message Put to Music." *Wall Street Journal*, September 25.

Oelsner, Lesley. 1970. "8 in 'Che!' Are Found Guilty of Obscenity." *New York Times*, February 26.

"Off-B'way 'Stag Movie' Keeps Going: Still a Public for Porno Legit?" 1971. *Variety*, March 3.

"Off Off Broadway Theater." 1969. *Screw*, May 16.

Oliver, Edith. 1970. "Off Broadway: *Isaac, Goliath,* and *James.*" *New Yorker*, February 7, 73–76.

Oppenheimer, George. 1976. Review of *The Club*. *Newsday*, December 17.

Oreskes, Michael. 1985. "Fiscal Crisis Still Haunts the Police." *New York Times*, July 6.

Papp, Joseph. 1970. "An Audience Guide: Program notes to *Mod Donna*" (Original Off Broadway production), dir. Joseph Papp.

Patient, Ray F. 1975. "Move Over, Miss Thing." *Spectator*, April 25.

Phillips, McCandlish. 1972. "Peep Shows and Massage Parlors Are Targets in City's Intensified Drive to Clean Up Times Square." *New York Times*, July 13.

Prial, Frank J. 1972. "Taxi Industry May Drop Theater Area Dispatchers." *New York Times*, January 12.

"Producer Denies Play Has Sex Acts: Says 'Let My People Come' Shows a 'Nude Ballet.'" 1975. *New York Times*, January 24.

Purnick, Joyce. 1986. "Homosexual Rights Bill Is Passed by City Council in 21-to-14 Vote." *New York Times*, March 21.

Quindlen, Anna. 1977. "'Skinny, Silly Schlump' Who Made It." *New York Times*, May 4.

Ragni, Gerome, and James Rado. 1966. *Hair: The American Tribal Love-Rock Musical.* New York: Pocket Books.

Ragni, Gerome, and James Rado. N.d. *Hair: The American Tribal Love-Rock Musical.* Production script.

Raymont, Henry. 1969. "'Che!' Tests the Limits of Sex Onstage." *New York Times*, March 24.

Rea, Charlotte. 1972. "Women's Theater Groups." *Drama Review* 16, no. 2: 79–89.

Reed, Rex. 1968. "Breakthrough by 'The Boys in the Band.'" *New York Times*, May 12.

Reed, Rex. 1976. Review of *The Club. Daily News*, October 15.

Reed, Rex. 1977. "*I Love My Wife.*" *New York Sunday News*, October 24.

Regelson, Rosalyn. 1969. "Is Motherhood Holy? Not Any More." *New York Times*, May 18.

Regelson, Rosalyn. 1977. "What Would *Psychology Today* Say?" *Soho Weekly News*, April 28.

Reif, Robin. 1983. "A 14th Birthday for Broadway's Long-Running Nude Musical: *Oh! Calcutta!*" *Playbill*, June 14–20.

Review of *I'm Getting My Act Together and Taking It on the Road.* 1979. *After Dark*, March.

Rich, Alan. 1976. Untitled review of *The Club. New York Magazine*, November 1.

Rich, Frank. 1989. "The Asterisks of 'Oh! Calcutta!'" *New York Times*, August 8.

Rich, Frank. 2000. "Conversations with Sondheim." *New York Times Magazine*, March 12.

Robbins, Tom. 2009. "Art D'Lugoff, Village Royalty, Gone Too Soon at 85." *Village Voice*, November 5, http://blogs.villagevoice.com/runninscared/2009/11/art_dlugoff_vil. php. Accessed July 28, 2011.

Roberts, Sam. 1985. "'75 Bankruptcy Scare Alters City's Plans into 21st Century." *New York Times*, July 8.

Rogers, John. 2009. "R.I.-Born Porn Star, 56, Found Dead." *The Providence Journal*, April 16.

Rossi, Lee D. 1975. "The Whore vs. the Girl-Next-Door: Stereotypes of Women in *Playboy, Penthouse,* and *Oui.*" *Journal of Popular Culture* 9, no. 1: 90–94.

Rudin, Seymour. 1969. "Theatre Chronicle: Winter-Spring, 1969." *Massachusetts Review* 10, no. 3: 583–93.

Russo, Vito. 1973. "I'll Take Manhattan: Politics, Actors, and the Theatre." *Gay*, May 21.

Russo, Vito. 1975. "Boy Meets Boy." *GPU News* 4, no. 8: 12–14.

"Sale of a Crime Book Is Blocked as City Takes 5 Sellers to Court." 1954. *New York Times*, September 11.

Sarracino, Carmine, and Kevin M. Scott. 2008. *The Porning of America: The Rise of Porn Culture, What It Means, and Where We Go from Here.* Boston: Beacon Press.

Schaefer, Eric. 2002. "Gauging a Revolution: 16mm Film and the Rise of the Pornographic Feature." *Cinema Journal* 41, no. 3: 3–26.

Schroeder, R. J. 1969. "The 1968–69 Off-Off-Broadway Season." *The Best Plays of 1968–69*, ed. Otis L. Guernsey Jr. New York: Dodd, Mead and Company.

Schulman, Bruce J. 2001. *The Seventies: The Great Shift in American Culture, Society, and Politics.* New York: Da Capo Press.

Schumach, Murray. 1971. "Tourist Business in Slump Here." *New York Times*, August 2.

Scott, Casey. N.d. DVD review of *Alice in Wonderland: An X-Rated Musical Comedy.* http://www.dvddrive-in.com/reviews/a-d/aliceinwonderlandx76.htm. Accessed October 28, 2010.

Sebesta, Judith. 2008. "Social Consciousness and the 'Search for New Directions': The Musicals of Gretchen Cryer, Nancy Ford, and Elizabeth Swados." In *Women in American Musical Theatre: Essays on Composers, Lyricists, Librettists, Arrangers, Choreographers, Designers, Directors, Producers and Performance Artists,* ed. Bud Coleman and Judith Sebesta. Jefferson, N.C.: McFarland.

Secrest, Meryl. 1998. *Stephen Sondheim: A Life.* New York: Knopf.

Senelick, Laurence. 1991. "Private Parts in Public Places." In *Inventing Times Square: Commerce and Culture at the Crossroads of the World,* ed. William R. Taylor. New York: Russell Sage Foundation, 329–53.

"Sex and the Theatre: Doing What Comes Naturally." 1980. *Dramatists Guild Quarterly* 17, no. 3: 22–33.

"Sextet." 1974. *Show Business*, March 7.

Shewey, Don. 2007. "Is He or Isn't He? *The Advocate*, January 30.

"Show in 'Village' Defended by Two: Mrs. Friedan and Toffler Back Sexual Musical." 1974. *New York Times*, December 24.

Siegel, Deborah. 2007. *Sisterhood Interrupted: From Radical Women to Grrls Gone Wild.* New York: Palgrave.

Simon, John. 1969. "Anemia and Impotence." *New York*, April 7.

Simon, John. 1973. Review of *The Faggot. New York*, July 9.

Simon, John. 1977a. Review of *The Club. New Leader*, January 17.

Simon, John. 1977b. Review of *I Love My Wife. New Leader*, May 23.

Simon, John. 1978. Review of *I'm Getting My Act Together and Taking It on the Road. New York*, July 3.

"S.L.A. Challenges Village Gate for Its 'Let My People Come.'" 1975. *New York Times*, January 21.

Slattery, William T. 1976. "City Locks Village Gate." *New York Post*, January 3.

Solomon, Alisa. 1993. "It's Never Too Late to Switch: Crossing Toward Power." In *Crossing the Stage: Controversies on Cross-Dressing*, ed. Lesley Ferris. New York: Routledge, 144–54.

Sondheim, Stephen. 2010. *Finishing the Hat: Collected Lyrics (1954–1981) with Attendant Comments, Principles, Heresies, Grudges, Whines and Anecdotes.* New York: Knopf.

Spear, Michael. 2002. "Lessons to Be Learned: The New York City Municipal Unions, the 1970s Fiscal Crisis, and New York City at a Crossroads after September 11." *International Labor and Working-Class History*, no. 62, *Class and Catastrophe: September 11 and Other Working-Class Disasters* (Fall): 89–95.

Stasio, Marilyn. 1969. "Theatre: We'd Rather Switch." *Village Voice*, June 26.

Stasio, Marilyn. 1974. "Sextet." *Cue*, March 11.

Stasio, Marilyn. 1976. "Let My People Come." *Cue*, September 9.

Stasio, Marilyn. 1977. "Scenes." *Penthouse*, April, 43.

Stewart, Michael. 1978. *I Love My Wife*. New York: Samuel French.

Stone, Elizabeth. 1976. "Welcome to *The Club*: Can a Rose Smell Like a Roast Beef Sandwich?" *Village Voice*, November 29.

Stratton, Jon. 2001. *The Desirable Body: Cultural Fetishism and the Erotics of Consumption.* Urbana: University of Illinois Press, 2001.

Strossen, Nadine. 2000. *Defending Pornography: Free Speech, Sex, and the Fight for Women's Rights.* New York: New York University Press.

"Supreme Court Actions." 1971. *New York Times*, December 21.

Swayne, Steve. 2007. *How Sondheim Found His Sound.* Ann Arbor: University of Michigan Press.

Sworowski, Roswitha. 1974. "Myrna Lamb's Sexual Economics." *Daily Californian*, February 1.

Talese, Gay. 1980. *Thy Neighbor's Wife.* New York: HarperCollins.

Tallmer, Jerry. 1969. "Tynan: A Show for the Thinking Voyeur." *New York Post*, April 9.

Tallmer, Jerry. 1970. "And Now...Women's Lib." *New York Post*, May 4.

Teal, Donn. 1969. "How Anguished Are Homosexuals?" *New York Times*, June 1.

"The Theater: New Musicals—A Guide to Modcom." 1969. *Time*, October 3.

"Theatre Unit Gives City New Sweepers." 1976. *New York Times*, August 5.

Thompson, Howard. 1974. "Witty 'Gay Company' at Little Hippodrome." *New York Times*, November 7.

Traub, James. 2004. *The Devil's Playground: A Century of Pleasure and Profit in Times Square.* New York: Random House.

Turan, Kenneth, and Joseph Papp. 2009. *Free for All: Joe Papp, the Public, and the Greatest Theatre Story Ever Told.* New York: Doubleday.

Tynan, Kenneth. 1969. "Pornography? And Is That Bad?" *New York Times*, June 15.

Untitled blurb about Marilyn Chambers. 1976. *Time*, March 29.

Valocchi, Steve. 2001. "Individual Identities, Collective Identities, and Organizational Structure: The Relationship of the Political Left and Gay Liberation in the United States." *Sociological Perspectives* 44, no. 4: 445–67.

Wadler, Joyce. 2006. "Theater: Breaking Character for the First Time in His Life." *New York Times*, November 26.

Ward, Jonathan. 2002. "Let My People Come: The Story of the Adult Musicals of the 1970s." June, http://www.furious.com/perfect/adultmusicals.html. Accessed January 22, 2008.

Watt, Douglas. 1976. "Looks Good but Falls Flat." *Daily News*, October 15.

Watts, Richard. 1974. "An Intimate Musical Comedy." *New York Post*, March 4.

Weales, Gerald. 1969. "The Stage: Beyond Burlesque." *Commonweal*, July 25.

Weber, Bruce. 2009. "Marilyn Chambers, Sex Star, Dies at 56." *New York Times*, April 14.

Weinraub, Bernard. 1969. "Obscenity or Art? A Stubborn Issue." *New York Times*, July 7.

Weiss, Frederic C. 1976. "Those Pornographic Liquor Licenses." *Soho Weekly News*, January 22.

Whitburn, Joel. 2000. *The Billboard Book of Top 40 Hits*. 7th ed. New York: Billboard Books.

Williams, Linda. 1999. *Hard Core: Power, Pleasure, and the "Frenzy of the Visible."* Berkeley: University of California Press.

Williamson, Bruce. 1969. "*Oh! Calcutta!*: Off-Broadway's Nudest Romp Unabashedly Satirizes—and Celebrates—Contemporary Sexual Mores, Hang-Ups and Diversions." *Playboy*, October.

Wilson, Earl, Jr. 1974. *Let My People Come: A Sexual Musical*. Original cast recording. Libra Records.

Wilson, Edwin. 1977. "*I Love My Wife*." *Wall Street Journal*, April 19.

"Wilson Jr. Says 'People' Turned to Porn" 1976. *New York Post*, August 17.

"Wilson Objects to New 'People.'" 1976. *New York Times*, July 15.

"The 'Wolf' Cry Is Real." 1971. *New York Times*, April 20.

Wolf, Stacy. 2002. *A Problem Like Maria: Gender and Sexuality in the American Musical*. Ann Arbor: University of Michigan Press.

Wolf, Stacy. 2011. *Changed for Good: A Feminist History of the Broadway Musical*. New York: Oxford University Press.

Wollman, Elizabeth L. 2006. *The Theater Will Rock: A History of the Rock Musical, from Hair to Hedwig*. Ann Arbor: University of Michigan Press.

Wollman, Elizabeth L., and Jessica Sternfeld. 2011. "After the 'Golden Age.'" In *The Oxford Handbook of the American Musical*, ed. Raymond Knapp, Mitchell Morris, and Stacy Wolf. New York: Oxford University Press, 111–24.

Zolotow, Sam. 1961. "Maidman Adding Two Playhouses: Developer to Open Mermaid and Midway on 42d Street." *New York Times*, August 15.

Zolotow, Sam. 1965. "The Theater Today: No Place for Drama." *New York Times*, June 21.

Zolotow, Sam. 1968. "Off Broadway Housing Shortage Leads to Plans for New Stages." *New York Times*, September 19.

# INDEX